Modern Chinese Literary and Cultural Studies

in the Age of Theory

a boundary 2 book

ASIA-PACIFIC: CULTURE, POLITICS, AND SOCIETY

Editors: Rey Chow, H. D. Harootunian, and Masao Miyoshi

Modern Chinese Literary and Cultural Studies in the Age of Theory: Reimagining a Field

Rey Chow, editor

Duke University Press · Durham and London · 2000

© 2000 Duke University Press
All rights reserved
Printed in the United States of America on acid-free paper ∞
Typeset in Dante by Tseng Information Systems, Inc.
Library of Congress Cataloging-in-Publication Data appear
on the last printed page of this book.

The text of this book originally was published as vol. 25, no. 3
(fall 1998) of *boundary 2,* with the exception of the following
additional material: Sung-sheng Yvonne Chang, "Beyond
Cultural and National Identities: Current Re-evaluation of the
Kominka Literature from Taiwan's Japanese Period" (originally
published in *Journal of Modern Literature in Chinese,* vol. 1, no. 1
[1997]: 75–107); Dorothy Ko, "Bondage in Time: Footbinding
and Fashion Theory" (originally published in *Fashion Theory,*
vol. 1, no. 1 [1997]: 3–28); and Paul A. Bové, "Afterword: The
Possibilities of Abandonment."

Contents

Acknowledgments

The bulk of this book was initially published in the journal *boundary 2* vol. 25, no. 3 (1998). I would like to thank Paul Bové for encouraging me to submit the original project proposal to the journal, and Reynolds Smith for helping to turn the special issue into a book.

Two essays have been added to the current volume: Sung-sheng Yvonne Chang's "Beyond Cultural and National Identities: Current Re-evaluation of the *Kominka* Literature from Taiwan's Japanese Period" (originally published in *Journal of Modern Literature in Chinese,* vol. 1, no. 1 [1997], 75–107), and Dorothy Ko's "Bondage in Time: Footbinding and Fashion Theory" (originally published in *Fashion Theory,* vol. 1, no. 1 [1997], 3–28). These essays are reprinted with the permissions respectively of the Centre for Literature and Translation, Lingnan University (Hong Kong, China) and Berg Publishers (Oxford, England).

Introduction: On Chineseness as a Theoretical Problem

Rey Chow

For several years now, with much fanfare and controversy, what is generally known as theory—by which is really meant poststructuralist theory
even though other types of discourses are sometimes included—has made
its way into modern Chinese literary (and of late, cultural) studies. Numerous publications, issued by university presses such as Stanford, Duke, California, and others, seem to respond to the consensus, among the younger
generations of scholars at least, that some use of or reference to theory
is a necessity.[1] While the most prominent example is probably feminist
theory and its corresponding investigations of women,[2] buzzwords such as
postcolonial, postmodern, the body, the subject, interdisciplinarity, and so forth
also seem ubiquitous and popular. The hostility toward "Western theory,"
which merely a decade ago was still predominant in the field of China
studies, has apparently all but become marginalized to the point of insignificance.

This enthusiasm for theory coincides, in many ways, with enthusiasm at
a different, though not unrelated, level—that of realpolitik. With the modernization campaign introduced by Deng Xiaoping after he resumed political centrality in the late 1970s, the People's Republic of China (PRC) has
been undergoing rapid, radical economic reforms, so much so that, by the
early fall of 1997, a massive plan to convert most of China's state-owned
enterprises into "shareholding" ones was announced in the Fifteenth Communist Party Congress, leaving many to wonder exactly what would still
be left of the Chinese government's avowedly socialist or communist ideological commitment. Taken in the broad sense of the word *economy,* such
openness toward economics may be understood, though with much debate, of course, as a pragmatic acceptance of an order that is capable of
managing things so that they *work*. For China at this historical juncture, the
economic order that works is one that is capable of successfully transform-

ing the existing, stored-up power of labor into energy that mobilizes and propels—into capital.

Much the same can be said about theory. As speculative labor, theory, too, seems to have acquired in the field of China studies something of the aura of a managerial economy that works, an economy that can transform the substantial accumulation of labor—in the form of knowledge—into a new type of force: cultural capital, the chief characteristic of which is its fluidity, its capacity for bypassing the cumbersome gravity of ironclad boundaries, be those boundaries national, racial, sexual, or disciplinary. If both economics and theory share a common new goal of turning things around where they have become stagnant, it is because they also share the telos of "progress," a rationalistic aspiration toward acceptance, recognition, and active membership on the global scene.

The Ethnic Supplement and the Logic of the Wound

The parallel between academic and political economies does not stop at the level of what works, be it in the form of cultural or financial capital. Both are marked, as well, by a recurrent symptom, the habitually adamant insistence on *Chineseness* as the distinguishing trait in what otherwise purport to be mobile, international practices. Just as socialism, modernization, or nationalism at the level of realpolitik has been regularly supplemented by the word *Chinese,* so, in the much smaller sphere of the academic study of China, is the word *Chinese* frequently used to modify general, theoretical issues such as modernity, modernism, feminism, poetic tradition, novels, gay and lesbian issues, film theory, cultural studies, and so forth. One can almost be certain that, once a new type of discourse gains currency among academics at large, academics working on China-related topics will sooner or later produce a "Chinese" response to it that would both make use of the opportunity for attention made available by the generality of the theoretical issue at hand *and* deflect it by way of historical and cultural characteristics that are specific to China.

This collective habit of supplementing every major world trend with the notion of "Chinese" is the result of an overdetermined series of historical factors, the most crucial of which is the lingering, pervasive hegemony of Western culture. "The West," in this instance, is, as Naoki Sakai writes, "not merely a geographic particular: it is an ambiguous and ubiquitous presence of a certain global domination whose subject can hardly be identifiable"; the West is what "peoples in the so-called non-West have to refer to and rely on

... so as to construct their own cultural and historical identity."[3] Against the systematic exclusivism of many hegemonic Western practices, the ethnic supplement occurs first and foremost as a struggle for access to representation while at the same time contesting the conventional simplification and stereotyping of ethnic subjects as such.[4] Nevertheless, even when such access is achieved, the mainstream recognition of non-Western representations is not necessarily, often not at all, free of prejudice. As I have pointed out in my discussion of contemporary Chinese cinema, there remains in the West, against the current facade of welcoming non-Western "others" into putatively interdisciplinary and cross-cultural exchanges, a continual tendency to stigmatize and ghettoize non-Western cultures precisely by way of ethnic, national labels.[5] Hence, whereas it would be acceptable for authors dealing with specific cultures, such as those of Britain, France, the United States, or the ancient Greco-Roman world, to use generic titles such as *Women Writers and the Problem of Aesthetics, Gender Trouble, Otherness and Literary Language, The Force of Law, The Logic of Sense, This Sex Which Is Not One, Tales of Love,* and so on, authors dealing with non-Western cultures are often expected to mark their subject matter with words such as *Chinese, Japanese, Indian, Korean, Vietnamese,* and their like. While the former are thought to deal with intellectual or theoretical issues, the latter, even when they are dealing with intellectual or theoretical issues, are compulsorily required to characterize such issues with *geopolitical realism,* to stabilize and fix their intellectual and theoretical content by way of a national, ethnic, or cultural location. Once such a location is named, however, the work associated with it is usually considered too narrow or specialized to warrant general interest. That this vicious circle of discriminatory practice has gone largely uncontested even by those who are supposedly sensitive to cultural difference is something that bespeaks the insidious hypocrisy of what purports, in North America at least, to be an enlightened academy. To this extent, authors who feel obliged to comply with this convention (of categorizing intellectual subject matter by way of ethnic labeling, which is deemed unnecessary in the case of whites and imperative in the case of nonwhites) are not personally responsible for the situation even as they perpetuate the problem by adhering to the convention. Such authors often have no choice.

In the case of China, the problematic of the ethnic supplement predates the current trends in North American academe. For a continuous period between the mid–nineteenth and the early twentieth centuries, China was targeted for territorial and military invasions by numerous Western powers as well as Japan, invasions that led to the signing of a series of what were known as unequal treaties between the Chinese government and various foreign nations, which were granted major monetary indemnities, territorial concessions, trading privileges, and legal exemptions (known as extraterritoriality) on Chinese soil. The unspoken rule of the scramble for China at the turn of the twentieth century was simple: attack China, then proclaim you're being attacked and demand heavy compensation; if China fails to pay up, attack it some more, demand more compensation, and so forth. The recent historic return of the British Crown Colony of Hong Kong to the People's Republic was, for Chinese populations all over the world, regardless of their political loyalties, a major watershed that put an end to this 150-year history of aggression and violence against China. And yet, even as the history of humiliation that officially began with the Treaty of Nanking (signed as the result of the First Opium War, which led to the ceding of Hong Kong Island to Britain in 1842) formally closed on 1 July 1997 — without violence or bloodshed — the media in the West, led by Britain and the United States, continued their well-worn practice of broadcasting all news about China as a *crisis*, picking on the smallest details in a militant goading-on of so-called democracy in order to demonize China and thus affirm Western moral supremacy.[6]

While this is not exactly the place to recapitulate modern Chinese history in detail — interested readers will be able to find volumes devoted to the topic easily — I highlight it for the purpose of underscoring the historicity behind the issue of ethnic supplementarity. Chinese intellectuals' obsession with China and their compulsion to emphasize the Chinese dimension to all universal questions are very much an outgrowth of this relatively recent world history.[7] In the face of a preemptive Western hegemony, which expressed itself militarily and territorially in the past, and expresses itself discursively in the present, Chinese intellectuals in the twentieth century have found themselves occupying a more or less reactive, rather than active, position. The subsequent paranoid tendency to cast doubt on everything Western and to insist on qualifying it with the word *Chinese* thus becomes typical of what I would call *the logic of the wound*. Beginning as a justified reaction to aggression, and gathering and nurturing means of establishing cultural integrity in defense, the logic of the wound is not unique to China. Nonetheless, it is something modern and contemporary Chinese culture seems enduringly reluctant to give up.

In the habitual obsession with "Chineseness," what we often encounter is a kind of cultural essentialism—in this case, sinocentrism—that draws an imaginary boundary between China and the rest of the world. Everything Chinese, it follows, is fantasized as somehow better—longer in existence, more intelligent, more scientific, more valuable, and ultimately beyond comparison. The historically conditioned paranoid reaction to the West, then, easily flips over and turns into a narcissistic, megalomanic affirmation of China; past victimization under Western imperialism and the need for national "self-strengthening" in an earlier era, likewise, flip over and turn into fascistic arrogance and self-aggrandizement. Among the young generations of Chinese intellectuals in the People's Republic, the mobilization of an unabashedly chauvinistic sinocentrism—or what I would call, simply, sinochauvinism—has already taken sensationally propagandist forms, typified by the slogan "China Can Say No." [8]

This paradoxical situation in which what begins as resistance to the discriminatory practices of the older Western hegemony becomes ethnicist aggression is part and parcel of what Etienne Balibar describes as the general displacement of the problematic of racism in the post–Second World War period. From the older racism based on biology and genetics, Balibar writes, the decolonized world has steadily shifted into a new, "differentialist racism," which finds its justification no longer in the absoluteness of blood but in the insurmountability of cultural difference. Ironically, this new, second-order racism has been encouraged in part by the ideologically humanistic, indeed antiracist, arguments of the postwar phenomenon of anthropological culturalism, which is "entirely oriented towards the recognition of the diversity and equality of cultures." Such an emphasis on cultural differentials has led to a situation in which "culture" itself and the aggressive racist conduct that is adopted to fortify cultural boundaries have become naturalized: "What we see here," Balibar argues, "is that biological or genetic naturalism is not the only means of naturalizing human behaviour and social affinities. . . . *culture can also function like a nature,* and it can in particular function as a way of locking individuals and groups a priori into a genealogy, into a determination that is immutable and intangible in origin." [9]

As China emerges as a world power at the end of the twentieth century, these volatile realities of ethnicity will inevitably have to become a central part of modern Chinese studies. It is in this context that we should rethink the use of the label "Chinese," which occurs as frequently as its status remains untheorized and taken for granted. In recent years, as various alternative forces have been gathering momentum, we have begun to see a gradual epistemic shift that seeks to modify the claim of a homogeneously unified, univocal China. Among such alternative forces are studies of China's minority populations (e.g., the Huis, or Chinese Moslems), continual demands for the liberation of Tibet, intermittent protests from Xinjiang and Inner Mongolia, repeated assertions of political and national autonomy by Taiwan, and concerted efforts for democratic government and the rule of law in post-British Hong Kong. As well, in the relatively new area of cultural studies, the notion of Chineseness as a monolithic given bound ultimately to mainland China has been interrogated and critiqued by scholars attentive to issues of the Chinese diaspora such as David Yen-ho Wu, Ien Ang, and Allen Chun.[10] However flawed and unsatisfactory, the modes of inquiries made under the rubric of identity politics have indisputably opened up new avenues of engaging with ethnicity, which is, strictly speaking, an unfinished process. (Conversely, it is because traditional literary studies have not provided tools for understanding the politics of ethnicity — even while such studies are fully inscribed in ethnicity's fraught articulations — that the foregrounding of identity constructions may help lead to new ways of reassessing literary theories and practices themselves.) As Stuart Hall writes, "We still have a great deal of work to do to *decouple* ethnicity, as it functions in the dominant discourse, from its equivalence with nationalism, imperialism, racism and the state. . . . What is involved is the splitting of the notion of ethnicity between, on the one hand the dominant notion which connects it to nation and 'race' and on the other hand what I think is the beginning of a positive conception of the ethnicity of the margins, of the periphery."[11]

It is such "splitting" of the notion of ethnicity that will, I believe, be instrumental to the reimagining of a field such as modern Chinese studies. Insofar as it deals with the politics of literary culture and representation, modern Chinese studies has, all along, we may say, been constructed precisely on the very ambiguity of the ethnic supplement — of the victim-cum-empire status of the term *Chinese*. Once ethnicity is introduced consciously as a theoretical problem, the conventions of understanding practices that are not explicitly about ethnicity as such take on new and provocative implications. For instance, what is Chinese about the Chinese language and Chinese literature? If *language* and *literature* in the narrow sense have been fundamentally dislocated in poststructuralist theory by way of the "differences" inherent to signification, *Chinese* language and literature must now be seen as a further dislocation of this fundamental dislocation, requiring us to reassess "ethnicity" (as a site of difference) not only in terms of a struggle against the West but also, increasingly, in terms of the permanently evolving mutations internal to the invocation of ethnicity itself, in particular as such mutations bear upon the practices of writing.

Within the institutional parameters of Chinese literary studies in the West, however, there is an additional ethnic factor that prohibits the problematization of ethnicity as I have suggested. This is the persistent orientalist approach adopted by some white China scholars toward their objects of study. Even at a time when race and ethnicity have become ineluctable issues in academic inquiry, such orientalism often continues bald-faced under the guise not only of "objective" but also of morally "progressive," indeed "theoretical," discourses.[12] To fully confront the issue of Chineseness as a theoretical problem, therefore, it is not sufficient only to point to the lack of attempts to theorize Chineseness as such. It is equally important for us to question the sustained, conspicuous silence in the field of China studies on what it means for certain white scholars to expound so freely on the Chinese tradition, culture, language, history, women, and so forth in the postcolonial age; it is also important for us to ask why and how one group of people can continue to pose as the scientific investigators and moral custodians of another culture while the ethnic and racial premises of their own operations remain, as ever, exempt from interrogation. The theorization of Chineseness, in other words, would be incomplete without a concurrent problematization of *whiteness* within the broad frameworks of China and Asia studies.[13]

Having raised these general issues of ethnicity that pertain to the field of China studies as a whole, I will now move on to a brief analysis of the more specific aspects of the relation between Chineseness and the study of Chinese language and literature.

The Language Issue

One assumption that binds the discipline of Chinese studies is that of a so-called standard language, by which is meant the language *spoken* in Beijing, Mandarin, which has been adopted as the official "national language" since the early twentieth century. Known in the People's Republic by its egalitarian-sounding appellation Putonghua (common speech), the hegemony of Mandarin has been made possible through its identification more or less with the written script, an identification that lends it a kind of permanence and authority not enjoyed by other Chinese speeches. Even in the instrumental uses of language, though, Chineseness—just what is Chinese about "standard Chinese"—inevitably surfaces as a problem. As John DeFrancis writes, "the 'Chinese' spoken by close to a billion Han Chinese is an abstraction that covers a number of mutually unintelligible forms of speech." [14] The multiple other languages—often known subordinately as "dialects"—that are spoken by Chinese populations in China and elsewhere in the world clearly render the monolithic nature of such a standard untenable. [15]

In the West, meanwhile, this untenable standard is precisely what continues to be affirmed in the pedagogical dissemination of Chinese. When there are job openings in the area of Chinese language and literature in North American universities, for instance, the only candidates who will receive serious consideration are those who have verbal fluency in Mandarin. A candidate who can write perfect standard Chinese, who may have more experience writing and speaking Chinese than all the Caucasian members of a particular East Asian language and literature department combined, but whose mother tongue happens to be (let's say) Cantonese would be discriminated against and disqualified simply because knowledge of Chinese in such cases really does not mean knowledge of *any* kind of Chinese speech or even command of the standardized Chinese written language but, specifically, competence in Mandarin, the "standard" speech that most white sinologists learn when they learn to speak Chinese at all.

Such, then, is the fraught, paradoxical identity of a non-Western language in the postcolonial era: Mandarin is, properly speaking, also *the white man's Chinese,* the Chinese that receives its international authentication as "standard Chinese" in part because, among the many forms of Chinese speeches, it is the one inflected with the largest number of foreign, especially Western, accents. Yet, despite its currency among nonnative speakers, Mandarin is not a straightforward parallel to a language such as English. Whereas the adoption of English in non-Western countries is a sign of Britain's colonial legacy, the enforcement of Mandarin in China and the West is rather a sign of the systematic *codification and management of ethnicity* that is typical of modernity, in this case through language implementation. Once we understand this, we see that the acquisition of the Chinese language as such, whether by environment or by choice, is never merely the acquisition of an instrument of communication; it is, rather, a participation in the system of value production that arises with the postcolonized ascriptions of cultural and ethnic identities.

In a context such as British Hong Kong, for instance, it was common for Chinese people in Hong Kong to grow up with a reasonable command of the Chinese language even as they were required to learn English. Nonetheless, with the systematically imposed supremacy of English in the colony, the knowledge of Chinese possessed by the majority of Chinese people, however sophisticated it might be, was generally disregarded as having any great value.[16] But the same was not true of Westerners: the rare instance of a Westerner knowing a few phrases of Chinese, let alone those who had actually learned to speak and read it, was instead usually hailed with wonderment as something of a miracle, as if it were a favor bestowed on the colonized natives. Similarly, in the West, knowledge of Chinese among non-Chinese sinologists is often deemed a mark of scholarly distinction (in the form of "Wow, they actually know this difficult and exotic language!"), whereas the Chinese at the command of Chinese scholars is used instead as a criterion to judge not only their ethnic authenticity but also their academic credibility. For the white person, in other words, competence in Chinese is viewed as a status symbol, an additional professional asset; for the Chinese person, competence in Chinese is viewed as an index to existential value, of which one must supply a demonstration if one is not a native of Beijing. And, of course, if one is not a native of Beijing and thus not bona fide by definition, this attempt to prove oneself would be a doomed process from the beginning. Those who are ethnically Chinese but for historical reasons have become linguistically distant or dispossessed are, without exception, deemed inauthentic and lacking.[17]

There are, in sum, at least two sets of urgent questions around the language issue. The first has to do with the "other" Chinese languages that have so far remained incidental realities both in terms of state policy and in terms of pedagogy. As the polyphony of these other speeches and their respective ethnicities is likely to become louder in the decades to come, it will be increasingly impossible to continue to treat them simply as the negligible aspects of a canonized discipline. Officials and scholars alike will undoubtedly need to respond to the plurality that has hitherto been suppressed under the myth of "standard Chinese." But such a response cannot simply take the form of adding more voices to the existing canon. The second set of questions, therefore, has to do with a much needed effort not only to multiply the number of languages recognized but also to theorize the controversial connections among language possession, ethnicity, and cultural value. These latter questions, which I believe are even more important than the first, have yet to begin to be raised in the field of modern Chinese studies.[18]

"Chinese" Literature: A Literary or Ethnic Difference?

Another major assumption that binds the discipline of Chinese studies is that of an unproblematic linkage between Chineseness as such and Chinese *literary* writing. In such linkage, what is Chinese is often imagined and argued as completely distinct from its counterparts in the West, even as such counterparts are accepted in an a priori manner as models or criteria for comparison.

To use a classic example in this systematically *reactive construction of a fictive ethnicity in literary studies,*[19] let us take the prevalent belief among some sinologists that ancient Chinese writing is distinguished by a nonmimetic and nonallegorical (as opposed to a mimetic and allegorical) tradition. This belief, I should emphasize, is fundamentally akin to the premise of postwar anthropological culturalism, namely, that there is a need to recognize cultural difference in a world still run by the erasure of such difference. At the same time, the assertion of the Chinese difference tends often to operate from a set of binary oppositions in which the Western literary tradition is understood to be metaphorical, figurative, thematically concerned with transcendence, and referring to a realm that is beyond this world, whereas the Chinese literary tradition is said to be metonymic, literal, immanentist, and self-referential (with literary signs referring not to an otherworldly realm above but back to the cosmic order of which the literary universe is part). The effort to promote China, in other words, is made through an a priori surrender to Western perspectives and categories.[20] Accordingly, if mimesis has been the chief characteristic of Western writing since time immemorial, then nonmimesis is the principle of Chinese writing.[21] Haun Saussy captures the drift and implications of these arguments in the following. According to the sinologists, he writes,

> Without "another world" to refer to, no Chinese writer can possibly produce allegories. There are only contextualizations. . . .
>
> . . . The secret of Chinese rhetoric is that there is no rhetoric. The seeming allegories, metaphors, and tropes of Chinese poets do no more than report on features of the Chinese universe. . . .

> . . . Metaphor and fiction, instead of being dismissed or bracketed as constructs of Western ontology, have now been promoted (as categories) to the status of realities. It is an astonishing conclusion.[22]

Such arguments about the Chinese difference, as Saussy points out, have been made with great erudition. In referring to them, my point is not to challenge the technical mastery and historical knowledge that unquestionably accompany their formulation. Rather, it is to foreground the fact that, in the insistent invocation of a Chinese tradition—and with it Chinese readers with Chinese habits, sensibilities, perspectives, points of view, and so forth—seldom, if ever, has the question been asked as to what exactly is meant by *Chinese.* Why is it necessary at all to reiterate what is Chinese in Chinese poetry by way of so-called Western attributes of poetic writing? What does it mean to supply this particular *copula*—to graft a term that is, strictly speaking, one of ethnicity onto discourses about literary matters such as allegory? If such erudite and authoritative accounts have succeeded in explaining the formal details of texts (by expounding on literary and historical commentaries that deal with the various uses of poetic conventions, for instance), little, if anything, has been done about the nonliterary term *Chinese* even as it is repeatedly affixed to such studies. The (rhetorical) status of the term remains external to the formal issues involved, and the question of cultural difference, which such discussions of literary matters are supposedly addressing, simply refuses to disappear because it has, in fact, not yet been dealt with.

What happens as a result of latching the investigation of literary specificities to this unproblematized, because assumed, notion of Chineseness is that an entire theory of ethnicity becomes embedded (without ever being articulated as such) in the putative claims about Chinese poetics and literary studies. For instance, when it is assumed that poets, literati, commentators, and readers engage in literary practices in the Chinese way, the discourse of literary criticism, regardless of the intentions of the individual critic, tacitly takes on a cross-disciplinary significance to resemble that of classical anthropology. And, once classical anthropology is brought in, it becomes possible to see that the practitioners of Chinese writing—or the Chinese practitioners of writing—are, in effect, read as ethnics, or natives, who are endowed with a certain *primitive logic.* As the paradigm of anthropological information retrieval would have it, such treasures of primitive thought, however incomprehensible to the contemporary mind (and precisely because they are so incomprehensible), must be rescued. The Western sinologist thus joins the ranks of enlightened progressives engaged in the task of salvaging the remains of great ancient civilizations. Since it is no longer possible to interview the natives of ancient China—the writers of classical Chinese narratives and poems, and their contemporary readers—the texts left behind by them will need to be upheld as evidence of their essential ethnic difference.

But what *is* this essential ethnic difference? As I already indicated, it is, according to these sinologists, nonmimeticism, a way of writing and reading that is said to be natural, spontaneous, immanentist—and, most important, lacking in (the bad Western attributes of) allegorical, metaphorical, and fictive transformation. While ostensibly discussing literary matters, then, these sinologists have, de facto, been engaged in the (retroactive) construction of a certain ethnic identity. The Chinese that is being constructed is, accordingly, a nonmimetic, literal-minded, and therefore virtuous primitive—a noble savage.

The implications of this are serious and go well beyond the study of an esoteric literary tradition. The characterization, however well intended, of an entire group of people (the Chinese of ancient China) in such cognitive, psychological, or behavioral terms as a disposition toward literalness, is, in the terms of our ongoing discussion, racist. Even though it takes the benevolent form of valorizing and idealizing a projected collective "difference," [23] such racism is, to use the words of Ang, "reinforced precisely by pinning down people to their ethnic identity, by marking them as ethnic." [24] To use the words of Balibar, this is a racism "whose dominant theme is not biological heredity but the insurmountability of cultural differences." Culture here functions as "a way of locking individuals and groups a priori into a genealogy, into a determination that is immutable and intangible in origin." [25]

From this it follows that it is antiquity that remains privileged as the site of the essence of Chineseness, which appears to be more bona fide when it is found among the dead, when it is apprehended as part of an irretrievable past. Within the field of Chinese, then, the dead and the living are separated by what amounts to *an entangled class and race boundary:* high culture, that which is presumed to be ethnically pure, belongs with the inscrutable dead; low culture, that which is left over from the contaminating contacts with the foreign, belongs with those who happen to be alive and can still, unfortunately, speak and write. It is not an accident that one of the most memorable studies of the ancient Chinese is R. H. Van Gulik's *Sexual Life in Ancient China,* a fascinating account in which, at the crucial moments, highly metaphorical passages about sexual activities, written in classical Chinese — already a challenge to the imagination with their allusions to dragons, phoenixes, cicadas, jades, pearls, clouds, and rain — are translated into Latin.[26] If the trends of modern and contemporary society move in the direction of fluidity and translatability between cultures, the sinologist, on the contrary, finds his vocation rather in the painstaking preservation of savage thought. He does this by rendering such thought indecipherable except to the learned few, West and East. Primitive logic, here in the form of the art of the bedchamber, is thus museumized and dignified, gaining its exotic value and authority at once through a punctilious process of fossilization.

Ridden with the contradictions of a modernist, rationalist attempt to redeem the past, Western sinology seems ultimately unable to extricate itself from a condition of captivity in which the only kind of specialty it can claim is, by logic, "hypotheses inimical to [its own] conclusions."[27] With the passage of time, sinology has hardened into an obstinate elitist practice with the presumption that Chineseness — that very notion it uses to anchor its intended articulation of cultural difference — is essentially incomparable and hence beyond history. One could only surmise that, if sinology had been a little more willing to subject the belief in Chineseness to the same fastidious scrutiny it lavishes on arcane textual nuances, the intellectual results produced would perhaps have been less ephemeral.

Literature and Ethnicity: A Coerced Mimeticism

The ideological contradictions inherent in the study of premodern Chinese writing are not exactly resolved in modern Chinese studies, but because of the conscious efforts to politicize historical issues in modernity, scholars of modern Chinese literature are much more sensitized to the inextricable relation between formal literary issues and nonliterary ones such as ethnicity. In modernity, the equivalence between Chinese literature and Chineseness enjoys none of the comfortable security of the dead that it has in sinology. Instead, it takes on the import of an irreducibly charged relation, wherein the historicity of ethnicity haunts even the most neutral, most objective discussions of *style,* resulting in various forms of mandated reflectionism.[28]

In his book *Rewriting Chinese,* Edward Gunn demonstrates how, in modern Chinese writing, style — a presumably formal matter involving rhetorical conventions that may be rationally explained through numerical analysis—has never been able to separate itself from tensions over *regional* diversities.²⁹ Since the early twentieth century, every attempt to stake out new ground in Chinese literature through recourse to more universal or global linguistic principles has, in turn, been weighed down and derailed by a corresponding set of demands about addressing specificities of native, local, rural, disenfranchised, and downtrodden voices, which, according to their defenders, have been left out and need to be given their place on the new stylistic ground. We think, for instance, of the May Fourth Movement of the late 1910s to the 1930s, with its advocacy of adopting Western linguistic styles in Chinese writing; the urbane Modernist Movement in the 1950s and 1960s in Taiwan, initiated by the Chinese elites who had left the mainland; and the renewed attempts at modernizing Chinese fiction and poetry in the People's Republic in the 1970s and 1980s after the climax of the Cultural Revolution. In retrospect, it is possible to say that the politics of style, like the standardization of language, is as much an index to the organization of ethnicity inherent to nation building as more overt bureaucratic measures, and that even the People's Republic's official strategies to *stylize* Chinese writing—to the extent of sacrificing the aesthetic value of the unpredictable—for the purpose of political cohesion must be seen as symptomatic of a postcolonial global modernity marked, as always, by massive ethnic inequalities.³⁰

Interestingly, if we read such *political* strategies (to stylize and stabilize language) from a *literary* perspective, we would have to conclude that in the global scene of writing (understood as what defines and establishes national identity), Third World nations such as China have actually been *coerced into a kind of mimeticism,* a kind of collective linguistic/stylistic mandate under which writing has to be reflectionist, has to be an authentic copy of the nation's reality. From the standpoint of the Chinese state, it was as if Chineseness had, in the twentieth century, become the burden of an ethnicity that was marginalized to the point of unintelligibility—and the only way to be intelligible, to regain recognition in a world perpetually ignorant of and indifferent to Chinese history, is by going realist and mimetic: to institute, officially, that writing correspond faithfully to the life of the Chinese nation as an ethnic unit.

In other words, the administering of writing in modernity, whether at the level of native intellectuals' advocacy for large-scale formal changes or at the level of explicit intervention by the revolutionary state, is always, ultimately, a regimenting or disciplining of ethnicity as a potentially disruptive collective problem. To this we may add the work of cultural critics (outside China) who are intent on arguing for the Chinese difference.[31] It is in this light—in the light of the politics of Chinese writing in *modernity*—that we may finally appreciate the full implications of sinological arguments about *ancient* Chinese writing. Like the Chinese political state, the sinology that specializes in Chinese poetics/narratology, insofar as it attempts to ground Chineseness in specific ways of writing, can also be seen as a kind of ethnicity-management apparatus. Once this becomes clear—that is, once the attempt to ground Chineseness is understood to be, in fact, a managerial operation dictated by extraliterary circumstances—the idealistic assertion of a nonmimetic, nonallegorical tradition that distinguishes Chinese writing, that makes Chinese literature *Chinese* literature, can only crumble in its own theoretical foundations. For isn't *equating* a definitive classification (the nonmimetic) with what is Chinese precisely a mimeticist act—an act that, even as it claims to resist mimesis, in fact reinscribes literary writing squarely within the confines of a special kind of reflection—the reflection of a reality/myth called Chineseness?

Mimeticism here is no longer simply a literary convention, however. Rather, it is a type of representational copula-tion forced at the juncture between literature and ethnicity, a reflectionism that explicitly or implicitly establishes equivalence between a cultural practice and an ethnic label—in the form of "this kind of poetic/narrative convention *is* Chinese." In this equation, this act intended to validate a particular kind of writing *as* ethnic difference per se, mimeticism, chastised though it may be at the formal level as an evil Western tradition, returns with a vengeance as *the* stereotyped way to control and police the reception of literary writing. In the hands of the sinologists, even ancient poems and narratives, it turns out, are documentaries—of what is Chinese. In the study of modern Chinese literature, such mimeticism between writing and ethnicity, which has all along been foisted on Third World literature in general, would receive a different name—national allegory—soon to be adopted widely even among Chinese critics.

Meanwhile, the émigrés who can no longer claim proprietorship of Chinese culture through residency in China henceforth inhabit the melancholy position of an ethnic group that, as its identity is being "authenticated" abroad, is simultaneously relegated to the existence of ethnographic specimens under the Western gaze. Worth mentioning in this context is the work of Tsi-an Hsia, who in the 1950s attempted, in Taiwan, to reinvigorate Chinese writing by advocating serious attitudes toward "new poetry," by borrowing the principles of the Anglo-American New Critics. One of the results of this attempt to rediscover the true poet's voice, however, was a further displacement of the ethnicity that such literary efforts were supposed to consolidate—the trend among Chinese students from Taiwan to study abroad in the United States, eventually bringing the habits of New Criticism to bear upon their reading of Chinese literature overseas.[32] As Gunn comments, "it is tempting to conclude that T. A. Hsia and his students had not brought modern literature to Taiwan but had moved Chinese literature to the United States."[33]

In exile, Chinese writing (first in Taiwan, then in the United States) is condemned to nostalgia, often no sooner reflecting or recording the "reality" of Chinese life overseas than rendering Chineseness itself as something the essence of which belongs to a bygone era.[34] Even so, the coerciveness of the typical mimeticism between representation and ethnicity continues.[35] No matter how nonmimetic, experimental, subversive, or avant-garde such diasporic writing might try to be, it is invariably classified, marketed, and received in the West as Chinese, in a presupposed correspondence to that reality called China. As in the case of representations by all minorities in the West, a kind of paternalistic, if not downright racist, attitude persists as a method of categorizing minority discourse: minorities are allowed the right to speak only on the implicit expectation that they will speak in the documentary mode, "reflecting" the group from which they come.[36]

Reimagining a Field

Although the abstract notion of the field of modern Chinese literary studies has hitherto been harnessed to the fantasy of an essentialized ethnicity, a standardized language, and a coercive equivalence between literary writing and Chineseness per se, even the most reactionary of the field's practitioners cannot be blind to the fact that, in the past decade or so, there has been an increasing noncoincidence between Chinese literary studies as such and what is actually taking place under its rubric. More and more scholars are turning to texts and media that are, strictly speaking, nonliterary (including film, television dramas, radio programs, art exhibits, and pop music), while non-China-related publications dealing with modernism, modernity, feminism, gay and lesbian studies, postcoloniality, philosophy, history, and so forth regularly fill China scholars' bibliographical lists. Against the rigidity of the norm of Chinese studies, then, a considerable range of discourses that are not Chinese by tradition, language, or discipline is making a substantial impact on the study of Chinese literature and culture. With the invasion of these foreign elements, how can the legitimating disciplinary boundary of Chinese versus non-Chinese be maintained? And, if we should attempt to redefine the field from Chinese language and literature to Chinese literary studies or Chinese cultural studies, what is the precise relation among these words—*Chinese, literary, cultural, studies?* Do Chinese literary studies and Chinese cultural studies mean the literary studies and cultural studies that are Chinese—in which case we would be confronted once again with the essentially external status of *Chinese* as an ethnic qualifier—or do these designations mean the studies of Chinese literature and Chinese culture—in which case we would face the same problem, which was in the past circumvented by a grounding in language and ethnicity, a grounding that must nonetheless no longer be taken for granted? (The same pair of questions can probably be asked of similar claims about British, French, or American literary and cultural studies.) In either configuration, what remains to be articulated is what, after the formulations of literature, culture, and literary or cultural studies, constitutes the ethnic label itself.

The essays collected in this volume make it clear that the old model of area studies—an offshoot of the U.S. Cold War political strategy that found its anchorage in higher education[37]—can no longer handle the diverse and multifaceted experiences that are articulated under the study of Chineseness, be that study through texts of fiction, film, history, art, subtitling, standup comedy, criticism, geographies of migration, or cultural studies. Instead, in the age of theory, new linkages and insights that may be at odds with more acceptable or naturalized conventions of interpretation continue to emerge, extending, redrawing, or simply traversing and abandoning existing boundaries of the field as such. *The interior of Chinese studies is now not so distinguishable from its exterior.* If there is one feature that all the essays in this volume have in common, it is not so much China itself as a sense of the mobility, permeability, and continuity between the inside and the outside of modern Chinese studies.

Readers will form their own judgments as to whether our collective effort at reimagining the field of modern Chinese studies constitutes any significant intervention in the long run. What is finally noteworthy, in my view at least, is that even as the notion of Chineseness is implicitly or explicitly deconstructed and critiqued, and thus becomes more and more of a catachresis in their readings, none of the contributors assumes that it is simply empty or arbitrary. Instead, in so many different ways, their arguments confront us with the same question: if, following Ien Ang's bold, diasporic reconceptualization, we may indeed say that Chineseness can no longer be held as a monolithic given tied to the mythic homeland but must rather be understood as a provisional, "open signifier,"[38] should we from now on simply speak of Chineseness in the plural—as so many kinds of Chineseness-es, so many Chinese identities? Should Chineseness from now on be understood no longer as a traceable origin but in terms of an ongoing history of dispersal, its reality always already displaced from what are imaginary, fantasmatic roots? As is evident in other intellectual movements, the course of progressivist antiessentialism comprises many surprising twists and turns, and the problem of Chineseness is, one suspects, not likely to be resolved simply by way of the act of pluralizing. (White feminism, which has taught us that the problems inherent in the term *woman* have not disappeared with the introduction of the plural, *women,* is the best case in point here.) And it is at this juncture, when we realize that the poststructuralist theoretical move of splitting and multiplying a monolithic identity (such as *China* or *Chinese*) from within, powerful and necessary as it is, is by itself inadequate as a method of reading, that the careful study of texts and media becomes, once again, imperative, even as such study is now ineluctably refracted by the awareness of the unfinished and untotalizable workings of ethnicity. The study of specific texts and media, be they fictional, theoretical, or historical, is now indispensable precisely as a way of charting the myriad ascriptions of ethnicity, together with the cultural, political, and disciplinary purposes to which such ascriptions have typically been put.

Only with such close study, we may add, can Chineseness be productively put under erasure—not in the sense of being written out of existence but in the sense of being unpacked—and reevaluated in the catachrestic modes of its signification, the very forms of its historical construction.

Notes

1 A short (and incomplete) list of scholarly works (in English) by single authors published in the 1990s includes, for instance, Michelle Yeh, *Modern Chinese Poetry: Theory and Practice since 1917* (New Haven, Conn.: Yale University Press, 1991); David Der-wei Wang, *Fictional Realism in Twentieth-Century China: Mao Dun, Lao*

She, Shen Congwen (New York: Columbia University Press, 1992); Yvonne Sung-sheng Chang, *Modernism and the Nativist Resistance: Contemporary Chinese Fiction from Taiwan* (Durham, N.C.: Duke University Press, 1993); Sheldon Hsiao-peng Lu, *From Historicity to Fictionality: the Chinese Poetics of Narrative* (Stanford, Calif.: Stanford University Press, 1994); Xiaomei Chen, *Occidentalism: A Theory of Counter-Discourse in Post-Mao China* (New York: Oxford University Press, 1995); Lydia H. Liu, *Translingual Practice: Literature, National Culture, and Translated Modernity—China, 1900–1937* (Stanford, Calif.: Stanford University Press, 1995); Tonglin Lu, *Misogyny, Cultural Nihilism, and Oppositional Politics: Contemporary Chinese Experimental Fiction* (Stanford, Calif.: Stanford University Press, 1995); Jing Wang, *High Culture Fever: Politics, Aesthetics, and Ideology in Deng's China* (Berkeley and Los Angeles: University of California Press, 1996); Yingjin Zhang, *The City in Modern Chinese Literature and Film: Configurations of Space, Time, and Gender* (Stanford, Calif.: Stanford University Press, 1996); Ban Wang, *The Sublime Figure of History: Aesthetics and Politics in Twentieth-Century China* (Stanford, Calif.: Stanford University Press, 1997); David Der-wei Wang, *Fin-de-Siècle Splendor: Repressed Modernities of Late Qing Fiction, 1849–1911* (Stanford, Calif.: Stanford University Press, 1997); Xudong Zhang, *Chinese Modernism in the Era of Reforms: Cultural Fever, Avant-Garde Fiction, and the New Chinese Cinema* (Durham, N.C.: Duke University Press, 1997); Sally Taylor Lieberman, *The Mother and Narrative Politics in Modern China* (Charlottesville: University Press of Virginia, 1998).

2   For an informed overview of Western scholarship, including feminist scholarship, on Chinese women, see Jinhua Emma Teng, "The Construction of the 'Traditional Chinese Woman' in the Western Academy: A Critical Review," *Signs* 22, no. 1 (autumn 1996): 115–51. For an argument about a predominant mode of literary representation of women—through recurrent tropes of hunger—in modern Chinese literature, see the essay by David Der-wei Wang in this volume. For arguments about how the curiosity about Chinese women as exotica is part and parcel of a long-standing orientalist fascination with China, see the essay by Dorothy Ko.

3   Naoki Sakai, *Translation and Subjectivity: On "Japan" and Cultural Nationalism*, foreword by Meaghan Morris (Minneapolis: University of Minnesota Press, 1997), 61.

4   A discussion that has been helpful to my formulation of ethnicity here is Stuart Hall, "New Ethnicities," in *Black Film, British Cinema* (London: ICA Documents, 1988), 27–31. Referring to the black experience in Britain, Hall writes: "The struggle to come into representation was predicated on a critique of the degree of fetishization, objectification and negative figuration which are so much a feature of the representation of the black subject. . . . The cultural politics and strategies which developed around this critique had many facets, but its two principal objects were: first the question of *access* to the rights to representation

by black artists and black cultural workers themselves. Secondly the *contestation* of the marginality, the stereotypical quality and the fetishised nature of images of blacks, by the counter-position of a 'positive' black imagery" (27; Hall's emphasis).

5 See the section "Chinese Film in the Age of Interdisciplinarity" in my *Primitive Passions: Visuality, Sexuality, Ethnography, and Contemporary Chinese Cinema* (New York: Columbia University Press, 1995), 26–28.

6 For a more sustained discussion of this point, see Rey Chow, "King Kong in Hong Kong: Watching the 'Handover' from the USA," *Social Text* 55 (summer 1998): 93–108.

7 As Naoki Sakai reminds us, this tendency toward self-referentiality on the part of the modern non-Western culture should be understood as always already operating in a *comparative* framework in what he refers to alternately as a "schema of cofiguration" or "regime of translation." See, in particular, chapter 2 of *Translation and Subjectivity*, "The Problem of 'Japanese Thought': The Formation of 'Japan' and the Schema of Cofiguration," 40–71.

8 See Song Qiang et al., *Zhongguo keyi shuo bu* (China can say no) (Hong Kong: Ming Pao, 1996); and *Zhongguo haishi neng shuo bu* (China can still say no) (Hong Kong: Ming Pao, 1996). For a discussion of the ramifications of such sinochauvinism, especially as it has surfaced in theoretical debates among contemporary PRC scholars, see the essay by Michelle Yeh in this volume. See also the essay by Chris Berry on the related problem of theorizing collective agency in the case of contemporary Chinese cinema.

9 Etienne Balibar, "Is There a 'Neo-Racism'?" trans. Chris Turner, in *Race, Nation, Class: Ambiguous Identities* by Etienne Balibar and Immanuel Wallerstein (New York: Verso, 1991), 21–22; Balibar's emphasis. Balibar is making his arguments primarily from the perspective of a culturally hegemonic postwar France, but they are also applicable to the attitudes typical of sinochauvinism. For another major discussion of the "new racism" (this time in contemporary Britain) that is based less on biological essentialism than on the notion of a pure and homogeneous cultural and national identity, see Paul Gilroy, *There Ain't No Black in the Union Jack* (London: Routledge, 1991). For an example of a collective attempt, prior to the introduction of poststructuralism, to rethink anthropology as a Western, in particular a post–Second World War, phenomenon, see some of the essays in Dell Hymes, ed., *Reinventing Anthropology* (New York: Pantheon, 1969).

10 David Yen-ho Wu, "The Construction of Chinese and Non-Chinese Identities," *Daedalus* 120, no. 2 (spring 1991): 159–79; Ien Ang, "On Not Speaking Chinese," *New Formations* 24 (winter 1994): 1–18; Allen Chun, "Fuck Chineseness: On the Ambiguities of Ethnicity as Culture as Identity," *boundary 2* 23, no. 2 (summer 1996): 111–38. For a related discussion of the way the governments in mainland

China and the Chinese overseas have interacted during alternating periods of strength and weakness in the Chinese polity, see Wang Gungwu, "Greater China and the Chinese Overseas," in *Greater China: The Next Superpower?* ed. David Shambaugh (Oxford: Oxford University Press, 1995), 274–96.

11 Hall, "New Ethnicities," 29; Hall's emphasis.

12 The best example in this regard is the use of feminist theory. One reason investigations of women are so popular in the China field, I think, is that gender serves in effect as a smoke screen, which enables Western women scholars to be both orientalist *and* politically correct at once—precisely by studying Chinese women—without having to come to terms with the exploitative implications of their own undertakings. While there is an abundance of research on ancient and modern Chinese women (ranging from wives and widows to maids and concubines or from writers and revolutionaries to factory workers and prostitutes), therefore, there is also a noticeable lack of inquiry into the racial and ethnic implications of the subjective structuring of these investigations.

13 See the essay by Stanley K. Abe in this volume for a critical reading of the orientalism prevalent in certain instances of Western appreciation of Chinese art and calligraphy.

14 John DeFrancis, *The Chinese Language: Fact and Fantasy* (Honolulu: University of Hawaii Press, 1984), 39.

15 See DeFrancis, *The Chinese Language,* 54–57, for a discussion of the controversy over the classification of different varieties of spoken Chinese, a controversy that constitutes part of the global problem of the relationship between dialect and language.

16 The devaluing of Chinese in Hong Kong continues in the post-British period. An ongoing controversy since 1 July 1997, for instance, has to do with the Hong Kong government's attempt to implement the use of Cantonese (the mother tongue of the overwhelming majority of the population) as the medium of instruction in the local education system. This has been met with severe criticism and opposition from large sectors of Hong Kong's Chinese population, who prefer to retain English as that medium. For a discussion of the inferior cultural position occupied by colonial Hong Kong vis-à-vis both mainland China and Britain, especially as this position is negotiated in fictional writing and literary criticism, see the essay by Leung Ping-kwan in this volume.

17 It should be pointed out that those who are considered "inauthentic" Chinese are often discriminated against in other major ways as well. For instance, in Southeast Asian countries such as Indonesia and Malaysia, where anti-Chinese sentiments are traditionally strong, Chinese people are discriminated against by not being allowed to *forget* that they are Chinese, even when their families have lived in those countries for generations and they do not speak Chinese languages at all. For a moving discussion of this vast historical scenario relating to

what are known as the Peranakan Chinese, see Ien Ang, "On Not Speaking Chinese"; see also Ang's essay in this volume for a critique of the recent discourse of "cultural China," which, despite its seeming openness, is in the end still deeply China rooted and hence unable to address such issues of Chineseness as those constitutive of the diasporic experiences of the Peranakan Chinese populations.

18 Even though it is not my main concern, a third set of questions around language can presumably be developed around the age-old myth of Chinese as an "ideographic" language. For an authoritative discussion that dispels this myth, see DeFrancis, *The Chinese Language*, 133–48. "Chinese characters are a phonetic, not an ideographic, system of writing. . . . There never has been, and never can be, such a thing as an ideographic system of writing," DeFrancis writes. "The concept of Chinese writings as a means of conveying ideas without regard to speech took hold as part of the chinoiserie fad among Western intellectuals that was stimulated by the generally highly laudatory writings of Catholic missionaries from the sixteenth to the eighteenth centuries" (133). Considering the centrality of the early work of a scholar such as Jacques Derrida for poststructuralist studies in general, and remembering how that work invokes Chinese "ideographic" writing as *the* metaphor for difference from "Western" phonocentrism—the heart of Derrida's critique—the implications of DeFrancis's assertion are staggering. For an analysis of the power-ridden relation between Chinese speech and Chinese writing in post-British Hong Kong, see the essay by Kwai-cheung Lo in this volume.

19 I borrow the term *fictive ethnicity* from Balibar, "The Nation Form: History and Ideology," in Balibar and Wallerstein, *Race, Nation, Class,* 86–106; see, in particular, the discussion on page 96.

20 In his study of Japan, Naoki Sakai perceptively calls this kind of effort to promote an ethnic culture mimetic: "The desire to identify either with Japan or the West is . . . invariably a mimetic one, so that the insistence on Japan's originality, for instance, would have to be mediated by the mimetic desire for the West" (*Translation and Subjectivity,* 52). As my arguments show, this mimeticism fundamental to modern East-West relations is further complicated in the China situation by sinologists' (ideological) insistence that classical Chinese writings are, in and of themselves, nonmimetic in nature.

21 For an informative discussion of the intellectual problems generated by such arguments in the field of ancient Chinese poetry and poetics, see Yong Ren, "Cosmogony, Fictionality, Poetic Creativity: Western and Traditional Chinese Cultural Perspectives," *Comparative Literature* 50, no. 2 (spring 1998): 98–119. In his well-known essay "White Mythology," Jacques Derrida, explaining the classical Western philosophical tradition, has suggested that, for a major philosopher such as Aristotle, mimesis "belongs to *logos*" itself and is "tied to the possibility of meaning and truth in discourse" in general. Accordingly, mimesis is "proper

to man. Only man imitates properly. Man alone takes pleasure in imitating, man alone learns to imitate, man alone learns by imitation. The power of truth, as the unveiling of nature (*physis*) by *mimesis,* congenitally belongs to the physics of man, to anthropophysics. Such is the natural origin of poetry, and such is the natural origin of metaphor" (*Margins of Philosophy,* trans., with additional notes, by Alan Bass [Chicago: University of Chicago Press, 1982], 237). Because my purpose here is to foreground the problem of ethnicity as it relates to literature (rather than the generality of mimesis [in writing] per se), a full-fledged discussion of the implications of Derrida's reading of Aristotle will have to be taken up on a different occasion.

22 Haun Saussy, *The Problem of a Chinese Aesthetic* (Stanford, Calif.: Stanford University Press, 1993), 27, 31. Saussy offers an informed discussion of the views that sinologists doing "comparative poetics" typically advance to support the claim that Chinese literature is nonmimetic and nonallegorical. See, in particular, chapter 1, "The Question of Chinese Allegory."

23 A good analogy here is Julia Kristeva's "positive" and laudatory reading of Chinese women by way of the psychoanalytic notions of pre-oedipality, motherhood, the semiotic, and so forth, in *About Chinese Women,* trans. Anita Barrows (London: Marion Boyars, 1977). For an incisive recent critique of this kind of essentialist reading of "ethnic" cultures by critics following theorists such as Kristeva, see Tomo Hattori, "Psycholinguistic Orientalism in Criticism of *The Woman Warrior* and *Obasan,*" in *Other Sisterhoods: Literary Theory and U.S. Women of Color,* ed. Sandra Kumamoto Stanley (Urbana: University of Illinois Press, 1997), 119–38.

24 Ien Ang, "The Differential Politics of Chineseness," *Communal/Plural* (Research Centre in Intercommunal Studies, University of Western Sydney, Nepean) 1 (1993): 25.

25 Balibar, "Is There a 'Neo-Racism'?" 21–22.

26 R. H. Van Gulik, *Sexual Life in Ancient China* (1961; reprint, Leiden: Brill, 1974).

27 "The juxtaposition of Eastern and Western poetics outlined by these critics seems to involve hypotheses inimical to their conclusions" (Saussy, *The Problem of a Chinese Aesthetic,* 34).

28 One such form is, I think, the genre known as reportage, which, as Charles Laughlin argues, should be dated from the 1930s rather than the more recent Chinese Communist period. See Laughlin's essay in this volume for the intricate relations between style (narrative subjectivity) and politics (the production of social space) in modern Chinese literature since the early twentieth century.

29 Edward Gunn, *Rewriting Chinese: Style and Innovation in Twentieth-Century Chinese Prose* (Stanford, Calif.: Stanford University Press, 1991).

30 Gunn writes: "the new political cohesion in China required predictability in language and writing to build the nation. . . . Style was fixed largely as it existed

in politically acceptable works of the late 1940's. . . . In stabilizing writing style to such a degree and greatly expanding the literacy rate, the PRC had to sacrifice the aesthetic value of the unpredictable, whether in the language-specific, metonymic range of regional vocabulary and grammar, or in the more metaphorically charged range of cohesion and disjunction" (*Rewriting Chinese*, 56).

31 For a related discussion, see, for instance, Anthony Kane, "The Humanities in Contemporary China Studies: An Uncomfortable Tradition," in *American Studies of Contemporary China*, ed. David Shambaugh (Washington, D.C.: Woodrow Wilson Center Press; Armonk, N.Y.: M. E. Sharpe, 1993), 65–81. Kane recapitulates the idealistic manners in which American China scholars in the early 1970s tried to defend the noble "difference" of PRC literature and art. What these scholars were really defending, he writes, "was the *politics* of contemporary Chinese literature and art while simply positing the existence of the literature and art itself. In the years since the death of Mao and the fall of the Gang of Four, the false optimism of the early 1970s has become the cause of much soul-searching and embarrassment, acknowledged and unacknowledged. Why, many wonder, were many in the field so determined to defend something that in retrospect seems so completely indefensible? . . . The mistake was not in trying to avoid being culture-bound; rather it was that in the process scholars suspended their disbelief to a point where they lost the ability to analyze critically" (69; Kane's emphasis).

32 The best example of the use of New Criticism to interpret modern Chinese literature remains C. T. Hsia's *A History of Modern Chinese Fiction*, 2d ed. (New Haven, Conn.: Yale University Press, 1971). Apart from the convention of Hegelian intellectual history, New Criticism is arguably still the predominant mode of analysis in modern Chinese literary studies today.

33 Gunn, *Rewriting Chinese*, 148–49.

34 See, for instance, Gunn's suggestive discussion of the renowned Taiwan author Bai Xianyong: "Taken as stories of the older generation of mainland émigrés, comprising its elite, Bai's portraits placed them, through his idealized style, in a museum of their own nostalgia, within the approved grammatical structures and lexical relics associated with that past and, more to the point, with *the* past. Just as their objective significance in society is displaced by the narratives to a focus on their subjective experience, so the style encases the characters in an ideal of prose features and associations recognized as signs of their archaism. Displaced from the center of an objective social reality, the émigré characters are gently set aside in a museum of prose that was both a tribute and an elegy. . . . *It is critical to the appreciation of Bai's style that it rests on a mimetic foundation, that it serves to authenticate both the existence of a social group and its retirement to a museum*" (*Rewriting Chinese*, 149–50; first emphasis is Gunn's, second emphasis mine). Gunn's description, which captures the sociological pathos of a

non-Western literary modernism, can also be used on numerous other novelistic treatments of the lives of Chinese people who moved from Taiwan to the United States (e.g., in the works of the woman author Yu Lihua). For another reading of the non-Western modernism occurring in Taiwan, see the essay by Christopher Lupke in this volume. See also the essay by Sung-sheng Yvonne Chang for a discussion of the legacy of Japanese colonialism that constitutes an important part of Taiwan's modern literary historiography.

35 In recent years, we have witnessed the emergence of another type of Chinese writing in exile — the genre of the post–Cultural Revolution confession/memoir, which is regularly read in the West as an authentic, factographic record of the monstrosities that took place in the PRC during the turbulent Cultural Revolution period. I am indebted to Christopher Lee for this argument.

36 Another familiar example along the same lines would be the attempts by critics (in Chinese studies as much as in other fields) to read writings by women by identifying feminine characteristics. Once identified in the mimeticist mode, however, such feminine characteristics are often judged to be a limitation. They are, accordingly, what make it impossible for women writers to attain the broad, universal visions found in the works of men.

37 For a sustained critique of the institution of area studies, in particular as it pertains to Asian studies, see H. D. Harootunian, "Tracking the Dinosaur: Area Studies in a Time of 'Globalism,' " in his *History's Disquiet: Modernity and Everyday Life* (New York: Columbia University Press, 2000). For discussions of related interest, see Harry Harding, "The Evolution of American Scholarship on Contemporary China," and Richard Madsen, "The Academic China Specialists," both in Shambaugh, *American Studies of Contemporary China*, 14–40, 163–75.

38 Ang, "On Not Speaking Chinese," 16.

Narrative Subjectivity and the Production of

Social Space in Chinese Reportage

Charles A. Laughlin

In a little-discussed 1932 work titled "Eventful Autumn" ("Duo shi zhi qiu"), Ding Ling illustrates the reaction of the people of Shanghai to the Japanese invasion of Manchuria in September of 1931.[1] The text opens, as many Chinese short stories and novels of the time do, with a bustling city scene described with a rich palette of sounds, colors, and movements and observed from the midst of the action. The scene envisioned is a large intersection on Shanghai's main commercial artery, Nanjing Road, from the point of view of the narrator on an approaching trolley.

> The trolleys' rumble mixed with the screeching of their wheels in the steel tracks, with a constant bell ringing on top of that, in the noisy clamor of the city, from the Jing'an Temple to Kade Road, the racetrack, finally coming to a rest on a wide avenue in front of Sincere Department store in the midst of a million even noisier city sounds converging.
>
> On the trolley platform countless people came forth, extending thin, blackened hands, and waving, calling out, wildly yelling unclear words, the sounds spewing forth from their dried throats were shattered into pieces in the clamorous sea of sounds, while in their other hand they held piles of newspapers and extra editions, sheets of paper flew up in all directions. They flew into the hands of some people standing nearby, then flew on to other places. (Autumn, 84–85)

As the opening paragraphs continue to describe the passage of the news of Manchuria's loss from extra editions of the newspaper into the hearts and minds of the bustling throngs and their confused collective reactions to the news, the reader begins to realize that no central characters will emerge and that the work, in fact, does not appear to be a short story at all.

The work's relative obscurity may have to do with the fact that it is *bao-gao wenxue* (reportage literature), a genre whose existence in China before 1949 has only been mentioned in an offhand manner in English-language studies.[2] *Baogao wenxue,* a translation of the French word *reportage* as adopted by the German proletarian literary movement, refers to consciously literary texts that narrate "real people and real events" (*zhenren zhenshi*) with a view to documenting social problems and momentous historical changes. Since the 1920s, reportage played a role in the international proletarian literary movement as a means of bringing intellectuals and the masses together through the investigation and documentary depiction of poverty and industrial working conditions. Reportage was thus introduced into China around 1930 via Japanese promoters of proletarian literature.[3] Ding Ling was a member of the League of Left-Wing Writers from its inception, and her literary activities until her arrest in 1933 demonstrate enthusiastic identification with the goals and artistic premises of the proletarian literary movement.

"Eventful Autumn" is comprised of six sections, narrating a series of highly localized incidents that occur on the streets of Shanghai over a two- or three-week period after the fall of Manchuria. The incidents themselves are not causally related to one another but attain unity in historical and social themes that arise through their narration and the comments of dozens of anonymous persons involved in or observing these incidents. The four principal events—students' organization of speechmaking teams to indoctrinate the city crowds throughout Shanghai; the spontaneous overthrow of a government-organized municipal rally by workers; a mass exodus of students to Nanjing to petition the government to declare war; and a police chief (You Bolu) ordering his men to open fire on an unruly crowd, killing many—exemplify in embryo characteristics of many different types of reportage that emerged and developed throughout the 1930s and 1940s. After using these incidents to illustrate how spontaneous, collective attempts to respond to the Japanese invasion are thwarted by the government and indirectly by the Japanese, leading even to bloodshed and tragedy, "Eventful Autumn" closes pessimistically as the patriotic energy that had been released in the schools and on the streets is co-opted and absorbed by government-organized, pseudomilitary training programs.

One reason for the inattention to "Eventful Autumn," and reportage literature in general, is that it does not fit into the literary aesthetic we commonly bring to our reading of modern Chinese literature. It has been observed that modern Chinese narrative art is dominated by a discourse of realism adopted uneasily from European fiction. However, if formal realism is limited from the point of view of Chinese writers and critics because of its social neutrality,[4] is this apparent neutrality not in itself ideological? Marston Anderson's study of modern Chinese "realism" reveals aspects of modern Chinese fiction that do not fit into the familiar realist paradigm, but it does not call our reading strategies themselves into question. If we understand fictional realism as a product of an Enlightenment confidence in the knowability and linguistic expressibility of the world and of human experience, realism should also be fundamentally complicit with that unassailable cornerstone of Enlightenment ideology, individualism.[5]

Reportage literature, on the other hand, presupposes a critique of the principles that underlie standards for literature prevalent in capitalist countries since the industrial revolution. By virtue of its point of view, "Eventful Autumn" can be viewed as a conscious critique of individualism. Calling this alternative worldview "Marxist" might create the impression that it is produced by and under the control of Communist critics and theorists alone. In fact, it extends well beyond the activities and social networks we usually call "leftist circles." The critique of individualism finds partial expression in the theoretical works of Marxist literary critics, but it is also manifested in the literary works of socially involved writers with a variety of political persuasions. It was an aspect of the general intellectual context of Chinese culture of the 1930s that was much more prominent and prevalent than we usually acknowledge.[6] Moreover, I am not treating the literary critique of individualism here as an articulated theory but rather as an ill-defined set of subject positions that underlay Chinese literary practice in the 1930s.

The method of reading I propose here attempts to do justice to the worldview from which "Eventful Autumn" is written by placing what appear to be two incompatible forms of subjectivity — the individualist rhetoric of interiority and the collectivist rhetoric of exteriority — on equal footing as alternative literary constructions of social space. The individual subject position expressed through interiority in literature already constitutes a form of literary space because its elaboration (beyond the level of internal dialogue) relies almost exclusively on spatial metaphors. Reportage works from these early years almost by definition do not elaborate interiority, yet they may be more "subjective" in that the author projects his or her emotions on the landscapes and events depicted. This is another approach to the elaboration of literary space, only it is no longer interior, no longer private, and as a result, I argue, no longer "universal" or "objective" in the sense these words are understood from the perspective of individualism.[7]

There are, in fact, at least three standards working together in conventional readings of modern Chinese fiction: that "good," "progressive" literature supports individualist values, that strict opposition between subjective and objective is employed, and that the subjective is identified with the interior, that the individual as situated as literature's proper subject. From the individualist point of view, a work like "Eventful Autumn" is read not as literature but as a factual, documentary form of narrative. As a result, any emotionally charged or judgmental content (that would not draw attention in a work of fiction) is viewed as a flaw in a work that is supposed to be objective. "Eventful Autumn" was written at a time and place in which the very idea of what is literary was in flux, and reportage, with its claim to veracity and conspicuous unconcern with aesthetics, posed a particular challenge to prevailing notions of the literary.

Unlike those who make utilitarian apologies for socialist literature, attempting to excuse its poor artistic quality,[8] I would prefer to view such works as embodying in their very modes of expression a critique of what their writers considered bourgeois ideology (individualism) in literature. It has been noted that the material and social condition of modernity in China never led, as in European modernism, to the artistic expression of alienation toward the modern, but rather to unbridled enthusiasm for it and an all-out critique of tradition.[9] Apt as this observation is, it overlooks what perhaps is China's principal contribution to the artistic response to modernity: modern Chinese writers' construction of alternatives to individual subjectivity, perceptual centers that are not anchored in an individual person but exist in relation to groups engaged in public events and are explicitly situated in a particular physical environment. Certainly many writers wished to write in a European-style modernist mode and identified with individualism in literature, but this was only one among many alternatives, and we tend to assume erroneously that it must have been the most reasonable and progressive form of identity and creative intervention available at the time.

The Limits of Individualism

The most influential approaches to modern Chinese literary studies in Europe and North America fall into two main categories. The first views modern Chinese writing as a passive reaction to superior Western models; critics and historians of this category identify with the cultural goals of the liberal humanist camp of the May Fourth generation and view later developments through the lens of their values. In the second category, the primary motivation for the study of modern Chinese literature seems to be to examine and describe the ways in which creative minds are suppressed in China and to champion figures who resist such suppression. What both these approaches have in common is the individualist assumption that the self-realization of the individual subject is the ultimate focus of political and artistic endeavors.

Zhou Zuoren is often identified with "humanism" because of his famous article "Humane Literature" ("Ren de wenxue"),[10] but on close inspection, humanism seems less important to him than individualism. In fact, what Zhou Zuoren promoted throughout his career was the literature of the individual, indifferent to saving the world, more attracted to "interesting" than "important" topics. The fusion of the individual with the human and the universalization of the individual's experience are the ideological gestures of the European Enlightenment, and Zhou Zuoren, along with Hu Shi (whose article on "Ibsenism" also promoted individualism), were perhaps the Enlightenment's most enthusiastic students in China. This legacy has not left us either; most humanists now would agree that universal values are the most important and that they should be centered upon the "natural rights" and desires of the individual.

But when we look at modern Chinese culture, it is not fair to uncritically identify humanism with individualism. The leftist critique of individualism also identifies with the humanist ideals of overcoming the spiritual dictatorships of religion and superstition, affirming the dignity of human life and faith in human progress. The individual is not natural or given, Marx and his followers say, but the instrument of bourgeois hegemony. The bourgeois use individualism not only to overthrow the aristocracy but to consolidate and strengthen their own dominance by concealing the historicity of their own values and the conflicts among classes in capitalist society. The Marxist critique of the Enlightenment (and, by extension, May Fourth liberal humanism) involves a redefinition of humanism, one that puts groups (the working class, minorities, women) rather than the individual at the center of attention. While Chinese writers may not have always been consciously concerned with critiquing the Enlightenment, their literary works often reveal a profound ambivalence about and even rejection of individualist values.

The view that the exploration of the individual soul is the proper trajectory of literature (particularly fiction) has contributed to the common perception of modern Chinese literature's inferiority, and particularly our puzzlement over the motivations behind Chinese leftist culture and its prominence in the 1930s. Despite the centrality of the individual personality within it, realism seems to demand "objectivity" from literary art as well: artistic exploration of the human and the social are only legitimate as far as they are dispassionate. But socially oriented Chinese writers rarely seek to be dispassionate or unbiased in their depiction of historical experience; this is most obvious in the case of reportage, which is supposed to depict actual people and events. More importantly, writers of such works do not locate the self in the individual ego but in the complex development of social events and human relationships. Since leftist fiction and reportage literature often tend toward the depiction of public historical experience from a deliberately emotional and subjective perspective, an individualist critic can perceive them only as immature and lacking in technical control.

Collective Identity in "Eventful Autumn"

What I am trying to circumvent here is neither the independence and autonomy of individual persons nor the assertion of individuality in society and art. What I refer to here as individualism is rather the raising of the private individual to the pinnacle of moral, political, and literary importance, his or her spiritual opposition to society, and the timeless universalization of the symbols, agonies, and ecstasies of his or her private world. Approaches to literature that are based on individualism require that a limited number of characters fill the narrative with their vivid personalities. Such characters must be "filled out" or "three-dimensional," which means that in addition to being behaviorally complex, they must be self-sufficient worlds unto themselves.

In "Eventful Autumn," however, even when characters are named, as occurs in the beginning of the student organization episode in section 2, they are not central to the narrated incidents. In fact, individual persons do not occupy the narrative spotlight even anonymously. Rather, the incidents are constructed of fragments of persons—voices, hands, collective movements—animated within specific scenes or environments that are brought together through the observing and participating consciousness of a narrator who herself is defined much less as an individual person than in terms of identification with a particular group (students and activist intellectuals) *as* a group.

The crowd began to thicken, most of them unschooled laborers and poor people, and children were also among them with wide open, curious eyes. They were all moved by these youthful, uncommonly pure, exuberantly patriotic hearts; limitless words and sentences, each word full of sincerity and excitement, becoming whole speeches, becoming forceful whips which fell upon the shoulders of the crowd, becoming fresh red blood raining down upon the hearts of the crowd. They wanted to cry out, they wouldn't leave, they wanted to hear more, know more. (Autumn, 89–90)

Moreover, the narrative focus is not limited exclusively to the actions of persons, even in groups. One of the most striking aspects of Ding Ling's text is its attention to the ways in which communications and transportation technology become extensions of human consciousness, particularly at times of historical crisis when such technology becomes essential to the achievement of goals of social intervention. "Eventful Autumn" opens dramatizing the process of distributing extra editions:

Countless hands also extended from the open windows of the trolley, and sheets of paper also found their way there. The trolley pulled away, and another pulled up.

The paper unfolded in thousands, tens of thousands of hands, and the airplanes and mortars of Japanese Imperialism in Shenyang, the weeping under the slaughter of artillery fire far away in the Northeast was brought before our eyes and settled into our hearts. Once settled in the heart, the news exploded and everyone leapt to their feet, making a greater sound wave in the midst of all the noise, so that the sound of the frightening news and reactions to it were spreading in all directions. (Autumn, 85)

Section 3 seems almost to take up where this narrative direction left off, dramatizing again the intense activity of the newspaper publishers and telegraph operators as messages are sent back and forth at a frenzied pace all over the world:

They were working overtime at the telegraph office, but they couldn't keep up. Dozens of provinces, thousands of counties, hundreds of thousands of organizations were competing to send telegrams with their declarations, regardless of length. The electric currents were filling the air. Consulates for all the nations of the world and the wireless communications for all important figures were unable to rest. Newspaper reporters were running all over looking for stories. Rest was even harder to come by for the workers in typeset rooms. The price of paper suddenly rose very high, partly because of the wild increase of papers, magazines, declarations and flyers, and partly because of the boycotts [including Japanese paper]. (Autumn, 91)

Not only are we presented with the laborers, clerks, and professionals working overtime and even around the clock to keep up with the pressure created by events, but we are also informed of the material effects (the shortage of paper and subsequent rise in price) and physical changes to the environment (the air filled with electrical currents).

These descriptions illustrate a collective, social physiology whereby momentous events (for example, the fall of Manchuria), which themselves start out as physiological experiences, are *communicated* about the country via technological means that interact with private bodies, even become part of a loosely defined, public body. The reception of the communication elicits the emotional sensations illustrated here, violent, explosive reactions that lead directly to powerful responses and decisive actions but never to doubt and confusion. By interacting dynamically with public events transmitted from afar, not only is the public "internalized" in the collective subject position, but thoughts, feelings, and reactions are externalized in speech, the movements of crowds, and the resolute actions of organized groups. Events of national import, communicated information, the media of communication, and the experience of the senses, emotions, and reason are all linked in a dynamic continuum whose motions resemble the interlocking waves and ripples of an agitated pool. This expansion of the subject to encompass the technological media of communication and transportation partakes not only of the leftist critique of individualism but the futurist enthusiasm for technological modernity, whereby leftist modernism is precisely the modernism that is *not* alienated by progress, only by the distribution of power and control.

At Critical Cross-Purposes: The Case of Ding Ling's "Water"

The characteristic group consciousness and identification with the environment exemplified in the aforementioned passages has been discussed to some extent. C. T. Hsia discusses a similar piece by Ding Ling written at about the same time, in this case a short story titled "Water" ("Shui,"

1931). "Water" narrates the ruin of a rural village by a flood; the people, starving and angered at the neglect of the government and local officials, organize themselves into a violent mob and revolt against their oppressors. Hsia's comments are prefaced by a long quotation of a scathing critique of similar works by Sha Ting, a critique that Hsia then goes on to illustrate by quoting a long excerpt from "Water" (translated unsympathetically) to make a burlesque of it. Hsia neither quotes nor even refers to a single positive response to "Water," adopting a tone of disingenuous bewilderment that the prominent writer Ding Ling could possibly write such a thing: "In view of the author's high reputation even among non-leftist quarters, one could only wonder about the *taste of the age* that could have accepted such a fraud" (*History*, 269; my emphasis). This comment leads to an extended meditation on the leftist mentality, the crux of which seems to be that leftist writers are either blind to or not interested in the physical experience of historical reality, what Hsia refers to here and elsewhere as "felt life":

> This blindness to physical reality, and to psychological and social reality, constitutes the one fundamental weakness of Communist writers, though ideally there is no reason why they should be so unobservant. Perhaps the type of mind which takes to the oversimplifying formulas of Marxism is naturally of an *abstract* order, incapable of much interest in the fascinating *concrete* phenomena pertaining to human existence. Nearly all proletarian stories by Communist writers of this period are duplications of *Water* against little-changed village, factory, and army settings. Such exceptions as Mao Tun's [Dun's] "Spring Silkworms" are the product of an *entirely different creative impulse*, in that they have achieved a degree of felt life. (*History*, 272; my emphasis)

The above passage is based on an opposition between the concrete and the abstract; Communist writers like Ding Ling are associated with an "abstract" conception of social reality that makes for insipid literature because it possesses none of the fascinating interest of concrete details, which, by implication, do not fit into neat Marxist formulas. However, Marxist discussions of creative literature also stress and appropriate the concrete, the details, as their own particular strength.[11] It is as if the concrete is the contested ground in ideologically driven polemics on literature; one's adversaries are always too abstract in their literary practice, while those one praises are immersed in the fascination of concrete detail.

The collectivist vision represented by "Water" elicits a full chapter—the final one—in Marston Anderson's *The Limits of Realism*.[12] "Water" is introduced by Anderson as a literary event of some moment: "After its publication in the inaugural issue of Ding Ling's own magazine *Beidou* (Big Dipper) in 1931, several critics credited Ding Ling with having invented a new form that overcame the individualism of May Fourth literature and took 'the unfolding of collective action' as its theme" (*Limits*, 184). This discrepancy from Hsia's treatment suggests less a disagreement about the artistic stature of a single writer than a fundamental difference in point of view: Hsia's discussion of "Water" not only does not mention these several critics' praise but also does not refer to the implications of the literary crowd for the May Fourth ideology of individualism as these critics do. At most, Hsia makes "Water" a seminal model for bad Communist fiction. As if in answer to Hsia's charge of blindness to physical reality, moreover, Anderson writes: "The real protagonist of much 1930s' fiction is no longer the individual struggling to achieve a critical perspective on a chaotic social environment . . . but a special kind of crowd, *abstractly conceived but possessed of an overwhelming physical immediacy*" (*Limits*, 182; my emphasis). Anderson then goes on to draw out perhaps the most important implication of the emergence of the crowd, its relationship with the May Fourth individual:

> In the works of Lu Xun, Ye Shaojun, and Mao Dun, crowds had largely been viewed through the eyes of a single protagonist; they were part of the social background against which the psychology of the individual was measured. "Water" and stories like it do not provide a single perspective through which to focalize the reader's view of the crowd. The reader must identify directly with the crowd as an entity in itself, as one identifies with an individual character in other kinds of fiction. (*Limits*, 185)

"Eventful Autumn" was written in very much the same way, but it does provide a single guiding perspective: that of patriotic activist students. Anderson imagines the crowd in "Water" as a homogeneous mass, a view derived in part from Elias Canetti's *Crowds and Power*. This is an oversimplification, though, that prevents a full appreciation of the expressive potential of the literary construction of collective consciousness. One of the most interesting aspects of "Eventful Autumn" is Ding Ling's depiction of crowds as heterogeneous and diverse; but the crowd is not a collection of individuals, it is a collection of groups. Ding Ling's representations of consciousness and identity in "Eventful Autumn" belong to groups (students, workers, police) that make up the crowd, not to the crowd as a whole. Thus the crowd, depicted by Ding Ling visually in terms of its movements or aurally as a montage of anonymous comments, takes shape not as a single character but a matrix or medium of social dialogue and interaction:

"What the hell? You start the meeting and then run off! . . ."
"Hey, what's up? What kind of game are they up to? . . ."
"It's not here! This is the director's podium! . . ."
"Where's the meeting? . . ."
With this there was a surge away from here to where the people were crowded more densely.
"Hey, who're you shoving!"
The Chairman was already there giving his report, one of the younger ones. The wind blew apart his speech, carrying detached words in all directions:
"Japan . . ."
"Compatriots . . ."
"Municipal rally . . ."
"The government . . ."
"The League of Nations . . ."
"Please voice your opinions . . ."
Upon which he retreated, and a tall, thin man came out.
"I didn't get a word he said! . . ."
"These officials, what are they up to, what do they think they're doing, dressed up all pretty like that? . . ." (Autumn, 94)

These constituent groups derive their identity from the social space they inhabit or from the positions they occupy in public space structured by events.

The Literary Construction of Social Space

Beyond the crowd itself there should be a larger frame of reference that can put the eruption of the crowd into literary perspective. I propose approaching such works as "Eventful Autumn" via the analysis of social space, specifically the literary or verbal construction of social space. Private individuality is of necessity enclosed, while collective identities are spatially external, out in the open, but by the same token are not given discursive access to enclosed individual identities. The literary techniques of crowd depiction are habitually confined to external "social surfaces," as the hostile critic (Han Shihang) cited by C. T. Hsia observes about Sha Ting's stories (*History*, 268–

69), but that does not prevent them from exploring subjective directions. The individual inhabits a private, isolated space, while the leftist collective subject moves about in public space, observing and participating in interactions among groups. Crowds can only attain unity (if not homogeneity) in the context of the literary elaboration of social space. The social space of "Eventful Autumn" is comprised of an entire matrix of subject positions with respect to a particular event in a particular place.

Marston Anderson's inventory of the 1930s leftist crowd-character, though, while observing many of its clichés and limitations, does not address one of its most potentially liberating attributes — its diversity. This is not a diversity of individuals (which cannot comprise a crowd) but a diversity of groups each with its own language, spatial position, dynamics, and relationship to the physical environment. It is not a question of whether individual or collective identity, individualism or leftism, is "natural" or "real," but a recognition that modes of identity are optional, shaped by circumstances, so the reader should be able to identify with the crowd experience as much as the psychological torment of the individual. Looking at this difference, these alternatives, from the point of view of social space allows them to be conceived not as diametrical or even incompatible opposites but as being alternative positions in the terrain of experience and consciousness, a "terrain" that can be superimposed figuratively on the depicted territory of China itself.

Leftist critics have been toying with the ideological and artistic production of social space throughout the century. One thinks of Walter Benjamin's reflections on Paris, Berlin, and Marseilles,[13] M. M. Bakhtin's carefully wrought notion of the literary "chronotope" (time-space),[14] and Georg Lukács's amplification of Marx's observations on the spatial and temporal logic of the industrial factory,[15] not to mention the emphasis placed on spatial configurations of social practice in Foucault, in Pierre Bourdieu's ideas of the *habitus* and the field of cultural production,[16] and Homi Bhabha's critical theory of nation space.[17] One thing these directions of inquiry have in common is to question and transcend many conventional oppositions of the social and the cultural, the historical and the literary, and the objective and the subjective; they aim at a general cultural theory without sacrificing the specificity of experience. Yet the proposal of a general theory of social space did not occur until the 1970s[18] and has only been marginally influential since then. Moreover, it is only recently that Lefebvre's conceptual apparatus has been brought into contact with the analysis of literature.[19]

A great deal more could be accomplished in this direction, particularly to avoid the influence of individualism and for the explication of leftist and socialist literature.

For Lefebvre, social space is not limited to physical, geographical space, a category that in its supposed objective neutrality is precisely the kind of Enlightenment concept to be circumvented. Lefebvre wants to break down the distinction between actual physical spaces and mental representations of space, and he proposes a new category of social space to encompass their productive interaction (Lefebvre, 11–14). The theory of social space views physical space (except when natural) as produced and encoded; it is the medium in which social environments are meaningfully configured. Social spaces manifest the physical traces of various modes of social practice; they may be constructed within the regimes of these practices, or they may appropriate and mold existing natural or social spaces as their own (164–68).

Social space is ideological insofar as its production relies on spontaneous collective contributions based on shared values and assumptions. It is defined by the activities of the groups that inhabit it, and it shapes their identity and subjective experience dialectically. Literature takes part in the production of social space; by depicting venues and events from certain points of view, those places and events are being produced as much as represented, and this production goes hand in hand with the construction and development of character and identity.

Revolutionary Social Space in "Eventful Autumn"

Especially in reportage, space is organized so as to bring out themes and achieve desired effects. In works like "Eventful Autumn" that emphasize collective action on the streets, this is commonly done by making the space theatrical. While the opening section depicting the dissemination of the news of Manchuria's fall is not as much theatrical as cinematic (reminiscent of a newsreel, with the narrator something like a voice-over), the ensuing scenes of a student organizational meeting, speechmaking teams on the streets, the municipal rally, the struggle over the train to Nanjing, and the climactic confrontation between the police and an angry mob after a soldier is arrested and beaten for posting anti-Japanese slogans, all imagine the streets as a stage on which acts of history are being played out.

I argue elsewhere that all types of reportage achieve artistic status by virtue of the symbolic manipulation of space, and that Chinese reportage can be classified into types on the basis of the different kinds of space each constructs.[20] "Eventful Autumn" belongs to the type I call urban protest reportage. The theatrical mode of spatial signification is only one among many, including the strategic/cartographic emphasis of war correspondence, the critique of ordered industrial environments like the shop floor and soup kitchens, and the utopian space of the Communist base areas and later the People's Republic of China.

The theatrical mode of depiction in "Eventful Autumn" is encouraged by the already theatrical nature of some of the events: the student organizers use the auditorium with its stage to put their oral propaganda plan into action, and the students who pour out into the Shanghai streets, especially targeting working-class and industrial neighborhoods, create stages by standing on raised platforms and talking loudly, bringing about the spontaneous formation of an audience. The municipal rally of 26 September, too, sets up a stage but actually ends up deconstructing the received theatrical paradigm of May Fourth texts.

> On the chairman's dais stood a couple of dozen handsome young men, all in Western suits and Zhongshan suits of first-class wool. They were looking down upon the masses below them, in tatters, boisterous and disorderly. They wore colored ribbons, all of them chairmen and representatives. Their hair was combed to gleaming perfection. Their leather shoes also glistened. Smoking cigarettes and cigars, they were the picture of contentment, putting on a great show on the dais!
>
> The workers in the crowd shoved their way up to the front, in blue cotton work clothes. Behind them were more workers, merchants in short vests, and scattered students looking about them in all directions. It was nine o'clock, and beneath the dais there was shouting:
>
> "What's the holdup?! . . ."
>
> "Not finished shitting yet? Motherfuckers, how long do we have to wait? . . ." (Autumn, 92–93)

Ding Ling narrates this event continuously from points within the crowd below the stage; there had been considerable confusion among illiterate workers as to where the stage was, and the hostility depicted here sets the tone for the entire episode. This municipal rally as a staged event is presented in ironic contrast to the intimate sincerity of the student speech teams haranguing passersby days before: the primarily working-class crowd, noisy, impatient, unruly, cannot make out the message of the overdressed young committee members and chairmen on the stage. The speakers' words are buffeted by the wind and by the obscenities of hecklers. The rally disintegrates as the crowd's hostility frightens away the slick speakers and as workers and students clad in blue cotton leap on stage and attempt to run their own rally, only to be forcibly removed by police and security guards.[21]

The episode plays on the complex flows of power within the staged event. Conventionally, the stage is a privileged platform that confers legitimacy on those who stand upon it; this is reinforced by the ways in which student activists adopt a theatrical structure of space to indoctrinate the masses and passersby in the second section of "Eventful Autumn." But the text progresses into a critique of the stage-structure as in the above passage, and perspective and identity are conferred through the narrator's positioning: the student speeches of the second section are narrated from the point of view of the students looking down sympathetically at the crowd they address, while the municipal rally is narrated from within the crowd, looking up with hostility at the people on the stage amid continual heckling.

The climactic episode in "Eventful Autumn" culminates in a district police chief named You Bolu ordering his men to open fire on a large, menacing crowd protesting police mistreatment of a patriotic soldier, killing several people (Autumn, 104–12). The narrative begins from the initial incident—a patrolman gets in a fistfight with a soldier who wants to paste a patriotic slogan on his police booth—and dramatizes the ensuing rapid growth of the crowd of onlookers and its descent upon the police station as the soldier is taken in for questioning. The crowd accumulates as its outer rings attract passersby asking what is going on and those at the crowd's margins explain and interpret. As the process continues, the police are increasingly accused by voices within the crowd of being traitors deliberately stopping patriotic acts out of fear of offending the Japanese. The soldier emerges, blood dripping from his forehead. He gets up on a flatbed truck (a makeshift stage that transforms the crowd into an audience) and tells them that it was only the pressure provided by the crowd that prompted the police to release him.

The crowd continues to grow, targeting the police station. Someone claims he saw Japanese entering the station. A student then jumps upon the truck and gives a speech ("waving a cap in one hand, the other a clenched fist" [Autumn, 107]) about the Japanese invading the Northeast, a speech full of rich, exaggerated images of bloodshed, chaos, and ruin. He then links the national crisis to the street incident, agitating the crowd to act against the police: "In their hearts once empty, once they heard some of his words, they felt like there was something in there, they felt like their hearts were going to explode. With this, some voices could be heard wildly shouting from within the crowd!" (Autumn, 107). The crowd starts chanting anti-Japanese and antigovernment slogans, and the street fills up completely, "all the way to the doors of the Commercial Press," becoming impassable for traffic. The sound of the speeches is lost in the clapping and chaotic shouting of the inflamed crowd. Police pour out of the station but are unable to act against the crowd.

The chief, You Bolu, emerges after calling in reinforcements and is showered with accusations, particularly about his relations with Japanese, demanding that he explain the situation. You's fury at the crowd is illustrated in a brief description of his thoughts, which shows the flexibility of reportage narrative technique. Though the focus of integration is not on the character but on the event, the reportage text can nevertheless exploit the techniques of illustrating character in the process. The crowd itself becomes the source of righteousness and authority, and all sorts of possible exercises of power bubble up from the crowd's anonymous voices: holding a "true" municipal rally; boycotting classes, commerce, sports, and work; even self-armament.

Suddenly, a car with a heavily made-up, middle-aged woman inside rushes into the crowd, hitting people and running over some. The infuriated crowd starts hitting the car, shattering one of its windows. You takes this as an opportunity to open fire on the crowd and gives the order, finally gaining some satisfaction from the situation. The crowd, some wounded and some killed, scatter. Like the third section in the story, this (fifth) section ends with a description of the desolate scene after the incident: patrolling armed police and the smoke of their guns and the bodies of the dead and dying. "Blood flowed in a number of places; the wind blew up some sand, and dust swept over it" (Autumn, 112).

While arguably theatrical, this episode also dramatizes the disintegration of spatial order and community in violence coming from both the crowd and the lawless police chief. As in the case of the municipal rally, the representation resists the newspaper versions, emphasizing the reversal of the flow of power from the stage down to the audience. The text thus produces revolutionary space by having the audience lunge out of its passive role, snatching the stage away from the state. Ultimately, however, even this gesture is tragically useless; the flow of power from the stage becomes a flow of murderous state violence, and the audience becomes carnage.

The theater makes an interesting analog to the reportage text in that it consists of actual physical space that is used to create imaginative space by means of a conventionally accepted system of signification. The audience enters the theater expecting to witness a depiction of an imagined world using real persons and objects; reportage uses actual events to depict the forces of history and the clashes of groups that are usually conceived in the abstract. The theatrical paradigm for imagining history was particularly important to the May Fourth generation in that they witnessed and participated in the adoption of Western-style theater (*huaju*) largely for the purpose of political indoctrination; their idea of what theater is and is for involved a conflation of political mission with a particular spatial order and system of signification.

Reportage, similarly, makes use of actual persons and events, deliberately situating them in suggestive spatial arrangements so that the actual persons are seen as embodying groups, classes, and historical processes. The particular characteristics of the theater that are most conspicuous in reportage's adoption of the theatrical paradigm are (1) the stage, a platform on which public attention is focused and on which occur momentous confrontations and symbolic interactions; (2) the audience, a heterogeneous crowd witnessing the events on the stage and reacting to them; (3) the play, based on an organized script of some sort, according to which the action unfolds with greater or lesser success depending on the circumstances; and, finally, (4) plot, a sense of dramatic action through which the audience is drawn together with the actors toward the enactment of a climactic moment.

The depiction of events in reportage also differs in significant ways from a theatrical performance: the "theatrical" space in reportage is not clearly demarcated; the audience is especially fluid; there are as many makeshift stages and quasi stages as actual ones. The narrator allows the reader's perception more freedom of movement, not limiting him or her to the audience position. Moreover, the "script" of a reportage narration is not composed beforehand but achieves narrative status only after the "performance." The reportage writer can be likened to a playwright composing the script after it has already been performed. I put it this way because the idea of scripting suggests much more than recording, which is what is normally assumed of the reportager; scripting involves the manipulation of characters within a space in which their very position (vis-à-vis stage and audience, for example) has significance.

In Ding Ling's text, being in the audience of onlookers to events means at once identification with a diverse public *and* proximity to a particular group within that public: the working class. This proximity has been one of the principal goals of Chinese writers from the early 1930s on and has been extended to soldiers and peasants. By positioning herself close to the workers in the unfolding of history's drama, Ding Ling's narrator is exploring one rather literal way of imagining the point of view of the working class. For Ding Ling, workers are not passive observers of the forces and tragedies that are played out on the city streets; rather, they react strongly (as indicated by their diverse and anonymous exclamations and discussions) and often act as well, as when they attempt to take over the municipal rally.

Ding Ling's use of the unruly diversity of the crowd is qualified, however, by her repeated emphasis on the importance of student leadership in all public, collective action. Ding Ling's narrator clearly identifies with student activists as a group, taking pains to justify their boycotting class and their promotion and adoption of violence. While the narrator seems to have access to all minds, it is the minds of students that are revealed to the reader at the greatest length and with the most overt sympathy. This indicates the persistence in Ding Ling of a discernible subject, even if it is a collective one; Ding Ling, after all, shared the intellectualist bias of the May Fourth period. At the same time, works from the 1930s like "Eventful Autumn" went the furthest in realizing reportage's departure from individualism.

Conclusion

The most conspicuous difference between urban leftist reportage and reportage written within Communist political jurisdiction is that the space of leftist reportage consists largely of the existing space of capitalist social life and industrial production, whereas socialist reportage inhabits the spaces consciously appropriated or constructed with respect to Communist ideology, usually natural spaces and socialist space that have been built more or less from scratch. The most curious attribute of socialist reportage from the Yan'an period (1937–45) on into that of the People's Republic is its qualified capitulation to individualism. Often viewed as a tightening of the screws of artistic repression, Chairman Mao's 1942 "Talks at the Yan'an Forum on Literature and the Arts" also signified an artistic retrenchment in leftist culture by which some of the subjective formulae of "bourgeois" art were surreptitiously put in the service of the party's propaganda.[22] This echoed the adoption of "socialist realism" in the Soviet Union as the approved vehicle of artistic expression, a politically safer, if poorly defined artistic regime introduced to draw writers away from other, more dangerously radical directions.[23] In both cases, although official rhetoric emphasized a break with bourgeois literature, what was encouraged in practice was, in fact, often a watered-down version of nineteenth-century European fictional realism. In spatial terms, even writers of reportage were exploring the interior spaces of subjectivity rather than the collective interactions of groups experiencing public events. The autonomous individual self that would previously have centered this interiority, however, had been replaced by the "spirit of the party" and of Communism.

Ideally, a spatial emphasis in verbal artistic expression empowers the writer through his or her work to critique conventional assumptions, to create an artistic whole without making obeisance to individualism. The critical aspect of my analysis lies mainly in targeting the predisposition toward individualism we bring to reading modern Chinese writing that leads to our aesthetic distaste and moral frustration; but the different, leftist convictions in response to which reportage literature is written can easily be manipulated in the service of nationalism, patriarchy, and fascism. At one extreme, the practice of reportage can act as a radical critique of Enlightenment values and the ideology of individualism. It comes closest to these potentials in the hands of writers like Ding Ling, who stand in an ambivalent political relation to the Communist cultural project to which they are thus contributing.

Despite the attention I am devoting to the leftist worldview, I want to maintain a distinction between the radical possibilities of reportage's literary construction of social space and the obstacles to those possibilities posed by leftist literature's authoritarian regimentation at the hands of the Communist Party's cultural apparatus. Thus I differ from C. T. Hsia mainly in affirming the way in which Chinese leftist literature experimentally and creatively critiques the individualist legacy of the May Fourth period, while I agree with him that the Communist literary organization has had the effect of stultifying creativity, reinforcing nonliterary features, and encouraging formulas. Even more important, however, is that I draw this distinction not on the basis of the presence or absence of individual creative freedom (praising leftist renegades and dissidents and blaming the party for criticizing them) but rather on the basis of the consistency of the work's critique of the individual subject position through the positing of a vibrant diversity of collective, public, and spatially dynamic subject positions in a social space of their own.

Notes

1 Ding Ling, "Duo shi zhi qiu," *Bei dou* (Big dipper) 2 (January and April, 1932): 1,
   3–4. Reprinted in Lu Fen, ed., *Zhongguo xin wenxue daxi 1927–1937 baogao wenxue ji*
   (Compendium of new Chinese literature, 1927–1937, vol. 13: reportage) (Shanghai: Shanghai Wenyi Chubanshe, 1985), 84–116. Quotations hereafter are cited
   parenthetically as Autumn; translations are my own.

2 Almost all existing English-language scholarship treats Chinese reportage as a
   post-Mao phenomenon: Xiaomei Chen, "Genre, Convention, and Society: A
   Reception Study of Chinese Reportage," *Yearbook of Comparative and General Literature* 34 (1985): 85–100; Thomas Moran, "True Stories: Contemporary Chinese
   Reportage and Its Ideology and Aesthetic" (Ph.D. diss., Cornell University, 1994);
   Rudolf G. Wagner, *Inside a Service Trade: Studies in Contemporary Chinese Prose*,
   Harvard-Yenching Institute Monograph Series 34 (Cambridge: Harvard University Press, 1992), 243–376; Zhang Yingjin, "Narrative, Ideology, Subjectivity: Defining a Subversive Discourse in Chinese Reportage," in *Politics, Ideology, and Lit-
   erary Discourse in Modern China: Theoretical Interventions and Cultural Critique*, ed.
   Liu Kang and Xiaobing Tang (Durham, N.C.: Duke University Press, 1993), 211–
   42; a notable exception is Chang-tai Hung, *War and Popular Culture: Resistance in
   Modern China, 1937–1945* (Berkeley: University of California Press, 1994).

3 The League of Left-Wing Writers' August 1930 resolution, "Wuchan jieji wenxue yundong xin de qingshi ji women de renwu" (New trends in the proletarian
   literary movement and our tasks), *Wenhua douzheng* (Cultural struggle) 1, no. 1,
   seems to be the first explicit promotion of reportage in Chinese. Reprinted in Ma
   Liangchun and Zhang Daming, eds., *Sanshi niandai zuoyi wenyi ziliao xuanbian*
   (Selected materials on left-wing literature in the 1930s) (Chengdu: Sichuan Renmin Chubanshe, 1980), 147–54. A discussion of the genre by Kawaguchi Hiroshi
   (Chuankou Hao) was summarized in early 1931 and published in translation in
   1932.

4 "The Chinese assumed that, once successfully transplanted, realism would encourage its readers to actively involve themselves in the important social and
   political issues confronting the nation. . . . But in its actual operation . . . realism
   is more given to encouraging an aesthetic withdrawal than an activist engagement in social issues" (Marston Anderson, *The Limits of Realism: Chinese Fiction
   in the Revolutionary Period* [Berkeley: University of California Press, 1990], 25).

5 While this association of realism with individualism may seem counterintuitive,
   it will seem less so to those familiar with the literary polemics of the May Fourth
   movement, in which the two terms are often interchangeable: For many in the
   "liberal humanist" camp of the May Fourth movement, the reality that must be
   expressed through the new literature is precisely the experience of the autonomous individual subject.

6 "The majority of fictionists, of course, were too much ridden by leftist attitudes to achieve individual distinction, but the very fact that there were so many of them and that they were so uniformly industrious bespeak the vitality of the period" (C. T. Hsia, *A History of Modern Chinese Fiction* [New Haven, Conn.: Yale University Press, 1971], 139).

7 From the point of view of the Enlightenment, the individual is of little importance if his experience is not universal; in the absence of religious faith as the wellspring of the knowledge of the cosmos, the individual is the means by which the (exhaustively intelligible) workings of the universe are understood and revealed. It is in this sense that I understand the individual's consciousness as being supposedly "universal" and "objective."

8 This is a common approach among literary historians in mainland China: acknowledging works' artistic inferiority and then accounting for it by appealing to the limitations and needs of the times. This "vulgar" Marxist approach is particularly blind to the literary implications of a radical critique of individualism.

9 C. T. Hsia, "Obsession with China: The Moral Burden of Modern Chinese Literature," in Hsia, *History of Modern Chinese Fiction,* 535–36.

10 Kirk Denton, ed., *Modern Chinese Literary Thought* (Stanford, Calif.: Stanford University Press, 1996), 151–61. See also C. T. Hsia's discussion of this essay in his *History of Modern Chinese Fiction,* 19–21.

11 See, for example, Hu Feng's discussion of reportage in "Lun zhanzheng shiqi de yige zhandou de wenyi xingshi" (On a combative artistic form in a period of war), in *Minzu zhanzheng yu wenyi xingge* (The national war and artistic character) (Shanghai: Xiwang She, 1946), 131–44.

12 Anderson, "Beyond Realism: The Eruption of the Crowd," in *Limits of Realism,* 180–202.

13 See Walter Benjamin, *Reflections: Essays, Aphorisms, Autobiographical Writings,* ed. Peter Demetz (New York: Schocken Books, 1986), 3–60, 131–62.

14 M. M. Bakhtin, *The Dialogic Imagination* (Austin: University of Texas Press, 1981).

15 Georg Lukács, "Reification and the Consciousness of the Proletariat," in *History and Class Consciousness: Studies in Marxist Dialectics,* ed. Georg Lukács (Cambridge: MIT Press, 1968), 83–222.

16 Pierre Bourdieu, *Field of Cultural Production: Essays on Art and Literature,* European Perspectives (New York: Columbia University Press, 1993), 176–91.

17 See, for example, his "DissemiNation: Time, Narrative, and the Margins of the Modern Nation," in *Nation and Narration,* ed. Homi K. Bhabha (New York: Routledge, 1990), 291–322.

18 Henri Lefebvre, *The Production of Space* (London: Blackwell, 1991); first published as *Production de l'espace* in 1974.

19 Kristin Ross, *The Emergence of Social Space: Rimbaud and the Paris Commune,* Theory and History of Literature (Minneapolis: University of Minnesota Press,

1988). Credit must be given to Gaston Bachelard for introducing space into literary theory and criticism in his 1954 *La Poétique de l'espace* (translated as *The Poetics of Space* [Boston: Beacon Press, 1964]). However, Lefebvre's theory is much more useful to this inquiry because of its potential as the basis of a critique of individualist literary aesthetics.

20 Charles A. Laughlin, "Narrating the Nation: The Aesthetics of Historical Experience in Chinese Reportage, 1919–1966" (Ph.D. diss., Columbia University, 1996).

21 Ding Ling notes that the newspaper coverage of the event erased the unruly crowd and the organizers' loss of control of the event; this is borne out, for example, by the rather detailed coverage of the rally (complete with photograph) in *Shen bao,* 27 September 1931, 13.

22 Mao Zedong, *Mao Zedong's "Talks at the Yan'an Conference on Literature and Art": A Translation of the 1943 Text with Commentary,* ed. and trans. Bonnie S. McDougall (Ann Arbor: Michigan Papers in Chinese Studies, 1980).

23 Régine Robin, *Socialist Realism: An Impossible Aesthetic,* trans. Catherine Porter (Stanford, Calif.: Stanford University Press, 1992).

Three Hungry Women

David Der-wei Wang

Women and hunger are most peculiarly linked in the configuration of gender, materiality, and revolution in modern Chinese fiction. Shortages of food, with their grave implications for national politics, economics, and even eugenics, have, of course, appeared all too often in China's quest for modernization.[1] But when hunger is treated in literary terms, it manifests itself in a wide variety of typologies, from famines caused by nature to "hunger revolutions" dictated by ideology. For Chinese writers since the May Fourth era, "having nothing to eat" not only reflects the agricultural crisis of an ancient nation whose roots are in the countryside (*yinong liguo*) but also concentrates the minds of a modern people who argue over "social welfare versus cultural nourishment" and "the survival instinct versus the body politic."[2] Above all, national hunger has been imagined in feminine terms, owing, perhaps, to women's somatic vulnerability during natural and man-made famines, or to women's conventional role in the semiotics of victimology. Hunger is a recurrent theme throughout modern Chinese history, and hungry women are recurrent protagonists in modern Chinese fiction.

The genealogy of literary hungry women can be traced to works by Lu Xun. For example, in the short story "The New Year's Sacrifice," the most memorable moment occurs when the narrator encounters the ill-fated wife of Xianglin on New Year's Eve. Ostracized by the townsfolk of Luzhen, Xianglin's wife has been living as a beggar (*yaofande*, literally, a food beggar) as the story opens. Upon meeting the narrator, however, this poor woman begs not for food but for the answer to her question, "After a person dies, does he turn into a ghost or not?" Completely caught off guard by such a question, the narrator can respond only by murmuring, "I am not sure."[3]

On this festive occasion, marked by the reunion of families and an abundance of edibles, Xianglin's wife impresses the narrator as a woman hungry for something other than food. But she readily swallows the narrator's empty contribution and eventually dies a pitiful death. Ironically enough, the pathetic situation of Xianglin's wife arouses the narrator's appetite: He may have failed to provide the hungry woman with a satisfactory answer, but, we are told, perhaps a bowl of sharkfin soup will give him peace of mind and satisfy his stomach. Where food is expected, meaning is requested; the words given are meaningless to the giver, but his emptiness can be filled with food.

Between Xianglin's wife and the narrator, there exists a cluster of images around the double functions of orality: eating and speaking. A beggar though she is, Xianglin's wife refuses to be fed with mere food and tries instead to articulate her puzzlement. Her attempt to speak out and to obtain some response is nevertheless thwarted by the narrator, who, as Lu Xun insinuates, can contribute to the woman neither anything edible nor anything thinkable. Drawing on Freudian theory, critics have argued about the shared motivational structure in eating and speaking: "Language is nothing other than the praxis of eating transposed to the semiosis of speaking: both are fundamentally communicative acts by which man appropriates and incorporates the world." [4] In the case of "The New Year's Sacrifice," one can talk about a short-circuiting of these two functions of orality. Xianglin's wife dies a mute woman, while her townsfolk consume their New Year's Eve banquet in a happy clamor. As Lu Xun would have it, she is the New Year's sacrifice served up at a cannibalistic banquet in honor of ancestors and deities.

As the archetypal hungry woman in modern Chinese literature, a long line of sisters follows Xianglin's wife. For instance, in Rou Shi's short story "Wei nuli de muqin" (A slave's mother), a hungry woman is sold as a surrogate mother by her husband to save the family from starving to death. In Wang Jingzhi's "Renrou" (Human flesh), a hungry woman is literally cut into pieces and consumed by a group of hungry men. In Wu Zuxiang's "Fanjiapu" (The Fan village), another hungry woman commits matricide after her mother refuses to lend her money to survive a drought. And in Xiao Hong's *Shengsi chang* (The field of life and death), hungry peasant women follow their men and stand up against Japanese oppression. The gallery of hungry women was well furnished by the early forties, and it culminates in Lu Ling's novel *Ji'e de Guo Su'e* (Hungry Guo Su'e).

For Lu Xun, as for those authors who followed him, hungry women are powerful tokens who inscribe the misery of the powerless in a cannibalistic society. The exuberance of these writers' words on behalf of hungry women, however, leads us to consider issues beyond the simple typology of social injustice and cannibalism. As indicated by the previous discussion of Xianglin's wife, one has to assess the following aspects of female subjectivity and its manifestation in modern Chinese literature: (1) the consumptive and enunciative capacities of women in quest of their social and economic self-hood; (2) the deployment of biological and gender resources in both the public and private spheres; (3) the mythification of hunger and femininity as an arguably male imaginary of the physical and metaphysical destitution that beset modern China.

These assessments take on a polemical dimension to the degree that they occur in the revolutionary discourse sanctioned by Chinese leftist politicians and progressive writers since the twenties. It is the juncture of biological and ideological hunger in Chinese communist revolutionary discourse, I argue, that renders the above issues all the more provocative. To exemplify my assessments, I will focus, in what follows, on three of these hungry women: Guo Su'e in *Hungry Guo Su'e*; Tan Yuexiang in *Yangge* (The rice-sprout song), by Zhang Ailing (Eileen Chang); and Cai Qianhui in "Shanlu" (Mountain path), by Chen Yingzhen (Ch'en Ying-chen). In each of these works, the writers observe how hunger affects a woman's fate, and, more poignantly, how writing about hunger entails a tension between digestive and diegetic imaginations, and metabolic and metaphoric actions.

Guo Su'e

In 1942, as Mao Tse-tung laid down the rules for a new communist literature in his Yan'an talks, nineteen-year-old Lu Ling was creating an independent piece of leftist fiction in Chongqing, Sichuan.[5] This work, which would bring him fame—and notoriety—was *Hungry Guo Su'e*. Published in 1943, the novel generated immediate controversy among readers for its daring revelations about wartime life at the lower depths and its stylized, almost self-indulgent description of sex, violence, and irrationality. At the center of the novel is Guo Su'e, a woman who is driven out of her hometown by famine and banditry, and, against her will, becomes the wife of a sleazy opium addict, Liu Shouchun, twenty-four years her senior. As hunger sets in, Su'e comes to realize that she has fallen into a more unbearable situation. In response to this, she develops a new appetite, an appetite for men. The title of the novel, *Hungry Guo Su'e,* therefore, invites the double interpretation that hunger for food is merely a prelude to hunger for the unspeakable.

Guo Su'e carries on an affair with a local worker, Zhang Zhenshan, while another worker, Wei Haiqing, secretly falls in love with her. But it does not take long for Guo's husband to discover his wife's adulterous behavior; he and other clan members catch her in flagrante delicto one night and put her on private trial. They humiliate and abuse her in a most horrific way until she loses consciousness. Later, a thug from the crowd takes advantage of her helplessness and rapes her. Guo is left alone in a temple and dies three days later from a lack of medicine and food.

To decipher the mysterious etiology of Guo Su'e's hunger, a standard answer can be found in Lu Ling's own commentary. For him, given all the miseries she has been through, Guo Su'e is "not a woman crushed by the old society"; rather, what he wants to "wastefully search for" in this woman is "the primitive strength of the people and the active liberation of personality." But Lu Ling wonders whether the "base aspect of the ancient China" can be reformed with ease, hence his note that before any hope of liberation comes in sight, "Guo Su'e will continue to degenerate, however temporarily, into promiscuous inertia and selfish stupor."[6] In the same spirit, Lu Ling's mentor, Hu Feng, one of the most tendentious in the vanguard of a "subjective" Chinese Marxism, wrote this famous comment in his preface to the 1943 edition of the novel: "Guo Su'e is a sort of woman from the old, feudal kingdom; but physical hunger not only cannot be numbed by moral prescriptions handed down from the ancestors, it also produces an even stronger spiritual hunger, hunger for a profound liberation, hunger for a firm and unyielding human nature. She uses a primitive fierceness to knock against the iron wall of this society but she pays the price and her life is tragically sacrificed."[7]

Given its provocative female character, its experimental narrative format, and its polemical debate over ideological orientations, *Hungry Guo Su'e* has, curiously, not drawn much attention from scholars in the English-speaking world. Of the handful of studies, Kirk Denton calls attention to the mythological themes evoked in Guo's delirium and desire, and he puts these themes in the context of Chinese Taoist dynamics. Liu Kang highlights the Lacanian state of the "imaginary" inherent in Guo Su'e's psychological makeup and the drama of Bakhtinian heteroglossia that informs the rhetorical gesture of the novel. Yunzhong Shu refers Guo Su'e's characterization to the revolutionary poetics conceived by Hu Feng and argues that by creating such a female figure, Lu Ling has taken issue with the formula Mao prescribed for leftist writers in 1942.[8]

I would offer a reading of *Hungry Guo Su'e* that places the novel in the context of left corporeal discourse and argues that, for all its conformist premises, it can best be seen as an unexpected response to the hungry dialectics of Chinese Marxism. Historians have pointed out repeatedly that hunger, as a result of both natural and man-made disasters, constituted one of the main causes of the Chinese Communist Revolution, particularly in the countryside.[9] As early as 1926, Mao declares in his "Zhongguo shehui jieduan de fenxi" (Analysis of class in Chinese society) that social disparity is often described in terms of unequal food distribution. In 1927, in his famous "Hunan nongmin yundong kaocha baogao" (Report on an investigation of the peasant movement in Hunan), he stipulates that "we must create a short reign of terror in all parts of the countryside. A revolution is not like having a dinner party, or composing an article, or doing embroidery, a revolution is an uprising."[10] Mao enumerates fourteen tactics that rebellious peasants used against the landlords, of which "eat the rich" (*chi dahu*)—eating the landlords' grain and livestock—stands out as an action that asserts most symbolically the proletariat's immediate needs.[11] Since the late twenties, hunger was a popular theme in Chinese communist literature, testifying to the writers' ideological commitment to recording reality and instigating extreme measures to change it.

From Jiang Guangci's *Paoxiao lede tudi* (The roaring land) to Ding Ling's "Shui" (Flood), from Mao Dun's *Village Trilogy,* "Chuncan," "Qiushou," "Dongcan" (Spring silkworms, Autumn harvest, Winter ruins), to Wu Zuxiang's *Yiqian babaidan* (Eighteen hundred bushels), poor, hungry peasants are portrayed as being driven to violence by an ever mounting threat of starvation, thus providing a major impetus to the oncoming revolution.

Whereas in an ordinary sense hunger represents a lack of physical resources—food, nutrition, and access to the normal circulation of foodstuff—in communist terms, it can mean something quite different. Under revolutionary circumstances, hunger drives one to the acute awareness of one's class status in the social hierarchy, thereby opening the way to radical solutions. On the other hand, in the same revolutionary circumstances, one's capacity to withstand hunger becomes a sign, through which one demonstrates one's physical and moral strength. From bodily destitution to political institution, hunger, as a spiritual state, has been reified, so to speak, in the discourse of revolution. For those who are willing to suffer for the truth of history, hunger is not only a cause of revolutions; it is a mark of the true revolutionary, the outward demonstration of political virtue.

Revolution, as Mao defines it, is not a "dinner party"; one must cease self-indulgence and begin a life of resolute action. If such arguments sound familiar, it is because they obviously recapitulate the neo-Confucian call for spiritual rectification at the price of bodily deprivation.[12]

But in Mao's and his literary cohorts' hands, the hunger motif acquires even more superstructural significance. Instead of *lack,* hunger comes to indicate its opposite, *excess.* Hunger is comparable to a libidinous drive — for revolution and for communism — that always remains insatiable. It is easy to fill a body with physical food, but the spirit can never have enough ideological food. After the actual revolution, Mao is equally deft at playing the politics of hunger on the level of the imaginary. The still unsolved but merely finite problem of physical satisfaction is superseded by the infinite problem of spiritual satisfaction. He constructs a mythology in which one's utopian desire cannot and should not be satisfied; hence the necessity of continued revolution. Ban Wang describes such a power in terms of the "Maoist sublime," meaning a range of figurative capacities by which "whatever smacks too much of the human creature — appetite, feeling, sensibility, sensuality, imagination, fear, passion, lust, self-interest, etc. — is purged and repressed so that the all-too-human is sublimated with violence into the superhuman and even inhuman realms." [13]

As early as 1940, Mao made it a crucial part of his policy to feed his "people" with proper "cultural food," [14] and almost at the same time, the term *spiritual food* (*jingshen shiliang*) appeared in communist publications.[15] In the following decades, his literary workers raised endless crops of "cultural food" to be harvested for mass consumption, on the pretext that, in the cornucopia of Maoist discourse, there can be no limit to the people's hunger. By the late forties, "antihunger" (*fan ji'e*) had become one of the most popular slogans of urban leftist intellectuals and students. And though they might never have experienced the food shortages firsthand, the intelligentsia felt no less strongly about spiritual hunger: Antihunger meant an effort both to prevent a lack of material food (attention: farm managers) and to ensure a limitless supply of spiritual food (attention: urban intellectuals).

Hungry Guo Su'e appeared as a most intriguing dedication to, and deviation from, the hunger discourse of the forties, and to that effect, it dramatized the intricate relations between Hu Feng's "spiritual hunger" and Mao's "spiritual food." Lu Ling created the character Guo Su'e presumably to illuminate Hu Feng's observation that Chinese humanity was experiencing spiritual hunger, a hunger that calls for a special remedy beyond mere edible

food. He (or even Hu Feng) would have concurred with Mao that, to satisfy her spiritual hunger, Guo would need an abundant supply of "spiritual
food," as best represented by revolutionary yearning and utopian vision.
What is now noticeable, however, is that in search of that spiritual food, Lu
Ling has taken a narrative path so idiosyncratic that it digresses from the set
course approved by Mao—or even by Hu Feng. And in so doing, Lu Ling
manages to push Chinese literature to a new stage in the assimilation of
modern literary consciousness.

■   ■   ■

The characters in *Hungry Guo Su'e* yearn for the fulfillment of an un-
identifiable desire. They suffer from symptoms such as hysteria, manic-
depression, nymphomania, and sadomasochism—presumably bodily signs
of their *ressentiment*—but physical and psychological ailments only intensify
their pursuit of the unattainable. C. T. Hsia finds in *Hungry Guo Su'e* a "hard-
core realism," a depiction of lowlife so raw as to turn aside all humanitarian
concern.[16] But when Lu Ling reveals the obduracy of suffering by taking
life's "hard-core" aspect literally, the most dismal circumstances are bound
up into a sensuous escapade that is both repugnant and seductive.

This is the juncture where Guo Su'e's sexual appetite meets her spiritual
hunger and thus renders a murky interpretation of Mao's body politic. In a
fervor, Guo Su'e pursues erotic satisfaction, but she is only temporarily sati-
ated and experiences a deeper sense of vacuity. She is trapped in cyclic elevation and depression, while her body succumbs to every external stimulus.
She cries and laughs vulgarly, and she quarrels, shouts, cheats, and backbites
as if possessed. A mood of macabre excitement prevails as Guo's mysterious hunger becomes more desperate. If one senses a neurotic inclination in
the vein of Zola's naturalism, one feels the romantic influences of Romain
Rolland and D. H. Lawrence; aside from Marxist philosophy, Lu Ling also
admired Freudian psychology.[17]

Thus Guo Su'e best acts out the "irrational" aspect of spiritual hunger
as she shuffles back and forth between apocalyptic visions and psychotic
hallucinations, between erotic appetite and political hunger. In the arms
of her lover Zhang Zhenshan, Guo Su'e is described as "transported; all
her worries, sadness, fear and anguish are gone"; she experiences "a foggy
and ebullient sensation of ecstasy"; her "vision blur[s] and she gasp[s], feeling delight . . . her soul [is] completely immersed in beatitude." When she
waits for another tryst with Zhang, she is "absorbed in her desires and aspi-

rations,"[18] and the uncertain future tosses her alternately in the moods of "bitterness and ecstasy."[19]

In his eccentric study of the "deep structure" of Chinese collective psychology, Sun Longki describes the Chinese as fixated on the oral stage, a stage that reveals the Chinese (male) infantile nostalgia and fear of full-grown sexuality.[20] Sun can find no better example than *Hungry Guo Su'e.* The novel appears irksome precisely because it brings forward such a confrontation between orality and sexuality and projects it onto a new ideological plane. Before Lu Ling came along, to be sure, there had been an array of communist writers who wrote about sexuality as either the incentive or impediment to revolution, Mao Dun being one of the most frequently cited.[21] What makes Lu Ling's voice more polemical is that sexuality in his novel bears no clear, logical relevance to the cause of revolution other than serving as a bodily index to the unpredictable and violent force in deference to the impending revolution.

Take, for instance, a figure such as Yang Xi'er, in the play *Baimao nü* (The white-haired girl), one of the most celebrated heroines of Chinese communist literature of the Yan'an period. In the original version of *The White-Haired Girl,* Yang Xi'er, after being raped, impregnated, and deserted by an evil landlord, runs to hide in the local mountains. To keep her newborn baby and herself alive, she steals food from a monastery and is accidentally mistaken by the superstitious village folk for the immortal White-Haired Girl. When the revolution reaches her village, Xi'er is eventually rescued, and she becomes a token figure who bears witness to the cruelties of the old society.[22] Whatever the nature of Xi'er's hunger, her tortured personal metabolism is easily understood as a metaphor for feudal suffering, which is, when seen from the point of view of the Marxist metaphysic, the necessary precondition of human progress.

Guo Su'e appears to be a counterexample to the model heroine Yang Xi'er, in terms of both characterization and the implied timetable ascribed to her salvation (or its absence). Yang Xi'er undergoes a metamorphosis that easily fits into the classic linear, progressive format, one that delineates how she is "transformed from a ghost into a human being" by the new society, as the most famous statement about the play puts it.[23] By sharp contrast, Guo Su'e's story fails to provide such familiar, progressive significance. Where Mao and his followers establish a symbolic linkage among material need, somatic constitution, revolution, and spiritual transcendence, Lu Ling reveals the ambiguous fissures in such "chains of being"; where Mao enshrines ideal communist womanhood in terms of saintly magnanimity, Lu Ling lodges, instead, souls tempted and engulfed by worldly desires. Hence Guo Su'e's ambiguous thoughts about her salvation:

> She has been thirsty for attaining a new life through sexual desire, and most of the time this thirst elevated her to dreams that she could revolt and thus leave her past behind. Although she works hard and appears extremely kind to neighbors, she cannot help displaying the look of a criminal, for which she is still considered to be a uniquely bad woman. But she ignores this and entertains a fastidious determination: she has hurriedly taken a stand on the shore of the sea of labor. No matter how unfathomable and horrible the sea is, the faster the strong wind blows behind her, the sooner she will jump into the sea.[24]

Of note here is the way Lu Ling (or Guo Su'e) renders the communist cliché "the sea of labor" through a sequence of metaphoric shifts. Guo fantasizes the salvation in the sea of labor as if she were yearning for her next depraved adventure, and she qualifies her final rescue in terms of an eternal fall. As a result, she leaves the reader wondering whether her thoughts are an eruption of fleeting impressions, subject to continued verbal and emotive displacements, or the emanation of a telos that will sublate all rhetorical contingencies.

This language of desire finds its preliminary expression in the desire for language. As Guo Su'e's and other characters' psychiatric symptoms surface as verbal symptoms, they signal that the linguistic process of representation becomes possible only when these characters' problems can no longer be contained within the order of reality and rationality. At the textual level, Lu Ling matches his characters' volatile fits and writes "wastefully" about their syndromes. His images, metaphors, and other rhetorical devices, from free indirect style to narrated monologue, proliferate in such a way that the whole narration dramatizes the frustration, rather than the fulfillment, of his characters' efforts to satiate deep-seated desire. His infatuation with language corresponds to an unexpected surplus of meaning, anathema to the Maoist economy of literature, in which there is only one true meaning.

If Maoist hunger discourse aims at soliciting from the literal and symbolic lack of food the "sublime" effect, an emotive response that overwhelms any human effort at corporeal and linguistic representation,[25] Lu Ling's may be seen as directed toward a subliminal realm, where language evolves amorphously in approximation of libidinal turbulences.[26] This subliminal realm can be understood in terms of Julia Kristeva's description of *abjection,* or repugnance as a reaction to an inability to transcend the base associations of the corporeal, such as food, waste, and gender differences. In contrast to the Maoist sublime, which hinges on the transcendence of the symbolic system of language and sign systems, the abject focuses attention on the "thresholds," which are manifested, among other ways, in those bodily orifices that blur the distinction between the inside and the outside, attraction and repulsion, Eros and Thanatos. Abjection appears, as one critic puts it, "where boundaries are traversed and unity punctured so that the resultant breach threatens to widen and overtake the whole."[27]

Kristeva's theory appears relevant to *Hungry Guo Su'e* in that it locates the site of abjection in women and links such a feminine abject state to the formation of a language system, on the one hand, and of the (psycho)somatic condition, on the other. If language is that which is predetermined by the patriarchal symbolic order, the feminine presents itself as an amorphous semiotic force coming from outside the male order. Contrary to the rational distinction based on the chain of language and naming, the feminine reestablishes these distinctions "by inscribing itself in sites of the body, particularly those bodily holes which confuse the boundary between inside and outside, and therefore between the Self and Other."[28]

The way Lu Ling straddles the realms of the sublime and the abject enables him to project Guo Su'e at the "threshold," so to speak, of the communist somatic/semiotic system. Guo's unpleasant appearance embodies the ambiguous zone one has to cross over in negotiating the metabolic hunger and metaphysic hunger. Incidentally, to redeem her sins, Xianglin's wife, in Lu Xun's "New Year's Sacrifice," is taught to donate a threshold, as her own bodily substitute, at a local Buddhist temple, to be trampled on by people. Where Xianglin's wife falls at the threshold of feudal ideology, Guo Su'e fights a fatal battle before the edifice of Chinese communism. That she dies in the middle of the narrative, therefore, is highly suggestive. Instead of providing an apotheosis, Guo Su'e's death resolves neither the novel nor the problem of hunger.

In the final hours of her life, Guo Su'e is taken to the back room of the Zhang Fei Temple and cries, "Don't touch me! I am a woman!" and "You scum who eat human flesh and don't spit bones!" She is forced to one corner of the room, her clothes torn to pieces, but her look is still defiant. As one of the clanswomen approaches her, "a devil suddenly comes out [of Guo Su'e].

This devil dishevels her hair, spits saliva, and jumps fiendishly onto the old woman, strangling the old woman [by seizing her] tender throat." [29] Infuriated by this unexpected move, Guo's husband and others tie her to a plank and sear her thighs with red-hot pokers, till, in excruciating pain, she loses consciousness. Then, "three days after that fearful night in the Zhang Fei Temple, she regained consciousness and groped her way out the hall door. She could move because . . . she felt she could live, and in the end, because she was hungry. But just as she had groped her way to the courtyard, she let out a shriek and fell to the ground as a white pus oozed out from below her belly." [30]

Guo Su'e's struggle to live thus ends with a slow and horrific degeneration to a state of total nullification; she dies after her voice fails to reach anybody and her need for food is left unfilled. Through the fatal denial of the fundamental needs of female orality, Lu Ling attacks the cannibalistic nature of the old society, while at the same time he has belied, however unwittingly, the call of the new communist society for a new, higher hunger. The corpse of Guo Su'e, rotting on the grounds of the feudal temple, prods one to question whether hers is just another heroic body to be added to the mausoleum of leftist victimology or, more pointedly, whether it is an abject reminder of the figural and figurative inadequacies of Stalinist/Maoist hunger symbolism.

Historical hindsight tempts one to read an allegory into Guo Su'e's hunger and death. Lu Ling was purged from the new communist society, together with other members of the Hu Feng gang, in the mid-fifties, *Hungry Guo Su'e* being only one of the examples of his ideological impurity. One recalcitrant fictional hungry woman had to be sacrificed so that postrevolutionary men and women could be nourished on more soothing fictional formulas. In the late fifties, as the whole country was happily digesting Mao's words—his spiritual food—rampant physical starvation was already under way. Millions of people paid their respects to Mao by dying, or killing and eating each other, in the name of spiritual truth.[31] When Lu Ling was at last rehabilitated in the eighties, he was already an old, schizophrenic man, thoroughly reformed and unable to write anything but slogans.[32] While his novels were altogether unknown to the general reader, the language revolution he quietly launched did inspire a new generation of writers in the 1980s, modernists such as Ge Fei, Bei Cun, and Yu Hua. Responding to a new kind of self-indulgent hunger that spread across post-Maoist China, these young writers scandalize orthodox Chinese readers with a literature that threatens to devour all certainties and to encourage feasting on possibility: They took up where Lu Ling left off.

Tan Yuexiang

Tan Yuexiang is the female protagonist of *The Rice-Sprout Song,* by Eileen Chang, one of the most important writers in Shanghai during the period of Japanese occupation. After the communist liberation in 1949, Chang first decided to stay in her beloved Shanghai, but political circumstances were such that she finally left for Hong Kong in 1952. During her stay in Hong Kong from 1952 to 1955, she wrote two novels in English, *The Rice-Sprout Song* and *Naked Earth,* under the sponsorship of the United States Information Service; she later rewrote these in Chinese. Both novels have clear anticommunist themes, and, to that effect, they can easily be taken as examples of Western propaganda of the cold war period.

The *Rice-Sprout Song* renders the horror and absurdity that the land reform movement brought to a southern village of China in the early fifties. The victorious revolution, followed by the redistribution of land, is supposed to "liberate" the peasants of the village. But contrary to their hopes, life does not change. As a result of both natural and man-made disasters, the peasants face yet another threat of famine, and China's involvement in the Korean War only deepens their misery. When they can no longer put up with pressure from local leaders to produce grain, the peasants take to bloody rioting. The local people's militia intervene, massacring the rioters and further tightening their control in the village. At the end of the novel, the survivors are forced to parade and take part in the New Year's celebrations.

Instituted as early as the forties, land reform was among the most important policies of the Chinese Communist Revolution in its early stages. At first glance, land reform appeared to be nothing more than a radical agricultural-economic policy. But the movement was never a mere attempt at revamping the rural infrastructure; rather, it was always given a superstructural dimension, as its implementation contributed to, and was conditioned by, a program of drastic changes in traditional Chinese morality, legality, and psychology. As early as the mid-forties, leftist writers such as Zhao Shuli, Zhou Libo, and Ding Ling were already engaged in writing about the triumphant consequences of the movement in northern China.[33] Their works do not stop at describing the redistribution to the many of the land that used to belong to the few. For these writers, reform of the Chinese landscape will lead to the reform of the Chinese "mindscape."

The Rice-Sprout Song rewrites this land reform discourse proffered by leftist politicians and writers. As if parodying the jubilant undertone of communist land reform novels, Chang maintains a festive atmosphere in *The Rice-Sprout Song*. But as her story develops, this festive atmosphere turns out to be a celebration of something ghastly and theatrical, the prelude to a *danse macabre*. She details the chilling fact of food shortages in the newly liberated south, traditionally the richest agricultural area of China, and reveals the desperate measures peasants took to survive the impending famine.

. . .

Hu Shi, one of the most important vanguards of the modern Chinese literary revolution, was among the first scholars to praise *The Rice-Sprout Song*.[34] He sees hunger as the theme of the novel, and credits Chang for her verbal subtlety and emotive control, which are a far cry from the "tears-and-blood" style of propaganda literature, communist or anticommunist. Following Hu Shi, critics have given credit to Chang's understated yet powerful narrative, but little has been said about the way she elaborates on the politics of hunger.[35]

Chang's question is, if the hunger revolution has been successfully implemented, why do the Chinese still suffer from hunger? The leftist writer Mao Dun had published, in the early thirties, the *Village Trilogy*, through which he made famous a paradox of production: The harder the farmers work, the less they earn; the more grain they produce, the hungrier they are. By means of this paradox, Mao Dun's *Trilogy* points to the irrationality of the prerevolutionary mode of agricultural production. *The Rice-Sprout Song* insinuates that the same paradox applies to the new mode of agricultural production. According to Chang, the old landlords may have been liquidated, but the communist government has become the single new landlord, with proportionately increased power and greed. Jingen and his wife, Yuexiang, the protagonists of the novel, work hard to meet the increasing demands of local cadres, only to realize that, however hard they work, they will never have enough to eat.

As the famine becomes more serious, Yuexiang, and not her husband, Jingen, emerges as the stronger one in the household. Before the land reform, Yuexiang worked as a maid in Shanghai, and was therefore more worldly than her husband and most villagers. She returned home at the governmental call to support rural work, and she realized only too late that life in the village was far worse than imagined. A pragmatic woman, Yuexiang understands that, to survive hunger, she has to store and ration food strictly; to that effect, she manages to cheat cadres, turns down her sister-in-law's requests, and even denies her own daughter's wish to have a bowlful of rice. But Yuexiang cannot prevent her husband from rioting. She is taken to the village barn by the local soldiers, and, after learning that Jingen was killed by the cadres, sets the barn on fire and burns to death.

In his reading of *The Rice-Sprout Song,* C. T. Hsia calls attention to Yuexiang's endurance and deep feeling for her husband and family. Hsia puts this female character in the humanitarian context of modern Chinese writing.[36] Granting its humanitarian context, I, however, would argue that the novel's power is derived not so much from Chang's compassion as from her lack of confidence in humanity and her idiosyncratic notion of individualism. For her, individualism is a euphemism for self-interest and self-protection; "selfish" as it may be to others, it is nonetheless the only way one can survive in a time of historical crises. It is this unique individualism that gives meaning to Chang's embrace of the material world, her aestheticization of eschatology, and her play with irony that subverts anything hailed as solid, including her own writings. And she does not hesitate to generalize these traits and associate them with her vision of femininity.

Yuexiang is a creditable female only by Eileen Chang's definition of femininity: selfish, earthy, and material. Although she may not appear as slick and sophisticated as those Shanghai ladies who crowd Chang's earlier fiction, she proves to be worthy of citizenship in Chang's female republic by fully representing what Chang calls "the most universal, the most basic of humanity: the cyclical movement of the four seasons; the earth; life, age, illness, and death; recreation and food." [37] Compared to the agenda of other feminist writers of her time, Chang's understanding of femininity may seem rather passive, if not reactionary. She is, nevertheless, a most somber guardian of her own space as a woman and as a writer. She knows well the importance of being not too earnest—or not too politically correct, in contemporary terms—whatever the cause.

At a time when most male and female Chinese writers were eager to exchange individual subjectivities for a collective, national subjectivity, Chang's own brand of "selfish" and "feminine" mannerisms stood out as a genuinely defiant gesture. As *The Rice-Sprout Song* develops, it is Yuexiang who sees through the myth of spiritual food and dares to cross political guidelines in pursuit of her family's livelihood. Reading Yuexiang against other communist figures in the novel, one wonders who is more sensitive to the material basis of life. Ironically, Yuexiang has to be killed, in the produce barn, to ensure communist spiritual abundance.

The significance of Yuexiang as a hungry woman takes on an extra dimension in the subplot of *The Rice-Sprout Song.* As the villagers are increasingly threatened by the shortage of food, Gu Gang, a scriptwriter, is sent from Shanghai to the country to "experience life." His mission is none other than to witness the "success" of land reform and write a movie script about the alleged abundances to be found in the new rural life. Gu Gang, however, soon suffers from writer's block because of his isolated status in the village and his discovery of the discrepancies between what he sees and what he is supposed to see, between what he can write and what he is supposed to write. But an even more immediate and embarrassing reason is that, once settling in the village, he, too, must deal with the lack of food in spite of his privileged class. Driven by the constant fear of hunger, Gu Gang racks his brain more often in search of food than of cinematic inspiration.

Gu's story drives home Eileen Chang's sarcasm about the myth of Maoist spiritual gastronomy. Before he can produce communist "cultural food," Gu Gang needs to feed himself, in the first place, with material food. He finds temporary solace only in Yuexiang, since she has been to Shanghai and appreciates his "culture"; even so, he cannot fully understand Yuexiang's need. As a self-conscious revolutionary artist, Gu hews to the party line regardless of all the visible, precipitate evidence in the village, and, in the most ironic twist of the novel, he finally completes his manuscript, finding inspiration in the villager's riots for food.

Thus, the peasant riot against the land reform movement provides the idea, in Gu's script, for a peasant riot scene against nationalist landlords. In the script, the reactionary landlords are seen "eating and drinking ferociously" behind closed doors, and there, in the midst of the secret banquet, stands a young woman who looks like Yuexiang: "Her main function in the scene is to lean slantingly against the table . . . thus lending an eerie and sensual atmosphere to the secret meeting among the landlords. Her appearance and dress look very much like Yuexiang's." [38] Nowhere else has Chang shown more bitter sarcasm about communist morality than in describing Gu Gang's final submission to the formulaic, feudal convention: A woman recklessly seeking food, in reality, has been demonized in light of the traditional stereotype of femme fatale, as a woman relentlessly hungry for sex in communist fictionality.

The story of Gu Gang may again illustrate the tension between the oppression of a totalitarian party and the creative freedom of a writer. But Eileen Chang gives this tension one more twist. Gu may have betrayed his political conscience by writing what he did not see and did not believe. He nevertheless settles with his artistic conscience because, party line notwith-standing, he has organized words, images, and symbolism into a verbal and visual extravaganza that meets his own satisfaction. Is Gu's script a decadent testimonial to, or the tendentious propaganda for, a certain ideology? Has he acted out the cause of "art for art's sake" under a regime that despises "art for art's sake"? Has he become a despicable accomplice in the collabo-ration of art with politics? And what is "art for art's sake," after all, if not the insatiable Maoist desire for ideological perfection?

In the afterword to the Chinese edition of the novel, Chang wryly tells us that *The Rice-Sprout Song* was inspired by a "reported" communist leader's confession about his failure to prevent a peasant riot during the land reform movement, and by a communist movie, which contained a plot of a barn fire set by nationalist spies. She turned these procommunist materials against themselves. Not unlike her character, Eileen Chang has enacted, on the scene of writing, a cluster of self-reflexive ironies on the mutual implication of history and fiction, and of imagined truth and materialized myth. Her sarcasm about Gu's mission to rewrite history reverberates from her own work, throwing open the question of its intentions. A writer who had been stranded in early fifties' Hong Kong, Chang was commissioned to write anticommunist literature — a genre thought not to be her strong suit. She nevertheless managed to work out her own version of anticommunist litera-ture, a version that has unexpected depths. Through Gu's story and her own afterword, Chang has written an allegory about the vulnerable situation of Chinese writers of the time, communist and anticommunist alike.

The final irony, perhaps, is that, forty years after the first publication of the novel, the hunger motif it so vividly portrayed has acquired a retro-spective poignancy. Recent studies by historians such as Jasper Becker have revealed that, between 1958 and 1962, at least thirty million Chinese per-ished in perhaps the worst famine in Chinese history, one caused not by nature but by Mao's ideological vanity.[39] This man-made disaster, and its scope, was hardly acknowledged at the time, partly because of tight govern-ment censorship and partly because of self-censoring China experts. When Chang wrote *The Rice-Sprout Song* in the mid-fifties, she had neither the intention nor the resources to predict the forthcoming horrors, but in an uncanny way, her novel foretold the cruel absurdities that Chinese would experience. A China watcher she was not, and yet she saw something inherently ominous by resorting to her "material," commonsensical vision. "Our age plunges forward and is already well on its way to collapse, while a bigger catastrophe looms."[40] A connoisseur of eschatology, Chang made this sober prediction in regard to the China of the forties; with *The Rice-Sprout Song,* this prediction proved all too true, and came to pass all too quickly, despite (or because of) all the official proclamations of an age of plenty.

Cai Qianhui

"When I first came to your family, I was ready to eat bitterness," the fifty-year-old Cai Qianhui, who lies in a hospital bed, recalls to her brother-in-law, Li Guomu.[41] Struck down by a mysterious illness, Cai Qianhui has been hospitalized for two months and is getting increasingly weak in spite of the nourishment and medical care she has received. She eventually dies, and the cause of her death is determined by a letter she leaves behind. Cai Qianhui is the protagonist of "Mountain Path," by Chen Yingzhen, one of the most important political fiction writers from Taiwan. First published in 1983, "Mountain Path" appears as the second story in a trilogy Chen wrote in memory of the "White Terror" of the fifties, an era that witnessed an increase in underground Taiwanese socialist activities, followed by massive crackdowns and bloody purges by the Nationalist party.

In Chen Yingzhen's narration, we are not fully informed of the historical background of the story until the end, when Cai Qianhui's letter is posthumously disclosed verbatim. Of the clues provided in the first part of the story, the most intriguing one is Cai Qianhui's revelation to her brother, quoted above: "When I first came to your family, I was ready to eat bitterness." "Eat bitterness" (*chiku*), a figure of speech that means "to endure hardships," suggests the life that Cai Qianhui must have lived. Indeed, as her letter reveals, for almost thirty years, she had helped the Li family survive all sorts of adversity, bringing it from the verge of starvation to the status of a comfortable urban middle-class household. Why, then, dying in a first-class hospital room, does she reiterate, nostalgically, her capacity to eat bitterness?

Unlike the two hungry women discussed in the previous sections, Cai Qianhui appears well fed. Though widowed since she came to the Lis', she is well respected by the family of her brother-in-law and is almost like a mother to them; and now, in the hospital, she is surrounded by doctors and all the food and medical supplies one could hope for to cure her mysterious disease. Yet Cai Qianhui fails to work up any appetite for food or anything else that can sustain her life. "She just became weak all of a sudden. Such a healthy person to become weak like that so suddenly."[42] When she dies, she dies as a woman remembering those hungry days she had had with her family.

It is in this enigmatic figure of Cai Qianhui that Chen Yingzhen has invested a touching allegory about political idealism and its betrayal and, as I will argue below, about the treacherous conditions of communist hunger aesthetics. A leftist writer based in Taiwan, Chen Yingzhen has had a career that may appear no less tortuous than those of some of the characters in his fiction. Chen was born into a pious Christian minister's family in northern Taiwan but grew up searching for his own beliefs. Chen was arrested in 1967 by the Nationalist party on a charge of leading procommunist activities, and he spent the next seven years in jail. After his release in 1973, he resumed his career as a writer, focusing mostly on the consequences of Taiwan's newly gained economic prosperity that resulted, Chen concluded, from American-Japanese capitalist imperialism, which began in the sixties. As he continued to hold on to his leftist idealism, the gradual revelation of the atrocities of the Great Cultural Revolution must have struck him as an unbearable departure from the expected course of global communist revolution. In the meantime, the death of Chiang Kai-shek in 1975 triggered a cluster of political metamorphoses in Taiwan, particularly the outburst of the Taiwan independence movement. Chen Yingzhen was faced with multiple challenges: How could a once noble revolutionary ideal have turned rotten so fast in the fresh air of history? How could unconditional dedication entail falsehood, betrayal, and self-destruction? Should a Taiwan leftist writer still endorse a Marxist regime that had caused such disaster in China?

. . .

"Mountain Path" must be read as a remarkable feat on the part of Chen Yingzhen to respond to these questions. From Cai Qianhui's posthumous letter, one learns that, as a teenage girl, Cai Qianhui was involved in a communist organization in northern Taiwan, in which both her brother and her fiancé, Huang Zhenbo, were members. Through this connection, Cai came to know the leader of the organization, Li Guokun, who stole her heart with his unconditional idealism. The organization was later suppressed by the Nationalist government. Li Guokun was put to death and Huang Zhenbo sentenced to life in prison; the informant was none other than Cai Qianhui's brother. To compensate for her brother's betrayal and to sustain her own revolutionary romanticism, Cai Qianhui decided to "marry" into the family, oddly, not of her fiancé, Huang Zhenbo, but of Li Guokun. She went to the poverty-stricken Li family, making up a story that she and Li had been secretly married, and vowed, as Li's widow, to endure with them all the hardships, or to "eat bitterness," for years to come.

Thirty years after she arrived on the doorstep of the Li family, Cai Qianhui, seated one morning in the comfortable living room of Li Guomu, her alleged brother-in-law, found out from the newspaper that Huang, her real fiancé, had been released from prison. Shamed by her betrayal of Huang Zhenbo and his comrades, and more by her ideological amnesia in recent years owing to the changes in Taiwanese lifestyle, Cai collapsed and thereafter lost her will to live.

I summarize the story at length because it is full of melodramatic surprises. But to anyone who criticizes its hackneyed plot, Chen Yingzhen would perhaps have retorted that the outrageous history of the White Terror, which affected so many people and families, would seem only more "unlikely" than the story. By the same logic, he could also have argued that if, for Cai Qianhui or Li Guokun, "revolution" meant acting to make the impossible possible, it ought to demand an extraordinary sacrifice of ordinary humanity. Thus the characterization of Cai Qianhui is credible precisely because she is capable of an incredible sacrifice; her story is a small-scale example of communist hagiography.

My reading suggests that Cai Qianhui be regarded as one of the last hungry heroines of modern Chinese communist discourse. Her appearance in Chen Yingzhen's fiction, across the Taiwan Straits and in the aftermath of the Cultural Revolution, recapitulates the metaphorics and metaphysics of hunger that have either enshrouded or enshrined so many modern Chinese female characters. There exists, however, a fundamental difference between Cai Qianhui and her other hungry sisters. Whereas characters such as Guo Su'e and Tan Yuexiang suffer egregiously from a lack of food, Cai Qianhui, as mentioned above, has come to have more than enough were it not for her antipathy to food and her inability to absorb nutrition. In the story, she is fed food and dutifully eats, but she cannot help the deterioration of her body, as if she has no control over it anymore.

From Cai Qianhui's mysterious withering away, one discerns an "anorexic logic." By this I do not mean merely an eating disorder that results from a physical and psychological repugnance to food, a symptom from which the term *anorexic* derives its primary definition. Rather, I mean a mode of thinking that compels one to configure one's body so as to express one's real relations to the world, in which consumption of food constitutes an embarrassment. At the core of such an anorexic logic is a tendency toward self-negation that drives one to despise or ignore one's corporeal constitution in anticipation of a higher, sanctified state of existence. The medical and imagined symptoms of anorexia and their consequences have become a popular topic in recent years. Leslie Haywood, for instance, delineates how anorexia has been borrowed as a trope to describe the "bony," "self-destructive" aesthetics of European high modernism and its inherent phallocentric agenda.[43] In her study of the phenomena of "fasting girls" in the Victorian period, Joan Brumberg differentiates two types of anorexic women: *anorexia mirabilis* and *anorexia nervosa*. Whereas the former is seen as the result of divine immanence and thus calls for religious sanction, the latter is associated with a hysteria that requires medical examination.[44] From *anorexia mirabilis* to *anorexia nervosa*, or from religious miracle to clinical illness, argues Brumberg among others, a process of rhetorical ambiguity is involved, and it is this process of ambiguity that informs the shift of episteme as well as the changed image of the modern woman at the turn of the century.[45]

Inspired by, but not limited to, these critical approaches, I find in the Chinese communist hunger discourse an uncanny counterpart to the medical, gendered symptoms of anorexia: a self-willed hunger motivated (possibly first) by historical circumstances but reinforced, and finally sanctioned, by ideological goals. As I discussed above, the Chinese communist hunger discourse has always entertained a component of self-willed hunger as a physical testimony to ideological strength. In theory, it reminds one of traditional religious fasting as a trial of self-purgation through self-negation, but in practice, it echoes more the (neo-)Confucian tenor of curbing one's corporeal welfare while asserting one's moral rectitude.[46] From the case of Boyi and Shuqi of the early Zhou dynasty to Liu Zongzhou of the late Ming, Chinese historiography is full of accounts of model figures who have starved to death to assert their moral or political integrity. And in terms of moralizing the relations between woman and food, what can be more striking than the statement by Song scholar Cheng Yi (1033–1107): "To die from hunger is an extremely trivial matter; to lose one's chastity is an extremely grave shame"?[47]

Cai Qianhui's case is challenging because at first glance she is neither anorexic in the strict Western medical sense nor a self-willed hunger heroine in the Chinese ideological sense. Her death, presumably from her body's resistance to any nutrition, came, at best, too late (and too gratuitously) to serve the revolution that failed. What is more, one finds in Cai Qianhui's life a cluster of ambiguities: a girl in the guise of the widow of someone other than her own fiancé; a virgin who assumes the image of "mother of the revolution" and who is sustained by "eating bitterness"; and a woman who denies her womanly qualities in the name of communist fraternity. This cluster of ambiguities culminates in her mysterious death, where the lines between medical pathology and ideological fanaticism, regret and bliss, alimentary nutrition and spiritual hemorrhage are blurred. Cai Qianhui never demonstrates the medical symptom of turning away food, but the point is precisely that she has developed such contempt for her body that food simply becomes a superficial reminder of the gap between what she is eating and what she wants to be fed.

Cai Qianhui's desire to relinquish her body, nevertheless, should be regarded only as the climax of an entire life dedicated to self-sacrifice. Taking another look at the "anorexic logic" implied in the Chinese communist hunger discourse, one realizes that throughout her life, Cai has lived to denounce her corporeal well-being. Cai Qianhui has, all along, seen the withering away of her virginal body as a way to live out the saintly bliss of the hunger revolution. But in the eighties, in Taiwan, she cannot figure out why her revolutionary life of "eating bitterness" ends up turning the family toward a heaven of capitalist expenditure. Material things have made her and her family "tame animals" of capitalism, yet she thinks back to her days of hardship, in search of the "proper" outcome: communist utopian life. Finally, as Cai Qianhui writes in her letter, "If the revolution fails on the mainland, does that mean [Li Guokun's] death and [Huang Zhenbo's] long-term imprisonment have turned into meaningless punishments more cruel than death or life in prison?" [48] For Cai, the only way to assure the meaning of life as it should be, as prescribed by the Communist Revolution, is to cut life (and time) short by losing her body, an act that could at least freeze her own history into the crystallized narrative form of History.

▪ ▪ ▪

Chen Yingzhen's negotiation with Chinese Marxist revolutionism does not, however, stop with his rewriting the hunger motif. Before he is an ideologue, he is, first and foremost, a strong writer. As in the case of Lu Xun,

Lu Ling, and Eileen Chang, Chen has always been self-conscious about the conditions of literature vis-à-vis the conditions of politics. In what sense, then, can we read "Mountain Path" not simply as a political allegory but as an allegory about the politics of writing?

Lu Xun and Lu Ling wrote about hungry women as a way of imparting their own political yearning, or hunger, for a national reform. Whatever their miseries, these hungry women are expected to inform a national aspiration for revolution, which would help feed Chinese with material and spiritual food. In "Mountain Path," however, Chen Yingzhen struggles to come up with a rationale after the Communist Revolution came to a disastrous halt and such noble hunger discourse had acquired the expected validation. If *Hungry Guo Su'e* marks the outbreak of the libidinous, political unconscious that knows no limits, "Mountain Path" faces the challenge of recalling, elegiacally, the bygone days of political fervor amid the ruins of revolutionary praxis. Instead of the primitive force driving Guo Su'e to consume and consummate her desire in the shadow of total destruction, Chen Yingzhen invests in Cai Qianhui's body politic a deep sense of irony: Her anorexic gesture is a retrospective visitation of the hunger spirit, and her suicidal motive is none other than the result of her historical hindsight. She has experienced both hunger and revolution, but these have resulted in a quite unexpected outcome. Hence Cai Qianhui's apprehension in her letter: "I have a feeling of desperate waste." [49]

What worries Cai Qianhui is not the bloody waste of life and idealism of one generation of Taiwanese revolutionaries but the threatening "meaninglessness" of that waste viewed in retrospect. Strangely enough, to act out her resistance to the wasted revolution, she chooses to waste her own body, as if only through the relinquishment of the body could she regain the pristine nature of her revolutionary selfhood.

Given Chen Yingzhen's Christian background, one can talk about a kind of religious martyrdom that underlies Cai Qianhui's political fanaticism. Feminists can charge Chen Yingzhen with indulging the idea of female self-effacement in support of a male-centered revolutionary cause, to the point where woman is transformed from a nobody in the revolution to a literal no body after the revolution. I suspect, nevertheless, that Chen Yingzhen is no more an ideological fanatic or a misogynist than he is a modernist informed by the (anti-)heroism of the absurd. Although allegedly dying for a revolutionary cause that has been invalidated in the postrevolutionary days, Cai Qianhui shows more determination to hold on to an idealism on her own terms. Her insistence intimates the mixture of both self-assertion and self-abandon, thereby bringing the absurdist double bind Chen Yingzhen describes as a "desperate waste." [50]

We then come to one last, poignant fact: Instead of any private but violent measures of suicide, Cai Qianhui dies in a slow and semipublic exhibition—a spectacle of a body wasting away. In this regard, she brings to mind Kafka's "Hunger Artist." The Hunger Artist, the reader will recall, cages himself as an art exhibit, and the subject of his performance art is the withering away of his own subjectivity. In other words, he acts out an art of deduction through his own self-deduction. With such a self-deductive and self-destructive character, as critics suggest, Kafka announces the coming of the age of modernism.[51] But in light of the Judaic mysticism behind Kafka's writing, this self-deduction may very well be regarded as the first step toward the plenitude of divine grace.

I have yet to find evidence of Chen Yingzhen's indebtedness to the Hunger Artist, although, considering his education, he should have been aware of the work. My point is, rather, that by describing Cai Qianhui's death in the manner of hunger artist-cum-ideologue, Chen has presented a provocative mixture of modernist aesthetics and Chinese Marxist ethics. But the story has something more to tell us about history and its artistic inscription. If writing can be treated as a "trace" in the poststructuralist sense, removed from the primal, phonocentric scene, which in its own turn is an *écriture* of the regressive ontological meaning, the fact that Cai Qianhui leaves behind a letter strikes a final self-ironic note. Written in a lyrical, nostalgic tone, the letter appears as a relic, something that will survive the erosion of time and bear witness to the truth that Cai Qianhui was unable to speak in her lifetime. But as remnants of the past, relics cannot retroactivate history per se but can only reaffirm the irretrievability of history. A sense of futility pervades the end of this story that aims to be the remainder and reminder of the past revolutionism. Questions must be asked: Hasn't Chen Yingzhen himself become a ghostlike chronicler of the glory of revolutionism? Would the meaning of Chen's corpus end up like Cai Qianhui's skeletal corpse, which asserts its protest to history by canceling its own existence?

Coda: The Daughters of Hunger

I have described the polemics of hunger in modern Chinese literature in terms of three "hungry women" as portrayed by Lu Ling, Eileen Chang, and Chen Yingzhen. By depicting the causes of these women's hunger and the way in which each one deals with the material consequences of hunger, I argue, these writers have achieved a special perspective from which to deal with the revolutionary discourse of modern China. Behind these women, moreover, lies the writers' own desire — hunger — for a better understanding of the metaphoric and metaphysic dimension of hunger as proffered by Chinese Marxist discourse. Thus, through a dedicated follower of Hu Feng's theory of Marxist spiritual food, Lu Ling reveals an eccentric self-indulgence when he "wastefully" parades the depraved deeds of the hungry Guo Su'e and people around her. His extravagant style betrays a textual desire that appears to contradict the stylistic manual prescribed by Mao. Eileen Chang, by paralleling Tan Yuexiang's desperate effort to survive the rural famine with Gu Gang's desperate effort to churn up cultural food for mass consumption, takes issue with the circulation of superstructural nourishment, which had been deemed unquestionable in an ideological system that otherwise favored infrastructural work. Chen Yingzhen, in a story about the waste of recollecting things past, ponders the authenticity of remembering and writing when political dedication had become a thing of the past.

All three writers start with a style of hard-core realism by depicting reality and by paralleling truth claims to linguistic make-believe. But while depicting hunger, they cannot help taking up the "side issues" of the aesthetics of hunger writing, which can be so polemical as to offend the political authorities. Hunger is no longer merely a theme or subject matter but a formal challenge, a body politic demanding its own literary politic. In Lu Ling's indulgence in textual desire, in Eileen Chang's flirtation with metafiction (a novel about the writing of a movie script about hunger), and in Chen Yingzhen's posthumous epistolary confession, one witnesses a most engaging dialogue between Chinese (anti-)communist writing and modernist sensibilities.

The hunger motif has remained a popular subject since the eighties. Both Zhang Xianliang's *Luhua shu sanbuqu* (Mimosa trilogy) and *Wo de putishu* (My own Bodhi tree), and Wang Ruowang's *Ji'e sanbuqu* (A trilogy of hunger) use hunger as a point of reference to chronicle the Maoist coercion of intellectuals. Lu Wenfu's "Meishijia" (The gourmet) and Ah Cheng's "Qiwang" (The chess king), on the other hand, approach hunger from the vantage point of either ironic recollection or critical lyricism. Liu Zhenyun's *Wengu 1942* (Remembering 1942) chronicles the famine of 1942, which took the lives of millions, using a complex of genres including reportage, newsreel, fictional reconstruction, and contemplative essay, whereas Yu Hua's

Huozhe (To live) portrays the forty years of PRC history as nothing but a record of survivalism.[52] And in Mo Yan's *Jiuguo* (The wine republic), Chinese cannibalistic desire comes full circle; instead of the Lu Xunesque "save the children," one hears the hungry calls of gourmets to "cook the children."

What about the fate of hungry women in end-of-the-century Chinese literature? The most unforgettable case, perhaps, is *Shafu* (The butcher's wife) by the Taiwan writer Li Ang. In this novella, a woman is forced to have sex with her husband, a pig butcher, in exchange for food. Driven by humiliation and hunger, she finally butchers her husband like one of his pigs. In Yu Hua's "Gudian aiqing" (A classical love story), a dark parody of the classical talent-beauty (*caizi jiaren*) romance, the beauty ends up becoming an "edible human" (*cairen*) in a year of famine—her limbs are chopped off and sold to the highest bidder. In Li Rui's *Wufeng zhishu* (Trees without wind), hungry women are sold as late as 1963 in the back country of Shan'xi to poor and deformed peasants as "public" wives. Across the Taiwan Strait, Tan Zhongdao publishes an equally ghoulish account of famine, "Canghai zhi yisu" (A tiny grain in the world) in which the hungry woman protagonist runs away from her husband's family, who were conspiring to eat her, only to be consumed by her own parents once she arrives home.

The latest addition to the century-long gallery of hungry women is the heroine in Hongying's most recent novel, *Ji'e de nüer* (The daughter of hunger). Written in the form of an autobiographical novel spanning the sixties to the eighties, *The Daughter of Hunger* relates the narrator's painful experience of growing up. Hongying was born in the heyday of the Great Leap Forward movement, when millions of people perished from the famine caused by Mao; worse, she was the illegitimate daughter of an illiterate woman. As the "daughter of hunger," the fictional Hongying was deprived as much by the natural environment as by the patriarchal social system.

The Daughter of Hunger should be regarded as one of the rare fictional accounts that confront the biological and psychological consequences of the national famine during the Great Leap Forward, whose atrocities still remain taboo today. Hongying tells how her mother ran away from an arranged marriage yet could not evade fate's blows in the years to come. During the great famine period, her husband was jailed on political charges. She and her children were close to starvation, but a young man came to their rescue and then fell in love with her. It did not take long before the affair was disclosed, and by then Hongying's mother had already become pregnant with her.

The story of Hongying's mother provides a striking parallel to Lu Ling's Guo Su'e. Both are hungry women who harbor a desire that cannot be settled by mere food. Given the horrible life Hongying's mother led after her adultery was revealed, one can well imagine what would have happened to Guo Su'e even if she had survived the private trial and lived to see the establishment of the People's Republic. The new society would have proven just as cannibalistic as the old one. Hongying's own experience growing up "almost" repeats her mother's. Her foster father is never able to convey his concern about her; her birth father never gets the chance to meet her until she is eighteen; and her first lover, ironically, her history teacher, who is twice her age, introduces her to sex but soon commits suicide because of his own political burden. "All three of my fathers—my foster father, my natural father, and my history teacher—betrayed me." [53] When she finds out that she is pregnant with her teacher's child, Hongying has an abortion, and she eventually leaves her hometown for good.

Her tumultuous life notwithstanding, "the daughter of hunger" grows up to become a chronicler of the famine that devastated China and that preceded the even more disastrous Cultural Revolution. Like thousands of women her age, Hongying has, all along, been troubled by a deep-seated hunger: She is fed up with the revolutionary spiritual food but starving for the more sensuous kinds of food, from a full meal, to love, to sex; even years after the hunger years, she can never forget her memory of deficiency and desolation. In both the literal and symbolic sense, hunger embodies her experience of growing up as a woman.

Unlike Xianglin's wife, Guo Su'e, Tan Yuexiang, and even her own mother, all of whom were muted by their societies and denied basic needs for survival, Hongying cries out and writes down, however painfully, the fears and desires, anxieties and aspirations shared by the new generation of daughters of hunger. "Perhaps someday, my born feeling of hunger can be cured by writing," [54] Hongying writes at the end of *The Daughter of Hunger*. While one is not sure whether writing will ever exorcise the hunger demon that has haunted her life, Hongying has at least made known her capacity to churn up her own kind of "spiritual food." By inscribing in her own way memories of the days of utter destitution, she has managed to turn the tables on formidable hunger discourse. Eighty years after Xiangling's wife falls on the snowy New Year's Eve and dies a silent death, a hungry woman at the end of the century can at last write a story of her own, answering some of the unpalatable questions posed by a cannibalistic century.

Notes

Throughout the text, I have referred to these works by their English titles, even though all have been published in Chinese and, with the exception of "The New Year's Sacrifice," *The Rice-Sprout Song,* and "Mountain Path," do not yet have English translations. Unless otherwise noted, all translations are my own.

1 For a comprehensive description of food shortages and their political and economic consequences in early-twentieth-century China, see, for instance, Walter Mallory, *China, Land of Famine* (New York: American Geographical Society, 1926); and John Lossing Buck, *Food and Agriculture in Communist China* (Stanford, Calif.: Hoover Institution Publications, 1966).

2 See, for example, Gang Yue's succinct analysis in "Hunger, Cannibalism, and the Politics of Eating: Alimentary Discourse in Chinese and Chinese American Literature" (Ph.D. diss., University of Oregon, 1993), which came to my attention after I wrote this essay.

3 Lu Xun, "The New Year's Sacrifice," in *Selected Stories of Lu Xun,* trans. Hsien-yi and Gladys Yang (Beijing: Foreign Language Press, 1978), 127.

4 James W. Brown, *Fictional Meals and Their Function in the French Novel, 1789–1848* (Toronto: University of Toronto Press, 1984), 12–13; Gang Yue, "Hunger, Cannibalism, and the Politics of Eating," 16; and Louis Marin, *Food for Thought,* trans. Mette Hjort (Baltimore, Md.: Johns Hopkins University Press, 1989), 35–38.

5 Lu Ling is the pseudonym of Xu Sixing. For more biographical information, see *Lu Ling ziliao xuanbian* (Research materials on Lu Ling), ed. Zhang Huan, Wei Lin, Li Zhiyuan, Yang Yi (Beijing: Beijing Shiyue Wenyi Chubanshe, 1993).

6 Lu Ling, *Ji'e de Guo Su'e* (Hungry Guo Su'e) (Beijing: Beijing Renmin Chubanshe, 1988), 103.

7 Hu Feng, *"Ji'e de Guo Su'e xu"* (preface to *Hungry Guo Su'e*), in *Lu Ling yanjiu ziliao,* 60. I am using Kirk Denton's translation, which I quote from "Mind and the Problematic of Self in Modern Chinese Literature: Hu Feng's Subjectivism and Lu Ling's Psychological Fiction" (Ph.D. diss., University of Toronto, 1992), 235.

8 See Kirk Denton, "Lu Ling's Literary Art: Myth and Symbol in *Hungry Guo Su'e,*" *Modern Chinese Literature* 2, no. 2 (fall 1986): 197–209; and also Denton, "Mind," 202–37; Liu Kang, "The Language of Desire, Class, and Subjectivity in Lu Ling's Fiction," in *Gender and Sexuality in Twentieth-Century Chinese Literature and Society,* ed. Tongling Lu (Albany: State University of New York Press, 1993), 67–84; and Shu Yunzhong, "Buglers on the Home Front" (Ph.D. diss., Columbia University, 1994), 156–89.

9 See Mallory, *China, Land of Famine,* and Buck, *Food and Agriculture.*

10 *Mao Zedong wenji* (Works of Mao Zedong), ed. Zhonggong zhongyang wenxian yanjiushi (Beijing: Renmin Chubanshe, 1981) 1:5–7, 15–16, 33, 44–45.

11 See Gang Yue's discussion in "Hunger, Cannibalism, and the Politics of Eating," 160–61.

12 Denton, "Mind," 129. The neo-Confucians had assimilated the language of Buddhist salvationism; Russian Marxists were assimilating the language of Orthodox Christianity into similar metaphors of revolutionary holiness.

13 Ban Wang, *The Sublime Figure of History: Aesthetics and Politics in Twentieth-Century China* (Stanford, Calif.: Stanford University Press, 1997), 1.

14 Mao Zedong, *Wenji*, 2:700.

15 See Gang Yue, "Hunger, Cannibalism, and the Politics of Eating," 162; see also his analysis of the increase in the use of the hunger motif in Yan'an literature, chap. 4.

16 C. T. Hsia, "Closing Remarks," in *Chinese Fiction from Taiwan: Critical Perspectives*, ed. Jeannette Faurot (Bloomington: Indiana University Press, 1980), 240.

17 Shi Shu, *Lixiang zhuyishe de jianying* (The silhouette of an idealist) (Taipei: Xindi Chubanshe, 1990), 149–50.

18 I am using Liu Kang's translations, in "The Language of Desire," 79–80.

19 Lu Ling, *Ji'e de Guo Su'e*, 37.

20 Sun Longki, *Zhongguo wenhua de shenceng jiegou* (The deep structure of Chinese culture) (Taipei: Jiegouqun, 1989).

21 See my discussion in *Fictional Realism in Twentieth-Century China: Mao Dun, Lao She, Shen Long Wen* (New York: Columbia University Press, 1992), chap. 3.

22 See Meng Yue's discussion in *"Baimao nü* yanbian de qishi: Lun Yan'an wenyi de lishi duozhi xing" (The transformations of *The White-Haired Girl* and its significance: On the polyphony of history in Yan'an literature), in *Zai jiedu: Dazhong wenyi yu yishi xingtai* (Reinterpretation: Popular literature and ideology), ed. Tang Xiaobing (Hong Kong: Oxford University Press, 1993), 68–89.

23 A statement made by He Jingzhi, one of the coauthors of the Yan'an version of *Baimao nü*; quoted in Meng Yue, *"Baimao nü* yanbian de qishi," 76.

24 Lu Ling, *Ji'e de Guo Su'e*, 22.

25 See Ban Wang, *The Sublime Figure of History*, chap. 1.

26 See Liu Kang, "The Language of Desire."

27 Robert Newman, *Transgressions of Reading: Narrative Engagement as Exile and Return* (Durham, N.C.: Duke University Press, 1993), 141; Julia Kristeva, *Powers of Horror: An Essay on Abjection*, trans. Leon S. Roudiez (New York: Columbia University Press, 1982); and Victor Burgin, *In/Different Spaces: Place and Memory in Visual Culture* (Berkeley, Calif.: University of California Press, 1996), 47–56.

28 Newman, *Transgressions of Reading*, 140.

29 Lu Ling, *Ji'e de Guo Su'e*, 81.

30 Lu Ling, *Ji'e de Guo Su'e*, 89. For Denton's translation, see "Mind," 231.

31 I am referring to the starvation that occurred during the Great Leap Forward

movement, from 1959 to 1962, in which millions of people perished. On the practice of cannibalism during the Great Leap Forward, see Jasper Becker, *Hungry Ghosts: Mao's Secret Famine* (New York: Free Press, 1996), chap. 14.

32 According to Wang Hui's report, Lu Ling resumed his career after rehabilitation. But the millions of words he produced turned out to be nothing but horrific repetitions—though in various forms—of slogans and propaganda he had been fed during the long period of imprisonment.

33 Zhao Shuli, *Lijiazhuang de bianqian* (1945) (Changes of the Li village); Zhou Libo, *Baofeng zouyu* (Hurricane); Ding Ling, *Taiyang zhaozai sanggan heshang* (The sun shines over the Sanggang river).

34 Hu Shi's letter to Eileen Chang, in *Zhang Ailing quanji* (Complete works of Eileen Chang) (Taipei: Huangguan Chubanshe, 1995), 1:4.

35 C. T. Hsia, *A History of Modern Chinese Fiction* (New Haven, Conn.: Yale University Press, 1961), 357–67; Long Yingtai, *Long Yingtai ping xiaoshuo* (Fiction criticism by Long Yingtai) (Taipei: Erya Chubanshe, 1985), 108.

36 C. T. Hsia, *A History*, 357–67.

37 Eileen Chang, *Quanji*, 3:87.

38 Eileen Chang, *Yangge* (The rice-sprout song), in *Quanji*, 1:189–90.

39 Becker, *Hungry Ghosts*, chap. 1.

40 Eileen Chang, preface to *Chuanqi* (Romance), in *Quanji*, 5:6.

41 Chen Yingzhen, "Shanlu" (Mountain path), in *Chen Yingzhen zuopinji* (Works of Chen Yingzhen) (Taipei: Renjian Chubanshe, 1998), 9:53.

42 Chen Yingzhen, "Shanlu," 38.

43 Leslie Haywood, *Dedication to Hunger: The Anorexic Aesthetic in Modern Cultures* (Berkeley, Calif.: University of California Press, 1995), 61–88; and Mark Anderson, "Anorexia and Modernism, or How I Learned to Diet in All Directions," *Discourse* 11, no. 1 (1988–1989): 28–41.

44 Joan Brumberg, *Fasting Girls: The History of Anorexia Nervosa* (Cambridge: Harvard University Press, 1988), 61–99; see also, Haywood, *Dedication to Hunger*, 72–73.

45 Brumberg, *Fasting Girls*, 99; Haywood, *Dedication to Hunger*, 73.

46 See Denton's succinct analysis in "Mind," 129, where he points out the link between Lu Ling and the Song and Ming neo-Confucian thoughts.

47 See Zhong Caijun's discussion in "Er Cheng shengren zhixue de yanjiu" (A study of the theory of sainthood by Cheng Yi and Cheng Hao) (Ph.D. diss., National Taiwan University, 1990), 234–43.

48 Zhong Caijun, "Er Cheng," 21.

49 Zhong Caijun, "Er Cheng," 21.

50 Shi Shu, "Taiwan de youyu: Lun Chen Yingzhen zaoqi xiaoshuo de yishu" (The melancholy of Taiwan: On the art of Chen Yingzhen's early fiction), in *Liang'an*

wenxue lunji (Critical essays on Chinese literature across the Taiwan Strait) (Taipei: Xindi Chubanshe, 1997), 149–65.

51 Manfred M. Fichter, "The Anorexia Nervosa of Franz Kafka," *International Journal of Eating Disorders* 2 (1987): 367–77; and Anderson, "Anorexia and Modernism," 28–41.

52 See Rey Chow's discussion in "We Endure, Therefore We Are: Survival, Governance, and Zhang Yimou's *To Live,*" *South Atlantic Quarterly* 95, no. 4 (fall 1996): 1039–64.

53 Hongying, *Ji'e de nüer* (The daughter of hunger) (Taipei: Erya, 1997), 322.

54 Hongying, *Ji'e de nüer*, 339.

Two Discourses on Colonialism: Huang Guliu and

Eileen Chang on Hong Kong of the Forties

Leung Ping-kwan

Before and after 1 July 1997, the day when Hong Kong was officially returned to China after more than a century of colonial rule under Great Britain, many summarized its past and speculated about its future. Critics have attempted to examine and define the cultural identity of Hong Kong. On the one hand, critics from mainland China overwhelmingly emphasize Hong Kong's identification with China's national culture; on the other hand, Western critics see Hong Kong as belonging unquestionably to a global community of postmodernism. Various critics also want to define and examine the "postcolonial" condition of Hong Kong. But before one can discuss the postcolonial situation of Hong Kong or try to apply postcolonial theory to the discussion of issues related to Hong Kong, one must understand the specific features of colonialism in Hong Kong and their effects, with references to political, social, and cultural specifics. This in itself is still an unfinished project.

In the study of Hong Kong literary culture, the lack of understanding about the complexities of indigenous cultural practices has often led to gross generalizations by critics from different positions. Statements such as, "The great Hong Kong novel has yet to be written" (typically made by Western critics), or, "There are not many literary works from Hong Kong that deal with colonialism, but the return to the motherland ends the ugly history of colonialism, and we can expect that major works will be produced in the future" (typically made by critics from China), though coming from different positions, share the same hypothesis that colonialism is directly responsible for the "lack" of good literature in Hong Kong, a hypothesis that is usually made without any effort to find out what has been written in Hong Kong. Hong Kong literature has yet to sort out its history and to compile its anthologies. But despite the fact that there is still, at this stage, a great need to produce literary histories, anthologies, in-depth research, and critical studies, not to mention translations and promotions for an outside audience, efforts have been made in recent years that may begin to help clear up some of the confusion and clarify speculative statements.[1] What have been put on the shoulders of present researchers are the burdens to rethink carefully various issues, to remap the existing territories, and to redefine the whole scope of studies.

In recent years, writers and critics have made various attempts to examine the intricacy of Hong Kong culture, and to see, despite all the limitations and appropriations, whether it is possible to argue for a kind of self-writing in the midst of various forces of colonialism and neocolonialism.[2] Postcolonial theory in general has alerted our attention to issues such as the relationship between the colonizer and the colonized, discourse and identity, representation and resistance, nationalism and hybridity, language and place, and global theory and local practices. In light of these issues, the challenges still remain: How can we reread the past critically and envision the future creatively?

This essay is part of a larger project of historical research that examines efforts to represent colonialism in Hong Kong fiction from the forties to the nineties and attempts to bridge some of the gaps in the studies of Hong Kong culture and literature mentioned above. In its present form, this essay is limited to the works of two writers from the forties, Huang Guliu and Eileen Chang, both of whom differ considerably in terms of political attitudes, class, gender, visions, styles, and textual strategies. What they have in common, however, is a history of being excluded. Both writers have been dismissed by critics from the Right and from the Left; they are usually not considered to be the most typical of Hong Kong writers, and certainly have not been examined together on their different attitudes towards colonialism. The following discussion will focus on their works as sites of contestation and struggle against various cultural and political forces. By doing this, I hope to call attention to the inadequacy of the existing literary histories and discussions of Hong Kong literature in relation to Chinese national literature, and to fill in some of the gaps in the explications of textual history in relation to literary and cultural contexts.

1

Huang Guliu's novel *The Story of Shrimp Ball* (*Xiaqiu Zhuan*) was first published in daily installments in the *Huashang Daily* in Hong Kong in 1947, with the help of the famous leftist writer Xia Yan, the editor in chief of the newspaper at that time. When Xia wrote the introduction to the reprint of the 1957 version of the novel (which was published in Canton as a revised version of the three-volume first edition originally printed in Hong Kong in 1948 and 1949), he emphasized Huang's career as a heroic and patriotic writer.[3] What Xia did not elaborate on in detail was the sad fate of Huang, who, in his later years spent in Canton, China, was criticized by northern leaders and purged at the time of the Cultural Revolution (1966–1976), which led not only to his resignation from work and the destruction of the manuscript of his new novel about the Korean War, but also to his bad health and premature death in 1977.[4] When Xia wrote the introduction to this new edition of *The Story of Shrimp Ball*, published posthumously in 1979, it was the first time since the late fifties that this book was back in circulation and the first time many readers discovered it.

The 1957 and 1979 versions of the novel begin with this sentence: "Around the dockyard in Hung Hum, Shrimp Ball had a hard time escaping from the chase of British policemen" (*XZ*, 3). This seems to set the tone of a story with an anticolonialist slant. Veteran Chinese writers, such as Mao Dun, complimented Huang on the merits of the novel, which, "through the lives of those living in the city evokes the dissatisfaction and rebellions against the present situation as well as yearnings for a new future."[5]

In spite of its unpredicted condemnation during a later period of political upheaval, the novel was duly recognized as representative of Huang's work. The novel is about a fifteen-year-old teenager, Shrimp Ball, who tries his best to earn a living during hard times but falls into the hands of criminals and gangsters. He is exploited by his boss in illegal deals, thrown into the hierarchic structure of the Triad gangs, and eventually jailed for stealing. Later, to his great surprise, he discovers that one of the victims whose pockets he picked is actually his father, who has returned after years of laborious work in the United States only to lose all of his savings. His father is so disturbed that he becomes mentally unstable. At the end of the first volume of the novel, Shrimp Ball, feeling guilty for what he has done and unable to find any other way out for himself or to change the society he lives in, decides to go to China to begin a new life. In the second and the third volumes, Shrimp Ball returns to Canton to join the guerrilla army, and, with his friends, he fights against the KMT army in the pre-1949 civil war and contributes to the building of the new nation.

Despite its pro-China tendencies, which echo other novels produced in

China during that period that celebrate the building of the nation, this particular novel differs formally in that it bears the traces of the specific cultural milieu of Hong Kong. It is written in simple vernacular Chinese, mixed from time to time with the Cantonese dialect and transliterations of English. Published in installments in the newspaper, each episode contains some action and some new development in the plot to arouse the reader's interest. The serial novel, which helps to make literature more accessible to the general public, follows a tradition set by the early newspapers in Hong Kong (e.g., *Xunhuan Daily,* which was established in 1874), which editors later adopted to attract a larger readership. In the introduction to the reprint of the novel, Xia himself revealed how Huang's novel developed from this particular form. Huang had completed the novel before he showed it to Xia, who liked it but thought it should follow the format of other novels that were published in installments in Hong Kong newspapers: Every thousand characters formed an autonomous unit, and included enough dramatic twists and turns to entice readers to read on. Huang accepted this condition with pleasure and commented that he would very much like to take this opportunity to learn the craft of serial novel writing in Hong Kong (*XZ*, 2).

We can see that, instead of being limited by an imposed formal constraint, Huang was actually able to make use of it to develop Shrimp Ball's eventful journey in and out of Hong Kong. His novel is, in this respect, not unlike the picaresque novel of the West, in which the protagonist encounters various people and events during his adventures, all of which help him establish his own sense of judgment and develop his own ways of dealing with difficulties, and eventually contribute to his self-education, character formation, and personal growth.[6] In *The Story of Shrimp Ball,* the protagonist leaves home at the age of fifteen, and the world he experiences is mainly the underworld of Hong Kong (though in the second and third volumes, he goes into southwestern China). We can also read the story as a bildungsroman, with the protagonist's typical search for the meaning of life in the process of growing up. This is especially true in the first volume, which focuses on Hong Kong, where Shrimp Ball is initiated into the world through his encounters with people who represent various social and political strata, encounters that are interspersed with vivid descriptions of the different urban spaces of Hong Kong.

His encounters with people from the underworld begin with Doggie Wong (Huang Gouzai), one of the gangsters who participates in illegal activities for Crocodile Head (Eyutou), a crooked businessman, and eventually end with the political figure Commissar Ma (Ma Zhuanyuan), an officer of the Nationalist party. In such a hierarchy of power, with representative types that illustrate the author's analysis of the structure of organized crime and its links to political authorities, Shrimp Ball occupies the lowest stratum. He enters as someone who is ignorant of this world, and through encounters with cunning tricks and criminal acts, he gradually learns more about it. One of the early discoveries comes at the end of chapter 3 and the beginning of chapter 4, when Shrimp Ball gets involved in an operation by the name of "Fishing," whereby Doggie Wong deals illegally with sailors on foreign ships who smuggle Western liquor and commodities. As the marine police suddenly approach, Doggie Wong, panic-stricken, leaves Shrimp Ball behind in a rush to escape. At this point, Shrimp Ball is alone in this hostile environment and learns for the first time to rely on his own cunning (*XZ*, 12–14). This is the first time that Shrimp Ball is betrayed by someone, but there are more betrayals to come. In chapter 8, he falls in love with A Ti (*XZ*, 27–28). In a series of events that contributes to Shrimp Ball's sentimental education, we see how he discovers the illusion of love, as portrayed in fairy tales, and comes to terms with his own feelings.

Huang's narrative links the representative character types to a specific set of local urban spaces and customs. Most of the events happen in Hong Kong. This is the Hong Kong of the forties, when there was no Mass Transit Railway or Cross Harbor Tunnel, when one could have noodles for thirty cents or congee for five cents, and a decent dinner cost only a dollar and a half. At the beginning of the novel, Shrimp Ball is selling breakfast in front of the dockyard in Hung Hum. He moves to Tsimshatsui, the center where everything happens. In the first chapter, we read about the foreign ships that anchor at the Hong Kong Wharf. The Peninsular Hotel, the central post office, and the train station clock tower are familiar landmarks of the area with links to Western cultures. We follow Shrimp Ball and his adventures throughout parts of Hong Kong. The locations are significant in highlighting class and ethnic differences: For instance, the wealthy smuggler Crocodile Head, who lives in the residential area of Tsimshatsui in a Western apartment, is, of course, a great contrast to the boat people and the shelters they occupy in Yaumatei, where A Ti and others reside.

The politics of place also plays a significant role in Huang's novel in that it defines the culture of Hong Kong. The description of the Wanchai football stadium area, where nightlife flourishes, is a revealing example. The playground is depicted as a kind of microcosm of Hong Kong, where various kinds of goods are for sale and where people from all walks of life crowd together to seek relief from stress:

> This is a strange world: The active ones are children, teenagers, young ones, and women, mature women, . . . an old man is rarely seen. Here, the phantoms driven by hunger follow everyone, chasing the failed ones among the crowd. People watch each other, spying on each other with anxious eyes. The couple dressed in costumes sells medicine, singing songs and beating the gong to attract spectators. The pickpockets wander around the spectators, the policemen patrol around the pickpockets, and the secret prostitutes watch with alert eyes the policemen on patrol. Some who suffer from the stress of daily work come here to find a temporary moment of intoxication. Shrimp Ball wanders around and around the district, and does not find any way of life that would suit his needs. (*XZ*, 16)

Everything that Shrimp Ball experiences in this market place in Wanchai is quite foreign to him, and he is unable to find any way of life here that would suit him. Subsequently, he encounters Sixth Auntie, a prostitute, who asks him to teach her to speak one sentence of the common Wanchai Chinglish: "Biao di fu ge er, wen na, duan di fa fu da la! Ao jia" (*XZ*, 16), which in English means "Beautiful girl, one night, twenty-five dollars, okay?" The strange transliteration printed in Chinese creates an absurd effect, alerting the reader to the kind of "mimicry" (in Homi Bhabha's sense) with which colonized people cope in the midst of an invasive foreign presence. Shrimp Ball refuses to say the words and goes on his way. As is typical of this picaresque novel, in the next paragraph, he soon finds himself in a very different space. He arrives at Shaukiwan by tram, where he passes a small alley "reminiscent of those in the interior province in China, on both sides of which are shops with low facades, with lights to attract customers from the boats. Shrimp Ball watches carefully; the one he looks for is not there" (*XZ*, 16). But here, which seems to be more "Chinese" in nature, he still can't find what he is looking for. He is even being chased from his newly found home in a temple. Again the question facing him is, "Where can he spend the night?" (which is also the title of this section).

Throughout the novel, Shrimp Ball is described as someone who has difficulty settling into any of the familiar places in Hong Kong, where he finds danger and hostility everywhere, and where criminal activity is commonplace. This failure to make Hong Kong a home triggers a sentimental longing for an idealized place beyond the space of the colony. It is at this point that Shrimp Ball and his friend Cowboy decide to climb beyond Lion Rock to go back to China:

> The two of them look at each other with friendly affection, and walk toward Lion Rock. Cowboy had climbed to Lo Fu Mountain alone before to learn martial arts. Now walking back to his own country, Shrimp Ball shares similar feelings. He loves the rifle of brother Ding, and he remembers Ding's words. He dreams of being able to use the gun, to learn to fight the war, and to be a decent Chinese who can contribute to his country. If only he can find a proper profession, not to disappoint Sixth Auntie, he'll be content. He thinks: I must find brother Ding, and learn to fight a guerrilla war with him. He is a good person, he will certainly take me in. They walk and walk, when the sun is in the middle of the sky they are halfway up the mountain; when the sun sets they have climbed over to the other side already. (XZ, 67–68)

Because Shrimp Ball has been described in earlier paragraphs as being unable to fit in either in the foreign or the Chinese sections of Hong Kong, it is less convincing here when he decides to go back to China. Here, Huang's novel follows a common practice of some Hong Kong leftist cinema and fiction of the fifties, which mechanically suggested that a return to mainland China could serve as a solution to the adverse living conditions and bad public order of Hong Kong.[7] But if we look back at the original version of the first volume of *The Story of Shrimp Ball* (1948), to our surprise, we will find that the ending is much more consistent with a childish dream. After the same beginning, the second sentence of the paragraph reads: "He loves the rifle of brother Ding: it can be used to shoot wild ducks, it can as well be used to shoot bandits. He thinks, I must find brother Ding and learn to shoot from him. He's a good man, he could not dislike children, could he?"[8]

It was only in the 1957 version, published in mainland China, that the ideas of returning to China to fight the guerrilla war, and of being a decent and useful Chinese are added to the narrative in the form of an afterthought, a kind of "repair." This revised version, however, became the model for later reprints.

The earlier version of this novel reveals Shrimp Ball to be in a kind of childhood fantasy at the end. Although *The Story of Shrimp Ball* does have a clear, political standpoint, which attacks the Nationalist party's government and defends the Communist party, it does not promote nationalism as a solution to the colonial situation. The single heroic figure, Brother Ding, whom Shrimp Ball mentions at the end, belongs to a self-defense troop that was formed by the people during the Sino-Japanese War; after the war, the troop was retained and hired by the British authorities to be a kind of self-defense force for the people. In this earlier Hong Kong version, Brother Ding is described as a man with a chocolate-colored face and a crew cut like a British soldier. These references to foreign products and foreign fashion, as well as the comradeship formed between members of the local Chinese self-defense troop and the English troops, are omitted in the later mainland version. Literature is consciously rewritten to serve national politics. Although in the original version, Brother Ding is a heroic figure, he is very much in line with the Hong Kong situation and its characteristically *open* relationship with various forces. *What has been added to the later version is an absolute distinction between China and the West, whereby foreigners are simply condemned as stereotypical colonizers.* Some English words, as well as allusions to sex (for example, A Ti places Shrimp Ball's hand on her breast [XZ 1948, 23]) are also omitted in the later version. Such omissions cast Shrimp Ball as a more positive yet puritan character, and the more colorful and lively descriptions of Shrimp Ball's psychological development and subject formation in a colonial situation become somewhat superficial and one-dimensional. In light of the more obvious political concerns of the later version, Huang, we may surmise, has revised his work in subservience to the new political agenda under the pressure of leftist critics.[9]

In the earlier version of the novel published in Hong Kong, the first sentence reads, "Near the dockyard, Shrimp Ball's morning business faces strong competition" (XZ 1948, 1). In the later version, it reads, "Around the dockyard district in Hung Hum, Shrimp Ball has great difficulties escaping the chase of British policemen" (XZ, 3). A later line, "This multicolored world is in front of him" (XZ 1948, 2), is changed to "This multicolored world ruled by foreigners is in front of him" (XZ, 4). At the beginning of the second section, a new sentence is added: "This colonial society of Hong Kong has many invisible nets hanging around to trap people" (XZ, 4). This new sentence seems to follow closely the discourse on colonialism promoted by the official party in China. While it provides one type of criticism of colonialism, it is not a particularly effective one. Because the attack on British colonialism relies merely on added sentences and rigid distinctions between black and white, it is hardly successful in capturing the nature and effects of colonialism in Hong Kong and the subtle, ambiguous transformations that take place in the lives of the colonizers and colonized alike.

2

Like Huang, who was excluded by most critics from Taiwan and Hong Kong in their discussion of Hong Kong literature mainly because of his leftist political position, Eileen Chang was ignored for many years by mainland critics. Chang, who also began her writing career in the forties, is a writer with a very different temperament and vision from Huang's. Coming from a traditional and prestigious family, she was influenced by her divorced mother, who spent most of her days traveling and working independently in Europe and Asia. Chang grew up in the city of Shanghai, studied at St. Mary's Hall Girls' School, and enrolled in the English Department at the University of Hong Kong from 1939 to 1941, but abandoned her studies and returned to Shanghai in 1942, after the Japanese had occupied Hong Kong. She became famous in the forties after publishing a series of short stories about Hong Kong and Shanghai, which she later grouped under the un-ambitious title *Chuanqi* (Legends, or Romances). Because she continued to publish in Japanese-occupied Shanghai, and because of her relationship with a notorious national traitor, Hu Lancheng, she was not highly regarded after the war, much less after the establishment of the People's Republic of China in 1949. Although she did finish two novels, *Eighteen Springs* (*Shiba chun*) and *Little Ai* (*Xiao Ai*) on the mainland before she left China in 1952 to return to Hong Kong, the publication in Hong Kong of two other novels, *The Rice-Sprout Song* (*Yangge*) and *Naked Earth* (*Chidi zhilian*), in which she criticized China's land policy in the fifties, led to her further marginalization. Her works were nowhere to be found in mainland China, and her name was not mentioned in literary histories. In 1955, Chang left for the United States, where she resided in exile until her death in 1995. Though her works were reissued in Hong Kong and Taiwan in the sixties and seventies, and in mainland China in the eighties, and have since tremendously influenced new generations of writers, her literary career has always been subject to controversy. The predominant accusation is that her works are trivial and narrow in scope, focusing only on love affairs and ignoring larger social and political issues.[10]

In this section, I will examine Chang's less-discussed short stories about Hong Kong, which she wrote in the early forties. Contrary to critics who think that the "personal" is necessarily divorced from the "political," I would like to suggest that Chang had made specific comments on the colonial situation of Hong Kong, where she placed her characters and their romances. In the order of publication, four of the first five stories which she published in Shanghai magazines, "Incense Ashes: The First Offering," "Incense Ashes: The Second Offering," "Jasmine Tea," and "The Love That Felled a City," were stories about Hong Kong, which Chang wrote shortly after her return from there. They are assembled with other stories about Shanghai in *Chuanqi,* her first collection of short stories.[11] The title of the collection refers, I think, more to the traditional genre of classical Chinese fiction that recounts strange events than to the usual English translation of the term *romance.* Romances though they are, Chang's stories usually contain baroque descriptions or tragic elements. She also makes use of another device: The narrator usually sets up a narrative frame (following similar devices used in traditional Chinese oral storytelling) that leads into and sometimes heightens the strange and exotic events narrated, creating a distance from which the audience can reflect on the unfamiliar.

One example of Chang's continuation and variation of the traditional account of the strange can be found in the story "Incense Ashes: The First Offering." After the protagonist, Weilong, visits the luxurious mansion of her aunt, Mrs. Leung, the narrator relates: "Weilong thinks of herself as the young scholar in *Strange Stories from the Liao Study,* who, after a visit to relatives in the mountain, finds that the grand mansion of wealth has turned into a huge grave. If that white house of the Leung family at this point turns into a grave, she won't be surprised" (*ZADX,* 292–93). This story does not follow the realistic mode of representation that Huang employs in his work. From the very beginning, the mansion is portrayed in strong, imaginative colors, and its eccentricity is obvious. The garden is depicted as "a gilded tray propped up high among the rugged mountains" (*ZADX,* 279), and the backdrop "is full of contradictions: all kinds of contradictory backgrounds, periods, and atmospheres, arbitrarily mixed and blended together to create a strange and unreal world" (*ZADX,* 280). This strange and unreal world, as it turns out, is the colonial space of Hong Kong. In this, Chang's description resonates with Huang's in that Hong Kong is seen as a "strange" place. But while Huang's story shows that it is not very difficult to escape from it, Chang's narrative goes on to show the colonial space as a haunted space in which people are trapped.

This strangeness is revealed in the description of the interior of the house, in which "the Oriental flavor seems to exist to please foreign friends. . . . The British have come such a long way to see China, we have to show them something Chinese. But the China here is the China in the eyes of the Westerners: absurd, exquisite, funny" (*ZADX*, 280). Immediately after this description, Weilong catches a glimpse of herself in the mirror: Looking at her "Chinese" costumes, which are designed for the Western gaze, she realizes that she herself is part of the Orientalism produced by the colonial legacy.

Weilong is a young student from Shanghai who is staying in the house of her aunt, Mrs. Leung. She feels trapped in the hybrid and grotesque place. In the scene mentioned above, when she leaves the house after her first visit, she imagines it to be a haunted house like those she knows about from classical ghost stories and fantasizes that she can remain safe as long as she remains aloof. Her fantasy, however, proves wrong. At the end of the story, Weilong ventures into the red-light district of Wanchai, which is described in a manner that is even more exaggerated and expressionistic than Huang's descriptions of the same area in *The Story of Shrimp Ball*: "The two of them walk on to browse through the things exhibited at the stalls. Here they sell everything, yet it is mainly people they sell. Under the bleak gaslight, there stands a group of girls, and because of exaggerated light and shadow, they all have pale blue noses, and green cheeks with patches of rouge turned purple" (*XZ*, 192–93).

This paragraph is preceded by more detailed descriptions of the commodities sold in the night market. Chang certainly exceeds Huang in her attention to detail, and her narrative thus conveys more layers of meaning. She sets the crowded annual New Year market of Wanchai—not unlike the grand mansion mentioned earlier that belongs to a different class of people—in the middle of a larger scene of desolation: "But beyond the lights, people, and commodities, there are the hollow sky and sea—boundless desolation, boundless terror. Her future perhaps is like that—she dares not think about it, otherwise she will be immersed in terror. She does not have a lifelong plan. Only in the trivial objects in front of her eyes, her timid and frustrated heart could find a moment of peace" (*ZADX*, 337).

The difference between Huang's and Chang's foci on the urban space of Wanchai is this: Huang's protagonist rejects the urban space and chooses to return to an idealized outside—China; Chang's protagonist sees no escape from this space. There is, in Chang's story, a possible point at which Weilong could have gone back to Shanghai, but her return is postponed by sickness (which may be an unconscious pretext to justify the delay, as hinted in the story). Her choice to stay is not so much affected by external factors as it is by the "irrational and savage passion evoked" (*ZADX*, 333) in her by her unreliable lover, George. Chang thus elaborates on colonialism through the subjectivity of her protagonist, showing Weilong first as a young girl who is innocent of the strange events taking place in the mansion but who becomes, after various struggles and defeats, resigned to being part of the "strangeness," which she had at first only glimpsed from the outside. Huang, by contrast, shows colonialism as something external, something realistic and geographical, something from which one can escape. For Chang, this is obviously not the case: Colonization could well be a *psychological* state, a condition that is internalized and thus much less clear-cut and more difficult to exorcise.

The frame Chang uses in this story is relatively simple. The narrator asks the reader to burn incense in an incense burner while listening to the narrator telling this story; when the story ends "the incense of Weilong will burn out soon as well" (*ZADX*, 339). This narrative frame prepares the reader for the transitions to the exotic story and strange events. But a frame can have significance in itself as well. At the beginning of "Incense Ashes: The Second Offering," the narrator chats with her friend Clementine, an Irish girl, in the library, while reading the historical account of Sir MacCarthy's visit to the Qing emperor, Qian Long, when he served as ambassador to China. Other than setting the scene for the story that follows, the frame used here, we eventually discover, complements the main body of the story as a comment on the strange consequences that result from the unequal encounter of Western and Eastern cultures. The story itself focuses on the expatriate circle in Hong Kong. At the beginning of the story, Roger, a chemistry professor and warden of a student dormitory, is preparing for his marriage to Susie, the youngest of an English widow's three daughters, who is twenty years his junior. Roger is optimistic and happy. In spite of his encounter with Susie's conservative and calculating mother and hysterical sister Phistine, who had an unhappy marriage with someone "abnormal," Roger has great hopes for his beautiful and innocent fiancée Susie, and he looks forward to their wedding. But things do not work out as planned. On their wedding night, Susie, who is inexperienced and perhaps influenced by her sister's prejudices against men, is frightened and flees in fear. She stays in the students' dormitory and, after being persuaded by the unknowing but self-righteous and overenthusiastic students, goes to see the vice-chancellor to seek advice in the morning. Chang does not dwell on the event itself but moves on to describe the *effects* this event has on the small expatriate community in Hong Kong by comparing them to the shadows produced by a dangling lamp: All common movements are enlarged ten times to become gigantic performances for the on-lookers. Roger's shadowy apartment, where he finally commits suicide, again seems to be a "haunted" place.

Chang, who has been criticized time and again for not dealing with the social situation of her time, is actually one of the few authors who has been able to write about the complex cultural relations that exist in the colonial situation.[12] If in "Incense Ashes: The First Offering" the focus is more on the hybrid culture of the upper and upper-middle classes and the colony's parasitic groups, in "The Second Offering," Chang seems to deal only with the expatriate circles, without any direct comments on their relations with the local people, except for the passing description of the unexplained enthusiasm of the students for reporting and condemning Roger, which may indicate a hidden hatred toward him which he has been unaware of. Chang's target of criticism is exactly the expatriates' ignorance and their lack of contact with the local people. At the moment when Roger is about to leave Hong Kong, he discovers he has nowhere to go. Hong Kong, a place he used to call a damp, humid, and foreign city, is now revealed to be his only home. But despite being alienated from his home country, he also has no real commitment to this colonial place:

> Fifteen years ago when he first arrived at Southern China University, he was a young man deeply in love with his work, and he sometimes stopped working to think for a while. But he felt the air in this university was not good for thinking. In the springtime, there were rhododendrons, red amid the entangling rain, falling and falling, red after red. In the summer, as he climbed the yellow slope to the lecture hall, the flowers were red and warm along the paths, like many suns burnt out of shape. In autumn and winter, the air was crispy and sweet, like biscuits. The wind from the mountain blew the brown, greenish, and graying trees into whistling. You just wanted to bring a few dogs whizzing up the mountains, do some exercises without tiring the brain. *Time passed just like that. For fifteen years, he had not changed his lecture notes. The research on physics and chemistry was forever going ahead, but he never read any new textbooks. The lecture notes he copied down when he studied in England twenty years ago, he still used as supplementary materi-*

als. From time to time, he would crack a few jokes in the classroom. He had done that for the past fifteen years. The chapter on carbon dioxide had jokes on carbon dioxide. In the same way, there were jokes about hydrogen, jokes about oxygen. He was such a person. If he had a sense of humor, he probably could not take himself very seriously. He did not regard himself highly, and hadn't had much confidence in the university education to which he had devoted half his life. Good or bad, he lived on in his own style for fifteen years. He did not bother anybody, he just did his share. Why didn't Susie, this girl with yellow hair, let him live on like this? (*ZADX*, 370–71; my emphasis)

Here again, we see the differences between Chang's and Huang's narrative strategies. Chang does not present to us a series of dramatic adventures; rather, she shows the serene life of the expatriates, which is so calm that one would not reflect on the strangeness of it until it suddenly breaks down in all its absurdity. Huang, for his part, sees colonialism in the form of an external kind of oppression and suggests the return to the national territory as an ideal solution. For Chang, colonialism is not only a mental state of the colonized; its damaging effects are revealed equally in the psychic condition of the colonizers, who, with their privileged positions, are actually living in a vacuum with no genuine human contact.

To a writer such as Huang, Chang probably is not enough of a critic of colonialism since she does not attack Westerners as he does, and even shows sympathy toward them. Yet in revealing that even the colonizers are victims, Chang is more observant and has offered more insights into the mechanism of colonialism:

[Roger] cannot explain clearly the misunderstanding against him even to his dearest friend. As for others, those British in the upper-middle class, to those people, what can he say? Those people, the men are like white tin alarm clocks, having set hours for eating, having tea, sitting on the toilet, sitting in the office. There is nothing in their minds except the tick tock of the clock. Maybe it is because of the hot weather in the east that the clock is not on time. Yet a clock is a clock. The women, knitting all day, their white faces become wool-like. Could he explain to these people what's missing in Susie's family education? Roger wants to be an ordinary person. Now, under these circumstances, when he's pushed outside the circle of the general people, he begins to see the stupidity within the circle—stupid and cruel . . . but isn't it equally terrible outside the circle? (*ZADX*, 369)

Such a critical portrayal of the British, written in the forties, has never created any controversy in Hong Kong. These comments have not been read as anticolonial discourse for several reasons: (1) Most of Chang's works are written in Chinese, and although some are available in English, they are not read by the English-speaking community, which is woefully negligent of Chinese writers; (2) the Chinese community, for its part, usually regards Chang as a popular author of romance and considers her works as mere love stories; and (3) academics trained in literary studies since the seventies for a long time read Chang's works through approaches such as New Criticism and psychoanalytic criticism, and although these readings would shed light on some aspects of Chang's works, they also render other aspects "invisible."[13]

Even though in "Incense Ashes: The Second Offering" Chang focuses on the isolation and the distorted mental states of the expatriates in the colony, she does not idealize the locals or see them as people who readily identify with national feelings of Chineseness. On the contrary, Chang is one of the most severe critics of nationalism at a time when the overwhelming emphasis in Chinese intellectual circles is on the "national characteristic" of literature. In "Red Rose and White Rose," the main character, Zhenbao, is described in the beginning as follows: "His whole being is an ideal modern Chinese, although what he encounters is not totally ideal, but when he reflects on himself and rearranges his perspective, all things become idealized, all fall into place" (*ZADX*, 57). One probably notices the irony in the latter part of the sentence, which forces the reader to question the phrase "ideal modern Chinese." Zhenbao is a man who is caught between two women, and his concern for social status and peer respect leads him to give up his true love, the woman known as "red rose," and endure an unhappy marriage with his wife, the "white rose," who cheats on him. At the end of the story, he is an unhappy and hypocritical person who has compromised his life. And when readers come to the end of the story and find Zhenbao shedding tears for himself, they probably find the irony of the phrase "ideal modern Chinese" to be all the more biting.

Chang's best-known story about Hong Kong, "The Love that Felled a City,"[14] can also be examined in relation to her idea of the nation and national characters. The female protagonist, Liusu, is called "a real Chinese woman" by the male protagonist, Fan Liuyuan, who continues with the following comments: "A real Chinese woman is the most beautiful woman in the world. She will never be out of fashion" (*ZADX*, 223). Yet one has to understand that Liuyuan was a second-generation immigrant who grew up in London and returned to China when he was twenty-four years old. On his return, he was greatly disappointed by the China that he had idealized in the past. This cultural background may provide a better understanding for the character of Liuyuan, who is often treated by critics and readers as merely a dandy. Liuyuan loves Liusu and thinks of her as the ideal Chinese woman, yet he worries that she is part of the trap of Chinese culture that wants him only for a convenient marriage. Therefore, he tries to take her away from China to Hong Kong the colony; he even considers taking her to Malaysia, to Africa, to primitive lands. Chang seems to suggest that all the reservations and pretensions that come with a cultural heritage that has a long history could be resolved only by a destructive war, which would return everything to normal. The playful relationship between Liusu, a husband-hunting widow, and Liuyuan, the flippant dandy, finally ends in a solid marriage because of the horrible threat of the war in Hong Kong. And it is only on that condition that they can marry without hesitation:

> The fall of Hong Kong has brought her what she always wanted. But in this world that has lost reason and logic, who knows what the cause is and what the effect? Who knows? Maybe just in order to please her, a city had fallen. Thousands and thousands of people died, suffered, then came changes that shocked the world. . . . Liusu doesn't feel that she played any important role in history. She just stands up laughing, kicking the mosquito-incense holder back under the table. (*ZADX*, 251)

The title, as well as the ending, compares Liusu to the ancient Chinese beauties that felled cities with their charm, only to highlight, in contrast, Liusu's banal and mundane qualities. The "ideal Chinese woman" is one who survives without her Chineseness.

"Jasmine Tea," which was written just two months before "The Love That Felled a City," could very well become its tragic counterpart.[15] Here, the protagonist, Nie Chuanqing, who suffers from being Chinese, faces the negative aspects of the Chinese tradition and family. His father, an opium smoker manipulated by Nie's practical stepmother, is quite domineering. Nie has a love-hate relationship with his professor's daughter, Yan Danzhu, who is described as someone more like a foreigner in her features and character: "Her curls are no longer curled, her hair is straight and hangs low, and she looks like the Native American Indian boy in American comics" (*ZADX*, 253).

Chinese ethnicity in the story is not depicted as an idealized source of origins. Nie, who is from Shanghai, is supposed to be superior in his mastery of the Chinese language and culture. Yet it turns out that he fails the subject of Chinese literary history and humiliates himself by failing to answer questions about the origins of classical Chinese poetry in front of the professor he admires. He is constantly scolded by his father, remains passive, and stays at home all the time fantasizing about his own biological origin—that he might, in fact, be the illicit son of Professor Yan, who had a brief love affair with Nie's mother. He has therefore developed a certain jealousy toward Danzhu, Professor Yan's daughter from his marriage to a woman from a southern province. Danzhu grew up in Hong Kong and is healthier, more open, and more popular, and seems to be better than him in every way. In the final scene, Nie's distorted state of mind drives him to the verge of a nervous breakdown when he shows excessive hatred as well as admiration for Danzhu. As he reveals his feelings, he finds himself being pitied by Danzhu and, suspecting that she despises him, he hits and kicks her, nearly killing her.

This is one of the rare moments of violence in Chang's writing, and it is ironic that the act is committed by a feminine-looking young man and that his victim is a more healthy-looking female character. Nie, who is from Shanghai, mainland China, lives in his Chinese-styled house with his old-fashioned father and stepmother, who regard the local Hong Kong students as inferior in their knowledge of Chinese culture and language, as Westernized, as wild and lacking in discipline. He dwells on his own fantasies and fragmented memories of the past as represented in old magazines. In a way, he is also living in an isolation not unlike that experienced by Roger and the expatriates in "Incense Ashes: The Second Offering." What these Chinese from the mainland and these expatriates have in common is a sense of superiority over the locals in terms of culture and a sense of living in a vacuum in which there is no concern for or interaction with others.

"Jasmine Tea," then, is unique in its severe implicit criticism of the national Chinese culture as presented by Nie's family, which is locked into a self-enclosed, self-indulgent existence with a sense of complacency. As a victim bred by this cultural conditioning, Nie envies Danzhu, who grows up in the colony with fewer restraints, but at the same time detests her and savagely denies the legitimacy of her existence. In the violent scene at the end, he "uses one hand to grasp her shoulder, the other hand to push her head down, as if he wants to push her head back into her body. She should not have been born; he wants her to go back to where she comes from" (*ZADX*, 277). This violent act toward the "other" is reminiscent of a colonizer's aggressive denial of the colonized's culture, but what makes it unique is that the perpetrator is a frustrated subject *within a national culture*. In its attempt to defend the purity of its origins, a national culture, too, can become violent: It must eliminate the hybrid to sustain the legitimacy of its own cultural supremacy. In writing about Hong Kong's colonial condition, Chang is one of a very few authors who, as early as the forties not only exposed, without sentimentalism, the ironic conditions of the colonizer and the colonized but also showed an astute wariness of nationalism as a collective discourse. Most of all, Chang alerts us to the fact that nationalism is not necessarily a realm into which one can *escape* to fight colonialism. The homogeneous and exclusionary attributes of nationalism, she warns, could very well be a force that contributes to the success of colonialism itself.

Notes

1   In the nineties, many books on the history of Hong Kong literature have been compiled by mainland Chinese scholars: Xie Changqing, *Xianggang xinwenxue jianshi* (A short history of new literature in Hong Kong) (Guangzhou: Jinan Daxue Chubanshe, 1990); Pan Yadun and Wang Yisheng, *Xianggang wenxue gaiguan* (An overview of Hong Kong literature) (Xiamen: Lujiang Chubanshe, 1993); Xu Yixin, *Xianggang wenxue guancha* (Observations on Hong Kong literature) (Guangzhou: Huacheng Chubanshe, 1993); Wang Jiancong, *Xianggang wenxueshi* (A history of Hong Kong literature) (Nanchang: Baihuazhou Wenyi Chubanshe, 1995); He Hui, *Xianggang dangdai xiaoshuo gaishu* (An introduction to contemporary Hong Kong fiction) (Guangzhou: Jingji Chubanshe, 1996); Liu Denghan, ed., *Xianggang wenxueshi* (A history of Hong Kong literature) (Hong Kong: Xianggang Zuojia Chubanshe, 1997). All except the last work were published solely in mainland China, and most have been written from a predominantly mainland Chinese perspective.

At the same time, editors and researchers in Hong Kong have published a number of anthologies and bibliographies of Hong Kong literature. There are also volumes of critical studies, but in general, further research is needed. The following are two useful reference books on Hong Kong literature that were compiled by Hong Kong writers: Wong Shuk Han, Sandy Yeung, and Anita Yu, eds., *Xianggang wenxue shumu* (A bibliography of Hong Kong literature) (Hong Kong: Youth Literary Bookstore, 1996); Liu Yichang, ed., *Xianggang wenxue zuojia zhuanlue* (Brief biography of Hong Kong writers) (Hong Kong: Public Library of the Urban Council, 1997).

For translations of Hong Kong literature into English, see the following special issues in journals: Eva Hung and John Minford, eds., "Special Issue: Hong Kong," *Renditions,* nos. 29 and 30 (Hong Kong: Research Centre for Translation of the Chinese University of Hong Kong, 1988); Eva Hung, ed., "Hong Kong Nineties," *Renditions,* nos. 47 and 48 (Hong Kong: Research Centre for Translation of the Chinese University of Hong Kong, 1997); *West Coast Line* 30, no. 3 (winter 1996–1997).

2   Rey Chow's article "Between Colonizers: Hong Kong's Postcolonial Self-Writing in the 1990s," *Diaspora* 2, no. 2 (fall 1992): 151–70, poses the question: "How do we talk about a postcoloniality that is a forced return to a 'mother country,' itself as imperialistic as the previous colonizer?" and speculates on the possibility for Hong Kong to find a third space to develop a new kind of self-writing. Matthew Turner, in *Hong Kong Sixties: Designing Identity* (Hong Kong: Hong Kong Arts Centre, 1995), examines the "Westernized" identity designed by the Hong Kong government for the people of Hong Kong after the riots in 1967 so as to prevent them from continuing to identify with mainland China. Ye Si, in *Xianggang wenhua* (Hong Kong culture) (Hong Kong: Hong Kong Arts Centre, 1995), examines various mainland and Western representations of Hong Kong, and looks at Hong Kong and its complicated relationships with the West and with mainland China. He uses the examples of cinema to discuss how, on the one hand, there is in Hong Kong a continuation of the less accepted cultural tradition from China, yet, on the other hand, Hong Kong cinema continues to problematize the idea of a national Chinese culture. Ackbar Abbas, in *Hong Kong: Culture and the Politics of Disappearance* (Hong Kong: Hong Kong University Press, 1997), discusses Hong Kong culture in terms of "disappearance" and argues that culture in Hong Kong cannot just be related to "colonialism" but must be related to this changed and changing space, which in many respects does not resemble the old colonialisms at all. In more recent discussions, there is also the view that denies a "Hong Kong identity" by insisting that there is only one Chinese identity (see, for instance, the series of essays that has appeared in *Ming Pao Monthly* since August 1996); there is also the concept of the "northbound imaginary," which holds Hong Kong to be the colonizer of mainland China (see, for example, Chen Qingqiao, ed., *Wenhua xiangxiang yu yishixingtai* [Cultural imaginary and ideology: Contemporary Hong Kong culture and politics review] [Hong Kong: Oxford University Press, 1997]).

3   Xia Yan, in his article "Guliu Remembered: An Introduction to the Reprint of *The Story of Shrimp Ball,*" writes that Huang joined the Nationalist army to resist the

Japanese invasion in the thirties, shifted his political sympathy from the Nationalist party (the KMT) to the Communist party because of the corruption he had witnessed in the government, and eventually joined the Communist party after he came to Hong Kong and established himself as a writer in the late forties. He volunteered to join the guerrilla army to fight in the southwestern areas of China before the liberation and again participated in the Korean War in the early fifties after the establishment of the People's Republic of China. This article is collected in Huang Guliu, *Xiaqiu Zhuan* (The story of Shrimp Ball) (Guangzhou: Renmin, 1979). Hereafter, references to this text will be cited parenthetically as *XZ*. This and all other quotations from Chinese texts discussed in this essay are my own translations.

4 Additional information about Huang was gathered from an interview I conducted on 8 September 1997 in Guangzhou with Xu Yixin, Huang's colleague and now a senior researcher at the Institute of Social Research in Guangdong.

5 Liu Denghan, *Xianggang wenxueshi,* 140.

6 For a discussion of picaresque literature, see Claudio Guillén, *Literature as System* (Princeton, N.J.: Princeton University Press, 1971), 71–106; and Harry Sieber, *The Picaresque* (London: Methuen, 1977).

7 See my article, "Cong Xianggang dianying li de dushi dao Xianggang de dushidianying" (From cities in Hong Kong cinema to urban cinema in Hong Kong), in *Fifty Years of Electric Shadows: The Twenty-First Hong Kong International Film Festival* (Hong Kong: Urban Council, 1997), 25–28.

8 Huang Guliu, *The Story of Shrimp Ball,* vol. 1, no. 1 (Hong Kong: New Democracy Publications, 1948), 60. Hereafter, references to this text will be cited parenthetically as *XZ 1948*.

9 Critics such as Shiyi have condemned the character of Shrimp Ball as lacking in political awareness. See Liu Denghan, *Xianggang wenxueshi,* 138–39.

10 An example of this kind of extreme criticism can be found in the works of Tang Wenbiao, who, at the height of the literary debates in Taiwan between the nativists and the modernists, condemned Chang as a writer with a very narrow range of subject matter, totally devoid of social consciousness, and unaware of the colonial situation she lived in. See Tang Wenbiao, ed., *Zhang Ailing zasui* (Miscellaneous writings on Eileen Chang) (Taipei: Lianjing Chuban, 1976). For more informative research and serious criticism, especially in recent years, see, for instance, C. T. Hsia, *A History of Modern Chinese Fiction,* 2d ed. (New Haven, Conn.: Yale University Press, 1971); Shui Jing, *Zhang Ailing de xiaoshuo yishu* (The art of Eileen Chang's fiction) (Taipei: Dadi Chubanshe, 1973); Chen Bingliang, *Zhang Ailing duanpian xiaoshuo lunji* (A critical study on Eileen Chang's short stories) (Taipei: Yuanjing Chubanshe, 1983); Zheng Shusen, ed., *Zhang Ailing de shijie* (The world of Eileen Chang) (Taipei: Yunshen Wenhua, 1989); and Rey Chow, "Modernity and Narration—in Feminine Detail," *Woman and Chinese Modernity:*

The Politics of Reading between West and East (Minneapolis: University of Minnesota Press, 1991).

11 These early stories were published in Shanghai magazines such as *Ziluolan* and *Zazhi,* and were collected in Eileen Chang, *Chuanqi* (Romance) (1944; reprint, Beijing: Renmin Chubanshe, 1986). A more popular reprint version authorized by Chang is *Zhang Ailing duanpian xiaoshuoji* (Short stories of Eileen Chang) (Taipei: Crown Publications, 1972). Hereafter, this work is cited parenthetically as *ZADX.*

12 Another story of Chang's, "Axiao's Grief for Autumn," is narrated from the perspective of an old-fashioned servant, Axiao, who comments in a casual and humorous way on her expatriate white male master and mimics his language and behavior with subtle irony. See *ZADX,* 125–49.

13 For one example of the criticism of "Jasmine Tea," see Li Zhuoxiong, "Linshui Zizhao de Shuixian" (Narcissus looks at his own reflection in water), in Zheng Shusen, ed., *Zhang Ailing de shijie* (The world of Eileen Chang) (Taipei: Yunshen Wenhua, 1989), 103–27.

14 The title of this story is usually translated as "Love in a Fallen City," but the original Chinese title is ambiguous: It could mean the love that leads to the fall of a city or the love that takes place during the fall of a city. I have taken the first interpretation, following Chang's own suggestion at the end of the story.

15 The story was written in June 1943; see Eileen Chang, *ZADX,* 107–33.

Beyond Cultural and National Identities:

Current Re-evaluation of the *Kominka* Literature

from Taiwan's Japanese Period

Sung-sheng Yvonne Chang

This essay is an offshoot of a larger, ongoing project that intends to deal with the relationship between various artistic formations and the dominant culture in Taiwan's post-1949 era. Though the lifting of martial law in 1987 has demarcated this era into two drastically different periods and a clearer contour of the new period has begun to emerge in the 1990s, various cultural forces are still busily negotiating with each other. Nonetheless, there seems to be a general consensus as to what constitutes the core of the new dominant culture: the spirit of *pen-t'u,* or a nativist imperative that obliges one to treat Taiwan as the "center" in one's cultural mapping. The primary driving force for this reconstitution of Taiwan's dominant culture undoubtedly came from the momentous changes in the political arena in the post–martial law period. This rather crude factor, however, should not obscure our vision of the longer, farther-reaching evolutionary process of cultural change in contemporary Taiwan. Simply put, since the early 1980s the older cultural hegemony has been seriously contested by forces coming from the Taiwanese cultural nationalism advocated in a vibrant *pen-t'u hua* (nativization) trend on the one hand and from various radical cultural formations on the other. Limited by space, this essay only deals with specific aspects of the nativization trend, with the main paradigm taken from the literary field. It begins with a brief overview of the indigenous literary discourse in Taiwan's post-1949 era, followed by analyses of recent scholarly re-evaluations of the *Kominka* literature from Taiwan's Japanese period.[1] Through this investigation, I hope to reach a better understanding of some important issues pertaining to contemporary cultural transformation in Taiwan such as the role of cultural nationalism, the problem of identity construction, and efforts toward institutionalizing Taiwanese literary studies as an academic discipline.

Reclaiming the Native: Indigenous Literary Discourse in Taiwan's Post-1949 Era

Historically speaking, modern Taiwanese literature was born in the 1920s amid the Taiwanese New Literature Movement.[2] From the point of view of mainstream literary production, however, there is little doubt that the legacy of this tradition has been minimal in Taiwan's post-1949 era. (The Taiwanese New Literature Movement here refers to the aggregate of literary conventions, critical discourses, aesthetic assumptions, and linguistic usage in creative works between the mid-1920s and the end of the Japanese period in 1945.) What is more, imprints of this modern literary tradition were considered suspicious and were painstakingly suppressed. Instead, the vigorous literary development in contemporary Taiwan has been largely nourished by traditions of nonindigenous origins: the lyrical-sentimental strands of the Chinese New Literature; literary modernism from the West; a nativist reaction to modernism, which nonetheless had recourse to an earlier Western importation, socialist realism; and various global trends of more recent years such as postmodernism and queer theory.

To be sure, despite the unfavorable environment during the martial law period, efforts to preserve an indigenous line of literary development have always been present. More notable activities include: the circulation in the 1950s of an informal newsletter, the *Wen-yu t'ung-hsun* (Literary correspondence) among a small number of Taiwanese writers; the founding of the Li shih-she (Poetry society of the bamboo hat) and the magazine *T'ai-wan wen-yi* (Taiwanese literature) in the 1960s; publication in the late 1970s of two literary anthologies on the Japanese period, *Jih-chu hsia T'ai-wan hsin wen-hsueh* (Taiwanese new literature under the Japanese occupation) (Ming-t'an, 1979) and *Kuang-fu ch'ien T'ai-wan tso-chia hsuan-chi* (Collected works by Taiwanese writers before the repatriation of Taiwan) (Yuan-ching, 1979); and appearance in the 1980s of a short-lived literary magazine, *Wen-hsueh chieh* (Literary world), and the (not officially recognized) Taiwanese Pen Association. These, however, occupied rather marginal positions in the general field of cultural production. Of much greater visibility and influence were politically informed intellectual discourses such as those generated by the *Hsiang-t'u wen-hsueh lun-chan* (Nativist literary debate) in 1977–78 and the *T'ai-wan yi-shih lun-chan* ("Taiwanese consciousness" debate) in 1983–84, which as a rule used literature as a way of avoiding direct confrontation with the government and of mobilizing crowds for specific forms of political intervention.[3]

Such high-profile debates, though primarily political in orientation, have inspired and provided ammunition for indigenous literary discourse and have created significant but perhaps unintended results. For instance, inspired by the Nativist literary discourse, Yeh Shih-t'ao, a veteran writer and literary critic from the Japanese period, affirms the cultural uniqueness of the indigenous Taiwanese literary tradition in his essay "T'ai-wan hsiang-t'u wen-hsueh-shih tao-lun" (An introduction to the history of Taiwanese nativist literature).[4] The essay's thinly veiled message deviated from the general ideological outlook of such leaders of the movement as Ch'en Ying-chen, and Yeh was consequently chastised for his "misguided separatist tendency."[5] Nonetheless, history has proven that the long-range impact of the Nativist Literary Movement has gone beyond the specific agenda of its earlier proponents, who favored socialist humanitarianism and voiced a nationalism calling for an undivided China. Many members of the baby boomer generation who arrived on Taiwan's cultural scene in the 1980s later professed that their consciousness of "Taiwanese subjectivity" was raised for the first time during the Nativist Literary Movement. Viewed with hindsight, the split in 1981–82 in the Nativist camp followed by the decline of the "Chinese nationalism" espoused by its leaders was not accidental. While it attacked the fictionality of the government-imposed cultural narrative and the repression of people's historical memory, the Nativist movement at the same time unleashed a hidden critical energy, which, once out, took on its own momentum. Different kinds of communal aspirations were expressed in the wake of the Nativist Literary Movement, and the particular visions of a core group of Nativist intellectuals had to compete with many others in the unusually lively cultural stage of the 1980s.

In a way, this unintended legacy of the Nativist Literary Movement supplied the animating force for the general field of cultural production in the 1980s. In particular, highly visible events in the literary sphere in the 1970s, generated by centrifugal forces radiating from the center of the Nativist Literary Movement, contributed significantly to the growth of a more broadly based "nativization" trend in the following decade. This trend included the resurrection of the legendary literary figure of Yang K'ui, the bestowal of posthumous fame on Chung Li-ho (unquestionably one of the finest writers in the modern literary history of Taiwan), and the reprinting of Wu Cho-liu's *Ya-hsi-ya te ku-erh* (The orphan of Asia), a novel that has inspired much discussion on the inherently traumatic nature of the "Taiwanese identity."[6] Even though a certain amount of camouflage was required at the time to win government approval (such as the coining of an image of the anti-Japanese, nationalist hero Yang K'ui and the stress on Chung's patriotic love for the Chinese motherland), there were notable consequences, including the fact that the status of indigenous Taiwanese literature was raised and selected samples of prewar Taiwanese literature became accessible to a wider circle of the intelligentsia. At the same time, even though the socialist appeals and left-wing ideology that dominated the Nativist writings in the mid-1970s have waned along with the movement, they have fostered a spirit of resistance that emphatically underscores such new brands of indigenous literature as saga novels (Li Ch'iao, Tung-fang pai, Chung Chaocheng, etc.), prison literature (Shih Ming-cheng, Yao Chia-wen, etc.), and works that either expose the crimes of the Nationalist government's political indoctrination (Lin Shuang-pu) or explore controversies surrounding taboo subjects such as the February 28 Incident.

For a trained literary historian, it is obvious that this literature is fully the product of the special dynamics of postwar Taiwan's sociocultural developments and can hardly be considered a return to the prewar tradition of the Taiwanese New Literature. For example, despite the historical subject matter of the saga novels, this literature has more to do with the contemporary than the Japanese period, and it is heavily indebted to the aesthetic assumptions advanced by the Nativist Literary Movement of the 1970s. Or, in the case of Lin Shuang-pu's exposé fiction, though thematically counterhegemonic, its stylistic traits amply suggest that the author has assimilated well the characteristic mainstream artistic criteria. Such observations, however, are only meaningful to people in the scholarly community. To the ardent revivalists of a distinctive Taiwanese culture, the historical continuity of an unadulterated literary lineage is essential and must be confirmed or constructed at any cost. Thus, a task that has engaged many nonacademic literary historians is the search for an axis along which the Taiwanese literary tradition has supposedly evolved. Many have subscribed to Yeh Shih-t'ao's vision that the "anti-imperial and antifeudalist" spirit is the true essence of the Taiwanese literary tradtion, and some have even taken the embodiment of this spirit as a criterion for "authentic" Taiwanese literature.

This phenomenon can of course be interpreted from a number of different angles. On the one hand, from the viewpoint of professional literary studies, one can easily point out that Yeh's proposition does not have much validity as a historical description. By virtue of its patent exclusiveness, it tells a partial truth and is unable to account for the extremely complex phenomenon of literary production in postwar Taiwan. And the fact that so much time and energy have been spent debating who should be considered "Taiwanese writers" makes it evident that the discourse on indigenous Taiwanese literature since the 1980s has been too often dominated by the political agenda of Taiwanese nationalism, in much the same way that the Nativist literary discourse was dominated by simplistic leftist views. The question as to whether Pai Hsien-yung, Yu Kuang-chung, and Wang Wen-hsing are legitimate Taiwanese writers only makes sense under the premise that postwar settlers (mainlanders) are dubious members of the Taiwanese political community.

On the other hand, however, the fact that discourse on indigenous Taiwanese literature has been subordinate to the political discourse of Taiwanese nationalism does not mean that these two discourses share the same orientations or the same goals. As John Hutchinson has argued, even though cultural and political nationalisms frequently converge in the same movement and are mutually inspiring, a distinction still can and should be made between the two. Political nationalists are primarily concerned with citizenship rights, and to "mobilize a political constituency on behalf of this goal, they may appeal to ethnic sentiments and in the process become 're-traditionalized.' . . . But their objectives are essentially modernist: to secure a representative state for their community so that it might participate as an equal in the developing world civilization" (emphasis mine).[7]

Cultural nationalists, on the other hand, perceive the nation as an organic entity and a creative force that is imbued with individuality. Their primary goal, therefore, is the moral regeneration of the community by means of evoking and appropriating "genuine communal memories linked to specific homelands, cultural practices and forms of socio-political organization."[8]

It is therefore more appropriate to look at Yeh's proposition as a performative speech act. Together with his voluminous reminiscences of prewar and wartime Taiwanese writers, his work sets the stage for the use of the tradition of the Taiwanese New Literature movement as a cultural symbol. Wielding this symbol, Yeh has played the role of a typical cultural nationalist in educating his fellow Taiwanese "to their common heritage of splendor and suffering" in order to inspire in them an emotional loyalty to this community and "to differentiate it against other communities."[9] As a survivor of a bygone era, Yeh's seemingly anachronistic evocation of the "anti-imperialism, antifeudalism" slogan (with the normally concurrent term *anticolonial* under erasure here) speaks to a deep impulse of many older Taiwanese who have been twice subjugated to colonial or quasi-colonial rules in their lifetimes. And Yeh's own personal career bears out the convoluted trajectory of the collective expression of this impulse, for his career has moved from tongue-in-cheek collaboration to explicit protest and defiant self-assertion. It is in this sense that the term *Taiwanese literature* has been imbued with the potency of a political sign.[10]

> Why do such myths and memories retain their hold, even today, to fuel the nationalist project? There is no single answer; but two considerations must take priority. The first is the role of ethno-history, its myths, values, memories and symbols, in assuring collective dignity (and through that some measures of dignity for the individual) for populations which have come to feel excluded, neglected or suppressed in the distribution of values and opportunities.[11]

This passage by Anthony D. Smith aptly defines a common drive — an aspiration for "a reversal of collective status, at least on the cognitive and moral levels" — lying behind the political and cultural nationalisms in Taiwan.[12]

But literary historians cannot afford to disregard the lack of sophistication, due to emotional motives, in the views repeatedly expressed by proponents of indigenous literature. The single-minded shallowness with which a host of literary debates were conducted in fact points to a deeper problem, an infrastructural deficit in humanities education in Taiwan's post-1949 era, for which individual participants of such debates naturally cannot take the entire blame. The structural factors — the ways in which resources are distributed in the field of cultural production — are even more relevant. It has been observed that Taiwanese cultural nationalists tended to be those equipped with less cultural capital or those who had to struggle with substandard resources.[13] What is needed, therefore, is a substantial overhaul in the entire field of literary studies.

And this appears to be happening in the 1990s. The lifting of martial law, the subsequent Taiwanization of the Nationalist Party, the Democratic Progressive Party's rise to power, and the transformation of the media — all these forces have initiated a process in which the status of indigenous cultural products is being reversed.[14] What we have been witnessing since the early 1990s may very well be a "reconstitution" of Taiwan's dominant culture in which formerly alternative or oppositional formations are being actively incorporated. All of these forces have given tremendous impetus to the study of modern Taiwanese literature. The resumption of the earlier journal *Literary World* under a new name, *Wen-hsueh T'ai-wan* (Literary Taiwan) (1991–), with professors at prestigious national universities joining the editorial board, marked the beginning of academic recognition of a hitherto suspicious category of scholarly pursuit. A particularly noteworthy event was the publication of the multivolume anthology *T'ai-wan tso-chia ch'uan-chi* (Anthology of Taiwanese writers) (1991–) by the Ch'ien-wei publishing house, which, by establishing an alternative canon, has effectively challenged the official genealogy of modern Chinese/Taiwanese literature. The government-supported "culture centers" at the subprovincial level, which are absorbing former members of alternative or oppositional formations, are spinning out publications of literary research materials and creative works of small commercial value. The fervor showered on Taiwanese literary studies reached an apex in the anniversary year of 1995, when an impressive number of conferences on the subject were held with handsome subsidies from the government, in particular the Council for Cultural Construction and Development of the Executive Yuan. Even though the public zeal for Taiwanese literary studies is soon likely to subside, the ecology of the field has been permanently altered.[15] Raymond Williams has identified three aspects in the general cultural process: tradition, institution, and formation.[16] We have already witnessed the unfolding of the nativization trend and the use of the tradition of Taiwanese New Literature as a cultural symbol. The next natural step should be the institutionalization of Taiwanese literary studies, which, in fact, is already very much on the horizon.[17]

Re-evaluating the "Traitor" Literature: An Identity Trap

The majority of serious scholars who have become involved in the study of Taiwanese literature share to an extensive degree the goals of Taiwanese cultural nationalism. As scholars, however, the problems they face are necessarily of a different nature. This section explores some of their basic problems by way of examining some of these scholars' re-evaluations of the *Kominka* literature.

Unlike the political nationalists, who primarily wish to promote the community's rights and prestige in a contemporary world, the cultural nationalists look to the past in search of the roots of a distinctive group identity. While doing so, it is impossible for the Taiwanese cultural nationalists to skirt the question of the community's historical ties to China. In order to legitimize communal aspirations against a competing Chinese nationalism, tremendous amounts of intellectual energy have been invested in redefining the Taiwanese ethnic and cultural identity in the last fifteen years or so, a process that has resulted in the rapid and vigorous evolution of the nativization discourse. Without attempting a systematic analysis of this discourse, I would like to observe that the literary scholars and historians partaking in this project seem to harbor a greater sense of ambivalence toward the Chinese heritage than do their counterparts in other intellectual spheres. For many of them, schooled in Chinese or history departments and intellectually nourished by the post-1949 dominant culture, the constant need to differentiate a "genuine" Chinese cultural heritage from the official version of it, which has been conceived within a discourse of power, can be emotionally taxing. Crucial questions pertaining to the future of the entangled identity issue — whether national, ethnic and cultural identities are in fact separable in the practice of everyday life — are relatively easy to handle. A prevailing attitude submits that everything in the long run will be resolved by political means. It is the questions regarding the past that demand concentrated deliberation.[18] Serious contemplations of the past thus involve an intellectual process ultimately determined by the moral and epistemic foundations of these scholars' knowledge.

The current re-evaluations of the literature written during the *Kominka* campaign in the 1940s may in one sense serve to illustrate the specific ways in which contemporary critics in Taiwan work out their ambivalence concerning the identity issue through the activity of literary interpretation. In another sense, these interpretive exercises are necessarily conditioned by the interpreter's general framework of knowledge and intellectual orientation, which goes beyond the interpreter's consciously taken stance on the question of identity. And whether these scholar-critics can develop an ability to critically reflect on the dominant framework of knowledge and intellectual tradition is crucially relevant to the future development of Taiwanese literary studies. The specimens of critical writings on the *Kominka* literature I have examined here were written mostly between 1993 and 1996. For the sake of comparison, I have also included a few papers authored by Japanese scholars. Since every sign indicates that scholarly work on Taiwanese literature of the Japanese period will continue to develop, I do expect to revise my views as more relevant materials become available.[19]

It is worth mentioning that within Taiwan's general intellectual circle the renewed attention to *Kominka* literature promptly elicited a knee-jerk response to the politically sensitive "traitor" issue. Such views, ranging from sympathetic understanding to outright condemnation, predictably diverge along ideological lines.[20] Public opinion of this sort and its facile verdicts fall short of acknowledging the complex reality experienced by veteran writers from that historical period—this can be easily proven. By contrast, however, even though the scholarly reassessment of *Kominka* literature invariably betrays personal predispositions (despite its claim of objectivity), the nature of such predispositions is seldom merely ideological.

The first type of scholar whose writings I have examined condemns the "traitor" mentality in principle. These scholars have, however, attempted to carefully discriminate between "genuine"—and thus unpardonable—*Kominka* works and works that are commonly labeled *Kominka* literature but nonetheless contain either implicitly or explicitly subversive elements. Their studies typically employ conventional methods like drawing evidence either intrinsically from the text or extrinsically from objective circumstances (such as whether the manuscript had been censored). This empirical approach, in a sense, also affects the way these scholars perceive formal matters. For example, in refuting the Japanese scholar Hoshina Kōshū's argument that Ch'en Huo-ch'uan's "Tao" (The way) embodies the dual quality of "*Kominka* literature" and "resistance literature," Lin Jui-ming argues that his reading of *Kominka* literature is predicated on a principle of morality and that in this crucial matter the Taiwanese, as descendants of the victims of imperialist aggression, do not have the luxury of tolerating thematic ambivalence.[21] At the same time, Lin approves of Wang Ch'ang-hsiung's story "Pen-liu" (Rapid torrents). Lin says that the author, by making his main characters, Itō and Lin Po-nien, represent two opposing attitudes toward the *Kominka* program, ultimately preserved (to some extent) the dignity of the Taiwanese as colonial subjects.[22] Similarly, Ch'en Wan-yi defends Wang by pointing out how each of the three main characters in his story is deeply tormented by the colonial condition: the dilemma of having to choose an identity, sometimes by radical means.[23]

The second type of scholar opts for an apologetic approach, focusing on the ways in which established Taiwanese writers responded to compulsory assignments to produce war propaganda. Works that receive special attention include, first, stories featuring the theme of *Jih-T'ai ch'in-shan*, that is, friendly social exchanges between Japanese and Taiwanese ("Yu-lan hua" [The magnolia flower], "Lin-chu" [Neighbors], and "Feng-t'ou shui-wei" [Barren land]), and, second, the more explicitly eulogistic works written after these writers were sent on official visits to military bases, mines, sea-shore salt fields, and factories producing war supplies. Since almost every well-known writer at the time—including Yang K'ui, Lu Ho-jo, and Lung Ying-tsung—wrote works of this sort, the critics are primarily searching these stories for traces of reluctance or resistance in disguise. One origi-nal—and persuasive—argument is presented by Shih Shu.[24] Shih contends that the exemplary portrayal of the working class in certain works by leftist writers, including Lu Ho-jo and Yang K'ui, surreptitiously introduces such conventions of proletarian literature as collectivism and ideological reform through labor, both prevalent in communist countries at the time. Thus, Shih suggests that these writers indirectly sabotaged Japanese imperialism and its fascist warfare, which they superficially endorsed.

Chung Mei-fang's well-researched paper represents a third type of criti-cal writing by Taiwanese scholars, one that perceives the Kominka campaign as an intensified version of the longer and more successful assimilation pro-gram of the second half of the Japanese period.[25] Interpreting Lu Ho-jo's "Shih-liu" (Guava) in an old-fashioned allegorical manner, Chung Mei-fang takes the pathetic death of the third brother—a young man who as a child was given to foster parents because of the poverty of his own and has re-cently gone insane for unclear reasons—as symbolically representing the younger generation of Taiwanese, who are simultaneously attracted to the heroic rhetoric of the Kominka campaign and disturbed by the discriminative practices of the colonizers in real life. With a wealth of historical materi-als (especially sources on a feud between the Japanese-sponsored magazine Wen-yi T'ai-wan [Literary Taiwan] and the T'ai-wan wen-hsueh [Taiwanese literature], in which many important Taiwanese writers were involved, and the newly recovered diary of Lu Ho-jo), Chung offers valuable evidence that seems to confirm the well-circulated view that, by depicting folk cus-toms and rural life, Taiwanese writers were at the time engaged in a form of "cultural resistance" against Japanese cultural assimilation, a practice that of course was especially meaningful in view of the ongoing Kominka cam-paign.[26]

All three groups of scholars discussed above share a strong empirical ten-dency and have supported their arguments with laboriously collected data. The historical research conducted by these highly qualified scholars is un-doubtedly much needed, and its accumulated results promise to form a solid foundation for the new field of Taiwanese literary studies. At the same time, however, scholars familiar with contemporary critical theories are likely to find their textual interpretations not sophisticated enough. Lacking interest in the formal dimensions of literary texts, these critics—with the possible exception of Shih Shu—seem to be single-mindedly concerned with the author's consciously encoded thematic messages in the story and they use these messages as a basis for a final judgment on the author's moral character. Occupying high moral ground, these critics by and large overlook—or purposefully defy—the relativism in values and belief systems found in different historical periods. In the field of modern Chinese literary studies, scholars have repeatedly pointed out that moralist imposition has been a major impediment to literary development in modern China. And it seems to me that these Taiwanese scholars are suffering from the same constraint. In what follows, therefore, I would like to propose an alternative model for analyzing the *Kominka* literature, with the hope of shedding some light on the inherent limitations of moralist criticism.

A central concept in the analytical model I endorse is that of hegemony, or the dominant culture, as defined by Raymond Williams. Simply put, hegemony is achieved with the tacit consent and active support of those being dominated, who have internalized the hegemonic values in the practice of everyday life. What is perceived to be a matter of moral integrity by these Taiwanese scholars, I would argue, has a great deal to do with individual writers' positions in relation to the dominant culture.

By way of illustration, let us take a brief look at Chou Chin-po's story "Shui-ai" (Mouth cancer). Toward the end of the story, the narrator, a Taiwanese doctor newly returned from Japan, laments the fact that he shares blood with a despicable country woman, the mother of a patient of his, whose ignorance and selfishness seem to him to be typical products of Taiwan's backward rural society. This rumination is followed by thoughts on the doctor's own responsibilities to enlighten his fellow countrymen, as it has dawned on him that his role is not merely that of a medical doctor but also that of a spiritual doctor to his people. There is, therefore, an apparent continuity that existed between Lu Hsun, Lai Ho, and Chou Chin-po: all three of them envisioned a "new, modern citizen" and their harsh criticism of the old customs of the traditional society was marked by a passionate love-hatred. There is, indeed, nothing inherently immoral about the author's thematic formulation. The real problem, of course, lies in the fact that he has unreservedly identified with the Japanese civilization and that, worse still, he has simple-mindedly suggested resolving the problems of Taiwanese society through the *"Komin*-cultivation program" (*huang-min lien-*

ch'eng yun-tung). But as a young writer in his early twenties Chou's belief in the movement might indeed have been sincere, as he himself suggested at a conference in 1994, and this might not even have been atypical of his generation of Taiwanese at the time.[27] Here we have encountered a crucial sociological factor: the widened gaps between generations in their cultural identifications. This is characteristic of the colonial rule in its early stage and must be given serious consideration in our reading of the *Kominka* literature. Generally speaking, the most active members of the literary community in the early 1940s were modern Taiwanese writers of the second generation, who were born in the second decade of the century and were intellectually nourished within the Japanese educational system, but whose sensitivity to racial discrimination was intensified by various fascist war programs pushed by the colonial government during the Pacific War.[28] This group included nearly all the writers mentioned above such as Lu Ho-jo, Ch'en Huo-ch'uan, and Wang Ch'ang-hsiung. Their relation to the dominant culture was considerably different from that of their immediate predecessors, such as Lai Ho and Ch'en Hsu-ku, whose much stronger cultural ties to China can be largely explained by the traditional Chinese learning acquired by members of the gentry in childhood. After the official ban on Chinese-language magazines in 1937, many members of this group reverted to writing traditional Chinese poetry. Newly arriving on the literary scene in the 1940s, then, was a group of even younger writers whose formative years fell entirely in the second half of the Japanese period, a time in which colonial assimilation was notably more successful than in the earlier period. Both Yeh Shih-t'ao (b. 1925) and Chou Chin-po (b. 1925) belonged to this group. The fact that Chou spent a large number of his formative years in Japan with his family and that Yeh began his literary career under the patronage of a well-known Japanese man of letters are additional factors that must have had significant bearings on these writers' relations with the dominant culture.

If contemporary Taiwanese critics have treated Chou Chin-po less harshly than they did another writer, Ch'en Huo-ch'uan (Chou seems to have been largely dismissed or considered unworthy of scholarly treatment), can we perhaps say that ambivalence is sometimes more offensive than outright betrayal? Or are these critics mainly looking for proof of the existence of a "Taiwanese consciousness" in defiance of colonial impositions and in doing so have unwittingly projected their own dilemma onto these literary texts? In either case, the contemporary critics have superimposed on the *Kominka* work a political concern from a different epoch and as a result they have only reiterated a universal moral standard to which they have a personal commitment. Their criticism is patently partial because of its arbitrary focus on the restricted domain of the authors' consciousness. A more historicized approach, one would argue, should instead aim at the multifarious configurations of the dominant culture in the literary text and at the complicated, often self-contradictory, tactics the writer employed to negotiate his or her identity. These configurations may be found in scattered, thematically irrelevant details in the text, which nonetheless reveal unexamined assumptions that these authors shared with a large number of their contemporaries. Indeed, despite their different thematic messages, all three stories — "Mouth Cancer," "The Way," and "Rapid Torrents" — have references to doubts about the *Kominka* movement among ordinary Taiwanese. At the same time, their authors shared assumptions that obviously were based on the same belief system that permeated the dominant culture of the time: the unquestioned "spirituality" of the Japanese civilization that finds its expression in *kendo* (the Japanese art of swordplay), mentioned in more than one story; the backwardness in rural Taiwan that has manifested itself in a pragmatic attitude and naked materialism; and the lamentable lack of integrity and idealism among ordinary Taiwanese. On the other hand, the authors' sense of mission and their desire to improve the society and enlighten the Taiwanese people seem to signal a common heritage of the Taiwanese New Culture movement. The only — albeit crucial — difference is that by the 1940s *Japanese civilization* had replaced such utopian terms as *modern citizen* and *new people,* which had appeared in Lai Ho's fiction (he had in turn inherited them from turn-of-the-century Chinese intellectual reformers through the writings of the May Fourth Movement), as a concrete embodiment of civil qualities in a modern society. A writer's attitude toward the dominant culture and its belief systems is of course closely tied to, but by far exceeds, his or her consciously taken stance regarding such topical issues as cultural and national identity or the controversial *Kominka* movement.

If a different approach is adopted, the most harshly condemned story, "The Way," with its relentless exposure of the inherently contradictory elements of the dominant culture and the traumatic effects they have created in the individual psyche, may even be regarded as the most subversive. The artistic merit of "The Way," as I see it, rests precisely in the successfully portrayed anxiety of the main character and his intense struggle to overcome this anxiety by self-inflictive, even sadistic means. The generic traits characteristic of confessional literature found in this story may not be accidental. Given what we know about the literary history of this period, it can be safely assumed that Ch'en Huo-ch'uan had been exposed to modern literary conventions from the West, not to mention the story's likely indebtedness to Japanese literary genres.[29] Ch'en's highly sensitive descriptions of the subtle differences between the Japanese and Taiwanese patterns of social interaction, of their differently conceived behavioral codes in the public and private spheres, of the repressive nature of Japanese men's avowed sense of honor, and even of the homoerotic relationships between the hero and his Japanese acquaintances are marked by an exquisite psychological realism.

In my view, therefore, what is needed for the study of Taiwanese literature to become a viable academic discipline is a refinement of its critical methodology. Since critical methodology nowadays is often equated with particular "Western" versions of it, objections to my view can be easily raised on nativist grounds. Rather than debating such hypothetical objections here, I would instead consider a more general problem confronting all nationalist/nativist projects in non-Western modern cultures. Partha Chatterjee has suggested that since "the new high culture" in these countries is essentially the product of an alien imposition, the following questions must be asked: "Can [this high culture] effectively supersede the various folk cultures and become a truly homogeneous national culture? Is there not a problem of incommensurability and inter-cultural relativism which the new national culture must overcome?"[30] A negative answer to the first of these questions and an affirmative answer to the second supposedly lay at the heart of Taiwan's Nativist Literary Movement in the 1970s. But while the movement has succeeded in raising people's consciousness the fundamental problems have remained largely unresolved.

In an earlier study on postwar Taiwanese literature, I came to the conclusion that the driving force behind Taiwan's Modernist Literary Movement in the 1960s and 1970s was precisely a desire to create an elitist institution of high art. And the Modernists believed that this could be effectively done only through assimilation of specific forms of aesthetic ideology from the West. The Nativists, while rebuking this effort and its complicitous role in the spread of Western cultural imperialism, nonetheless had recourse to an earlier Western importation, socialist realism, which had enjoyed high cultural status both on the Chinese mainland and in Taiwan in the prewar era. Indeed, many proponents of Taiwanese indigenous literature, including the preeminent Yeh Shih-t'ao, have repeatedly referred to the fact that the introduction of contemporary Western high culture was more success-fully accomplished in the Japanese period than in Taiwan's post-1949 era.

The situation is further complicated by the fact that, whereas the mod-erates following the liberal-humanist tradition are often regarded as com-pradors for the imperialists, left-wing ideology is a long-term ally of the nativist resistance. The split in Taiwan's Nativist camp in 1982, which ended the temporary coalition between the two groups in the 1970s against a com-mon enemy, was at least partially caused by incompatibility between the socialists' internationalism and the cultural nationalists' primordialism. In the post-Nativist nativization discourse, with the anti-imperialist impulse being absorbed largely by the overriding imperative of "desinicization" (*ch'u Chung-kuo hua*), hostility toward Western cultural influences has been much more relaxed.

Moreover, in the 1990s, riding on the high tide of the globalization trend, public and private sectors in Taiwan have aggressively tried to promote national, corporate, or personal interests by creating cultural spectacles on the international stage (such as the staging in the West of Lin Huai-min's modern dance and the Chinese-opera version of *Macbeth* and efforts to mar-ket art films at international film festivals). As active participants in cultural politics at the domestic level, proponents of indigenous Taiwanese litera-ture have also begun to stress the importance of "internationalizing" Tai-wanese literary studies, and major transformations of the discourse seem to be fermenting.

Indeed, the discourse on indigenous Taiwanese literature has appeared to be quite susceptible to the influence of the latest Western intellectual fashions. For instance, in a 1995 essay, "T'ai-wan wen-hsueh-shih fen-ch'i te i-ke chien-t'ao" (A re-examination of the periodization of Taiwanese literary history), Ch'en Fang-ming adumbrated a number of ideas from an impres-sive array of contemporary critical theories.[31] Assigning "postcoloniality" to Taiwan's post–martial law period, Ch'en used the term *second coloniza-tion* to characterize the earlier postwar period (1945–87) and presented argu-ments about the resistance nature of Taiwanese literature in that period. To conclude the essay, he further appealed to a utopian vision supposedly em-bodied by postmodern pluralism and feminist egalitarianism as providing hope for the future of cultural reconstruction in contemporary Taiwan.

In an earlier stage of the nativization discourse, the pure/impure bi-nary opposition and the concept of "origin" featured prominently, and one frequently encountered the fetishized image of the "land" and "mother tongue." [32] Such romantic notions, however, have been harshly criticized in intellectual circles, and recently we have seen a notable change in strategy employed by proponents of the revivalist Taiwanese language movement. For instance, with tactics of identity politics inspired by the discourse on multiculturalism, Lu Hsing-ch'ang has effectively justified his promotion of the Taiwanese language movement as an effort to remove the "sino-centrism" (Han-tsu chung-hsin chu-yi) so far dominating language use in contemporary Taiwan. [33]

True enough, scholarly and nonscholarly appropriations of Western critical theories in Taiwan are more often than not superficial and marked by a layman naïveté. Nonetheless, given Taiwan's cultural environment, in which Western cultural products continue to enjoy lofty status, the immediate effect of using these Western theories is empowerment. Moreover, history has taught us that imported ideas often have tremendous potential in transforming indigenous cultures and societies in unpredictable ways. Trained as a literary comparatist, I am inclined to accept the general premise that cross-cultural fertilization is a positive force behind human civilization, and I am more concerned with the practical problem of how to improve the quality of scholarly work related to Taiwanese literary studies. As I see it, the most serious problem faced by Chinese literary comparatists and perhaps by scholars of Taiwanese literary studies as well is the difficulty of combining theoretical approaches with empirical data. While Western critical theories hold great promise for producing sophisticated literary interpretations, the greatest pitfall is that they also tend to dictate the issues that would receive the primary attention of critics. Methodology in many cases determines the content of criticism. How to employ interpretive frames with greater heuristic power but at the same time resist their restrictive effects seems to be an urgent task for scholars of Taiwanese literature. In the remaining part of this section, I offer a critical analysis of two Japanese scholars' critical writings on the Kominka literature as an illustration of this task.

Unlike the traditional approach employed by an earlier generation of Japanese scholars of Taiwanese literature, which focuses mainly on dating, textual verification, and meticulous construction of literary chronology, works by Tarumizu Chie and Fujii Shōzō are unmistakably informed by the latest findings of such Western critical theories as postcolonial discourse, Jürgen Harbermas's theory on the public sphere, and Benedict Anderson's idea of "imagined communities." In her essay on "Ch'ing-ch'iu" (Clear autumn) by Lu Ho-jo, for example, Tarumizu suggests that the hero in the story has an "imperfect identification" (or "hybrid identity") and that his inner conflict mirrors the inherently contradictory relationship between "modernization" and "traditionalism." [34] In another essay, "Chan-ch'ien 'Jih-pen yu' tso-chia: Wang Ch'ang-hsiung yu Ch'en Huo-ch'uan, Chou Chin-po chih pi-chiao" ("Japanese-language" writers in the prewar period: a comparison between Wang Ch'ang-hsiung and Ch'en Huo-ch'uan, Chou Chin-po), Tarumizu observes how a story like Ch'en Huo-ch'uan's "The Way," which delineates in minute psychological detail the soul-rending sufferings of an individual Taiwanese in his effort to transform himself into a Japanese, inevitably forces a sense of guilt upon the Japanese colonizers.[35] Representing Japan's younger postwar intellectuals as being haunted by a sense of guilt for Japan's military atrocities in the Second World War and for its larger imperialist project, Tarumizu has expressed a sentiment that finds its counterpart in Western academe's critical bashing of the modern Enlightenment project and its complicitous relationship with imperialism.

Another Japanese critic, Fujii Shōzō, argues that a distinctive new group identity among educated Taiwanese had emerged by the 1940s.[36] Using literacy in Japanese as an index for the general educational level in Taiwan, Fujii suggests that the success of Japanese-language education in Taiwan was the essential enabling condition for the emergence of a reading public for literary magazines and for the subsequent formation of a local literary community, the *T'ai-wan wen-t'an,* distinct from the Japanese literary centers or *chung-yang wen-t'an.* And the Taiwanese writers' collective endeavor to write about the experience of the war helped to shape an "imagined community" that distinguished itself at once from Japan and China. The multilingual ability of the Taiwanese gave them a sense of superiority in relation to the people they came in contact with in South China and Southeast Asia during the Pacific War. New perceptions and a new structure of feelings were gained, especially among the younger generation of Taiwanese fluent in the Japanese language. The Japanization program had thus created an unintended result: instead of converting the Taiwanese into loyal Japanese citizens, it gave birth to a unique community identity, which is very similar to what is now referred to as the "Taiwanese consciousness." The fact that Fujii considers the remarkable success achieved by the Japanese in modernizing its first colony to have been an essential foundation of Taiwanese nationalism is reminiscent of a theory proposed by South Asianists on the relationship between the British Empire and India, which suggests that the former's colonial discourse provided a model for the latter's nationalist thoughts in the postcolonial period.

What interests us here is not the Japanese scholars' ideologically de-termined moral inclinations but rather their Western-influenced method-ological approach. This approach at once provides a contrast with the em-pirical methodology of the more conventional scholars and exemplifies ways in which these Japanese scholars' perceptions of the issue were condi-tioned by the methodologies they employed, for their work often contains inadvertent oversights.

Tarumizu has dealt with the significant topic of modernization, a topic conspicuously absent in Taiwanese scholars' writings on the *Kominka* litera-ture. Both essays, however, may still be faulted for insufficient contextual-ization and lack of acknowledgment that the attitude toward modernity is precisely a contested area among Taiwanese intellectuals of different gen-erations. Perhaps I may repeat some of the observations that I have made elsewhere. Many of the first-generation writers of the Taiwanese New Lit-erature embraced modernity as an advanced stage of civilization, but the passion was expressed in vacant terms, for essentially they never had any real experience of a truly modernized society.[37] (A good example would be the moralist philosophical underpinnings of Lai Ho's negative criticism of "law.") Most of the second-generation writers, pressured by wartime lit-erary politics, engaged in indirect resistance by means of asserting nativ-ism, notably by decreasing their criticism of the traditional, feudalist traits of Taiwanese society. However, if some of these writers consciously deni-grated modern urban civilization, symbolically represented by the Japanese metropolis, still others held exactly the opposite stance. In works of the younger writer Chou Chin-po, who opted to side with progress, a promi-nent theme was the urgency to modernize in view of the obvious bene-fits that modernity could have brought to the Taiwanese people. As Japan is equated with civilization, these writers ardently supported Japanization, albeit not without doubts from time to time.

Fujii's theoretically sophisticated essay is significant in that it calls our attention to the collective experience of educated Taiwanese in the 1940s. Taking a sociological approach, it focuses primarily on the intelligentsia rather than the thinking elite, and therefore it completely disregards the resistance activities the Taiwanese scholars have always emphasized in a perhaps exaggerated manner. As compulsory assimilation under the inten-sified assimilation program enforced by the colonial government since 1937 necessarily heightened the awareness of racial discrimination, one wonders if the rekindled yearnings for a now much alienated China, as documented in Lu Ho-jo's diary and elsewhere by the works of Wu Cho-liu, were not indeed echoed among the broader social group of educated Taiwanese.

Resisting Tendentious Scholarship

In the first section of this essay, I suggested that the tradition of the Taiwanese New Literature was virtually nonexistent in the mainstream literary institution of Taiwan's post-1949 era, that the honor bestowed on such writers as Chung Li-ho and Yang K'ui in the wake of the Nativist Literary Movement was mixed with misrepresentation, and that the recent elevation of the Taiwanese New Literature tradition to the status of cultural symbol serves the goals of Taiwanese nationalism more than those of literary studies. While several academic studies devoted to the literary history of the Japanese period have been published in the last few years, scholarly treatment of "the legacy of Japan in the literature of postcolonial Taiwan," in whatever marginal or oppositional form, seems to be lagging behind. In what follows, I would like to offer some preliminary thoughts on this important topic.

In an essay presented at a 1995 conference, Chang Heng-hao eloquently appealed to his peers to depoliticize critical judgments of Taiwanese literature. Chang first pointed out the ironic fact that the inclusion of an inferior story by Yang K'ui, "Ya-pu-pien te mei-kui-hua" (An uncrushable rose), in middle-school Chinese textbooks was actually based on a misinterpretation on the editor's part (a misinterpretation that fit Yang's story into the official ideology) and that, for similarly blatant political reasons, an artistically more accomplished, award-winning story by the same author, "Sung-pao-fu" (The newspaperman) remained largely unknown to contemporary readers.[38] He went on to call for a criticism that would defy the shifting paradigms that are extrinsically originated and instead take into consideration only the artistic merits of the work. These remarks are immediately reminiscent of critical doctrines propounded by Taiwan's postwar Modernists, doctrines that served as powerful weapons of resistance against political and moralist impositions deeply rooted in the Chinese literary tradition.

Of course, while reasserting the value of the artistic merit of literature, Chang could not have forgotten that the Modernists' New Critical textual approach, which privileges intrinsic, artistic qualities, was a critical paradigm passionately renounced by the Nativists in the 1970s. Chang's own essay, in fact, suggested something more. By documenting the political manipulations behind the reception of Yang K'ui's work, Chang demonstrated the primary importance of a contextual approach for literary historians of Taiwanese literature. Indeed, a rigorous contextual study of the trajectory in which a few Taiwanese writers carried on the tradition of the Japanese period in Taiwan's post-1949 era would be a significant undertaking that promises to illuminate not only works by these writers but also the politically induced rapid shifts of the dominant culture in contemporary Taiwan. To redress the numerous misconceptions built around the stigmatized Taiwanese writers from the colonial period, misconceptions that grow from either ignorance or political bias, it is particularly important to attend to what Pierre Bourdieu has stressed: the position and position-taking strategies of individual writers in the general field of cultural production.

Whereas the interest of many critics of the indigenous camp has been preoccupied with KMT (Nationalist Party) bashing, in reality the different types of peripherality assigned to these writers for different nonartistic reasons reveal a much more complex picture of the post-1949 cultural field. For instance, the fact that Chung Li-ho spent many years in Manchuria and North China and wrote excellent Chinese certainly helped him win a prize in the literary contests in the 1950s, when language usage, and even style, were seen as symptomatic of ideological allegiance. Yet his truly superior literary talent did not earn him an important position in the cultural field since he lacked other kinds of capital deemed useful at the time.

Chung's alleged "China complex" has been a focus of attention in the recent "unification versus independence" debate. The fact that Chung eloped with a sweetheart of the same clan name—they were forbidden to marry by local custom—to Manchuria and then to North China—which were then within the sphere of Japanese political influence—instead of to Japan, could indeed have been motivated by pro-China nationalist sentiments, as has been widely claimed (see Chang Liang-tse, Lan Po-chou). The heroic stories of colonized Taiwanese searching for identity in the Chinese motherland, which have been lamented by Hsieh Li-fa (with reference to the musician Chiang Wen-yeh) and admired in Lan's work and Hou Hsiao-hsien's movies, need to be better contextualized. More research in this direction would be a valuable contribution to our understanding of the educated class in Taiwan in the 1940s and would either modify or complement the picture portrayed in Fujii Shōzō's essay.

The current discourse on Taiwanese literature has apparently established its own hierarchy. In fact, the higher status or visibility enjoyed by certain writers is undoubtedly derived from the political influence of their activities. For instance, the merits of the personal memoirs of Wu Cho-liu, a journalist in both profession and writing style, which have registered Wu's searching reflections on identity and his historical witness of a turbulent age, certainly far surpass those of his novel *The Orphan of Asia,* which is filled with trivializing melodramatic episodes.

Yang K'ui and Yeh Shih-t'ao were perhaps the best-known writers from the Japanese period but not necessarily the most artistically accomplished. Yang's prestige comes partly from his activism as a respectable leftist intellectual, and Yeh's capacity as a spokesman for the bygone era in the nativization movement derives primarily from his personal participation as a young protégé of Nishikawa Mitsuru in the literary circles of the early 1940s, which were led by the latter's Japanese magazine *Literary Taiwan.*[39] Yeh had a glimpse of something like a golden age of Taiwanese literature, but unfortunately that ephemeral moment happened to coincide with a dark period historically marked by turbulence and treachery.

In contrast, the names of Lu Ho-jo and Chang Wen-huan, probably the two finest Taiwanese writers of the 1940s, have just begun to be known to the public. The fact that they wrote in Japanese was of course the conspicuous reason for their lack of recognition in the post-1949 era. But even in the course of their resurrection primary attention has been given to Lu's mysterious death in the early 1950s in the armed rebellion at Lu-k'u, which made him a leftist martyr to the Nationalist government's White Terror. As a matter of fact, the distinctively different fiction of Lu and Chang represented a high-water mark in twentieth-century Taiwanese literature under Western influences; the fact that their works' ideological affiliations belong, respectively, to the leftist and liberal-humanist traditions must be seen as historical inscriptions deserving greater critical attention. Contrary to the legendary manner in which Lu ended his life, Chang chose a nonresistant path by retreating to a business career before he took up the pen again in the mid-1970s. The novel he completed in 1978, *Kun-ti lang* (The man who crawls on earth), synthesized several major lines of thought found in his works of the early 1940s. But because the novel was written in Japanese and published in Japan, it has remained peripheral to the discourse of Taiwanese literature.

As for more aesthetically oriented writers such as Lung Ying-tsung and Lin Heng-t'ai, the impact of the change in political regimes was less but still significant. I personally object to the claims that are sometimes made about their pioneering status with regard to the Modernist Literary Movement of the 1960s and 1970s, for it is easily demonstrable that the main thrust of the movement, as part of a larger, liberally inclined cultural formation, came from elsewhere. I would argue instead that at the beginning of Taiwan's post-1949 era what confronted such writers as Yeh Shih-t'ao, Wu Cho-liu, Chang Wen-huan, and Lung Ying-tsung, was the instant devaluation of much of their previously earned cultural capital. What these writers have eventually achieved, therefore, has invariably been the result of constant efforts to negotiate with a new set of laws upon which the field of cultural production now operates.

In conclusion, I would suggest that the literary conventions, aesthetic assumptions, and language usage of the Taiwanese literary tradition in the Japanese period are of such a rich diversity that any political appropriation of this tradition is ultimately rendered meaningless. In fact, one distinctive value of studying Taiwanese literature is precisely this: its inherent hybridity and conspicuous deviation from the norm of a national literature force us to recognize the futility of attempts to contain the complexly interactive nature of any literary tradition, cultural heritage, or personal life within a teleologically conceived narrative. Such an understanding would effectively challenge the very foundation of the prevalent moralist approach to *Kominka* literature, an approach that is based on a binary opposition. Evidently, the moralist critics' purist and exclusionary attempt to distinguish acts of furtive resistance from unrepentant sellouts among the *Kominka* writers relegates all other positions on the spectrum to the status of unimportance or unintelligibility. Nevertheless, the most common reactions to high-handed political programs, be it the *Kominka* campaign or the Nationalist "anticommunist" program of cultural mobilization of the 1950s, are by no means the extreme ones and cannot be easily fit into the binary mode. Here I would like to mention a dramatic event that will probably help to confirm this observation. In a frequently cited incident at the Taiwanese War Literature Conference of 1943, in order to fend off threatened or insinuated punitive measures to be taken against Taiwanese writers for their unenthusiastic participation in Japanese war projects, the Taiwanese representative Chang Wen-huan supposedly declared: "There is no non-*Kominka* literature in Taiwan. Anyone who produces non-*Kominka* literature should be shot." [40] Chang's utterance appropriated the official language of labeling in such a blatant manner that it foreclosed any further interlocutory attempts; its conspicuous ambivalence was thus left unquestioned. Years later, the ambivalence was echoed by Yeh Shih-t'ao when he asserted in an interview that " 'Taiwanese literature' is nothing other than 'literature of the Three Principles of the People [of Sun Yat-sen].' " [41] The immediate contexts of these two utterances were no doubt dissimilar, and the moral verdicts that have been passed on the two speakers are quite varied. Perceived from another angle, however, in both cases meanings assigned to the pernicious political lingo are fluid and become self-deconstructing. What compels our attention here, then, is strictly speaking neither a "spirit of resistance" nor obsequious conformism. Instead, it is a flaunting of the will by redefining terms in a way that rivals, by means of mimicking, the political authority's willful abuse of language and its categories. As these utterances of ambivalence register a coercive external condition that demands the submission or collaboration of the speakers, the utterances are ultimately accompanied by a sense of shame and humiliation, of being dominated by power, which the speakers may or may not be willing to verbally acknowledge. The work of Taiwanese writers from the Japanese colonial period, which survives with an invisible stigma, is filled with complex emotions of the sort still awaiting proper analysis by literary historians.

Notes

This essay was completed with a grant from the Pacific Cultural Foundation. I would like to thank Professor Ping-hui Liao for having included me in a research project, sponsored by the National Science Council of the Republic of China, at the National Tsing Hua University in 1994. Much of the material on which my arguments are based was collected during a seven-month stay in Taiwan that year. In addition, a research grant from the Center for Chinese Studies in Taipei for 1992–93 enabled me to begin my research on the broad subject of Taiwan's contemporary literary discourse.

In observation of the Chinese naming convention, the names of Chinese scholars in this essay are given in the original word order, that is, surname first, followed by the given name.

1   *Kominka* literature refers to literary works written by Taiwanese writers, voluntarily or involuntarily, in support of the coercive Japanization program promoted by the colonial government during the Second World War. *Kominka* literally means "to be transformed into a subject of the (Japanese) Emperor."

2   See Hsu Chun-ya, *Jih-chu shih-ch'i T'ai-wan hsiao-shuo yen-chiu* (A Study of Taiwanese fiction in the Japanese period) (Taipei: Wen-shih-che, 1995); and Liang

Ming-hsiung, *Jih-chu shih-ch'i T'ai-wan hsin-wen-hsueh yun-tung yen-chiu* (A study of the Taiwanese New Literary Movement in the Japanese period) (Taipei: Wen-shih-che, 1996).

3   See Sung-sheng Yvonne Chang, *Modernism and the Nativist Resistance: Contemporary Chinese Fiction from Taiwan* (Durham: Duke University Press, 1993); and Shih Min-hui, ed., *T'ai-wan yi-shih lun-chan hsuan-chi: T'ai-wan chieh yu Chung-kuo chieh te tsung chueh-suan* (A collection of essays on the Taiwanese consciousness debate: the final confrontation between the China complex and the Taiwan complex) (Taipei: Ch'ien-wei, 1988).

4   Yeh Shih-t'ao, *T'ai-wan hsiang-t'u tso-chia lun-chi* (Essays on Taiwanese nativist writers) (Taipei: Yuan-ching, 1979), 1–25. The essay first appeared in the magazine *Hsia-ch'ao* (China tide) in May 1977.

5   Ch'en Ying-chen, "Hsiang-t'u wen-hsueh te mang-tien" (The blind spots of nativist literature), *T'ai-wan wen-yi* (Taiwanese literature) 55 (1977): 107–12.

6   In *Wu Cho-liu tso-p'in chi* (Collected works of Wu Cho-liu) (Taipei: Yuan-hsing, 1977). For political reasons, this multivolume collection does not include Wu's famous memoir *Wu-hua kuo* (The fig tree).

7   John Hutchinson, *Modern Nationalism* (London: Fontana Press, 1994), 43.

8   Hutchinson, *Modern Nationalism,* 20.

9   John Hutchinson, *The Dynamics of Cultural Nationalism: The Gaelic Revival and the Creation of the Irish Nation State* (London: Allen and Unwin, 1987), 16.

10 To assert the cultural uniqueness of the community, historians have rewritten the history of Taiwan in a number of different ways. The literary historians, for their part, have been most concerned with Taiwanese New Literature, which has developed since the 1920s, as opposed to the traditional literature of the first half of the colonial period. One obvious reason is that the New Literature was severely suppressed in the martial law period due to its affiliation with the "shame" of Taiwan's colonial history.

11 Anthony D. Smith, "Towards a Global Culture?" in *Global Culture: Nationalism, Globalization, and Modernity,* ed. Mike Featherstone (London: Sage Publications, 1990), 182.

12 Smith, "Towards a Global Culture?" 182.

13 See Helmut Martin's observation on Yeh Shih-t'ao in his "The History of Taiwanese Literature," *Chinese Studies* 14, no. 1 (June 1996): 37.

14 Cultural sections in newspapers now feature reports on local histories of different regions of Taiwan. Mainstream writers join in public efforts to create more narratives about Taiwan's past that depart from the official version of this history in the martial law period.

15 By enlarging the pool of students from which future scholars will be produced, this temporary rage for Taiwanese literary studies has a predictable long-term

benefit. Another relatively new phenomenon is that younger scholars with training in Western critical methodology — many trained in comparative literature — have also begun to work on Taiwanese literature.

16 Raymond Williams, *Marxism and Literature* (Oxford and New York: Oxford University Press), 115.

17 The spring 1995 public hearing on a new law requiring all newly founded colleges to have a Department of Taiwanese Literature and the 1996 proposal to found graduate institutions of Taiwanese literature in the Liberal Arts College of National Taiwan University are just such examples.

18 For instance, nationalist historians have been most interested in either the precise moment of the historical awakening of the Taiwanese with regard to the problematic identity issue or the suppressed historical possibility for the Taiwanese in forming an independent political entity. Lin Jui-ming's excellent work on Lai Ho, Ch'en Fang-ming's book on Hsieh Hsueh-hung, and Wu Mi-ch'a's writing about the short-lived *T'ai-wan-kuo* are examples. Lin Jui-ming said at a 1994 conference that, from an anthropological point of view, the religion, language, and customs of the Taiwanese after a half-century of Japanese colonization were still primarily Chinese. That a *T'ai-wan-shan* (Taiwanese-style shirt) is essentially a *t'ang-shan* (Chinese-style shirt) is evidence to this effect. And Lin continued to suggest that the awakening to the possibility of a distinctive Taiwanese political identity was inspired by the liberation discourse on self-determination by "poor and weak peoples of the world" following the First World War.

19 It is regrettable that I was not able to take into consideration views expressed in papers delivered at a conference on Lu Ho-jo held in Taiwan in November 1996, when this essay was just being finished. It is interesting to note that this conference was sponsored by the mainstream literary journal *Lien-ho wen-hsueh* (Unitas, a literary monthly), which proves that the subject has moved farther toward the center of Taiwan's cultural stage. In a forthcoming article, "Ts'ung tang-ch'ien tui Jih-chu shih-ch'i wen-hsueh te hsueh-shu t'an-t'ao k'an 'T'ai-wan wen-hsueh yen-chiu' t'i-chih-hua te chi-ke mien-hsiang" (Perspectives on the institutionalization of Taiwanese literary studies: a review of current scholarship on literature of the Japanese period), I have included some discussion on the more recent developments of *Kominka* literary studies in Taiwan.

20 The latter's attitude is best illustrated by public indictments articulated by Ch'en Ying-chen, a leading intellectual of the Nativist Literary Movement in the 1970s and staunch advocate of Chinese nationalism. Ch'en publicly castigated the lack of nationalist consciousness among Taiwanese, which he considered shameful in contrast to anti-Japanese sentiments militantly expressed by the Koreans.

21 Lin Jui-min, "Sao-tung te ling-hun: chueh-chan shih-ch'i te T'ai-wan tso-chia yu Huang-min wen-hsueh" (The disturbed souls: Taiwanese writers and *Kominka*

literature in the war period), in *Jih-chu shih-ch'i T'ai-wan shih kuo-chi hsueh-shu yen-t'ao hui lun-wen* (Proceedings of the international conference on Taiwanese history of the Japanese period) (Taipei: National Taiwan University, 1993), 458–59. The article was reprinted in Lin Jui-ming, *T'ai-wan wen-hsueh te li-shih k'ao-ch'a* (A historical examination of Taiwanese literature) (Taipei: Yun-ch'en wen-hua, 1996), 294–331. Hoshina Kōshū's argument referred to by Lin is found in "Jih-chu shih-tai te T'ai-wan hsiao-shuo: kuan-yu 'Huang-min wen-hsueh'" (Taiwanese fiction from the Japanese period: on "*Kominka* literature"), in *Er-shih shih-chi Chung-kuo wen-hsueh* (Twentieth-century Chinese literature) (Taipei: Hsueh-sheng shu-chu, 1992), 64.

22 Lin, *T'ai-wan wen-hsueh te li-shih k'ao-ch'a,* 311.

23 Ch'en Wan-yi, "Meng-ching yu hsien-shih: ch'ung t'an 'Pen-liu'" (Dream and reality: rereading "Rapid Torrents"), in *Yu wu-sheng-ch'u t'ing ching-lei: T'ai-wan wen-hsueh lun-chi* (Listening to thunder at a silent place: collected essays on Taiwanese literature) (Tai-nan: Nan-shih wen-hua, 1996), 143–66. This essay was originally presented at the conference Lai Ho chi ch'i t'ung-shih-tai te tso-chia: Jih-chu shih-ch'i Tai-wan wen-hsueh kuo-chi hui-yi (Lai Ho and His Contemporaries: An International Conference on Taiwanese Literature in the Japanese Period), held at National Tsing Hua University, Hsin-chu, Taiwan, November 1994.

24 Shih Shu, "Shu-chai, ch'eng-shih yu hsiang-ts'un: Jih-ju shih-tai te tso-yi wen-hsueh yun-tung chi hsiao-shuo chung te tso-yi chih-shih fen-tzu" (Studio, city, and village: the leftist literary movement and leftist intellectuals in the fiction of the Japanese period), *Wen-hsueh T'ai-wan* (Literary Taiwan) 15 (summer 1995): 97. An earlier version of the essay was presented at the Lai Ho conference.

25 Chung Mei-fang, "Lu Ho-jo ch'uang-tso li-ch'eng ch'u-t'an: ts'ung 'Shih-liu' tao 'Ch'ing-ch'iu'" (A preliminary study of the creative process of Lu Ho-jo's "Guava" and "Clear Autumn"). Paper presented at the Lai Ho conference, 1994.

26 Lu wrote in his diary that he was deliberating on the idea of incorporating more materials from China and that the "nationalist cause" must now take precedence over other concerns in fiction writing. Lu's diary thus offers persuasive evidence for the popular critical opinion that the core group of writers associated with *Taiwanese Literature* employed strategies of cultural resistance. These strategies included deliberate depiction of local customs as a means of resistance to the exoticization of Taiwanese landscape and folk customs for Japanese audiences.

27 At the concluding session of the conference on Lai Ho and his contemporaries, several veteran writers from the Japanese period were present (Wu Yung-fu, Yeh Shih-t'ao, Ch'en Ch'ien-wu, Lin Heng-t'ai, Chou Chin-po, Yang Ch'ien-ho, and Wang Ch'ang-hsiung), representing a broad spectrum of attitudes. Chou Chin-po, the unrepentant *Kominka* writer now in his seventies, declared in a touching manner that "the motives behind the story 'Chih-yuan ping' [The volunteer sol-

dier] were sincere and that the motives of those young Taiwanese volunteers were also sincere." "The Volunteer Soldier" is a much criticized *Kominka* story by Chou. Chou's speech was delivered entirely in the Japanese language.

28 Lai Ho (1894–1943) and Ch'en Hsu-ku (1891–1965) belonged to the first generation; Chang Wen-huan (1909–78), Lu Ho-jo (1914–51?), Lung Ying-tsung (b. 1911), and Wang Ch'ang-hsiung (b. 1916) belonged to the second generation; and Yang K'ui (1905–85) was between the two.

29 I would especially like to thank Professor Robert Hegel for reminding me of the stylistic affinity between "The Way" and the Japanese "I-novel."

30 Partha Chatterjee, *Nationalist Thought and the Colonial World: A Derivative Discourse* (Minneapolis: University of Minnesota Press, [1986] 1993), 6.

31 In *T'ai-wan wen-hsueh fa-chan hsien-hsiang: wu-shih nien lai T'ai-wan wen-hsueh yen-t'ao hui lun-wen chi* (Literary developments in Taiwan: proceedings of the Conference on Taiwan Literature in the Last Fifty Years), 2 vols. (Taipei: Wenchien-hui, 1996), 2: 13–34.

32 See A. Taiwaner, "Pseudo Taiwanese: *Isle Margin* Editorials," trans. S. Yvonne Chang and Marshall McArthur, *Positions* 4, no. 1 (spring 1996): 145–71.

33 What further complicates this situation is the fact that the mother tongue for many younger people living in the urban areas of Taiwan is no longer Taiwanese.

34 Tarumizu Chie, "Lun 'Ch'ing-ch'iu' chih ch'ih-yen chieh-kou: Lu Ho-jo lun" (The *différance* structure in "Clear Autumn": a study of Lu Ho-jo). Paper presented at the Lai Ho conference.

35 Tarumizu Chie, "Chan-ch'ien 'Jih-pen yu' tso-chia: Wang Ch'ang-hsiung yu Ch'en Huo-ch'uan, Chou Chin-po chih pi-chiao" ["Japanese-language" writers in the prewar period: a comparison among Wang Ch'ang-hsiung, Ch'en Huo-ch'uan, and Chou Chin-po], in *T'ai-wan wen-hsueh yen-chiu tsai jih-pen* (Studies of Taiwanese literature in Japan), ed. Huang Ying-che, trans. T'u Ts'ui-hua (Taipei: Ch'ien-wei, 1994), 87–107.

36 Fujii Shōzō, " 'Ta tung-ya chan-cheng' shih-ch'i T'ai-wan tu-shu shih-ch'ang te ch'eng-shou yu wen-t'an te ch'eng-li: t'sung Huang-min-hua yun-tung tao T'ai-wan kuo-chia chu-yi chih tao-lu" (The maturation of a reading market and the establishment of literary circles in Taiwan during the "Great East Asian War" period: the journey from the *Kominka* movement to Taiwanese nationalism). Paper presented at the Lai Ho conference.

37 See Sung-sheng Yvonne Chang, "Modern Taiwanese Literature and Its Colonial Context," in *Taiwan: A History, 1600–1994,* ed. Murray Rubinstein (Armonk, N.Y.: M. E. Sharpe, 1999), 261–74.

38 Chang Heng-hao, " 'Ch'un-kuang kuan pu chu' te ch'i-shih" (The lesson of the story "The Light of Spring Cannot be Shut In"), in *T'ai-wan wen-hsueh fa-chan hsien-hsiang,* 2:123–36.

39 For a discussion of Yang K'ui in English, see Angelina C. Yee, "Writing the Colo-

nial Self: Yang Kui's Resistant Texts and National Identity," *Chinese Literature: Essays Articles, Reviews* 17 (December 1995): 111–32.

40 This incident is described in Lin, "Sao-tung te ling-hun," 296. Lin cites various previous records of this incident in note 21.

41 Yeh Shih-t'ao, "T'sung hsiang-t'u wen-hsueh tao san-min chu-i wen-huseh: fang Yeh Shih-t'ao hsien-sheng t'an T'ai-wan wen-hsueh te li-shih" (From nativist literature to literature of the Three Principles of the People: an interview with Mr. Yeh Shih-t'ao on the history of Taiwanese literature), in *Wen-hsueh hui-yi lu* (Recollections of literature) (Taipei: Yuan-ching, 1983), 255–56, 288–89.

Wang Wenxing and the "Loss" of China

Christopher Lupke

1. The Historical and the Personal

During the Cold War, a recurrent issue in Chinese studies, particularly that strain connected to American foreign relations, was the question of who "lost" China; whose fault it was that the disintegration of China during the first half of the twentieth century did not lead to the ultimate reunification under a regime friendly to the United States and one that upheld "our" values. China's "loss" to the Communists set it on a trajectory whose recognition by the United States was long in coming. In Taiwan, "Free China," as it was known, many historical novels were written, particularly in the 1950s, narrating a version of the events during the War of Resistance to the Japanese and the civil war between the Nationalists and the Communists. The structure of such novels as Wang Lan's (b. 1922) *The Blue and the Black* (*Lanyu hei*) resembles the expansive style of historical romance: loosely written, exhaustive in detail, and expressing a singular point of view toward the consequences of the civil war.[1] In some ways, it seems, the current rhetoric toward China conjures these Cold War images of a brutal regime on mainland China, a place where even the preposition "on" as opposed to "in" suggests a degree of uneasiness with the permanence of the People's Republic of China (PRC) as a legitimate nation-state. Not everyone has accepted the phrase "*in* the PRC," and as a result, some are still more comfortable with the characterization "*on* the mainland." What this seemingly minor choice of prepositions implies is that the last battle of the Cold War, always fought on the terrain of ideology and discourse, has not been waged. And yet in the years since the publication of Cold War classics such as *The Blue and the Black* a different set of texts, whom many have referred to as "modernist," have been written and published in Taiwan that refract the historical image of twentieth-century China. For instance, Wang Wenxing's (b. 1939) novel *Family Catastrophe* (*Jiabian*) provides a different version of history, but not just one in content alone.[2] Indeed, as many critics have suggested, it is precisely the structure of *Family Catastrophe* that represents an innovation in Chinese literature.[3] What is it about this radically constructed novel that not only has raised serious questions about modern Chinese writing but now, one could say, even has implications for the apparatus by which we understand China and it understands itself? In answer to that question, I would like to suggest that the so-called loss of China which so plagued the Cold War discourse and representation of the PRC in the United States, and in some ways continues to do so, be examined in its complex multivocalities, and that in so doing we might arrive at a better understanding of some of the issues central to Chinese intellectuals throughout the twentieth century.

First of all, how do we think of the notion of loss? One way, of course, is to repeat the stale Cold War debates over what happened to China, a set of issues that continue to be recast into questions such as "What will happen?" in China. Prognostication has for quite some time been the chief mode in which China experts assert their opinions. Attendant concerns are usually framed as "When will China modernize?" "When will it become a civilized member of the world community?" "When will it be free?" Those interested in modern Chinese culture instead should be asking what has happened and how these past events are rendered into text. What is the nature of the multivalent "loss" that underlies Wang Wenxing's novel, and how is it best understood? As I will suggest in the ensuing pages, Wang Wenxing is influenced in sophisticated ways by the modes of modernism, and still he manages to forge both his knowledge of and facility with Western aesthetics and his consciousness of China's past into a creative expression of inimitable brilliance and complexity. I am particularly interested here in Wang's ability to shape a literary narrative that fundamentally reshapes the historical narrative of the so-called loss of China in 1949. And this political loss is overlayed with the deeper, more profound loss of traditional Chinese values. Wang ingeniously weaves these two together with the personal loss of the protagonist's father in *Family Catastrophe*.

In Western theoretical discourse, when we think of "loss," we often think of the Freudian metaphor. In his 1927 article "Fetishism," Freud argues that a fetish is "a substitute" for that which is lost.[4] Freud has suggested problematically that the perceived lost object is the mother's penis, that there is some sort of primordial wholeness that, while always already absent, points toward an irretrievable time in which it did exist. Thus, the lost object is not simply a loss but a fracture of a prior unity that is no longer accessible. *Family*

Catastrophe is just such a narrative of loss. The family has "lost" its father, and the novel consists of a search to regain him. Perhaps this loss of the father in Wang's narrative signifies the highly reified quality of China's patriarchal tradition, the absolute supremacy above all other relationships of the filial bond. While in Western society certainly there can be no question of the dominance of patriarchal values, the preeminent status of filiality as a device for the formulation of subjectivity in the Chinese tradition nevertheless is not matched by the more individualistic sense of subjectivity found in Western society. The other component of this machine of subject formation is the role of language. In the Chinese tradition, filiality, language, and subjectivity are inseparable. It is therefore not without reason that in the process of his narrative of the father's loss, Wang Wenxing is drawn into a fascination with language.

This remarkable obsession with the play of language has been the source of much criticism of Wang's writing. Some even have asserted that Wang's language play is a distraction to the primary subject matter of the novel. Two early symposia on this novel were largely conducted along such negative lines. Zi Yu has criticized the novel for developing a compelling theme in language that is alienating. Every time one gets drawn into the novel, Zi Yu observes, the language thwarts this identification and distances the reader from it. Later critics, including myself, would contend that this is exactly the point of the technique, or at least an important aspect of it. Criticism of Wang's language in these symposia include assertions that the innovations are "unnecessary" (Zhang Jian), "too lyrical" (Lo Men), or "unrealistic or uncharacteristic of ordinary life" (Lin Haiyin and Zhang Xiguo).[5] But if we remember the connection made by Freud between the fear or trauma of loss and the need to fasten oneself to another, ulterior object, in this case language itself, then the reason for Wang's fascination becomes clear. Language becomes the fetishistic substitute for that which is lost—the loss of the father, the loss of one's home on mainland China, and perhaps even the loss of tradition in an era not just of vast change but of the hegemony of Western values. These various levels of trauma are worked and reworked in the language of the novel until they take on an aesthetic form. Wang's literary project simulates the structure of a dream in the sense of working through and then textually resolving what is a personal example of a broader set of historical issues—the fissure of Taiwan and mainland China, the disintegration of traditional Chinese values.

Wang's trauma is further elucidated by reference to a related article of

Freud's, "Splitting of the Ego in the Defensive Process." [6] In this article, Freud observes that the fear one encounters when confronting a risky desire is resolved through a "splitting of the ego." The ego is able to ignore any prohibition and at the same time recognize the danger of reality. In *Family Catastrophe,* the protagonist, Fan Ye, undertakes just such a course of action. He searches to restore order to the family structure while simultaneously disclosing the reason that no such restoration is possible. The novel consists of a "split" narrative. This split narrative is reminiscent of Freud's "rift in the ego." The rift never heals and tends to deepen over time. It is the price one must pay to indulge an instinctual desire and in the same breath to acknowledge its danger. The attack on traditional Chinese values seems reminiscent of Freud's discussion of risky desires, for what could be more dangerous than the repudiation of one's cultural icons? [7]

The twentieth century in general has been a period during which Chinese intellectuals have looked to the West for all sorts of models whereby to reconceptualize cultural values in China. This process itself reflects the rather unequal ideological relationship between China and the West, with traditional Chinese values characterized as "backward," "superstitious," and even "cannibalistic." Lu Xun's famous "Diary of a Madman" is considered the locus classicus of this radical critique of the Confucian tradition, an orthodoxy that, the madman observes, orders its adherents not to revere and respect but to "eat people!" [8] Could it possibly be a coincidence that the madman discerns this from the *language* while carefully reading a book of *history*? In contrast to the rather inflammatory imagery used to describe and assess the Chinese tradition — by its own modern intellectuals — Western literature and thinkers generally have been assigned a privileged status in the twentieth century. Marx, Nietzsche, and Hegel have all been influential. Freud, too, has had his role, perhaps more so in the literary realm than in the political. In the 1930s and 1940s, in particular, there was a great deal of translation of Freudian texts and terminology in China. The Shanghai modernists were one group fascinated by the unconscious, the subjectivity of perception, fantasy, and in some cases what could be considered, in Freudian terms, sexual perversion. [9] During the Maoist period in China, Freud, of course, was banned.

But his influence still was felt in Taiwan as much as that of anyone else associated with modernism. During the 1960s, modernism was the most influential movement in Taiwan, flourishing under the leadership of writers such as Wang Wenxing, Bai Xianyong, Chen Ruoxi, and Ouyang Zi. The major journal *Modern Literature* contained many short stories that could be described as modernist—using interior monologue and alienation as a theme, or taking a certain stance that evoked the iconoclastic elitism of Pound and Eliot. These writers and others, such as Franz Kafka, Virginia Woolf, and D. H. Lawrence, were translated and published in this journal. In 1972, the year that *Family Catastrophe* was published, *Modern Literature*, of which Wang Wenxing was a founding editor and one of two or three of its most important voices, devoted two parts of two issues to a symposium on the relationship between psychoanalysis and literary art. This symposium included translations of Freudian interpretations of literature—*Moby Dick* was one, Kafka's *Trial* was another—as well as translations of works by Freud himself such as "The Moses of Michelangelo" and "Dostoyevsky and Parricide." [10] There is no question that Wang Wenxing, a highly literate and well-educated member of the intelligentsia, was very familiar with the major works of Freud and probably influential in choosing the theme of this particular double issue. As we will see, the theme of the Oedipus complex figures prominently in his novel.

I would maintain, however, that the turn to Freud is not simply a study in the influence of one major Western thinker on a Chinese writer, even if it is complicated by the subtle ironies of various power dynamics—West versus China, intellectual over the mass public, and so on. One could look at the work of Ouyang Zi, a contemporary of Wang's in Taiwan and a writer whose work almost always involves some Freudian theme, to illustrate that Wang Wenxing's work is far too sophisticated, complex, and unresolved to sustain a simple influence study. We should keep in mind that what Freud was most interested in was foregrounding the unconscious. The limitations of a writer such as Ouyang Zi do not rest in any stylistic flaw, for she is a careful craftsperson of language. The problem with such pieces as "The Vase" is that the Freudian metaphor is almost always *too* literal, *too* clear, that is, too *conscious*. [11] In Wang Wenxing's work, the issues are fraught with complexities, and Freud's influence is not restricted to the Oedipal theme. His work forces us to reassess the value of history and, in fact, what counts for history. For is history foremost composed of the major political events of an era, or is it made up of the minutiae of social interactions that together form some sort of picture of the rituals and cultural norms that pervade a given society? Is the representation of history always straightforward and objective, or is it twisted and reconfigured according to the restrictions of individual perspective? Investigating the fundamental relationships in *Family Catastrophe*, the way certain events are emphasized and others are diminished in stature, will help ascertain those aspects of the narrative that are least discernible, most repressed, and closest to the *unconscious*. What we discover is a fascination with language that nevertheless suggests the personal loss of the father as well as the larger loss of China, and most assuredly the loss of the traditional scaffolding of Confucian values. We also find a structure that is broken in two, in a manner that indicates that the loss is not just a loss but also a split, a bifurcation, an absence of the wholeness that, as we read the work, seems at one time to have been present but is now gone forever. To fully comprehend this, we must first examine the exact structure of this novel that is so unique yet so heavily weighted by history and influence.

2. Fan Ye and the Predicament of Universal Subjectivity

In addition to being written in three long parts, *Family Catastrophe* consists of a bifurcated narrative, a novel divided into two alternating modes of development. These two halves develop in two different strains of the story, proceeding in a contrapuntal back-and-forth through the end of the novel. The first begins with the departure of Fan Minxian, the head of the household, from his home. This mode then develops the narrative of Minxian's son, Fan Ye, or Mao Mao, searching the island for him. This quest proves futile, for once the father has left home he is never heard from again. Each of these chapters, as I will call them for lack of a better word, begins with a letter, so that the novel progresses from A to O. Within each of these lettered chapters is the other narrative mode, numbering from 1 to 157. The numbered sequence of episodes traces the biography of Fan Ye from the time he first learned to read up to the present. The syntax of the novel becomes more convoluted as the narrative develops, and Wang has been variously applauded and impugned for mixing classical grammatical patterns with vernacular ones, for adopting English syntax, and for simply creating his own private language. He often reverses the order of Chinese characters in two-character combinations, purposely misuses diction, and chooses obscure forms of individual characters.

As Ouyang Zi has shown, each of these two separate narrative modes has its own tone.[12] The lettered chapters describe Fan Ye in the narrative present. The narrative present is the point at which the reader finds Fan Ye during his search for the father, though it begins with the father escaping the house. Fan Ye endeavors to restore the family order to what it supposedly used to be before his father's disappearance. His entreaty at the beginning of each of these chapters, written in the literary language, is a nostalgic reminder of what that order comprised: filial trust in the father's ability to resolve all the family's problems. Read within the Chinese context, the father would be culturally marked as the ultimate power figure and as a sort of conduit to the traditional social formation in general, for he is the fulcrum of the filial relationship. The tone that this particular narrative develops is challenged by the action as retold in the numbered sequence of episodes embedded within the lettered chapters. In this numbered sequence, we learn of the gradual metamorphosis of the family, from a social unit that provides economic security and spiritual comfort to some sort of a prison. In chronological time, the events in the numbered episodes, which describe the family's disintegration, would naturally precede the action of the lettered chapters, the search for the father. But the narrative trajectory dictates that the quest precede this description. The quest, then, is encountered prior to the unraveling of the familial bond, although the narration of this quest is not apprehended by the reader "intact." This structure creates a doubly inscribed narrative tone, one in which each of the narratives, presented almost in conjunction, perpetually strives to displace the other. The skeletal structure of the novel can be diagrammed in this manner:

I. Beginning of the novel.
   A. The father surreptitiously leaves the home.
   B. Fan Ye and his mother realize the father is gone, and Fan Ye begins the search.
       1. The history of the family is narrated beginning with Fan Ye as he learns to read characters.
       2. The history proceeds, set in the past.
   C. The chapter begins with the entreaty to the father written in classical Chinese. Then, Fan Ye's search is described in the present.
       3. More of the history, still set in the past, is given.

The narrative continues in sequence, with four, five, six, and so on. Eventually there is a new lettered chapter, D, followed by more numbers and then E, and so on. About one-third of the way through the novel, the second part begins, then more lettered chapters, some number sections, and so forth. Finally, the novel concludes with the third part, comprising chapters N through O and episodes 124 through 157. The basic result is two narratives that eventually merge: the lettered chapters written in the present interspersed with the numbered sequence of episodes telling the history of the family.

This double inscription is the source of moral ambivalence that destabilizes the text. The development of the novel along two strains, wherein these narrative modes vie with each other, the first telling of the dutiful son's search, the second depicting his loathing for the father and the ritual of filiality that serves to symbolically imprison Fan Ye within the family unit, raises the issue of closure, a topic I will address below. The numbered sequence increasingly becomes a narrative of Fan Ye's rage toward his father. For example, he begs his mother, Ye Qiufang, to repay a small debt his father has incurred with a relative. Fan Ye is likewise enraged when his father is cheated in a quick-profit money scheme. And he feels humiliated by his father's enfeebled behavior in old age. In one interesting scene, he becomes livid when his father gets up in the middle of the night and urinates loudly into a chamber pot for all the neighbors to hear. This loathing reaches a climax with Fan Ye's nightmare that he has stabbed his father in a fight. Of course, the anger he feels for his father, a fury that drives him to harass his father with greater frequency, most likely precipitates his father's flight from the family. And although he demonstrates sincerity in scouring the island in search of his father, he finally resigns himself to a peaceful life alone with his mother, thereby completing a symbolic Oedipal replacement.

The disturbing feature of this type of critique is that the Oedipus complex is invested with universal or archetypal significance by its exponents (or, conversely, dismissed as categorically false by its critics) while the implication is that the practice and ideology of filiality is specific to Chinese culture.[13] Thus the appropriation of the classic Oedipus complex of challenging, defeating, and replacing the father as a method of critiquing the cultural production of filiality typifies the universal/particular dialectic that leads to pathological descriptions of writers "obsessed" with China.[14] This type of reading is not restricted to Chinese novels but is, in fact, extended to them from a pervasive style of reading virtually all non-Western literature by a First World audience. A cursory glance at the back cover of almost any non-Western novel will usually reveal some sort of comment such as this: "It's not just about the local situation; it rises to the level of universality and speaks to the problems that all mankind faces." It stems from what I would call a modernist, universalist style of reading that is still ubiquitous. A fascinating example is the back cover of a pocket edition of *Robinson Crusoe*, not a non-Western novel but nevertheless a classic "colonial" one: "For this story of the young seaman concerns not only an almost universal human dream but also an almost universal human speculation. As we follow the detailed account of the castaway's twenty-five solitary years, we find ourselves inevitably asking what we would do if faced with the same problems, how we would go about building a life with only the slender resources of nature and with no aid or comfort from any fellow being [*sic*]." [15] The most eloquent articulation of this sort of reading can be found in Dorothy Van Ghent's chapter on *Lord Jim*: "Jim himself is not enigmatic. The wonder and doubt that he stirs, both in Marlow and in us, are not wonder and doubt as to what *he* is: he is as recognizable as we are to ourselves; he is 'one of us.' " [16] Van Ghent even goes so far as to say that there is nothing really interesting about the native Jim beyond the mystery of his character, which reminds us of ourselves. According to this reading, then, we need only dispense with all those elements in the native's character that are different, and he is then "the same as us." Even the translation of *Family Catastrophe* has been packaged in a book cover that is seemingly straightforward yet still very ideological. On the front, almost as a subtitle, are the words "A Modernist Novel"—essentially dictating the way in which we are to read it. On the back is a quotation asserting that "the novel's artistic excellence and its universal theme . . . promise to provide an aesthetically gratifying experience for general readers as well." I would suggest that while it is true that the novel is an enormously accomplished work of literary mastery—and difficulty—the theme is not necessarily "universal." We should not read it solely for its formal excellence. Equally important is its ability to engage the specific historical situation of China and the diaspora and render it in a manner that also implicates certain trends in Western theoretical discourse and subject formation. The engagement of the predicament of universal subjectivity, which Naoki Sakai has referred to as a "particularism thinking itself as universalism," is what makes this work indeed appealing to the general reader. [17]

A closer examination of how the ritual system of filiality develops in the novel will begin to illuminate the connection with Wang's critique of subjectivity. [18] In an early scene, Fan Minxian accuses a young and willful Fan Ye of being unfilial. But the mistrust he and his wife feel stems from a fear that their son will not support them in their old age. The father looks at Fan Ye's face and concludes that the boy is rebellious and ungrateful, and that he will someday abandon his parents. Episode 93 begins like this: "No doubt about it, the child has no respect, no filial feelings whatsoever. People say, 'Store grain for the lean times, rear sons for old age,' but from what I can see, neither of us can count on this son for our future. We've raised him for nothing. Brand new, top quality gym shoes bought especially for him, but does he appreciate them? No!" (*FC*, 96; 112). For the first time in the novel, Fan Ye is shown bearing great resentment toward his father. When, throughout the novel, the father reflects on his suspicion that his son will abandon them, he often threatens to disappear and resort to life as a monk. In one such scene, Fan Ye is described as filled with a sorrow that stabs him in the heart, thus foreshadowing in an ironic way his subsequent dream of stabbing the father. In other scenes, he flaunts his disdain for filial rituals. To Fan Ye, who has been schooled in Western learning, the whole enterprise of ancestral worship seems empty, facile, and, most of all, superstitious. His anger and humiliation stem from the feeling that no "modern" individual should subjugate himself to another. The thrust of this issue becomes so strong that at one point it seeps into the third-person narrative as well. Perhaps to undercut any possible power that the notion of filiality may contain, Wang puts the term *filiality* in quotation marks. However, the statement "This sort of superstition should never have been allowed to exist!" is not in quotation marks. Thus, the power of Fan Ye's emotion has broken through his own speech and permeated the third-person narrative.

Fan Ye is confounded by his father's role in all this for one important reason: His father was a foreign exchange student in France. In his reckoning, then, Fan Ye feels his father should have been able to internalize "universal" values of meaning and thereby debunk the Chinese myth of filiality and ancestral worship. The reason he fails to do this, however, stems from the fact that Fan Minxian was never really a serious student when abroad, that he never became a sincere inductee into the world of Western values. This too is a source of great pain and humiliation for Fan Ye, since he grew up thinking of his father as one of the educated elite who had returned early from Europe only because he had to tend to his own father's illness. Even if it were true that Fan Minxian came back to care for his father, why he exhibited this sort of filial conduct is lost on Fan Ye. Fan Minxian has proven impervious to "Westernization," but that fact, his continued adherence to filiality, is ignominious in the judgment of the son. Thus, since Fan Ye has invested Western values with a certain privileged status, he comes to view his father as a failure for not having emulated them. Fan Minxian's direct encounter with things Western, his excursion abroad and so forth, either never made an impact on him or inspired him to recede further into a "nativist" consciousness. Fan Ye, on the other hand, is disgusted by this retreat. One could argue with equal force, however, that it is the son whose mind has been "colonized" by ascribing such a privileged position to Western values.[19]

The most poignant contrast between what is viewed as the superiority of Western values versus the primitiveness of Chinese values comes in Episode 152, Fan Ye's diary chapter. In this scene, Fan Ye contemplates the need for a family as well as the importance of filiality. The characters for filiality are set off in quotation marks as if both to invoke them and to distance the reader from this invocation. Fan Ye cites a work of Western literature as proof of the moral inferiority of filiality. Wang Wenxing inherits this anti-Confucian cultural critique from the antitraditionalism of the May Fourth era, but as an author he carefully conceals or at least complicates his own views. In spite of its devastating attack on the cultural norms of Chinese society, Fan Ye's diary passage is poorly reasoned. Wang Wenxing's insertion of this reference to a Western literary work establishes a clear intertextual link between the characters in his work and those in the Western novel. It is reminiscent of a technique of ironic manipulation that Yu Dafu uses in his short story "Sinking" ("Chenlun"). In this May Fourth work, Yu Dafu often contrasts the florid prose of his self-absorbed hero with the English of such writers as Wordsworth. The effect is to mock the intellectual featured in the story, for that young man's melodramatic soliloquies are no literary match for his great romantic mentor's verse. Yu and Wang both develop a critique of the Chinese intellectual by textually juxtaposing him to a superior Western counterpart. This results in a cultural "subaltern" that incessantly conceives of the Western model in terms of a universal standard and the Chinese one as stricken, diseased, or otherwise bereft of moral value.[20]

The problem for Fan Ye is how to avoid a repetition of this predicament. Since repetition and recurrence seem to be favored techniques of the novel, one must therefore ponder whether any avenue of escape for this young Chinese intellectual is attainable. Fan Ye's development as a human subject in the novel is described as a series of reflections and repetitions of his parents, leading to his self-loathing. In several early passages, Fan Ye is shown repeating lyrics, traditional phrases, and even basic characters as a way of developing his language. When he recognizes that his self-identity is constructed of ever more embellished repetitions of his parents' habits and physical characteristics, his revulsion forces him to seek refuge in his bedroom. The bedroom becomes from this point on a symbolic extension of his own isolated and individuated subjectivity, a place where he can shut himself off from his family. Beyond a means of escape from his parents, this room provides a partitioned space where Fan Ye can recede deeper into his books of Western literature and philosophy. His reading constitutes the other source of socialization that he is receiving, and it clearly runs against the grain of the socialization he is receiving from his parents. The result of these two forms of subjective development is an internal conflict in Fan Ye that leads him to despise any vestige of his resemblance to his parents.

The permutation that modernism takes in Taiwan, then, is that while the alienated intellectual is present, he is not alienated from the world at large, as in European modernism. Nor is he alienated from the colonizing West, as in other non-Western modernisms, such as Chinua Achebe's fiction. He is, rather, alienated from the Chinese world. He lives with the "affliction" of his feudal ancestors. His internal division against himself is the chief antagonism that typifies the modernist style of Wang Wenxing. The struggle between the mind and the body epitomizes the "split" that I referred to in the first part of this essay, the loss of the tradition that results in a splitting of the ego. Wang Wenxing inherits this conflict between traditional and Western values from the May Fourth iconoclasts. Even if Fan Ye is alienated and reified, then, in fact, by virtue of this alienation, his character is a synecdochical component of a larger cultural issue affecting Chinese intellectuals in general. He is not really a decentered subjectivity but one that attempts to recenter subjectivity in the form of a new hybrid cogito that attacks its own cultural reproduction by internalizing the European ideology of (what some have described as) the colonial subject. This cultural reproduction pertains specifically to the Chinese condition as enshrined in the critique of filiality. Thus, just as Fan Ye has caused one loss by driving the father into flight, he also is an emblem of the more philosophical notion of the loss of traditional Chinese values. However, the division caused by history, the unsalvageable loss of the homeland, is no better expressed than through the predicament of Fan Ye's awkwardly positioned brother.

3. Fan Lunyuan and the Predicament of Historical Particularity

The above analysis of Fan Ye's psyche is actually only possible by bracketing the issue of historical particularity. More precisely, modernism owes its attraction to the reader's complete attention to the universality of this subject. Any references to particulars should either support this reading or at most be ancillary to it. But such an attempt at reading *Family Catastrophe* according to the rhetorical modes of Western modernism belies a self-consciousness of its status as non-Western. Thus, the reading of non-Western literature, and even the appreciation of non-Western art, is often justified in terms of its reputed transcendent value—it articulates the universal concerns of the human condition that "we all" share in spite of its historical particularities. Wang Wenxing's novel does indeed contain important elliptical references to history. But they are disclosed in repressed, almost lyrical ways. So, in contrast to the expansive historical romances of the 1950s, *Family Catastrophe* foregrounds the theme of exile and the stakes involved in historical representation by inverting the emphasis placed on the historical background. The historical reality of the family's life in Taiwan is displayed in ways that may be inexplicit but are nevertheless quite pervasive. Fan Ye's mother does not allow him to play with the neighbors. Second Brother is forbidden from cavorting with Taiwanese women. Fan Minxian leaves his identity card but takes with him a photograph of his deceased wife and eldest son, who were abandoned on the mainland. And ironically, Fan Ye takes up the study of history at a university in Taibei. It is as if his profession has turned out to be exactly that which the text tries so hard to suppress. A closer examination of Second Brother's situation illuminates this contrast between the notion of a universal subject position and the historical situatedness of this novel.

The specificity of the critique as centered on the Chinese self becomes no clearer than when one considers that the principal discursive unit of civilization in China is not the individual subject but the family. The reader is tempted to think that the family disintegrated when Fan Minxian left home, that there was something wrong in it that drove him to flee. In fact, though, the historical situation in which they exist, their status as a family dislocated on Taiwan, enjoys a repressed presence in a novel having much to do with the dissolution of the familial structure itself. Left back on mainland China prior to the 1949 Liberation, Eldest Brother appears only as a distant memory in the novel. Moreover, if Fan Ye provides a convenient template on which the problem of individual subjectivity can be mapped, then this mapping is only conceivable by virtue of the fact that the reader must temporarily hold in abeyance Fan Ye's status in the family, not as an only son or even as the eldest son but as Third Brother. With a preponderance of the depiction centered on Fan Ye, then, the other family members tend to fill supporting roles in what could perhaps be characterized as a non-

Western bildungsroman. By contrast, however, Second Brother's disjointed and maladjusted status in the novel as the son who probably should have stayed behind but didn't quite seem to fade out of the novel is a vestige of the historical predicament in which the family is caught. Fan Ye's crisis, on the other hand, necessitates displacing the historical context in which he has been born. The foregrounding of this predicament, as encountered by an alienated individual subject, conjures notions of a transhistorical human condition. With Second Brother, Fan Lunyuan, however, no possible imagination of him disconnected from his role as brother, son, stepson, husband, or father exists. He serves as a reminder that the historical situation is always immediately real and inescapable. The problems he faces thus all revolve around this historical connectedness.

Fan Lunyuan is indifferent to the father's disappearance from the outset. He does not share in the search for the father and merely cooly asks after Ye Qiufang, the stepmother whom he refers to as "Auntie" and with whom he does not enjoy a close relationship. Ye Qiufang treats Fan Lunyuan with suspicion and hostility. In one telling scene, they differ over how to take a set of family pictures. The episode ends with a great deal of tension. Divided by the partitioning of China and the memory of a previous life on the mainland, all the weight of the family's unsuturable historical predicament flows into Lunyuan's hand as he ends the photograph session with an unceremonious snap of the lens cover. Fan Lunyuan's presence in the novel never allows the reader to forget this dislocation that, in spite of whatever conflicts are to follow, already exists long before the father's disappearance from the home. In this sense, Fan Lunyuan embodies the historical and political loss of China.

Qiufang's silent contempt for Lunyuan turns to open suspicion of him in Episode 67, the long scene in which Lunyuan and Fan Ye go to a Peking Opera. In this scene, the mother, whose increasing paranoia will be dealt with below, explicitly warns Fan Ye that his brother may be dangerous. At this point in the novel her paranoia does not prevent the boys from going out to see the opera. Involving the great Song dynasty general Yue Fei, who was martyred by the corrupt leaders of the Southern Song regime, the opera plays to the national pride in Taiwan audiences—especially mainlanders. The opera praises service to the country, service that may entail the sacrifice of oneself and one's familial relationships, since Yue Fei's wife must remain back in China to demonstrate her chaste loyalty to her husband on the front. This opera assumes a somewhat allegorical role, since it implies a connection with the current political situation in China, a view of China under siege by the Communists. Fan Ye, and even Second Brother himself, find themselves absorbed in the drama of the play, the sensitivity of the love scenes, and the great acting by the beautiful Xia Peili, who stars in the role of Yue Fei's wife. Their impression is ruined, though, when, having forgotten their raincoats, they return to see the actress with the makeup smeared from her face, which "appeared a scummy yellow, making her look much older than before" (*FC,* 76; 85). She also exhibits some rather crude behavior in front of them, shouting out an expletive now and then. What the two brothers witness perhaps disillusions them. It certainly serves as a stark reminder of the distinction between fiction and reality, for the opera that had briefly smitten them has been undercut by the very real situation before their eyes. As they once again depart for home, this time in silence, Fan Ye may still be thinking of his shattered love for Xia Peili, but Fan Lunyuan is thinking of the historical reality that no drama has the power to change: They are on Taiwan permanently. The next time Fan Lunyuan appears in the novel, his attention has clearly focused on initiating a relationship with a woman on Taiwan.

Fan Lunyuan's development of a stable relationship with a Taiwanese woman leads to the severance of his relationship with his father. In Episode 88, the family goes on a day trip to a park, but while the bulk of the description involves the natural setting, the amusement park where they play, and the picnic lunch they eat, the central issue of the scene is carried out peripherally. This issue is Lunyuan's discussion with his father on the subject of his girlfriend: His father opposes the relationship. By the end of the scene Lunyuan has resigned himself to his father's stand, so he decides to terminate the relationship with this woman. In Episode 113, however, Lunyuan returns to the narrative with another girlfriend. Now that this issue has arisen again, Lunyuan is determined to seek a different outcome. Lunyuan's situation has progressed since his relationship with the first girlfriend: By this time he is older and gainfully employed. Nevertheless, Minxian opposes the relationship not only because she is Taiwanese but because she is a bar girl, too.

Lunyuan's financial independence affords him the power to resist his father's opposition this time, though the victory he obtains may be a Pyrrhic one. As Yan Yuanshu has shown, the accumulation of capital has been Lunyuan's only means of achieving the requisite autonomy to maintain his relationship and eventually marry this Taiwanese woman.[21] The price, of course, is the irreconcilable break with his father, a rupture that may have been inevitable anyway. Throughout the novel, Fan Lunyuan has been unsuccessful in neutralizing the tension between the family's past and its present. In an ironic way, he now takes the first step toward its future. His financial independence partially evokes the notion of reification that eventually envelops the character of his younger brother.[22] Yet this too is ironic, since at this juncture in the novel Lunyuan is not escaping to his bedroom, as Fan Ye is, but is set free to do as he pleases unrestricted by the family. He is the closest of any of them to obtaining any sense of freedom, not because he can return to the mainland nor because he has discovered the means to suture the wound of historical displacement, but because he alone has come to accept a permanent life on Taiwan.

Fan Ye's visit to his brother near the end of the novel in Chapter N underscores the irony of Fan Lunyuan's position in the novel. Although disowned by the father, and although his relationship with Qiufang has been distant throughout, Fan Lunyuan has performed the ultimate filial act: He has produced a male heir. Admittedly, the father's severance of their relationship may annul any of the spiritual significance of the birth of a son. Nevertheless, the boy's surname is Fan and he is thus the ineluctable vessel that perpetuates the lineage into one more generation. The description of him and his wife as well fed and plump signifies the prosperous conditions in which they now live. And, of course, the most ironic aspect of this encounter between the two brothers is that Fan Ye does not even know his own nephew's given name.

Straddling the fissure between the family's past on mainland China and the reality of its present in Taiwan, Fan Lunyuan crystallizes the conflict between a universal humanistic discourse and the inexorability of the historical predicament in which they find themselves. I have suggested at the outset that Wang Wenxing's narrative style represents a departure from the expansive anti-Communist novels of the 1950s. There is still a residual strand, however, of the Cold War discourse embedded within the modernist, humanistic ideology informing Wang Wenxing's narrative. As William Pietz has observed in arguing that the structure of Cold War discourse resembles that of the colonialist language of orientalism, the "totalitarianism" of Communist states such as the Soviet Union, and, by extension, the People's Republic of China, derives from a submerged connection with the roots of these non-Western nations that, according to the Western account, are characterized by "oriental despotism." Pietz's analysis of George F. Kennen's writings, among others, suggests that the Cold War discourse sought to privilege "the values of Western Civilization" and set up the descriptions of the Communist bloc as straw men against it.[23] What this entails for Wang Wenxing's text is that the emergence of Fan Lunyuan serves as a reminder to us of the historicity of this predicament. While the narrative of the embattled human subject, as "universal" as that may seem, is the dominant theme of the novel, there are other crucial voices at work that serve to temper, complicate, and perhaps even implicate the narrative voice in other ways. Fan Lunyuan reminds us that this "loss" of China was indeed very palpable for the family, and, in fact, perhaps because of the great trauma of the loss, necessarily repressed or refracted in the narrative. Even the so-called universal theme itself is one perhaps more nostalgic for the days of high modernism than anything else. The other important aspect of the brother's role is this repressed or refracted quality. Much like the structure of a dream, the historical reality of the situation is not laid out evenly or openly but rather is buried deep within the recesses of the novel's structure, and thus seems more like the sorts of irruptions from the unconscious that Freud describes in his notes on that elusive terrain.

4. Ye Qiufang and the Loss of Language

Wang Wenxing's portrayal of Fan Ye's mother, like the critique of filiality, is in part influenced by the May Fourth critique of feudal attitudes toward women. Ye Qiufang is a pathetic figure whose resentment toward established social mores (as embodied by the father) grows from grievance to paranoia and jealousy until she eventually succumbs to near complete delusion. In an early scene in the novel, she gives birth to a baby girl, but after three months the child dies. She deeply resents the fact that her daughter did not receive adequate health care, since Minxian was unwilling to borrow money to purchase the necessary medicine to treat her illness. In addition, while her own father had encouraged her to study, her mother felt it was improper for women to have an education, so she was forced to withdraw from school. As a result, she never properly learned Mandarin, effectively nullifying any chance for her to become conversant in mainstream or "high" cultural institutions such as writing and the knowledge of literature, history, and thought. While Fan Ye's illness as a child is rendered from his perspective, highlighting his own resentments, this resentment is mitigated by the mere fact that at least he received medical attention. That his younger sister is neglected and eventually dies can only be understood as a classic example of the importance placed on sons over daughters in traditional Chinese values (*zhongnan qingnü*).

If Fan Minxian to an extent represents the decay of the educated elite, scholar-gentry class, of which his wife is also a descendant, then Ye Qiufang's character, by virtue of her gender, is severely undermined by illiteracy. In spite of her own disdain for the common ways of the native Taiwanese, she comes to represent the "superstitious" side of feudal Chinese culture. Throughout the novel, there are references to her ritual practice of ancestral worship and remonstrances against inauspicious behavior and speech. For example, Ye Qiufang cautions her son against discussing the death of a neighbor when his funeral procession passes by their house (*FC*, 36; 42); while his father recites Song dynasty lyrics, his mother suggests a home remedy for relieving hiccups (*FC*, 44; 51); and after they move to Taibei, Fan Ye, still rather young, discovers a shrine in a dark corner of their home: "Behind the rice barrel was a gloomy, dank, dead-end corner, full of spider webs. Ma had pasted an amulet here, and this was where she made her sacrifices to the gods. He dreaded this corner and kept away from it as much as he could. In fact, he had never dared look directly into it. Of all the corners of the house, this one aroused the worst fears in him" (*FC*, 62; 70). The motif of his mother worshiping gods and ancestors in the home as contrasted with Fan Ye's antipathy for them develops into one of the main subplots of *Family Catastrophe*. It reaches a climax with the scene in which Ye Qiufang tries to force Fan Ye to kowtow before the candles lit for ancestral worship. As crucial to the reading of the novel as Fan Ye's rejection of this ritual is, it is important to note the insistence on the part of the mother to uphold these rituals as well. And yet, when asked why she performs them, for what purpose, and why in this manner, she is at a loss to explain it. Like other women in modern Chinese literature, such as Lu Xun's Xianglin Sao, Zhang Ailing's Qiqiao, and Bai Xianyong's Madame Qian, Ye Qiufang is a complex character who has not mastered the language or understanding to articulate the contradictions of traditional society under which she suffers.

Possibly, it is this incapacity that brings her to the realization that she lacks power, in her relationship with her husband and in society. Certainly an attendant concern of hers is the lack of economic means or independence. Although Fan Minxian did not have the will to borrow money to save the life of their daughter, for example, he seems to have no problem borrowing jewelry from Qiufang's trousseau to pawn for cash. Finances are a salient topic in her relationship with Minxian, usually involving his spendthrift habits and insatiable appetite for her jewelry box. In Episode 47, Qiufang finally refuses to yield to his incessant lifting of her jewelry for pawn:

> "Nothing doing. Redeem it indeed! Which of my pieces would you redeem first? My earrings, my necklace, or my gold bracelet? When you have the money, whenever that might be, you'd find other more important things to attend to. Once you've pawned them, my things are lost forever and ever. I'm not going to let you trick me again this time. Among the many things Ma left me, this is the dearest to me. Don't you be looking at it with those hungry eyes of yours." Her tears came pouring down with this torrent of words.
>
> "All right, all, right, don't give it to me then!" Papa snorted at her resentfully.
>
> "I won't give it to you no matter what. If you need money, go borrow some. Or ask somebody to help you out. Don't pin your hopes on my letting you have my ring. Go wait for whatever you like," she retorted. (*FC*, 50–51; 58)

Ye Qiufang's lack of control over her situation, her impoverished status, the raiding of her dowry, and, perhaps most important, the lack of a fully developed language in which to articulate her grievances, lead to ever increasing bouts of paranoia and delusion. (Madness has been a major theme in literature of the May Fourth era and throughout the twentieth century, for that matter.) Her paranoia begins as part of a misrecognition of the family as perhaps a more highly structured and fortified unit than is natural. She has paranoid delusions that Second Brother, because he is not her biological offspring, is therefore a threat to the safety of Fan Ye. The tension between stepmother and stepson is first extensively illustrated in the picture-taking episode, as the discussion above has shown. This tension develops into fear by Episode 67, the theater episode, when Second Brother is asked to take Fan Ye to see a production of Yue Fei. Ye Qiufang takes Fan Ye aside and warns him that Second Brother could hurt him: " 'Listen to me. If, later, your Second Brother suggests that you go somewhere else with him, don't go, no matter what. You understand?' He said, 'Uh . . . why not?' Mama looked momentarily embarrassed, recovered quickly, and said, 'Nothing really. Just in case. . . . You and him, you didn't come from the same belly, you know. I'm just afraid he might take advantage of you' " (*FC*, 71; 80).

The competition between wives and concubines, another classic sub-motif in the depiction of women in Chinese literature, both modern and premodern, seems to inform this tension. Female power in the family usu-ally stems from the ability to produce a male heir. In this case, however, due to the political reality of their refugee status in Taiwan, Second Brother is, in a way, "stranded" between the connection with his deceased mother on the mainland and his unavoidable life on Taiwan. In any event, it is quite extreme and rather strange that his stepmother has taken such a dislike to him. He reminds her of a past of which she was not part, an element of their history that does not help foster the sense that this family is cohesive, nor-mal, and without a traumatic past. On the contrary, Second Brother, as I have attempted to show above, is the best example that this is not a "univer-sal" predicament at all, but rather one that is quite particular and, in fact, one that the family is always anxious to escape. The fact that she cannot es-cape the historical situatedness of their predicament means that Ye Qiufang must be considered one of the most important characters in this dubious tradition of madwomen. Illiterate and impoverished, she is unable to fully account for her own place in the family.

Her paranoid outbursts become more pronounced over time and even-tually result in complete non sequiturs: fits of jealous rage toward her hus-band that are absolutely groundless; attacks, such as the one in which she falsely accuses a washerwoman of stealing a handkerchief; and fanatically protective behavior toward Fan Ye. In one such episode, she sequesters the young boy inside, not allowing him to be exposed to the hot Taiwan sun in order to preserve his pearly white skin. Perhaps this overprotectiveness is connected to the notion in elite traditional Chinese culture that darkened skin is an indication of working in the fields and thus an emblem of peasant status—something to be avoided by the gentry. So while Ye Qiufang desires to participate in elite culture and exhibits elite attitudes numerous times in the novel, she does not, in fact, inhabit this exclusive zone. Her grasp of spoken Mandarin is very uneven, and her financial savvy is practically non-existent. Encoded into the novel as the character least able to make sense of the historical and cultural situation in which she resides, Qiufang is never secure in her stature as mother or as wife. Thus, at several points in the novel she demands love and allegiance from her son Fan Ye, and at other points she vehemently accuses Fan Minxian of unfounded transgressions, such as having affairs with other women. As the character most dependent on the family for survival, since she can neither flee on her own nor retreat into the world of literature and history books, she is the only one for whom the option of escape is precluded. Qiufang's paranoia arises from this displaced lack of control in her life and also a lack of the means to fully understand, articulate, or critique her subaltern status. Ironically, then, Ye Qiufang serves almost as an alter ego for her son. She does not possess the language that comes with developing into an intellectual. She lacks what he has. On the other hand, she still clings to the elite values that are enshrined in this language. By virtue of her lack of education, and one could certainly say her gender, she does not have the means actually to occupy the role that she so desperately covets. Fan Ye, on the other hand, despises the elite, traditional Confucian system of beliefs as well as those of popular religion. He certainly possesses the language to articulate them, but by virtue of his education he rejects them just as he perhaps unconsciously causes the banishment of his own father. The cathexis of language in this novel, this fascination with its form and ideological implications, both in the third-person narrative as well as in the characters' use of and attitudes toward it, betrays the profound sense of loss of traditional Chinese values.

5. The Fetishization of Language

Ye Qiufang's outrageous public displays of emotion are an embarrassment to Fan Ye, the most self-conscious member of the family when it comes to how those displays are viewed by others in the community. Fan Ye is quite worried about the issue of "face." One can practically define the border of this family by the recurring image of the fence around their house, periodically adorned with the eyes of neighbors peering over it to see what is going on. The fence is one of the first images recorded in the novel, with the father casting a glance back at it as he slips out of the house. It is a dilapidated, bamboo fence, perhaps described to illustrate its stark contrast to the imposing walls erected around scholar-gentry homes in the premodern period. The fence or wall is a significant demarcation in traditional Chinese culture, designed not simply to physically keep out those on the outside but also to define spiritual space. Whatever is on the inside is part of "us," a certain notion of Confucian subjectivity (actually deriving from *The Book of Changes* [*Yijing*] and notions of geomancy), and whatever is outside is part of "them." This rickety fence, then, is a paltry reminder of the glorious walls of wealthy homes in premodern China. The most famous literary example of this sort of walled-in home would be "Prospect Garden" (*daguanyuan*) from *The Dream of the Red Chamber* (*Honglou meng*). In *The Dream of the Red*

Chamber, however, the development of the novel is connected to the resolution of the plot, referred to in traditional fiction as "the grand reunion"
(*datuanyuan*). In *Family Catastrophe,* by contrast, just as there is no wonder-
ful prospect garden, but only a grim shadow of it, the weedy, unkempt tiny
little yard of the Fans, there is similarly no grand reunion either.[24] The father
never returns and is never found. Thus, as the novel proceeds and more and
more embarrassing incidents occur, stimulating people to gather around
the bamboo fence for a peek, Fan Ye becomes more and more deeply humiliated. He thus more readily envisions the fantasy of himself dissociated
from the family, taking up a position on the other side of the fence.

The subjectifying gaze in this case is not only that of the reader into the
novel. As is the case in many instances in modern Chinese literature, the
role played by the gazing bystanders is crucial to understanding the whole
situation, because the issue of "face" is always present. "Face" is an important component in the construction of subjectivity in traditional Chinese
culture. I have already argued above that the novel is composed of two contending narrative modes intertwined. The power of *Family Catastrophe* to
persuade the reader of a conflict between the modern and the traditional,
between the strength of the atomized, Western subjectivity over and above
the sort of relational, superstitious, near supine subjectivity of the feudal-
istic tradition, rests in its ability to present a coherent contrast between
itself and this premodern sensibility. If it were able to carry this out, then
it would be part and parcel of the May Fourth ideological tradition. But it
is not fully able to do so. Instead of creating two cohesive narratives that
discretely contrast with one another, Wang Wenxing has established an unstable, doubly inscribed text that throws into question the whole project
of Chinese modernity. In Episode 5, for example, Fan Ye as a little boy has
a vision at night of a monster. While the narrative is written in the third
person, it states, "He was not dreaming." Thus, the omniscience of the narrative voice, its ability to seep into the mind of the child and take on *his*
voice, creates problems of distance and of credibility for the narrator. In the
final analysis, we are reading the account of an unreliable narrator. The narrative basically is conducted in the third-person voice, even though it is told
from the point of view of Fan Ye. In some cases, however, the use of the
first person, "I," slips into the third-person narrative. The first example of
this occurs when young Fan Ye is closed up in the house while his mother
goes shopping in Episode 81. Fan Ye becomes psychologically absorbed with
himself precisely as he is physically closed within the confines of the home.[25]

At other points in both the lettered and the numbered narrative, such as Episode 118, Fan Ye's thoughts and feelings are narrated by the third-person narrator in such a way that it almost seems as though it were Fan Ye doing the talking. In Fan Ye's long dream episode, number 149, a bizarre sequence in which he imagines his father has killed him, as Fan Ye stands over his own vanquished body, the narrative once again slips into the first person. And while most of these examples occur in the numbered sequence, there is one instance in Chapter H where in a prayer of petition for the return of his father, the narrative again slips into the first person. In fact, the last such instance occurs in Episode 153, shortly after Fan Ye severely attacks the values of his parents, when he again takes over the narrative in a moving expression of remorse and sympathy for his father: "Do I really not love my own father? No, in actual fact, I do. Deep in my heart I love him. If he were to become critically ill, I would, without hesitation, use all my resources, sink every cent I have into making him well again, even if it meant getting myself into serious debt. So thinking, he felt the burden lift and fall away into insignificance. And thus calmed, he drifted serenely into the land of sweet and peaceful dreams" (*FC*, 185; 236).

This consistent slippage of the narrative voice and referent leads to the instability of the narrative. On its face, this novel seems like a radical critique of traditional Chinese cultural institutions from the point of view of May Fourth iconoclasm. Although that is certainly one possible reading of the novel, *Family Catastrophe* is a far more carefully constructed and important work than most of those written during the Republican period in China. This is a complex, multifaceted, and brooding narrative containing many cobwebs. The result of the incoherent narrative voice is not simply that the *narrative* tone is unclear at points but that the *moral* tone is complicated and unclear also. The questions concerning ethics are reflected in both the structural and the stylistic, or linguistic, construction of the novel. In the final pages of the book, for example, a fascinating intersection occurs that undercuts any cohesive assessment of the novel's moral tone.

The final numbered episode in the novel, 157, is written from the perspective of Fan Minxian instead of from that of Fan Ye. All but a few of these scenes, which generally recall the life of Fan Ye, are written in the third person from the son's perspective. This last one, however, takes the father's point of view, describing him as he leaves home. It therefore completes the narrative that began in Chapter A at the beginning of the novel, although the language is different. A literal translation of the last two sentences might take this form: "Not a day or two after that, this father, he—with utmost stealth, no one knowing his motives—went out that door, vanished" (*FC*, 194; 248). The last clause, *de chumen bujianle*, does not make clear grammatical sense with the "de" particle at the beginning of a clause, but it is the function of a "suspension" of the actual action of the sentence so that this main clause is modified by a string of loosely structured dependent clauses. This suspension also invests the short, staccato monosyllables of the main clause with an onomatopoeic finality to the description. This method of linguistic structuring is rather unique to Wang Wenxing, although he himself claims that it is an example of what he would call "unplanned speech."[26] Whatever the case, the conscious shift in point of view in this numbered sequence cannot have a stabilizing effect on the reading of the text. Indeed, the final chapter of the novel, O, shifts the perspective as well, though in a much subtler fashion. The lettered chapters have charted Fan Ye's progress searching the island of Taiwan for the father. Chapter O nullifies the search since it depicts the young man in his "present home, he and his mother, living a simple life together, seeming to get along much more happily than it appeared they did in their previous situation" (*FC*, 195; 248). The two juxtaposed scenes supply the final element in the Oedipus complex. With one scene described rather sympathetically from the point of view of the father, and with the other described with equal sympathy from the point of view of the son, judging the parties would be futile. Thus, the reversal in tones, the sympathetic portrayal of the father in contrast to the animosity directed toward him in the rest of the numbered sequence, along with the mother and son's acceptance of his loss in the final lettered chapter, is emblematic of the ideological conflict between Confucian filiality and anti-Confucianism. Ultimately, this conflict, which originates in style and structure, is elevated to the plane of moral value. The ideological implications for Wang Wenxing's novel are thus quite significant, for as the text remains ambivalent in the final analysis, the moral value is a question that is similarly left unresolved.

To return to the issue of reification mentioned earlier, this novel that interrogates the traditional Confucian virtue of filiality as expressed in ritual form, linking it to a reified subjectivity that becomes atomized in a system of commodity relations, is still a work that resists such commodification itself. Wang Wenxing's inimitable art sets itself up as the last vestige beyond this set of relations based on exchange. Within the ideology of the aesthetic, there is nothing that can stand in place of the work of art. Of course, this too is doubly inscribed, since every linguistic "transgression," if Wang's lexical and syntactic liberties can be called such, is answered with the repetitive entreaty written in the form of a newspaper advertisement that begins almost every lettered chapter. This entreaty is inscribed in the formal and regular literary language that Confucius himself strove for in his appeal for a rectification of the names. Wang Wenxing's interrogation on this level destabilizes the referential code of the novel itself. The language of *Family Catastrophe* accomplishes an extraordinary feat: It manages to become a unique, almost bizarre creative expression and at the same time performs the struggle and resistance against tradition. This fascination with, or, if you will, fetishization of language itself establishes Wang Wenxing as one of the consummate stylists of his age.

6. The Loss of the Loss

Why should Wang enact such an unflagging critique of the culture and language of China? A partial answer derives, perhaps, from the marginalized historical situation in which he finds himself as an intellectual shut out from the educated elite in China and from the majority of Taiwanese in Taiwan. Another factor is the power of Western literary tropes and techniques, features of the hegemonic discourse that have trickled into vernacular Chinese through the process of Europeanization. Thus Wang Wenxing's situation may be said to resemble that of Franz Kafka, who was writing as a "minor writer" in the "major language" of German. In their study *Kafka: Toward a Minor Literature,* Gilles Deleuze and Félix Guattari argue that Kafka was culturally marginalized as a Jewish intellectual in the diaspora, conversant in a language that was always already foreign to him. Estranged from the source of dominant cultural expression, Kafka sought to "deterritorialize" the German language by consciously disorganizing the conventions used to write it. Thus, instead of repressing the historical fact of cultural life on the margins, Kafka embraced it and even extended it.[27] Similarly, Wang Wenxing upsets the conventional modes for narrating a text and thereby accentuates his own marginality as a Chinese intellectual cut off from his roots on the mainland. Instead of depicting the historical predicament by emphasizing the major events that occurred at that time, he chooses to ignore them altogether. In a classic modernist turn, he inverts the emphasis by focusing only on the minute aspects of life. The family's flight from the mainland is mentioned in only one short, imagistic sentence, and nothing is ever stated about the historical reasons for that flight (*FC,* 42; 49). The importance of the East-West dynamic is similarly not disclosed in an overt fashion, but rather insinuates itself in the text in subtle, complex, often masked ways. The father's education abroad and his "failure" to imbue himself with the cultural constructs of the West diminish Fan Ye's respect for him. And structurally, the parodic depiction of Fan Ye as the universal subject trapped in the historical specificity of a Chinese body subverts the dominant trope whereby characters epitomize the universal problems of the human condition. Accordingly, this subversive gesture disappoints any desire on the reader's part to "identify" with the protagonist.

If anything in the novel is offered as the stable ground upon which the author deterritorializes the Chinese language, it is the work of art itself. Like the ultimate legitimacy of the pristine work of art in modernist discourse, *Family Catastrophe* does at times revalidate art itself. Episode 101 finds Fan Ye actually "worshiping" art. He even replaces one of the religious idols that sits in a niche with one of his paintings. "He adores this dark blue watercolor painting," the text reads. "He placed it far away from himself and worshiped it. To worship it, he set it high up on the white wall in the niche where an idol goes" (*FC*, 101; 119). But this "hybrid" form of modernism, one that resides in the specific locale of China yet appropriates the tropes of the master discourse, never fully commits itself to any such validation. Homi Bhabha's thesis that the seeds of colonialism's critique are sown in the colonial discourse itself, yielding agency out of the authoritative discourse, complements Deleuze and Guattari's thesis on deterritorialization. For Wang Wenxing's narrative does not simply interrogate the mechanisms of the dominant discourse of modernism. It creates a counterdiscourse, one that might not be imitated but that nevertheless stands on the frontier of contemporary Chinese literature by disorganizing the standard idiom from which it emerges. Thus, if any word could summarize the novel it might be *neologism*. *Jiabian* is ultimately untranslatable not because of convoluted sentence patterns or complicated subject matter but because it is so jarring in the original Chinese that there are no established conventions for ascertaining a stable text. The new, the previously unspoken, has no basis on which to be translated into another language. The resistance to domestication, then, lies in the fact that any strategy for entry into the novel is, in fact, a highly fraught attempt to reterritorialize it. Therefore, Wang Wenxing's monument to linguistic anarchy,[28] like the characters in his book, attempts to negotiate the infirm ground of a non-Western world, a world where the native place itself is as much contested as it is sought after.

With regard to language, it was the early critics who expressed the most consternation about, and the most detailed analysis of, Wang's writing. Zhang Hanliang's defense of Wang's style includes examples of how the author merges classical and vernacular terms into one sentence and even combinations of words. Yet, while Zhang's impassioned plea on behalf of this writer is detailed and precise, his appeal to an Eliotic ideal of organic language can only partially account for Wang's innovation.[29] It is true that Wang Wenxing seems to have made a concerted effort to create hybrids, for even the title itself is an instance of the transitional nature of what the author is trying to describe. *Jiabian* is the sort of classical structure in which the first word, *jia* (family), a noun, is modified by the second, *bian* (to change), a verb. These sorts of structures could actually be freestanding sentences in classical Chinese writing. Many, in fact, have become "combinations" or complex single words in modern vernacular Chinese. The "combination," *jiabian*, epitomizes the two antithetical tendencies of this novel: the stability and constancy of "family" and the instability of "change." It is true that the word *bian* can also mean "incident," or "tragedy." Thus, the translator's use of the title "Family Catastrophe" is not without merit. However, neither it nor any other English title could adequately convey both the meaning and the structural importance of the original Chinese. The compact quality of classical Chinese, not to mention the neologistic aspect, is lost in any translation that makes sense. Nevertheless, I would translate it as "Family Metamorphosis," since the word *metamorphosis* both conveys the idea of gradual change and carries a certain negative connotation for the modern reader who, inevitably, would be familiar with the work of Kafka.

The crucial difference between Kafka and Wang Wenxing, however, is that while the former was interested in a critique of *individual* subjectivity, given the historical context of European thought and culture, Wang Wenxing naturally takes the family as the irreducible unit of critique. Wang Wenxing is operating in the Confucian sphere. And clearly it is Confucian authority that Wang is most interested in attacking. Confucius, in fact, as Fan Ye argues in this novel, suffered his own loss. Fan Ye suggests that it was Confucius's loss of his own father that served as his impetus to seek office and to develop his philosophy. Interestingly, then, this loss of the father has resulted in a system of thought that pervades traditional Chinese culture. Perhaps Confucius's own attempt to "rectify the names," a project implicitly attacked in the novel, is motivated by this loss. The loss of the father in Wang Wenxing's novel, then, works on several levels at once: It intersects with this original loss of Confucius, but it also attacks the institutions that have grown up as a result of it. And it establishes an important articulation of the fractured state of affairs that still dominates, and will continue to dominate, the concerns of the Chinese state, the whole issue of national identity and cohesion, of which the world outside China is now only beginning to hear. But this analysis of Wang Wenxing's literature within the context of China, this argument against reifying "Taiwan," is not an argument for a third "United Front" for China, an attempt to elide the differences between mainland and island (*tongpai*). Nor is a recognition of the importance of cultural production in or associated with Taiwan an argument for a separate culture or state outside the PRC (*dupai*). Rather, assigning a deserving place to literature such as *Family Catastrophe* is more a recognition of many lesser Chinas vying for space in which forced continuities tend to obscure our vision of what China is. The loss that Freud speaks of is best understood as a split, the split in language, the split of the psyche, of the family, of mainland China and Taiwan, of the *jia* and the *bian*, of tradition and modernity. If we can bracket the oppressive image of a cohesive nation-state, China will not seem lost at all. It is, on the contrary, our lens onto this constellation of cultures, histories, and minor literatures that needs to be recovered and that occasionally requires a good polishing.

Notes

This article is a revision of a portion of one chapter from my Ph.D. dissertation, "Modern Chinese Literature in the Postcolonial Diaspora" (Ithaca, N.Y.: Cornell University, 1993). I have delivered it in different forms at the MLA Annual Conference, Chicago, 1990; the University of Michigan, Center for Chinese Studies, 1991; and at a conference on Taiwan literature at the University of Colorado, Boulder, 1991. I would like to express my appreciation to the following colleagues and students whose insight has improved this work: John Berninghausen, Yvonne Chang, Robert Eskildsen, Yi-tsi Mei Feuerwerker, Howard Goldblatt, Edward Gunn, Theodore Huters, Joseph Lau, Shuen-fu Lin, David Ralston, Abigail Ryan, William Tay, Jing Wang, and Meredith Wu. A particular note of gratitude goes to Rey Chow for many meticulous and insightful suggestions for revision. All remaining lapses are my own.
1   Wang Lan, *Lanyu hei* (Taibei: Chunwenxue Chubanshe, 1958).
2   Wang Wenxing, *Jiabian* (Taibei: Huanyu Chubanshe, 1973; reprint, Taibei: Hongfan Chubanshe, 1978). *Jiabian* was first serialized in *Zhongwai wenxue* (Literature east and west) in 1972 and 1973. All references are to the standard Hong-

fan edition. Susan Wan Dolling has completed an excellent and elegant translation titled *Family Catastrophe* (Honolulu: University of Hawai'i Press, 1995). I have generally followed her translation in the quotations contained herein with a few exceptions for precision. Subsequent references will be made parenthetically within the text and abbreviated *FC* with the page number from the Hongfan edition first, followed by that from Dolling's translation.

3   Edward Gunn's characterization of *Family Catastrophe* as a "Brechtian epic," a novel that develops momentum and then undercuts it by changing structure abruptly, thus "alienating" the reader, is still one of the best insights into the overall structure of the novel. See his "The Process of Wang Wen-hsing's [Wang Wenxing's] Art," *Modern Chinese Literature* 1, no. 1 (September 1984): 33.

4   Sigmund Freud, "Fetishism," trans. Joan Riviere, in *Sexuality and the Psychology of Love,* ed. Phillip Rieff (New York: Macmillan, 1963), 215.

5   See Lin Haiyin et al., "Jiabian zuotanhui" (A symposium on *Family Catastrophe*), *Zhongwai wenxue* 2, no. 1 (June 1973): 164–77; and Wang Dingjun et al., "Tan Jiabian" (On *Family Catastrophe*), *Shuping shumu* 6 (1973): 80–113. In an eloquent defense of Wang Wenxing's linguistic project, not to mention a highly detailed semantic analysis of *Family Catastrophe,* Zhang Hanliang suggests that, as T. S. Eliot says, it is the writer's responsibility to preserve the language by expanding it. Wang Wenxing's mixture of vernacular (*baihua*) and literary Chinese (*wenyan*) is a move toward modifying modern Chinese, equipping it for the future, so that it can remain an elastic and viable modern language. See Zhang Hanliang, "Qian tan 'Jiabian' de wenzi" (A preliminary discussion of *Family Catastrophe*), *Zhongwai wenxue* 1, no. 12 (May 1973): 122–41.

6   Sigmund Freud, "Splitting of the Ego in the Defensive Process," trans. James Strachey, in Reiff, ed., *Sexuality and the Psychology of Love,* 220–23. I also have referred to the father/son conflict in *Family Catastrophe* as an Oedipus complex, but I have not cited Freud for this. The Oedipus complex is so pervasive in a wide variety of cultural texts, West and East, and it is so obviously a part of the writing of this novel, that Freud need not be cited. What I am suggesting, however, with respect to the notions of "loss" and the "splitting of the ego" is a certain reading that addresses several levels of the novel at once as well as the methods of reading it.

7   In his important article "Iconoclasm in Wang Wen-hsing's [Wang Wenxing's] *Chia-pien* [*Jiabian*]," James C. T. Shu, in *Chinese Fiction from Taiwan,* ed. Jeanette Faurot (Bloomington: Indiana University Press, 1980), 179–93, reads Wang's novel in the tradition of May Fourth anti-Confucianism, particularly as it relates to filiality.

8   Lu Xun, "Kuangren riji," in *Lu Xun Quanji* (Lu Xun's complete works), vol. 1 (Shanghai: Renmin Chubanshe, 1981), 425.

9   See Jingyuan Zhang, *Psychoanalysis in China: Literary Transformations 1919–1949* (Ithaca, N.Y.: Cornell East Asia Series, 1992).

10 See *Xiandai wenxue* (Modern literature) 47 and 48 (1972): 5–130 and 220–49, respectively.

11 Ouyang Zi is an accomplished minor writer. See her short story collection *Qiuye* (Autumn leaves) (Taibei: Chenzhong Chubanshe, 1971). She is also one of the best critics of her generation. I nevertheless would suggest that she is not in the same league with Wang Wenxing as a creative writer. Of course, such an extensive comparison would require a whole other article.

12 Ouyang Zi's "Lun 'Jiabian' zhi jiegou xingshi yu wenzi goufa" (On the structure, form and literary style of *Family Catastrophe*), *Zhongwai wenxue* (Literature east and west) 1, no. 12 (May 1973): 50–67, is the first analysis of the narrative point of view of the two sequences. She suggests that the lettered chapters are written in the voice of an omniscient, distanced narrator and that the numbered episodes are closely associated with Fan Ye's point of view. This is generally true, but perhaps by virtue of this general tone in the novel certain "transgressions" that occur serve to undermine the attempt to establish a stable reading of the text.

13 Lü Zhenghui, for example, posits a universal subject: the father/son conflict. While this conflict is universal, he argues, the family (*jiating*) is a problem specific to Chinese discourse. See his "Wang Wenxingde beiju" (The tragedy of Wang Wenxing), *Wenxing* (Literary star), n.s., 102 (December 1986): 115. This seems somewhat strange, since his use of Lukács (see note 22, below) would suggest a very historicist reading of the novel precluding any sense in my mind of a universal subject or conflict.

14 C. T. Hsia's "Obsession with China: The Moral Burden of Modern Chinese Literature," in his *A History of Modern Chinese Literature*, 2d ed. (New Haven, Conn.: Yale University Press, 1971), 533–36, is the locus classicus for this influential method of viewing China. Subsequent notable examples include inter alia Leo Lee, "Literary Trends I: The Quest for Modernity, 1895–1927," in *The Cambridge History of China*, vol. 12 (Cambridge: Cambridge University Press, 1983), 451–53.

15 Daniel Defoe, *Robinson Crusoe* (New York: Washington Square Press, 1974).

16 Dorothy van Ghent, *The English Novel: Form and Function* (New York: Rinehart and Co., 1953), 229.

17 "And," he continues, "it is worthwhile doubting whether universalism could ever exist otherwise." What Sakai is suggesting here is that the notion of a universal is really historically and ideologically produced to legitimate the dominant role of the West. Indeed, this dominance itself is, due to its historical situatedness, a particular. In order for it to function as a legitimating ideology for colonialism, however, it must portray itself as a universal. See Naoki Sakai, "Modernity

and Its Critique: The Problem of Universalism and Particularism," in *Postmodernism and Japan,* ed. Masao Miyoshi and H. D. Harootunian (Durham, N.C.: Duke University Press, 1989), 98.

18 See A. R. Zito, "City Gods, Filiality, and Hegemony in Late Imperial China," *Modern China* 13.3 (July 1987): 333–70. Also useful are Emily Ahern, *The Cult of the Dead in a Chinese Village* (Stanford, Calif.: Stanford University Press, 1973); and Patricia Ebrey, *Confucianism and Family Rituals in Imperial China: A Social History of Writing about Rite* (Princeton, N.J.: Princeton University Press, 1991).

19 One could chart the son's attitude toward his father's training in France as it deteriorates through the course of the novel. In the first instance, Episode 40, the young boy is very impressed with his father's overseas experience. In Episode 110, Fan Ye is appalled by his father's superstitious ways, gasping, "And to think that he had been abroad to study in Europe!" By Episode 126, Fan Ye has concluded that his father never really received even the most rudimentary education in France but had, in fact, only participated in a brief excursion. A more telling characterization of his father's educational preferences is revealed in a much earlier episode in the novel, number 32. In this scene, Fan Minxian is described as reciting traditional Chinese poetry, indicating his induction into the elite culture of China's traditional scholar-gentry class.

20 Wang Wenxing also resembles the romantic writers in his interesting uses of nature imagery, both that of the third-person omniscient narrator and that more specifically pertaining to the thoughts and feelings of Fan Ye. Particularly in the episodes from 68 to 86, the developing adolescent Fan Ye is fascinated with romantic poetry and images of nature such as sunny days, the wind and rain, leaves, and so on. It is reminiscent of the work of writers such as Yu Dafu, as well as Guo Moruo, Xu Zhimo, and others. This romantic strain in twentieth-century Chinese literature is closely connected with the emergence of individuality. See Leo Lee, *The Romantic Generation of Chinese Writers* (Cambridge: Harvard University Press, 1973).

21 Yan Yuanshu, "Kudu xipin tan 'Jiabian' " (A painstaking reading and analysis of *Family Catastrophe*), *Zhongwai wenxue* (Literature east and west) 1, no. 11 (April 1973): 73. A very careful and sympathetic analysis, his article typifies the times, asserting that Wang's novel is much like a combination of D. H. Lawrence's *Sons and Lovers* and Joyce's *Portrait of the Artist as a Young Man.*

22 For the concept of reification, the standard text is Georg Lukács, *History and Class Consciousness,* trans. Rodney Livingstone (Cambridge: MIT Press, 1971). See especially "Reification and the Consciousness of the Proletariat," 83–223. Also utilizing Lukács, Lü's "Wang Wenxingde beiju," 113–17, suggests that the contradictions in Fan Ye's character are caused by rapid Westernization—especially of the education system. See also Sung-sheng Yvonne Chang's highly informed analysis of *Family Catastrophe,* which includes a discussion of Lü's article, in her

Modernism and the Nativist Resistance: Contemporary Chinese Fiction from Taiwan (Durham, N.C.: Duke University Press, 1993), 112–24.

23 William Pietz, "The 'Post-Colonialism' of Cold-War Discourse," *Social Text* 19–20 (1988): 55–75, esp. 58, 59.

24 Chen Wanyi compares Fan Ye to the protagonists of *The Dream of the Red Chamber* (*Honglou meng*) and the May Fourth novel *Family* (*Jia*), Jia Baoyu and Gao Juehui, respectively. His article is an important and detailed analysis of the family as it has evolved from the late Qing dynasty, through the May Fourth period, into the present, and even speculates on where it may go from here. See his "Nizide Xingxiang: Jia baoyu, gao juehui he fan ye de bijiao" (The image of the unfilial son: A comparison of jia baoyu, gao juehui, and fan ye), in *Wenxing* (Literary star), n.s., 102 (December 1986): 125–29.

25 Regrettably, the translator has overlooked this slippage in the Chinese and translated what appears in the original text as "I" (*wo*) as "he."

26 Wang Wenxing suggested in an interview with me that these and other seemingly convoluted grammatical structures were actually what sounded to him like speech. Wang Wenxing, "Interview" (Taibei, 11 December 1988).

27 Gilles Deleuze and Félix Guattari, *Kafka: Toward a Minor Literature,* trans. Dana Polan (Minneapolis: University of Minnesota Press, 1986). David Lloyd has expanded upon Deleuze and Guattari's thinking on "minor literature." He provides an excellent elucidation of how a work on the margins of modernism can undermine the process of identification that goes on in reading by creating "a disjunction between the desire of the characters and the effort of the text." His notion of a "parodic mode of minor literature" is quite similar to that used by Wang Wenxing. See his *Nationalism and Minor Literature: James Clarence Mangan and the Emergence of Irish Cultural Nationalism* (Berkeley: University of California Press, 1987), 19–26.

28 As Edward Gunn might refer to it. See his *Rewriting Chinese: Style and Innovation in Modern Chinese Prose* (Stanford, Calif.: Stanford University Press, 1991), 161.

29 Zhang Hanliang, "Qian tan 'Jiabian' de Wenzi," 140–41.

If China Can Say No, Can China Make Movies?

Or, Do Movies Make China? Rethinking National Cinema

and National Agency

Chris Berry

Writing about national cinemas used to be an easy task: film critics believed all they had to do was construct a linear historical narrative describing the development of a cinema within a particular national boundary whose unity and coherence seemed beyond all doubt. — Mitsuhiro Yoshimoto, "The Difficulty of Being Radical: The Discipline of Film Studies and the Postcolonial World Order," *Japan in the World*

1

Mitsuhiro Yoshimoto's enumeration of the problematic elements of the national cinema paradigm in film studies is elegant and concise. But one element is missing: national agency. For an underlying assumption of the paradigm is that films from a certain country are somehow the expression of that country, that in some sense the nation authors them. In 1996, a nationalist and anti-American book called *China Can Say No* took the Chinese book market by storm,[1] reportedly selling out its first print run of 130,000 copies in a matter of weeks.[2] The title implies that the nation called "China" is a collective agency, a conscious being that can speak, in much the same manner that national cinema assumes nations make movies. For many years, this was not so much a theoretically articulated paradigm as implicit and taken for granted. Over the last decade or so, the nation, including the nation in China, has come into focus as an object of critical and theoretical interrogation.[3] Yoshimoto's remark registers the impact of this shift on the national cinema paradigm and also seems to beg the question of what should take its place.

After all, once one starts to think about it, the idea of a nation speaking or shooting movies can seem like quite a ridiculous fantasy. And for those of us predisposed against nationalisms of all sorts, the temptation to redefine the nation as a discursive fiction and to dismiss the whole issue of national collective agency and its mobilization in relation to cinema must be strong. Indeed, although a number of works have engaged the national cinema paradigm very productively in recent years, I believe there has been a tendency in this direction of eliding or foreclosing upon consideration of the national as a collective agency with a putative collective consciousness. However, whether he mentions national agency or not, Yoshimoto's statement has stuck in my mind for some time now. Despite the growing number of new works on the national cinema paradigm, as far as I am aware, there has been little detailed discussion of national agency as a problematic in regard to Chinese cinema. Maybe that is why his statement has stayed with me. Clearly it is time to ask again what we mean when we talk about "Chinese cinema," and whether or not and under what conditions we should speak of "Chinese cinema" (or "French cinema" or "Italian cinema") as a national cinema or even a number of national cinemas.

In what follows, I discuss what sort of theoretical reorganization is necessary if we are to begin to answer these questions. I believe that in order to rethink the issue of the national and cinema, it is necessary to return to the question of national agency and other types of collective agencies. It is necessary to examine their forms, their modes of agency, and their legitimization, and the cinema's participation in all these regards. Maybe China *can* make movies after all, but maybe not in the expressive and monolithic sense assumed by the national cinema paradigm (or, I suspect, by the book title *China Can Say No*). Drawing on theories of the performative, I will argue that the making of "China" as national agency is an ongoing, dynamic, and contested project. In a paradoxical fashion, statements such as that of the book title or the complex significations of the cinema participate in the constitution of "China" as national agency by signifying the existence of this collective entity prior to the very statements that constitute them. However, the variety of such significations itself belies their frequent significations of "China" as singular, essential, and naturalized, revealing instead not that "China" is a nonexistent fiction but that it is a discursively produced and socially and historically contingent collective entity. In this sense, it is not so much China that makes movies, but movies that help to make China.

In order to reach this conclusion, I first examine the relative absence of detailed discussion about collective agency and national cinema in English-language studies on Chinese cinema.[4] I argue that this may be the result of the very same factor that makes Chinese cinema a particularly compelling site for this project, namely the evident difficulty of knowing what the Chinese nation is. Underlying this particular difficulty are broader questions about the conceptual status of the nation itself. I then turn to recent works on other cinemas that engage in the national cinema problematic to see what they can offer, as well as a recent critique of those works by Michael Walsh. Walsh argues that, in their invocation of Benedict Anderson's "imagined communities," many recent works lean toward reinstalling the Lacanian Imaginary and the nation as a collective version of the universal subject. However, I find that Walsh's own argument responds to these problems in conceptualization by moving away from the issue of collective agency and its constitution altogether. In contrast, I argue here that a deeper engagement with this concept is necessary.

In the wake of Anderson's work, the imagined community-as-nation is sometimes understood as only a textual trope and therefore a social fiction to be dispelled and replaced with empirical truth. In contrast, I argue that Anderson's concept participates in that larger range of work that recasts the concept of being, previously understood as essential, natural, and given ("I think therefore I am"), and places it as discursively constructed and historically and socially contingent. From this perspective, the nation is not merely an imagined textual object but a historically and socially contingent construction of a form of collective agency. Here, I draw upon Judith Butler's work on performativity. In these circumstances, if "China" can say no, we need to ask about the circumstances of the constitution of this collective agency. Similarly, rather than arguing for the total abandonment of the concept of national agency in regard to national cinema, I argue for recasting national cinema as a multiplicity of projects, authored by different individuals, groups, and institutions with various purposes, but bound together by the politics of national agency and collective subjectivity as constructed entities. In regard to China, this recasting, then, means that Chinese national cinema is not simply the same as all cinema produced within Chinese territories or by Chinese people. Instead, we have to speak of Chinese national cinemas and distinguish their specific circumstances as socially, politically, and historically specific projects contesting each other in the construction of Chinese national agency, which is itself defined in various ways.

2

At first, the lack of detailed attention paid to Chinese cinema and the issue of national cinema may seem odd. The eagerness with which the Japanese government pursued the project of constructing Japan as a modern nation and nation-state well before the invention of cinema might excuse the ready assumption of the national cinema model in that case (although, of course, that assumption also needs interrogation).[5] But one glance at twentieth-century Chinese history should make immediately obvious the problem of assuming a national cinema in the Chinese case and its potential productiveness as a site for the investigation of the issue. Yet maybe it is the very obviousness of the difficulties presented by the uniqueness of the Chinese situation—the existence of two political regimes, the People's Republic of China and the Republic of China, each claiming to be the one and only Chinese nation-state, and the separate but not national space of Hong Kong—that is still inhibiting discussion.

Certainly, that obviousness has not stopped us from sidestepping the problem in the past.[6] In the introduction to their remarkable website on Hou Hsiao-Hsien's *City of Sadness* (*Beiqing chengshi*), Abe Mark Nornes and Yeh Yueh-yu note, "The preference for mainland China studies over other Chinese areas (e.g., Taiwan and Hong Kong) has also been replicated in film studies. As a result, Chinese-language films from Taiwan and Hong Kong were relatively ignored under a specious definition of 'Chinese' identical with the People's Republic of China. Therefore, the politics of choosing *City of Sadness* . . . can be seen as an intervention against the monolithic perspective dominating the definition of 'Chinese' cinema in film studies."[7] Nornes and Yeh emphasize a bias toward socialism. They note that Jay Leyda, author of the first major text in English on the Chinese cinema, had an explicit interest in leftist politics and the "wave of pilgrimages to post-Mao China" upon invitations in the late 1980s.[8] While I am skeptical about the existence of any Communist plot to seduce American film academics, Taiwanese and Hong Kong cinemas certainly were relatively overlooked. No doubt the long-prevailing interest in art-house and "high-culture" non-Hollywood cinemas over popular and "low-culture" non-Hollywood cinemas played a part in this, particularly in the case of Hong Kong cinema, which rightly or wrongly is so often perceived as an archetypal popular and "low-culture" cinema. But I would argue that the national cinema framework was also important. Hong Kong was a colonial territory, and the primary market of Hong Kong cinema is as much the Chinese global diaspora as it is the population of Hong Kong itself. It simply does not fit the national cinema paradigm, and attempting to examine Hong Kong cinema would inevitably have threatened that model. For different reasons, much the same is true of Taiwanese cinema. The Kuomintang KMT Nationalist party maintains it is the government of all China despite being confined to the island of Taiwan for almost fifty years now. Writing about Taiwanese cinema would require paying attention to this peculiar situation, again potentially undermining the convenient epistemological fiction of national cinema.

Despite this history of avoidance, some work has touched upon the national issue. The recent *New Chinese Cinemas* volume does cover the People's Republic, Taiwan, and Hong Kong. In his introduction, Nick Browne does not sidestep the question of how these territories are related to each other and to Chinese culture but makes comparisons and traces connections. It is in the tracing of connections that the issue of national cinema is alluded to. For, having stated that "the presumption that Chinese cinema is the monolithic cultural expression of a Chinese nation has been dramatically undercut by history," he goes on to speak of "a common cultural tradition of social, ideological, and aesthetic forms that stands behind and informs Chinese cinema as a whole."[9] Although there can be no doubt that shared elements inform certain films from different Chinese territories, this is a rather strong statement. Here, I believe, there is a risk of replacing the discredited essentialized and transcendent nation as the author of national cinema with an equally essentialized and transcendent "common cultural tradition." Although there is nothing to suggest that either the editors of the book or specifically Browne's introduction intend to engage in such a move, it must be pointed out that this repositioning risks appropriation by those cultural nationalist forces eager to mobilize one or another form of "Greater China."[10] Retrospectively constructing a common cultural tradition is one of the most basic moves in the mobilization of modern nationalism, if not indeed a precondition for it.[11] But pointing to common cultural characteristics across certain periods and territories as informing cinema from those territories does not have to be done in a manner that invokes the type of transcendent cultural identity that would subtend Greater China–ism. To avoid this danger requires the conceptual and theoretical frameworks that would enable such distinctions to be made. In other words, it requires a rethinking of the conceptual framework surrounding culture, agency, and cinema as surely as rethinking national cinemas requires rethinking national agency.

A second book that invokes issues of collective agency in relationship to cinema is Rey Chow's *Primitive Passions,* in which she speaks of contemporary Chinese cinema as "a kind of postmodern *self-*writing or *auto*ethnography." [12] As far as I can tell, Chow does not explicitly address the connection between this concept of autoethnography and the issues I am raising here, but insofar as *ethnos* means "people," I understand that issues of collective agency and authorship are at stake here, too, although it must be emphasized that Chow insists this process is always already a cross-cultural one. I will return to this and to Browne's concept of a common cultural tradition as interesting and important ideas that invoke collective Chinese agency exceeding the modern Chinese nation-states after I consider other current work on other cinemas that is attempting to move beyond the old national cinema paradigm. [13] Perhaps such work can provide the concepts and tools needed to rethink Chinese cinema and the issue of national cinema.

3

In a recent article, Michael Walsh surveys a number of books on national cinemas. [14] Perhaps unsurprisingly, he finds that, "of all the theorists of nationalism in the fields of history and political science, Anderson has been the only writer consistently appropriated by those working on issues of the national in film studies." [15] Anderson's felicitous term "imagined communities" has been the trigger in many fields for rethinking the nation, not as something taken for granted but as a socially and historically specific idea of community. As an ideal concept at least, the nation is defined by unity and shared characteristics among its national citizenry, as opposed to the hierarchies of differences structuring the subjects of monarchies, empires, and religious realms. [16]

Walsh then focuses on and questions what he perceives as the dangerous slide from Anderson's use of the word *imaginary* to its conflation with the Lacanian concept of the Imaginary in much of the work surveyed. His objections are numerous but can be summarized as a concern that this implies a return to an already discredited Marxist-psychoanalytic structuralist approach that is essentialist, unified, and ahistorical in its pretense to scientific objectivity and universal truth. This untenable essentialism manifests itself not only in the positing of the nation itself as a collective subject but also in the relations between the film and the spectator, whereby the cinema is said to participate in the constitution of that subject. This does not allow for the heterogeneity of cinematic texts, the range of spectator responses, and the instability of the subject, be it individual or collective. He cites the example of the New Zealand films *The Piano, Heavenly Creatures,* and *Once Were Warriors* as evidence of a "plurality of conceptions of the nation and of identity within nations."[17]

However, Walsh also acknowledges that the works he is considering are short on explicit theoretical exposition and that he is extrapolating from what is often only implicit in the adoption of the language of Lacanian-Althusserian film studies. His critique certainly highlights an aspect of these recent works that lacks adequate theorization, although I suspect this general elision of explicit and theorized discussion of collective agency and its construction, rather than wholesale and unquestioning acceptance of the Lacanian-Althusserian paradigm, may be the problem. And insofar as Walsh is arguing that the model of the psychoanalytic subject cannot be assumed to be universal, seamlessly complete, or the only model of subjectivity and agency available or suitable, I am in complete agreement with him. Despite the fact that I have frequently deployed concepts derived from psychoanalytic theory in my work on Chinese cinema, I want to emphasize that I have no interest in privileging that conceptual framework over others. And in recognition that there is a real (if sometimes inadvertent) danger of suggesting such a position by using terms like "the national imaginary" and "the national subject," I will continue to use what I hope will be accepted as less specifically psychoanalytic terminology such as "agency" and "collectivity" here. But I am afraid that in his concluding paragraphs Walsh makes his own slide from questioning the universality of the Lacanian-Althusserian paradigm toward abandoning questions of national agency and its construction altogether. He concludes by suggesting, "If the term [national imaginary] simply refers to a body of conventionalized imagery related to nations and nationally-bounded groups, I would argue that more interesting theories of national and transnational cinema could be produced by simply talking about conventions rather than this proliferation of imaginaries."[18]

Perhaps we can get a stronger idea of the type of work Walsh is advocating by looking at his citations. In passages prior to the one quoted above, writers such as David Bordwell and Noël Carroll, along with literary formalism, are mentioned with approval. Walsh points out quite rightly that attention to formal categories need not entail lack of attention to sociohistorical grounding and conditions of production. Indeed, Bordwell's meticulous attention in his book on Ozu to the filmmaker's biography, the institutional conditions within which he worked, and other proximate and material evidence could all be cited as examples for similar work on cinema and national identity.[19] Also, in what is probably the most popular academic introduction to the field of film studies today, David Bordwell and Kristin Thompson define national cinemas in terms of, first, films made within a particular nation that share formal features and, second, filmmakers who share assumptions about filmmaking and work within a common production structure.[20]

Certainly, there are considerable benefits to be derived from focusing on concrete analysis and socially and historically located discussion of the texts involved in relation to the construction and signification of national agency and nationalism, rather than simply assuming that all films from a particular country express some national essence. Indeed, I believe that many of the works Walsh cites attempt to do just that. In addition to the examples he gives, I would add Tom O'Regan's more recent book on Australian cinema. O'Regan's book explores a variety of competing representations of Australian national identity and national culture in the manner suggested by Walsh's citation of New Zealand films. He also moves away from automatically encompassing all Australian films in a discussion of national cinema. Instead, he locates national cinema as a project developed in response to American Hollywood domination of certain territories, noting, "In Australia's case, the project of national cinema did not emerge until 1969."[21]

With this approach to replace the concept of national cinema itself, two different but potentially linked areas of work on cinema and the national appear. One consists of mapping patterns of film discourse that signify the nation in various ways. The second concerns locating institutions involved in the production of national cinema, whether conceived of in terms of locally based industry or in terms of a local industry that also produces and promotes cinematic constructions of the national. This second project can also be expanded into the investigation of groups of filmmakers working toward such goals with or without institutional support.

In the case of Chinese cinema, this approach can yield a number of potentially productive projects that move beyond the old national cinema concept to distinguish different textual and institutional concepts of national cinema and the national. For example, the film policies pursued by the government of the People's Republic of China after 1949 were heavily informed by a particular conception of national cinema and the Chinese nation. These policies entailed nationalization of studios not only to put them into state ownership but also to secure the leadership and control of the state through the Film Bureau in the Ministry of Culture and an entire administrative structure that was constructed under it. The import of American films was terminated, and the circulation of existing prints came to a halt with China's involvement in the Korean War in the early 1950s, effectively reversing American domination of the Chinese market and replacing it with a near monopoly of Chinese films. In addition to this institutional transformation of the cinema, a series of policies were instituted concerning cinematic content and form. What is particularly interesting here is the intersection of socialism and nationalism under the rubric of the "New China," as opposed to the "Old China." In other words, as a project of the revolution, the Chinese nation was understood to be undergoing a transformation in which the undesirable was being discarded and the new was being built. Notable here is the *gongnongbing* (worker-peasant-soldier) policy, which not only placed an emphasis on themes concerning workers, peasants, and soldiers but also emphasized a style appropriate to audiences composed of such people. Among other things, this involved the endorsement of clear moral plots in which other people, such as landlords and capitalists, appeared as villains. Often their villainy was signified not only by class treachery but also by betrayal of the nation to foreign enemies. This cinema was part of a broad media complex that communicated the message that in the People's Republic of China not all China's citizens were members of the "people."

Most of the details in the brief sketch I have provided above have been drawn from Paul Clark's history of the Chinese cinema between 1949 and 1981.[22] But it would be interesting to carry out further research that examined those details in regard to the particular ways in which the revolution's dual emphasis on the nation and socialism had a mutually transforming effect in both matters of policy and cinema aesthetics over the years. These details could then be contrasted, say, to the policies in the cinema pursued by the KMT in Taiwan. In the case of the People's Republic, it may be particularly interesting to trace the production of "New China" and the national cinema that participated in that production as a dynamic, contested, and ongoing process of sorting and categorizing, a process that excluded not only certain foreign things but also much of "old society," forming the backdrop for the 1980s films that rediscover prerevolutionary China as an exotic and, one could even say, foreign culture.[23] This applies not only to the ornate and invented rituals and details of Zhang Yimou's films, which have been much discussed and branded by some critics in China as self-orientalizing products designed for foreign consumers,[24] but also to a wide range of other less well-known works made primarily for contemporary Chinese viewers and sufficiently welcomed by them that they have become a staple genre of contemporary Chinese cinema.

In this sorting process, differing interpretations of revolutionary politics mandated the acceptance of certain things as part of this new national collective cultural formation and the rejection of others, and the things accepted and rejected could be both foreign and Chinese in origin.[25] The connotations of costume are a relatively simple example. Wang Ping's 1958 film *The Unfailing Beam* (*Yong bu xiaoshi de dianbo*) is a typical spy drama set before the revolution. Unsurprisingly, Chinese who are traitors are marked by foreign clothes and habits. However, these are not just any foreign clothes and habits but those marked as bourgeois and Western, that is, those of the imperialists. Liu Nina, the main collaborator with the Japanese, has a Western given name. When she first appears, she is sitting in the back of a car, wearing heavy makeup, a wide-brimmed hat with flowers and fruit, prominent earrings, a fitted white suit that clings to her body, and a dark cape. Other male collaborators putting in later appearances wear aloha shirts patterned with palm trees, wide ties, and white, double-breasted Western suits. Liu Nina is chauffeured to a large hotel, where a flunky in a uniform opens the car door for her. The positive characters also appear in costumes that could be said to be foreign in origin, such as modern army uniforms, overalls, and simple, less extravagant Western-style clothes. Here, the soldier- or worker-class connotations of their clothing make them an acceptable part of the new Chinese nation. In rural films like the numerous versions of *The White-Haired Girl* (*Baimao nü*), where most if not all the characters typically wear Chinese-style clothing, class again determines what is and what is not part of the new Chinese nation, with landlords distinguished by their robes as opposed to the working clothes of the farmers. This sorting process in the construction of the new Chinese national is found in other elements, including modes of speech, gesture, religion, and so forth.

The authors who accuse Zhang Yimou of making prerevolutionary China exotic in order to catch the eye of foreigners also often accuse him of catering to them by adopting Hollywood techniques.[26] This ignores the fact that the whole of Chinese cinema between 1949 and 1979 was also dominated by a realism itself drawn from Western culture, and especially Hollywood. The history of realism in Chinese cinema is a complex topic, probably deserving of a book in its own right. However, in regard to the sorting process mentioned above, it seems the imperialist and foreign pedigree of the dominant realist form in much of People's Republic cinema has been buried. Two factors may have contributed to this. One is the detour via Soviet cinema that overlays the Hollywood origins of this model with a revolutionary pedigree, making it acceptable for adoption as part of the new Chinese national culture. The other is the retrospective search for local forms similar to realism in order to legitimate its adoption as the dominant form in the literature and the arts of the People's Republic via nationalism.[27]

Another interesting area for further research linked to the above projects would be the "Progressive Left-Wing" cinema of the 1930s and its late 1940s follow-up. Here again, a project of national construction and mobilization in response to the Japanese invasion was clearly a major element in the 1930s, and disillusion with the KMT was clearly an important element in the late 1940s. But the question of whether this cinema was directed by the Communist Party of China or whether these filmmakers of the 1930s and 1940s should be seen as part of a social realist cinema as opposed to socialist realist cinema remains unresolved and requires further analysis of both the films and the circumstances of their production.[28]

I have tried to sketch out these possible projects according to my understanding of what Walsh sees as the positive directions in the new scholarship that has succeeded the old national cinema paradigm. I have focused on various discursive patterns and conventions signifying the national and on the relevant institutions and policies whose determination upon the texts is relatively material, direct, and traceable. I have carefully avoided concepts and rhetoric relating to identity or the imaginary that might invoke the psychoanalytic in any form. Certainly, I believe this approach is an important advance on the old model, and no doubt a considerable number of other projects along these lines and relating to Chinese cinema could be proposed. However, before we start introducing more such projects, it is necessary to ask whether this new conceptual framework is adequate.

4

Unfortunately, I believe the new conceptual framework sketched out above, although a very important move forward, is still incomplete. Wittingly or unwittingly, it performs a sort of short circuit that forecloses consideration of what is most crucially at stake in cinematic significations of the national. It highlights discursive patterns within the texts and the immediate material circumstances of their production, but downplays consideration of the ways in which these texts usually attempt to solicit recognition of membership in a collectivity and to signify that this collectivity extends to include both the audience and the filmmakers. Yet I believe that this must be one of the core issues in any consideration of cinema and the national. For whether or not such cinematic efforts to participate in the construction of collective agency are effective, this is their aim. And in the case of Chinese cinema, where there are clearly so many different and competing efforts to constitute Chinese collective agency, the development of an adequate conceptual framework for thinking about this issue is particularly important.

How is it that Walsh's discussion slides away from this core issue? Two tendencies can be observed. One is his insistence on locking discussions of collective agency into a rigid Lacanian-Althusserian model of subjectivity, which excludes it from further consideration. The second is his failure to question the individual as subject or the issue of collective agency in regard to groups, which amounts to a simple equation of subjectivity and agency with individual identity. At one point, Walsh remarks, without further justification, "I would argue that personal identity, especially in the way psychoanalysis conceives of it, is much more fixed and marked by at least the conscious illusion of unity, than is national identity." [29] I find this an intriguing and, dare I say it, symptomatic remark. For, first, it reveals Walsh's understanding that the models of subjectivity he critiques assume the successful production of a fixed, essentialized unity. And second, it reveals his tendency to downplay the problems in assuming any such unity in the case of the individual subject, leading him to speak of filmmakers and critics without questioning the constitution of their subjectivity. His thoughts are contrary to my reading of psychoanalytic theory. The origins of psychoanalytic theory lie in the questioning of the seemingly natural self, by placing an emphasis on the tenuous and contingent nature of any seeming unity, be it individual or collective, and its constructedness. Having downplayed the problem of the constitution of the individual subject, Walsh's discussion of the social impact of discursive constructions of the national is confined to the advocacy of learning theories to understand how individual audience members respond to such textual figurations, and then to the tracing of institutionalized critical responses that feed back into state policy. The constitution of collective agency is in danger of disappearing from view again. This in itself is an ideological move, conscious or not, that follows the liberal individualist tendency to deny the collective and draw attention away from it, as exemplified in Margaret Thatcher's notorious remark to the effect that society did not exist, a comment she made while in an office that empowered her to transform the very entity she denied.

To move beyond this deadlock requires rethinking theories of subjectivity, including psychoanalytically derived ones, rather than rejecting them *tout court.* After all, if Walsh can rescue literary formalism from charges that it is ahistorical by anchoring textual studies socially and historically, there is no logical reason that theories of subjectivity, including but not only those that draw on psychoanalytic concepts, cannot be socially and historically grounded. If we return to Anderson's discussion of "imagined communities," his intervention and the vast quantity of writing that has followed it join a larger conceptual shift that works to erase the naturalized realm of the essential, the absolute, and the universal, and to re-situate it as historically and socially constructed, as contingent. This shift should be understood as applying not only to the national as textual figurations but also to national agency as a mode of being itself. National agency does not just disappear with the discrediting of discourses that place it as essential; rather, it reappears as a contingent formation.

From this perspective, psychoanalysis and psychoanalytically derived theories along with other models for understanding various forms of agency and their constitution become cultural patterns that do not pre-exist the discourses that speak them but subtend the various social institutions and texts that circulate those discourses. Walsh objects to Susan Hayward's nomination of the relationship of French national cinema to Hollywood in terms of a relation to the Other, and to Homi Bhabha's discussion of colonialism as fetishistic on the grounds that these arguments necessarily slide back into the universalism and essentialism of Lacanian-Althusserian psychoanalytic theory.[30] But it is not at all clear to me that the deployment of these and related terms by Bhabha, Hayward, and others is necessarily essentialized and not the description of a historically and socially located discursive pattern. Certainly, there is no reason to confine ourselves to psychoanalytic terms in such discussions, and indeed there are almost certainly many other patterns and models to be discerned. For example, in the last pages of the revised edition of *Imagined Communities,* Anderson compares the way modern individual life history is constructed through the writing of biography with the writing of histories of modern nations.[31] And in the specific case of China, it is important to undertake genealogical research to trace the specific local inflections in the terms that are used to speak of the national and collective agency in regard to cinema.[32]

With this understanding, to invoke collective agency, and the nation as a form of it, does not necessarily entail a slide back into essentialistic, universal, unified categories, psychoanalytic or otherwise. And with this in mind, we can turn again to the connection between Chinese cinema and the constitution of Chinese national identities, not as absolute or unified but as contingent, dynamic, contested, and often competing. In some cases, we do not have to rely only on the evidence of the discursive patterns found across bodies of films for this discussion. In the case of post-1949 People's Republic of China cinema, for example, its deployment in support of efforts to construct a national agency can be traced quite clearly with the type of proximate material evidence Walsh advocates. If one consults the media coverage of any film, one will find numerous accounts that place a film in precisely this way, connecting and often conflating nationalism and socialism in the manner suggested above. Critical articles on a film explicitly focus on the issue of whether or not and in what ways leading characters are suitable for audience emulation. In addition, there are numerous reports on film study groups that are formed to encourage this emulation by relating the film characters to people among the local audience. This discourse in itself is highly unified, policed and disciplined as it was by the administrative mechanisms of a totalitarian state, that is, a state that admits of no more than token internal difference and allows no competing institutions within the borders of its territory. Of course, it must be noted that the existence of this discourse with its structures to engage cinema spectators does not necessarily mean it succeeded entirely in doing so. But finding the material traces of any such failure may be more difficult.

In understanding mobilizations of national agency such as the one I have described for the post-1949 period in mainland China and the cinema's participation in that effort, a useful model that might be excluded by any taboo on psychoanalytic terminology is the work of Judith Butler and others on performativity. I believe Butler's work is particularly useful here precisely because it offers an account of the construction of subjectivity and agency that is neither universalist, nor determinist, nor devoid of historical and social specificity. As such, it may offer the possibility of tracing and accounting for the ways in which Chinese cinema participates in the construction of a variety of possible Chinese national collectivities. Butler's work produces an account of subjectivity and agency that is grounded by the concepts of citation and iterability. In so doing, she utilizes Althusserian ideas like interpellation to note the paradoxical discursive effect whereby subject positions are implied to pre-exist the very texts that construct them. This insight re-locates "being" from transcendent space into the materiality of discourse. Butler further grounds her observation socially and historically by noting that each such citation is part of a chain that links different times and places, making it different from the original it claims to repeat but simultaneously conditioned by that original it requires for the work of citation. In other words, each citation is necessarily a mutation, in the Foucauldian sense of the term. Sometimes, the forces deploying such mutations will strive to minimize or erase their difference from the original. At other times, they may use the original strategically to push in new directions. It is this under-standing of performativity that enables her to state of interpellation, "If the one who delivers it does not author it, and the one who is marked by it is not described by it, then the workings of interpellative power exceed the subjects constituted by its terms, and the subjects so constituted exceed the interpellations by which they are animated."[33] Perhaps this concept can be extended to provide a model of national agency as performed, and as always exceeding and exceeded by, in contingent ways, both those who author it and those it attempts to recruit. I believe that with this model of performa-tivity we can begin to think of cinema in a dynamic relation to the national, as something that mutates in every citation and every screening (which is a form of citation in itself). And we can also think of filmmakers and audi-ences in relation to those cinematic invocations of the nation without re-ducing them to mere functions of those invocations.[34]

5

As I indicated at the outset of this article, I think the complex question of what the Chinese nation is places particular pressure upon us to develop such an understanding of collective being as contingent and performative, rather than eliding the issue. Instead of having to answer this question in the singular, we now have a flexible conceptual framework that suggests any identity is infinitely plural because it exists only in its infinitely differ-ent citations. Yet, at the same time, these citations are linked into clusters and chains that can be treated as bundles. For example, rather than try-ing to abstract an effort toward a singular construction of Chinese national agency in the People's Republic of China after 1949, we may be able to trace a chain of citations in which this collectivity that links the national and the socialist undergoes various mutations. These mutations might include, for example, greater emphasis on class struggle at certain times and greater emphasis on patriotic unity at others and would be bolstered by critical writings citing party line, Mao's thoughts, and so forth. However, the possibilities for "perverse" citation within cinema itself were always limited by the tight institutional controls that prevailed during this period. By way of contrast, the Fifth Generation films often stand as greater mutations of the originals they cite, empowered by the internal devolution and exposure to foreign culture inspired by Deng's reforms. From this performative perspective, a film like *Yellow Earth* (*Huang tudi*) cites well-established socialist narratives about revolutionary history and the horrors of life in the prerevolutionary countryside and equally well-established character types, such as the tragic child-bride, the earnest and sincere revolutionary soldier, the superstitious and impoverished peasant farmer, and so on. But, as is commonly noted by critics, it also cites Chinese traditional landscape painting styles, which are translated into cinematography, and the codes of certain types of European art cinema, including a minimization of dialogue, the latter legitimated by critical citation of the Dengist call to "modernization," in this case as the "modernization of film language." The incorporation of these additional elements, in turn, opens up the film because it replaces the didactic linearity of the socialist realist mode with contemplative ambiguity and distance. The resultant variety of interpretations ranges from the completely conventional, which allowed it to be passed by the censors, to scandalous readings that break the line between new and old China to see the prerevolutionary as a metaphor for postrevolutionary society. A reading along these latter lines, then, impacts upon the kind of collectivity the film can be said to construct, shifting it from a simple investment in the revolutionary vision of a new China to a broader perspective that exceeds that particular nation-state project and questions its inclusiveness. It is in this sense that I would refer to it as mobilizing or attempting to mobilize a "postsocialist" Chinese collective perspective.

From this example, it is possible to see that with a model of national agency that is plural and performative another question about cinema and national agency can also be considered productively in the Chinese context. The existence of two nation-states claiming to be the one and only China and, until 1997, Hong Kong's existence as a colonial territory, taken together with the Chinese diaspora, all suggest that China exceeds the nation-state in a way that may be more obvious than is the case in many other places, such as Japan, which I mentioned at the beginning of this essay. In these circumstances, then, is it possible to think of some of the "Chinas" that are making movies as collective agencies other than the nation-state, or as performative mutations that move away from that model?

The example of certain readings of *Yellow Earth* I have just given is one possible instance of that. However, it must be noted that China's post-socialist condition is characterized by continuing strict political and ideological controls operating simultaneously with economic and cultural diversification. In these circumstances, it is difficult to tell if films like *Yellow Earth* should be read as voluntarily subscribing to a position that eschews any readily visible advocacy of an alternative nation-state project or as doing so as a survival tactic.

I think Browne's discussion of a "common cultural tradition," however problematic I have suggested that term can be, also invokes the possibility of collectivity that moves beyond nation-state projects. And I also think this is what intrigues me about Rey Chow's use of the term *autoethnography* in *Primitive Passions*. In part, Chow uses this term to invoke the self-alienation and even self-orientalism in which some of the so-called Fifth Generation filmmakers can be said to engage in their images of either historic or out-of-the-way parts of China. But I think it is also fair to say that if these filmmakers are engaged in writing-themselves-as-a-people, which is what both the term *autoethnography* and the metaphorical possibilities of films like *King of the Children* (*Haizi wang*), *Raise the Red Lantern* (*Da hong denglong gao gao gua*), *Red Sorghum* (*Hong gaoliang*), and *Judou* suggest to me, then perhaps they can be said to be engaged in the effort to produce a collective agency. However, Chow does not use the term *national* in regard to these films. I would suggest one way of understanding this is that it precludes any confusion of the self that is producing this ethnography with the self that is invoked by the nation-state of the People's Republic of China, and the type of collectivity that model invokes. For, to give an obvious example, if all those evil patriarchs in Zhang Yimou's films can be read as allegorical representations of China's current regime by some viewers, then these films may be understood as producing a kind of collective Chinese agency that claims to be a popular one distinct from the nation-state as it currently exists. I might note here that for Walsh and other analysts who place a premium on proximate material evidence, such an interpretation, which is unsupported by recorded audience response or critical writings from within the People's Republic and is based on wholly allegorical reading, will seem flimsy at best. While I understand this concern, I can only point out again that in a situation in which the practices of the regime attempt to rigorously police any explicitly oppositional statements, this is hard to avoid, and indeed this is what makes cinematic discourse particularly interesting. Jing Wang, in *High Culture Fever,* notes that the national continued to be an overarching sign of legitimacy in the People's Republic throughout the 1980s, so that different intellectuals contesting one another's power or (usually implicitly) the power of the nation-state consistently laid claim to the national in attempts to authorize themselves. However, the question that a performative understanding of the national begs is what sort of "nation" these various discourses invoke, and in particular whether or not it is a "nation" that can be accommodated within the modern, unified nation-state model or one that exceeds it. Perhaps the Fifth Generation films can also be placed in this context.[35]

Finally, if a performative model of collective agency allows us to begin to speak of Chinese national cinemas that construct collectivity distinct from the existing nation-states, I would like to raise the question of how we should understand the type of collectivity and agency that Hou Hsiao-Hsien's *City of Sadness* can be understood as enabling. As is, I think, well-known, the film deals with a major event in Taiwanese history, discussion of which was suppressed for forty years. This is the so-called February 28th Incident of 1947, in which a revolt by the local Taiwanese Chinese against the new KMT government on the island was put down brutally with considerable loss of life. However, the film does not depict the incident directly, focusing instead on its effects on an extended family living in the hills outside Taipei. Furthermore, the main character in the film is a deaf and mute photographer who seems to stand in for the filmmaker. As Ping-hui Liao points out about the film in his commentary on the contemporary debate around the incident, "By using a deaf and mute character, the filmmaker can maintain an ambivalence that allows him at once to say nothing or anything about the character (and the Incident). . . . Hou consistently—and redundantly—turns his gaze away and focuses on the landscape that, in its permanent silence, seems to witness the loss of human lives and nevertheless survives."[36]

Certainly this use of the photographer character and the grassroots focus of the film made it difficult to mobilize as a tool in the production of Taiwanese anti-KMT feeling, as Liao notes and Nornes and Yeh also discuss in their website. How, then, should we understand the agency the film constructs? Is this a purely individual agency, quite apart from any kind of national or other collective agency and sense of selfhood, an agency similar to the seemingly private agency of the photographer and his wife, who it seems would prefer to disengage from any involvement in public affairs? Can it be understood as a broad Taiwanese sense of self, resistant to the projects of both the KMT and Taiwanese nationalism? Or is it part of an even broader Chinese cultural consciousness resistant to state projects and politics?[37] Rather than attempting to answer these questions in any definitive way, I would suggest that if agency and consciousness are understood as performative, we need only look to the various mobilizations of this ambiguous text by different audiences and critics to understand how each is a different and specific citation of both the text and, via the interpretations of it, the agency, whether individual, Taiwanese, Chinese, or a combination of these three. But I would also add that what interests me most about the *City of Sadness* in terms of the topics raised in this essay is not only its potential for the mobilization of a Taiwanese collectivity that, like the films of the Fifth Generation, exceeds the unified collectivities invoked by the nation-state and modern nationalisms at the same time that it registers the violence perpetrated by them. I am also particularly interested in the insistent heterogeneity of that collectivity as it is inscribed in the film by different dialects, languages, personal histories, and so forth, which to me invokes a collectivity and perhaps even a "common cultural tradition" that not only exceeds but resists cooptation into modern, unified national formations.

Notes

1   Song Qiang, Zhang Zangzang, Qiao Bian, Tang Zhengyu, and Gu Qingsheng, *China Can Say No (Zhongguo keyi shuo bu)* (Beijing: Zhonghua Gongshang Lianhe Chubanshe, 1996). In an interesting response to this volume and the issue of nationalism today, "Thoughts on Reading the China That Can Say No," *Sinorama* 21, no. 10 (October 1996): 76–96, Ju Gau-jeng points out that the title is adapted from Ishihara Shintaro and Morita Akio's 1990 bestseller *The Japan That Can Say No*.

2   Charles Hutzler, "Anti-US Sentiment Swells in China, Threatening Improving Ties," <http:sddt.com/files/librarywire/96wireheadlines/08_96/DN96_08_12/DN96_08_12_1b.html>. Rone Tempest, in "Close-up: China's Youth Find It's Cool to Be Seen As Anti-American," <http://www.seattletimes.com/extra/browse/html/altchin_070896.html>, quotes Song Qiang as saying that China needs its own ultranationalist like the Russian Zhironovsky.

3 On the importation and deployment of the concept of the nation in China, see in particular Prasenjit Duara, *Rescuing History from the Nation: Questioning Narratives of Modern China* (Chicago: University of Chicago Press, 1995).

4 In regard to the conception of the "national" at least, I believe that Chinese-language film theory and criticism remains somewhat autonomous from English-language theory and criticism. Therefore any proper study of the issue in Chinese-language film theory and criticism, although certainly desirable and necessary, would require separate attention extending beyond the range of this essay.

5 Carol Gluck, *Japan's Modern Myths: Ideology in the Late Meiji Period* (Princeton, N.J.: Princeton University Press, 1987).

6 I include myself in the list of guilty parties here. In the introduction to *Perspectives on Chinese Cinema,* ed. Chris Berry (London: British Film Institute, 1991), which includes what could be seen as only token articles on Hong Kong and Taiwan, I simply ignore the problem entirely.

7 Abe Mark Nornes and Yeh Yueh-yu, "Introduction," ⟨http://cinemaspace. berkeley.edu/Papers/CityOfSadness/table.html⟩, 4.

8 Jay Leyda, *Dianying: An Account of Films and the Film Audience in China* (Cambridge: MIT Press, 1972). On the alleged "pilgrimages," see Hu Ke, "Contemporary Film Theory in China," trans. Ted Wang, Chris Berry, and Chen Mei, in *Screening the Past,* ⟨http://www.latrobe.edu.au/www/screening the past/ reruns/hkrr2b.html⟩ (25 March 1998).

9 Nick Browne, introduction to *New Chinese Cinemas: Forms, Identities, Politics,* ed. Nick Browne, Paul G. Pickowicz, Vivian Sobchack, and Esther Yau (Cambridge: Cambridge University Press, 1994), 1.

10 Jing Wang points to some of the complicated and contradictory articulations of various Greater China projects in *High Culture Fever: Politics, Aesthetics, and Ideology in Deng's China* (Berkeley: University of California Press, 1996), 65–73, 327–28 n. 34.

11 See, for example, the essays collected in Eric Hobsbawn and Terence Ranger, eds., *The Invention of Tradition* (Cambridge: Cambridge University Press, 1983).

12 Rey Chow, *Primitive Passions: Visuality, Sexuality, Ethnography, and Contemporary Chinese Cinema* (New York: Columbia University Press, 1995), xi.

13 Zhang Xudong also has a chapter on Fifth Generation as "national cinema" in *Chinese Modernism in the Era of Reforms* (Durham, N.C.: Duke University Press, 1997), 347–66. However, what constitutes the national and how it is to be understood theoretically is not a major issue in the chapter.

14 Michael Walsh, "National Cinema, National Imaginary," *Film History* 8 (1996), 5–17. The main works Walsh surveys are: Susan Hayward, *French National Cinemas* (London: Routledge, 1993); Ella Shohat and Robert Stam, *Unthinking Euro-*

centrism: Multiculturalism and the Media (New York: Routledge, 1994); Sumita Chakravarty, *National Identity in Indian Popular Cinema, 1947–1987* (Austin: University of Texas Press, 1994); Stuart Cunningham, *Featuring Australia: The Cinema of Charles Chauvel* (Sydney: Allen and Unwin, 1991); and John King, Ana M. López, and Manuel Alvarado, eds., *Mediating Two Worlds: Cinematic Encounters in the Americas* (London: British Film Institute, 1993).

15   Walsh, "National Cinema," 6.

16   Benedict Anderson, *Imagined Communities: Reflections on the Origin and Spread of Nationalism,* rev. ed. (London: Verso, 1991).

17   Walsh, "National Cinema," 12.

18   Walsh, "National Cinema," 16.

19   David Bordwell, *Ozu and the Poetics of Cinema* (Princeton, N.J.: Princeton University Press, 1994).

20   David Bordwell and Kristin Thompson, *Film Art: An Introduction,* 3d ed. (New York: McGraw-Hill, 1990), 371.

21   Tom O'Regan, *Australian National Cinema* (London: Routledge, 1996), 51.

22   Paul Clark, *Chinese Cinema: Culture and Politics Since 1949* (Cambridge: Cambridge University Press, 1987).

23   This idea underpins Chow's discernment of primitivism and autoethnography in Fifth Generation cinema in *Primitive Passions*; see esp. 142–45.

24   The best-known example translated into English is Dai Qing, "Raised Eyebrows for *Raise the Red Lantern,*" trans. Jeanne Tai, *Public Culture* 5, no. 2 (1993): 333–37. Chow discusses this critique of Zhang in "The Force of Surfaces," in *Primitive Passions.*

25   Clark sets up the useful device of a spectrum between hard-line Yan'an politics and softer, less class-struggle-dominated Shanghai politics to examine these shifting political sands in the film industry.

26   For a sophisticated example of this type of critique, see Dai Jinhua, "Liegu: Jiushi niandai dianying biji zhi er" (Rifts: Notes on nineties cinema, part 2), in Dai Jinhua, *Dianying lilun yu piping shouce* (Handbook of film theory and criticism) (Beijing: Kexue Jishu Wenxian Chubanshe [Science and Technology Documents Press], 1993), 82–86.

27   David Holm, *Art and Ideology in Revolutionary China* (Oxford: Clarendon Press, 1991), 57–58.

28   For an analysis that favors a "social realist" reading of these films, see Leo Ou-fan Lee, "The Tradition of Modern Chinese Cinema: Some Preliminary Explorations and Hypotheses," in Berry, ed., *Perspectives on Chinese Cinema,* 6–21.

29   Walsh, "National Cinema," 11.

30   Walsh, "National Cinema," 11.

31   Anderson, *Imagined Communities,* 204–6.

180 · Chris Berry

32 *Minzu* is one term that has already received attention in English-language scholarship, although so far only in regard to issues of race. Chris Berry, "Race: Chinese Film and the Politics of Nationalism," *Cinema Journal* 31, no. 2 (1992): 45–
58; Yingjin Zhang, "From 'Minority Film' to 'Minority Discourse': Questions of
Nationhood and Ethnicity in Chinese Cinema," *Cinema Journal* 36, no. 3 (1997):
73–90.

33 Judith Butler, *Excitable Speech: A Politics of the Performative* (New York: Routledge,
1997), 34.

34 However, at the same time we must also be careful not to elide issues of access
to discourse and public visibility as though all were equally empowered to cite
and transform originals. I have discussed these issues further in relation to performativity in the films of Zhang Yuan in "Staging Gay Life in China: Zhang
Yuan and *East Palace, West Palace*," *Jump Cut* (1998).

35 Jing Wang, *High Culture Fever*. Particularly relevant to this essay is chapter 5,
"Romancing the Subject: Utopian Moments in the Chinese Aesthetics of the
1980s," in which Wang considers the Chinese adoption and utilization of the
concept of the "subject," including and in particular the collective and national
subject (195–232). As mentioned in note 13, Zhang Xudong does place these films
within this "national" context but without problematizing or retheorizing what
is meant by the "national" itself.

36 Ping-hui Liao, "Rewriting Taiwanese National History: The February 28 Incident as Spectacle," *Public Culture* 5, no. 2 (1993): 294.

37 Discussing another of Hou's films, Nick Browne, in "Hou Hsiao-hsien's *Puppet-
master*: The Poetics of Landscape," *Asian Cinema* 8, no. 1 (1996), also writes of
Hou's grassroots perspective and use of landscape, arguing that "politics has
real effects and consequences, but they are viewed as incidental and temporary
against the landscape and the larger pattern of life. The value of any post-colonial
critique must confront and come to terms with the aesthetic ontology of Hou's
work and the equivocal place it accords to political administration" (37).

Look Who's Talking: The Politics of Orality
in Transitional Hong Kong Mass Culture

Kwai-Cheung Lo

Future historians of modern China will probably give a prominent place to the historic return of Hong Kong's sovereignty to the People's Republic in 1997. They may celebrate that Chinese people were heading toward a national unity in the new millennium. But this problematic transition, whereby Hong Kong people have supposedly become part of a "reunified" Chinese subject, cannot be easily accounted for by the macro-explanation of the long-term rationality of history. Hong Kong people are now solicited — or interpellated, as Louis Althusser puts it — by a new system of representations in which they must see their specifically designated place in a historically changing, peculiar cultural and sociopolitical formation as inevitable, natural, and real in order to meet the demands of their current conditions of existence.[1] However, the transition to the new representational framework may not be as smooth as one assumes. After all, the transition of power means more than a substitution of the British colonial flag with the new logo of the Special Administrative Zone and the Chinese five stars. There are many possible ways to examine how Hong Kong people will be reconstituted and transformed in the posttransitional period into the new form of social reality and subjectivity, as well as how they, consciously and unconsciously, counteract the ideological solicitation.

In this essay, I choose to deal with the above problem from the perspective of language used in mass culture, since many cultural critics have already pointed out that the so-called Hong Kong cultural identity is derived from the former colony's idiosyncratic use of the Chinese language. Cantonese, the mother tongue of the majority of Hong Kong people, is not exactly a written language and has to be "transcribed" in the proper form of standard Chinese, namely, Mandarin or Putonghua. Over the last two decades, with the increasingly engulfing influence exerted by Hong Kong mass culture, Cantonese has become the dominant language in many popular writings, which will definitely create difficulties for Chinese readers from other places. Yet the vitality of Hong Kong's language, many believe, lies precisely in its intractability to the taming by standard Chinese. Hong Kong is a perfect example of how the use of language constitutes a contested terrain in which a local identity strives to come into being. At the same time, discussion of the language problem can also highlight the idea that the world of words creates the world of things. Language has the power to seize and change human desire, and to unite a community with the bonds of its symbolic commerce. In the light of all this, I would like to use the language issue to further illustrate the process of "subjection" taking place in the re-formation of national subjectivity in posttransitional Hong Kong.

Modern concepts of the sign may help us better understand the cultural politics of Hong Kong in the posttransitional period.[2] According to the Genevan linguist Ferdinand de Saussure, a linguistic sign unites not a name and a thing but rather an acoustic image (what he calls a "signifier") and a mental concept (what he calls a "signified"). Meaning is generated by signifiers not just in relation to their signifieds but also in differential relation to other signifiers. There is never a natural, nonarbitrary one-to-one link between a signifier and a signified; instead, an effect of a signified is generated by the movement from one signifier to another. The unification of Hong Kong and China, if understood in such a linguistic perspective, should no longer be conceived as a simple representation of a new Chinese identity. Rather, the "value" of this unity lies precisely in the difference articulated by Hong Kong in relation to what it means to be "Chinese" (that is to say, how Hong Kong can offer a new understanding of this nationality when it is integrated with China). The reconstruction of Hong Kong's national identity could be approached by questioning the established notion of "Chineseness." If Hong Kong is perceived as a signifier that has no clearly determinate meaning or identity but that designates only a configuration of differences under changing circumstances, the return of its sovereignty to China now gives the port city a particular positive nationalized content. However, this content is always posited as something purely contingent. As Jacques Lacan's modification of the Saussurian sign shows, it is the signifier, not the signified, that has the capacity to combine with other signifiers to form meanings. The return of Hong Kong to mainland China does not necessarily mean an elimination of the differences between the two places.

On the contrary, it is precisely this integration that may lead to a cultural transgression of Chineseness as a presumed stable signified itself, because the secure realm of the signified is now facing the threat of being penetrated by a material but elusive signifier.

I would like to make clear at the beginning that in referring to the linguistic implications of Hong Kong's cultural politics in terms of its relation to China, I am not proposing that China and Hong Kong are two opposing terms that defy any reconciliation.[3] But, if Chinese cultural studies tend to be a discourse preoccupied with the notion of a unified Chineseness, I propose, first, that it is difference that is constitutive of its origin, and that its practice should be grounded on the disjunction and fragmented historical configurations of various Chinese communities. Thus, second, it is impossible to assume that the studies of different Chinese cultural spaces can be conducted in a homogeneous way, since the differences among them are qualitative. Willingly or reluctantly, Hong Kong culture is moving toward becoming an integrative part of China's cultural whole. What should be problemized, then, is precisely Chineseness itself as a presumed referential unity in the cultural studies of various Chinese communities. Third, I would argue that in the process of Hong Kong people's resubjectivization, or "becoming Chinese," some revealing moments may appear that could be illuminating to the studies of national culture and related issues.

I will use two forms of signification—subtitling on Hong Kong television and the emergence of stand-up comedy—as examples to investigate the operation of resubjectivization within the posttransitional period. Both forms are relatively new phenomena of the 1990s, and they specifically represent certain points of rupture in the transition process launched by the linguistic nationalist project, although neither subtitles nor comedies are unfamiliar to Hong Kong mass-culture consumers. I see subtitling as a strong case of the failure of resubjectivization, even if Hong Kong people are willing to embrace their new Chinese identity, whereas stand-up comedy is a good example of how the subject position constituted by the local residents themselves, in opposition to China's nationalist calling, could be both politically enabling and paralyzing.[4] Whether or not Hong Kong people are willing to accept the national identity imposed in the new political context, the unpredictable contradiction and subversion appearing in the process of resubjectivization may compel scholars of Chinese cultural studies to rethink the question of cultural totality and national unity.

Subtitling: The Violence of Writing and the Elusiveness of Voice

In Hong Kong, subtitles conventionally appear in foreign movies in order to help local viewers understand the dialogues spoken in different languages. Some filmmakers prefer dubbed versions of their works when they are released overseas because they believe subtitling is distracting and interferes with the visual experience of a film. It has been a strange custom for a long time that Hong Kong movies, even those released locally, are always shown simultaneously with English and Chinese subtitles. In order to reduce the production cost, the film industry may not want to incur the expense to provide a version without subtitles to the local market. And Hong Kong viewers may accept it as a ritual and never complain of such visual distraction. Interestingly, the local television channels also began subtitling their programs in the early 1990s, but this tells a different story about the cultural changes in the posttransitional city.

That the Chinese language is made possible by one single scriptural economy has become a widely believed myth. It is generally thought among the Chinese themselves that, although Chinese of different regions speak many different dialects, when they write, they write in a unified fashion. According to this belief, the multiple, if not conflicting, voices are under the governance of the scriptural, which separates itself from the barbaric world of voices. Writing is not merely an act that traditionally distinguishes the educated from the illiterate; it also serves as the ideological apparatus that helps create the concept of cultural nationalism. Written language, accompanied by print-capitalism, constitutes the basis for national consciousness by unifying the tools of exchange and communication and by hierarchizing one dialect over the others.[5] This scriptural economy could be compared to the economy of perspectivism, which conquers the space of exteriority from a dominating geometral point of vision. The field of language is turned into a place of production for the mastery of the writing subject. Writing enables the subject to occupy a position from which to manage his space, a space that is distinct from others, and in which he or she can carry out his or her own will. Jacques Derrida may in fact not be right when he says that writing is the forgetting of the self and that voice is closest to the signified.[6] In many cases, writing, in fact, inscribes the mastering subject in his space of articulation, whereas voice is driven outside the scriptural empire to collide with the slippery chain of signifiers.

An example of this is a television documentary on Hong Kong history, entitled *Hong Kong: One Hundred Years* (*Xianggang cangsang*), aired by China's central station in early 1997. It represents the scriptural enterprise that seeks to forge a new space with respect to the past, to write itself anew, and to produce a consistent and unified national history. Since the documentary was first nationally broadcast on the mainland and only later on the Hong Kong cable network, apparently the primary political aim of the program was to reeducate the mainland Chinese audience about the colonial history of Hong Kong in order to celebrate and propagate the return of the former colony to the Chinese homeland. Using the conventions of documentary, *Hong Kong: One Hundred Years* is built around a series of interviews, with a combination of voice-over narration and compilation of historical footage. However, like many propaganda films made by the Chinese government, its voice-over narration is authoritative rather than neutral, and does not hesitate to make judgments about political and historical events, notwithstanding its attempt to extensively interview people with different points of view. There is a segment in which mainland Chinese reporters interview passersby on a Hong Kong street. They ask them why a street in Hong Kong Island is named "Station Street" (the Chinese name of the street is "Shuikengkou" meaning, literally, puddle's mouth). It was, of course, a leading question, asked for the simple purpose of proving the ignorance of Hong Kong people about their colonial history: The street is named after the first instance of the British army's garrison on the island in the nineteenth century.

An interview is like a written record of voices. Every enunciation of the interviewees is defined and measured by the system of language established by the scriptural production. Even though the program in question is full of voices (those of the interviewees and that of the narration itself), these voices are all used for a collective fabrication of national unity. In theory, there is no need for the diversification of these voices in the process of writing or rewriting the nation. The early colonial history of Hong Kong is construed by the documentary as the history of a national struggle against the British imperialists, with the Chinese side always remaining a unified front. Nevertheless, there are some revealing moments when the scriptural system obviously attempts to write *over* those voices and to put them in a "proper" place in the text.

Orality has to be written in the national discourse as much as the "voice of the people" has to be written in the official historiography. The audible must be transformed into visual texts for the consumption of craving eyes. The documentary subtitles the words of its interviewees, although most of them are speaking in Mandarin. It may be said that, in some cases, since a few Hong Kong interviewees who are Cantonese fail to speak proper Mandarin in conformity with the standard of mainland China, subtitles become necessary. But when even interviews of the mainland Chinese who speak "properly" are subtitled, it becomes an implicit acknowledgment of the political chaos caused by the voice, a chaos that disrupts the tidiness and self-transparency of the logos that is the nation. To a certain extent, the documentary does prove that there is relatively much more freedom of speech in China nowadays, since people are allowed to voice their different opinions on camera. The national and political discourse at least seems to concur that there is something significant expressed by these voices, but it also assumes that these forms of utterance do not fully comprehend the importance of their own voices. Thus, the scriptural system must take the responsibility to clarify and explicate the "hiddenness" of these voices by transcribing them into written text.

In the politics of subtitles, therefore, we are witnessing a subtle form of power manipulation. In the cultural politics between mainland China and Hong Kong, there is no longer any simple suppression of different voices. Instead, there now exists a mechanism that seeks to eliminate the radical ambiguity of the voice by translating it into a "comprehensible" as well as a "readable" scriptural message, and this is precisely the function of the subtitles. The transcription of the oral into the written becomes a legitimate operation because the production of "meaning" depends on the textualization — that is, elimination — of all hidden or indistinguishable voices. In short, through these subtitles, the self-transparency of the nation as a logos is no longer hindered or obstructed by the disruptive, senseless voices. Voice is now brought under control by the rational articulation of the written, so that it will not pose a threat to the established order fixed by writing.

The language of Hong Kong has been considered by many scholars to be a "unique" phenomenon, for its form of orality is a schizophrenic contextual combination of the vernacular Cantonese, the written form of Chinese, and verbal, written, and broken English.[7] Many cultural critics of Hong Kong are proud of this hybrid language, and they see in this linguistic predicament and language incompetence a *positive* opportunity both for constructing a critical discourse against the pure Chinese national tradition and for problemizing the classic binary opposition between East and West.[8] One critic even states that Hong Kong's hybrid culture is a new source of imagination for Chinese culture: "Every old civilization needs a 'savage' to rejuvenate itself. It is what Africa means for modern European arts, what the West means for American spirit . . . what Hong Kong means for China, and what 'bantangfan' (half-Chinese and half-Western) means for Hong Kong." [9] However, the optimistic view of the cultural impact of Hong Kong on mainland China could be hit hard by the reality of the city's self-adjustment and its eagerness for cultural assimilation into China in the transitional era.

In the early 1990s, rather than introducing more Mandarin programs, Hong Kong television stations began captioning their own Cantonese programs, including news broadcasts and soap opera series, in standard written Chinese. These subtitled programs are meant, it is claimed, to cater to the needs of the new non-Cantonese immigrants from mainland China. But there is a joke that the captions are provided for the interest of the non-Cantonese-speaking Communist high officials who may take duty trips to Hong Kong and by chance watch the local programs. Since they can now understand what the soap operas say, they would not mistake them as political innuendo against the party (for a while vilified images of mainland Chinese often appeared in Hong Kong cinema and television). The captioning of Hong Kong television programs does not, of course, necessarily mean that Hong Kong's voices are subordinated to the authority of the scriptural text or that the hybridity of these voices is vanishing into an integrated national form of speech. As I mentioned earlier, it has been a longtime practice of the Hong Kong film industry to subtitle their productions in both Mandarin and English for overseas marketing. Thus, are we overreacting to the significance of the phenomenon of subtitling on Hong Kong television? After all, isn't it just another strategy by the cunning Hong Kong people for marketing their products to the mainland Chinese? I believe that the act of subtitling on TV in the 1990s implies something entirely different.

Derrida's critique of phonocentrism is that the voice produces an illusion of hearing oneself speak and provides the speaking subject with the sense of an immediate transparency of self-presence. Now the majority of Hong Kong's audience, who are Cantonese, are watching television programs in their own language and at the same time hearing themselves speak; but whatever illusion of self-identity they might get from the voice alone is regularly punctured and corrected by the written words on the screen. When interviewees on news programs are stuttering or saying something redundant, for instance, the subtitles immediately tidy up their words in order to clarify their thoughts. So the excess of spoken words and the inaccuracy of verbal expressions are steadily being eliminated in the written form. The "cleaning" performed by the subtitles also points to the fracture and the insurmountable difference between the voice and the text. The text endeavors to cite and alter the voice, but it is not able to erase the specificities of speech within the parameters of scriptural reconstruction except by simply ignoring them. What this means is that a Hong Kong audience can hear itself speak but cannot hear itself think or rationalize, for its voice fails to coincide with the distinct logic of meaning and thinking offered visually by the written Chinese text. To use Derrida's argument, writing (or subtitling, in this case) does, in one way, supplement the voice. But writing has also become usurpatory, and the production of the meaning is now, from an official viewpoint, confined to the written text alone. Voice, meanwhile, has not disappeared. Instead, it has turned into an opaque object that continues to render the self-presence of the written subject impossible. In other words, it is voice, not writing, that now occupies the place of what Derrida refers to as the "dangerous supplement."

What then is the political implication of this dissolution of self-identity in the cultural relation between Hong Kong and China? The return of Hong Kong to China is overdetermined by a narrative that emphasizes ethnic reunification and a national totality. In the (post)transitional period, Hong Kong people are already undergoing the process of resubjectivization as "Chinese" citizens under the polity of one nation. Insofar as a Hong Kong individual is a captive of the signifier of the other, he is, we might say, inevitably inscribed in the universe of the other's (China's) desire (he desires what China desires). The example of TV captioning, then, can be read as a Lacanian *capitonnage* (quilting operation) of this national resubjectivization project, which attempts to anchor Hong Kong people to a unified image of identity. What results, however, is something different: Even though the individual is captioned/quilted by the other's signifier, he is not in reality inscribed squarely in the other's desire and cannot become a subject that desires exactly what the other desires. His path toward subjectivity is undermined by an excess—the voice that eludes the scriptural conquest. The hindrances embodied by this obscure voice undercut the self-presence of the national subject and ensure that the identity imposed by writing will always be forced from its trajectory by nontranscribed or nontranscribable differences.

The Ambivalent Hailing of Stand-Up Comedy

Voice, in many theoretical discourses, is considered a significant factor in the process of subjectivization. The most typical one is, of course, given by Althusser, who describes an everyday-life scene in which an individual walking along the street is hailed from behind by the voice of a police officer: "Hey, you there!" The individual turns around, believing that the call is for him. As Althusser puts it, "By this mere one-hundred-and-eighty-degree physical conversion, he becomes a *subject*."[10] The calling of the voice solicits an individual to become a subject and confers on him an identity. But such a subjectivization through voice not only designates the becoming of the subject but also denotes the reality of subjection. In short, a subject is produced by its readiness to submit to the voice of the law, and this submission is redeemed by the assurance of one's own existence.[11]

How does this subjectivization through voice illuminate the cultural politics of Hong Kong in the 1990s? Undoubtedly, the Hong Kong culture industry has always been voice-dominant. Many local residents sing karaoke, frequent Canto-pop concerts and listen to loud music on their stereos. Here I would like to look at another example of voice-signification of Hong Kong mass culture: stand-up comedy. Stand-up comedy is verbal entertainment presented by one person to others. It is a monologue spoken to and for the audience, and its purpose is not to inform but to invoke the audience's response. It is a speech that always presupposes a reply. Applause and laughter are the audience's answers to the address of the comedian. Surprisingly, stand-up comedy has yet to become very popular with Hong Kong consumers.[12] Unlike its American counterpart, stand-up comedy in Hong Kong is not a kind of quotidian entertainment. No comedy club or venue holds stand-up shows regularly, and there has never been any TV broadcast of a live, concert-length performance of stand-up comedy. However, there is one comic, Wong Tze Wah, who is regarded as the representative of Hong Kong stand-up comedy. He has been performing once a year on stage since the early 1990s, and his shows are generally well received. He attracts many Hong Kong people to their first live performance of stand-up comedy and has popularized the art form in the city.

The market for one-person performance has been very limited in Hong Kong. Average listeners or viewers prefer duos or trios on radio or TV talk shows because it is believed that drama and humor could be better achieved by the coordinating efforts of a comedy team.[13] So Wong's stand-up comedy is seen as unprecedented—a new kind of theater art that has cracked the local entertainment market, although most people have come to know him through the videos of his performances.[14] Wong's stand-up comedy has been contrasted with the dominant *muleitou* (senseless) comedy, in which meaning itself, however readily recognized it might be, is always undermined by a characteristic senselessness. Viewers are not encouraged to think or understand the jokes but are only asked to laugh at them simply because they are jokes. The consumption of senseless comedy does not require the mediation of a seriously contemplative subject. The fun will be lost if too much rationality is involved.

By contrast, Wong's comic performances are considered "intellectual" because they require that his audience reciprocate with intelligence. Voice in Wong's stand-up is no longer meaningless noise. In other words, his comedy is a kind of "mind game" that calls for the presence of a thinking subject. At the thematic level, his jokes are targeted at the history and city life of Hong Kong and criticize the politics of mainland China. Though his presentation is hilarious, the concern is often serious. He is even considered by some to be the voice of ordinary Hong Kong people and a symbol of conscience and justice.[15] This is the reason that only Wong's stand-up comedy has become arguably the most popular entertainment in Hong Kong. With the political handover, Hong Kong people may have no choice but to embrace the terms by which they are interpellated by the official national discourse. But Wong's performances perhaps provide a different kind of calling, which may recast the power that constitutes Hong Kong people as the power to resist. I will return to this point.

Wong's personal background also helps create the character of his shows. A former student of philosophy who devotes himself to the acting business but is not appreciated by the commercially oriented culture industry, Wong is a frustrated artist whose ideals are always challenged by the cruel reality of show business and a culture of instant gratification. His background becomes his stage persona. His first concert-length show, "The Bloody History of the Entertainment Industry," was about how he struggled to find an identity for himself.[16] The punchlines of his jokes primarily have to do with his failure in finding recognition in the entertainment industry:

> One day I was at the TV station. I saw the director whom I worked
> with several times walking towards me. God knows why I suddenly
> bumped into him. When I wanted to say sorry, he turned around,
> looked at me, then looked past me and said, "Oh, what happened? I

felt I was hit by something. But there wasn't anyone. Was it a ghost?" Then I understood, in the eyes of the director, I do not exist.

The biggest reason for me to believe that film industry is a triad society is: If it is not a triad society, how come I can't get in?

Every time you see the actors playing their roles on the screen and know that some of their roles should have been played by you, you inevitably feel cuckolded. I hate those male leads. They always cuckold me! [17]

By portraying oneself as a small and despicably comical person, one attains the enjoyment of overcoming one's own inferiority. The subject Wong establishes in his humorous and self-mocking discourse is either an invisible subject or a subject that is rejected or humiliated. A subject that is not recognized by others or given a proper place in the world, this "small person" can only come into being through language, through the verbal joke. Entirely constructed by language, this "subject" can only exist in the form of an effect. By means of language, an individual becomes a subject, but, simultaneously, he or she is also alienated as an object of verbal ridicule. In other words, the subject formation in the self-ironic jokes is at the same time an objectification of the subject itself. The subject has no choice but to identify himself as a ridiculed object in his self-teasing discourse. Indeed, Wong's stand-up routines are quite successful in dramatizing the predicament of this ironic and self-objectifying subject. Paradoxically, only by embracing the terms that belittle and injure him can he resist and oppose them. Wong never hides his eagerness to establish his identity in society, even though he has to yield to the rules that disavow him. What Wong demonstrates is that subjectivization cannot occur without the readiness or anticipatory desire on the part of the one subjected, because one's narcissism will inevitably latch onto any term that confers social being on one.

The subject portrayed by Wong is a middle-class Hong Kong single male who is attempting to maintain his masculinity through verbal forms of sexual aggression.[18] Socially powerless, and conforming to the majority, he is also quite bitter and discontented about the status quo. Audience members may easily find traits in him with which they can identify. Wong tends to make fun of his audience's intelligence by laughing at its unexpected ability to grasp his humor and his "profound" political jokes. Like many intellectuals, Wong distrusts the intellect of the mass audience. Meanwhile, like many intellectuals in the capitalist world, he has to restrain his prejudice in order to earn applause and recognition from an audience he instinctively distrusts. In his interaction with the audience members, Wong always tricks them by isolating a few individuals as the objects for his jokes in order to highlight the aggressiveness of the majority. A sense of equality between the comedian and the audience is rare. In a television interview, Wong claimed that he loves the ordinary people because they have no position.[19] What he implies could be interpreted in two ways: Either the ordinary people have no position and no voice of their own, so he can speak for them, or the ordinary people cannot be represented because they are too dispersed, divided, and dislocated, so it becomes possible to ventriloquize their opacity and inaccessibility from an elitist intellectual perspective.

In addition to being a comedian and an entertainer, Wong likes to assume the position of a teacher who tells his audience about the politics and history of China and Hong Kong. "Settling Accounts before the Autumn Harvest" (1997), a show that makes fun of modern Chinese history and China–Hong Kong politics, is named after a phrase often used in Chinese political struggles—"Settling Accounts after the Autumn Harvest." The Chinese Communist government and its leaders are always the targets of Wong's derision, but he does not spare Hong Kong people either. In one of his shows, "The God of Money" (1994), he told the audience a long story of how the elder generation of Hong Kong people came from mainland China as refugees and made their living in the colony. Precisely because people in Hong Kong do not want to become "comrades" (the Chinese term referring to both mainland Chinese and gay men), they work only for economic self-interest, which has led to the economic boom today. But the lack of political idealism also goes hand in hand with the absence of political correctness. For example, Wong compares Hong Kong to a small toilet: The first user will never want to share it with the latecomer. Like the toilet user, Wong gibes, Hong Kong people love to say they have come here first and then reject the Vietnamese refugees and the new immigrants from the mainland.[20]

In "Doubles" (1995), a stand-up show Wong performs with another comedian, he jeers at Hong Kong people's blind faith in English: "When you speak English, you are assumed to be omnipotent. Your mom will say: 'You know English, help me fix the washing machine; you know English, tell me what that Japanese said.' " Hong Kong's English colonization also makes its people look down on the Chinese language: "You just don't know how to deal with your Chinese teacher. Respect him? Or pity him?" In the same show, Wong's teammate mocks the absurdity and fragility of the patriotic education provided by the left-wing schools in Hong Kong. The fantasy of nationalism is easily shattered by the economic reality of the colonial city. In Wong's jokes, Hong Kong people, rather than being enthusiastic about the return of the colony to China, lament the disappearance of colonialism. By ridiculing his audience and aiming the jokes at them, Wong also performs the discursive function of constituting a subjectivity for the heterogeneous mass: "Hey, you audience are this!" "You audience are that!" This symbolic calling of the audience is similar to the way Wong portrays himself as the subject in his self-mocking jokes. A certain Hong Kong identity is constituted through Wong's sarcastic and injurious language that nevertheless resignifies and unsettles the presumed subjection to the nationalist interpellation.

In another show, Wong, taking a cynical view of Hong Kong people's lack of patriotic fervor, pronounces that horse races could be more tragic to them than the 4 June Tiananmen Square incident because they care more about their loss of money than the lives lost in a pro-democracy movement. Hong Kong's energy is largely channeled into the fun-loving behavior patterns—what Wong calls "Seven-Elevenism": Just as the Seven-Eleven convenience store is open twenty-four hours a day, Hong Kong people indulge in leisure activities around the clock. However, the city's prosperity, which is a result of the incredible vitality of Hong Kong people, pales in comparison to the extensive capitalization launched in China. He mentions the population figures of Hong Kong and China: "Do you know what the difference between six million and 1.2 billion is?" Wong asks. "If you have a meal that costs 1.2 billion dollars in a fancy restaurant, do you know how the waiters will react if you only tip them six million? They'll throw it right back at you!" In other words, in the face of the huge market and the tremendous manpower of China, Hong Kong's significance dwindles. The well-being of Hong Kong's stock market, he says, depends on the condition of the testicles of the Chinese leader (in 1995 Deng Xiaping was believed to have prostate cancer, and the news immediately triggered a drastic plunge in the Hang Seng Index).

Wong intends for his comic description of China–Hong Kong relations to get on the nerves of Hong Kong people. The common view (and Wang's) is that Hong Kong's anxiety over the handover is due not only to the possible restriction of freedom but also to the possible loss of its economic advantage over China. In Wong's discourse, many Hong Kong residents are still unaware of the imminent loss; they are like frogs being boiled in cold water: If frogs are thrown in hot water, they will struggle because of the heat and the pain. But if they are put into cold water and then boiled, they are never aware of the impending danger. In the optimistic atmosphere of celebrating the return of Chinese territories to the Chinese, Hong Kong people are lured into a dangerous situation that they wrongly assume to be favorable.

So Wong reminds the audience where their interests stand in relation to mainland China. Of course, the ironic posture of Wong's jokes is not meant to overcome or transcend history and supplant it with a more justified conception of one's ability to control one's own destiny. On the contrary, the ironic consciousness is depicted as inadequate both to the comprehension of reality and to the exercise of any control over it. Although it is a consciousness that marks the failure of action, it is still a form of consciousness that adheres to the ordinary people. It is a subject position that has nothing to do with the agency of freedom or the mastery of one's own universe but, rather, with a being that is subjected to the surrounding circumstances. Perhaps Wong wants to share his "subjectivity" with his audience. The position of Hong Kong is analogous to that of the stand-up comedian himself: the subject is laughing at his or her own ego as an object of manipulation while he or she recognizes the lack of a solution to the problems it experiences.

The jokes in Wong's stand-up shows do not reveal anything new to his audience, although they are interwoven with both abstract and concrete references to the local city life and Chinese politics in a playful, and sometimes allegorical, manner. There is no particularly deep content, analysis, or insight in his routines that would give new meaning and direction to the reality Hong Kong people are confronting. Wong's jokes themselves are not what make his stand-up performances popular, however. The main attraction of his shows is their form. In a verbally sophisticated society like Hong Kong, no joke is completely "original" and the meaning of any joke, however new, is always redundant. In stand-up comedy, ideas and stories are always already familiar to the audience so that it can easily understand, consume, and identify with their humor. What matters most, therefore, is the form—the process of juggling and transforming certain serious ideas into comical signifiers. Stand-up comedy is the art of mastering language or the pure skills of speech. Through Wong's jokes about Hong Kong and its relation to China, Hong Kong people are illusorily reconstituted as a subject who can now speak "properly" and "eloquently" to China, a formidable interlocutor with whom Hong Kong could not formerly engage in dialogue.

On the other hand, the idea in the joke is not represented but is reduced to a signified that, through the signifier, becomes self-identical only by referring to other signifieds. The identity of the signifieds, like the Chinese Communist Party, Hong Kong's handover, and other national and political concerns, are articulated by the signifieds of trivial anecdotes and erotic material, and conceived merely as effects of the signifier, since the signifier embodies the process of signification in terms of the differential relation. The current social and political issues now no longer weigh as heavily as they used to on Hong Kong people, insofar as the priority of the referents has shifted under the play of differential articulation. This is not to say that the referents totally become meaningless. Rather, while being presented in the jokes, they are emptied of their seriousness. Losing their proper place in the signification, the signifieds of the "serious" concerns are now juxtaposed with obscene subject matter in order to produce the same comic effects for the audience.

What the audience responds to in the jokes is not their specific messages but their form, which is specifically addressed to it (the audience). Like the comedian who reinvents himself as a laughable object in humorous discourse, the audience members can identify themselves in the stand-up show but only by losing themselves in it like objects being called upon. If the official discourse of Hong Kong's return to China seeks to accomplish a full-fledged national identity for Hong Kong people, Wong's stand-up comedy, which perhaps is another kind of ideological apparatus, also functions to interpellate its audience, but it does not subjectivize them into a distinct identity with a full representation. It is true that the audience is already hailed by the discursive form of stand-up comedy and surely is structured by the law of subjectivization. However, its identity is not a fully totalized one because it has been objectified as a ubiquitous laughing voice that does not designate a definitive presence. By listening and responding to the humorous narration of China–Hong Kong politics in Wong's jokes, the audience recognizes and reiterates itself in a site where any unified identity is bound to be contested. Those jokes that are directed at Hong Kong people can be heard or understood as an affirmation *or* as a ridiculing of their existence. So the hailing of stand-up comedy simultaneously constitutes the subject and produces its subversion. Indeed, no Hong Kong individual becomes a national Chinese subject without being subjected to the voice of the dominant discourse. The voice of Wong's stand-up comedy, on the one hand, provides a way of locking individuals into a certain subject position vis-à-vis mainland China, but on the other hand, it disturbs the facile conferral of identity, even though it is powerless to alter the law of subjectivization.

These forms of orality, subtitling and stand-up comedy, give us a glimpse of how ambiguity could subvert the system of subjectivization. Even though Hong Kong people may politically "consent to" their subjection to the hailing of Chinese identity in the (post)transitional period (since they have no choice in the matter), there may always emerge some forms of alienation or foreignness that have the potential to alter or deflect the representation imposed on them. If resubjectivization is based on a smooth transition from one signifier to another, we may say, with regard to both subtitling and stand-up comedy, that a piece of invocatory material is somehow always going to fall out of the signifying chain and cannot be successfully reintegrated into the formation of a clear-cut identity with self-transparency. The trend toward reconstituting a new Chinese identity is unstoppable, but the process of subjectivization is never going to remain pure and unruffled either. Whether in the form of the excessive voice defying any attempt at rational subtitling or in the form of the self-mocking humorous voice in stand-up comedy, the kinds of rupture points signified by Hong Kong mark a fundamental failure in China's linguistic nationalist project.

Notes

1   See Louis Althusser, "Ideology and Ideological State Apparatuses (Notes towards an Investigation)," in *Lenin and Philosophy and Other Essays,* trans. Ben Brewster (New York: Monthly Review Press, 1971), 127–88.

2   By modern concepts of the sign I mean those proposed by Ferdinand de Saussure, Roman Jakobson, Jacques Lacan, Roland Barthes, and Emile Benveniste. See, for instance, de Saussure, *Course in General Linguistics,* trans. Wade Baskin (New York: McGraw-Hill, 1966); Jakobson, "Two Aspects of Language and Two Types of Aphasic Disturbances," in *Fundamentals of Language* (The Hague: Mouton, 1956); Lacan, *Ecrits: A Selection,* trans. Alan Sheridan (New York: Norton, 1977); Barthes, *Elements of Semiology,* trans. Annette Lavers and Colin Smith (New York: Hill and Wang, 1973); and Benveniste, *Problems in General Linguistics,* trans. Mary Elizabeth Meek (Coral Gables, Fla.: University of Miami Press, 1971).

3   In order to attain "reconciliation," we do not have to "overcome" the scission between the two parties. We only need to construct a new frame of reference and insert the conflicting parties in the new symbolic order.

4   According to Matthew Turner, the so-called Hong Kong identity was carefully designed by the British colonial government after the 1967 anticolonial riot in order to alienate the Chinese population from Communist China. Because of the social and political changes that have taken place over the past two decades, Hong Kong lifestyle has been displacing traditional cultural attachments to China. In the mid-1980s a great majority of the local population identified themselves as "Hong Kong people," not "Chinese people." But the return of sovereignty to China forced Hong Kong people to rethink their identity and relation to China. See Turner, "Hong Kong Sixties/Nineties: Dissolving the People," in *Hong Kong Sixties: Designing Identity,* ed. Matthew Turner (Hong Kong: Hong Kong Arts Center, 1995), 13-34.

5   See, for instance, the argument posed by Benedict Anderson in his *Imagined Communities: Reflections on the Origin and Spread of Nationalism* (New York: Verso, 1983), 41-49.

6   Jacques Derrida, *Of Grammatology,* trans. Gayatri Chakravorty Spivak (Baltimore, Md.: Johns Hopkins University Press, 1974).

7   Hong Kong Chinese is not exactly a written language, though it sometimes has been textualized in writing. But it is criticized as bad Chinese or a language that contaminates Chinese writing. The Hong Kong form of orality that is found in popular writings is generally consumed as entertainment rather than as an anchorage of serious meaning.

8   See, for instance, Quentin Lee, "Delineating Asian (Hong Kong) Intellectuals: Speculations on Intellectual Problematics and Post/Coloniality," *Third Text* 26 (spring 1994): 11-23.

9   See Chan Koon-Chung, "Bantangfan—Meixue biji" (Half-Chinese and half-Western—Notes on aesthetics), *Mingbao Daily,* 10 Oct. 1997, D4. Chan himself is the founder of *City Magazine,* which advocates the use of hybrid language in writing. Its style of writing has been characterized as a major feature of Hong Kong culture. For Chan and his cultural enterprise, see Jianying Zha, "Citizen Chan: Is Hong Kong Poised to Take over Mainland China?" *Transition* 65 (1995): 69-94.

10   Althusser, "Ideology and Ideological State Apparatuses," 174; emphasis in the original.

11   This notion of subject formation, according to Judith Butler, is full of religious implications. The interpellating call comes from God and is figured as a demand to align oneself with the law through the appropriation of guilt. The submission to the law is a necessity to prove one's innocence in the face of accusation. Butler points out: "To become a 'subject' is thus to have been presumed guilty, then tried and declared innocent." See her *Psychic Life of Power: Theories in Subjection* (Stanford, Calif.: Stanford University Press, 1997), 118.

12   The talk show is another form of voice-signification which is not particularly

popular in Hong Kong. Talk shows or call-in shows are mainly confined to the radio. TV talk shows are simply celebrity or star interviews. Ordinary people are probably still too timid to voice their personal opinions on current issues in front of the camera, and stars are the ones who boost the TV ratings. Nonetheless, contrary to the American example, the talk show in Hong Kong is by no means a channel for viewers to release and express their feelings of anger and pain.

13   The best comedy team of the nineties is "Hard and Soft Masters" (Ruan-ying tianshi), who made their name first on radio. Although comedy films are popular in Hong Kong (Michael Hui and Stephen Chow are the comedy kings), they have not encouraged comedians to do stand-up comedy shows.

14   Since its first appearance in Hong Kong, stand-up comedy has been compared with "xiangsheng," a traditional Chinese folk cultural form of two performers telling jokes. An ethnographer insists that a similar form of stand-up had already appeared in the 1930s in Hong Kong. During that time, a street performer named Shenggui Zhuo (Wicked Zhuo) also performed stand-up comedy in Yaumati. In spite of the foreignness of stand-up comedy, therefore, it has been quickly domesticated and absorbed into the body of national culture. The nationalization of the imported art form is one of the readiest strategies used in the local assimilation of Western culture.

15   "The Common Sense," Jade Channel, TVB, 9 Nov. 1997.

16   The show was transcribed in Wong Tze Wah, *Yulequan xieroushi* (The bloody history of the entertainment industry) (Hong Kong: Chuangjian, 1990), which could be considered Wong's attempt to establish his voice with the written text. But the book was not popular. Perhaps audiences identify only with the evanescent moments of joke telling and are not interested in the history of stand-up comedy. Since then, Wong's shows have not been transcribed into book form.

17   Wong Tze Wah, *Yulequan xieroushi*, 73, 87, 88.

18   A large number of Wong's jokes are obscene or about men's sexual interest in women. Apparently, his jokes conform to the taste of male audiences since research in social psychology demonstrates that men tend to laugh more readily than women at aggressive and sexual humor.

19   "Common Sense."

20   Wong's comparison of Hong Kong to a toilet indicates his view of Hong Kong people's irrational obsession with their place, which may not be as invaluable as they believe.

Bondage in Time: Footbinding and Fashion Theory

Dorothy Ko

When Pierre Cardin staged a historic fashion show in Shanghai in 1978, the Chinese and Europeans alike took the occasion as an announcement that Maoism was buried along with Mao jackets. There was no disagreement that fashion was as Western and capitalist as Kentucky Fried Chicken. More recently, cultural critics have sought to wrestle fashion away from its exclusive European heritage by redefining it as a dynamic between body and social habitus of which all people at all times have partaken. Jennifer Craik, for example, conceives of fashion as "clothing, body and decorative techniques that are instrumental and pragmatic" instead of embodying absolute or essential meanings.[1] These theoretical reorientations, although salutary and necessary, should not obscure the historical fact that the equation of fashion with Western modernity is centuries old and has been embraced by many people outside the West. It remains the dominant view among the majority of Chinese today.

Without reifying the divide between the West and non-West, I wish to revisit the "only Europe has fashion" construct by looking from the outside in, by exploring the terms with which European travelers perceived Chinese dress and bodies from the sixteenth to the nineteenth century. It is my intention to show that the equation of fashion with Europe would not have worked without its corollary: the absence of fashion in the rest of the world. Hence, this essay is about the history of perceptions, the history that matters most.

Footbinding and Alterity

From Marco Polo in the fourteenth century to friars and traders in the sixteenth, European travelers never failed to notice what the Chinese wore. The images of China in European eyes, however, were composed as much from hearsay and imagination as from anything witnessed. As a unique

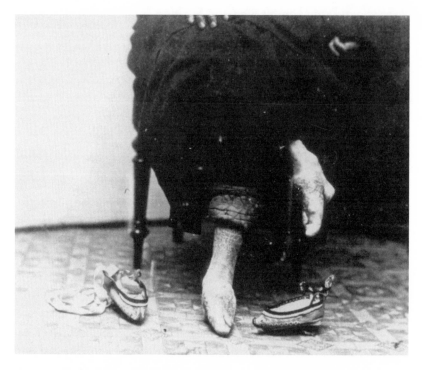

Figure 1. Footbinding as Concealment: The decay of the flesh is in striking contrast with the ornateness of the shoes. No wonder when footbinding was in its heyday a woman would not have unwrapped her binding even for her husband's eyes, and pictures like this were unthinkable. (Courtesy of the Peabody Essex Museum, Salem)

element of Chinese attire that the foreigner was not allowed to see, foot-binding posed a vexing challenge. Not only were footbound women be-hind close doors, but the rationale and rituals of the practice also seemed opaque. Hence, from the start footbinding was construed as the ultimate sign of China's uniqueness and Otherness, and it has continued to fuel the Euro-American's imagination of a mysterious, exotic, and barbaric Orient.

It was not until the nineteenth century that raw flesh and bare bones were exposed to foreign eyes. Dr. Lockhart, a medical missionary, explained what he saw:

> To produce the diminution of the foot, which is the object of the ban-daging, the tarsus, or instep, is bent on itself; the os calcis or heel-bone, is thrown out of the horizontal position, and what ought to be the pos-terior surface brought to the ground. The ankle is in this way forced

higher up the leg than is natural, producing, in fact, *talipes calcaneus;* the four smaller toes pressed down under the instep, are checked in their growth, until at adult age they are like flakes of skin, folded under the ball of the great toe. Thus, all that is left to go into the shoe, is the lower end of the os calcis, and the whole of the great toe.[2]

This precise medical description and the flood of photographs from the same period have obscured a larger truth: that the exposure itself spelled the demise of footbinding, the attraction of which lies in concealment.

The visual potency of footbinding as concealment has not been taken seriously by social reformers and scholars alike in their eagerness to condemn the practice. Many theories have sprung up to attempt an explanation of footbinding, viewing it an instrument of gender separation, female oppression, class distinction, and so on. To my mind, these functionalist explanations are not entirely satisfactory, based as they are on an assumption that footbinding embodies an absolute and essential meaning. In contrast, my premise is that the meanings of footbinding are historical and multiple; they are always constructed and so are always entangled with the politics of seeing.

In particular, in this essay I show that European perceptions of footbinding and fashion changed radically in the nineteenth century, as Europe adopted a different vision of itself. My source is the vast body of travel accounts and general descriptions of China published in Europe from the sixteenth to the early twentieth centuries, many in the original, held in the James Duncan and Stephen Phillips Libraries of the Peabody Essex Museum in Salem, Massachusetts. This essay offers my personal reading of a handful of related tropes crucial to the European way of seeing; readers interested in a comprehensive history may consult Donald Lach's monumental series, *Asia in the Making of Europe.*[3] My purpose is not to juxtapose the Euro-American myth with Chinese sources to prove it wrong but to argue for the power of images and the imagination in constructions of believable "reality." As Michael Taussig has put it: "The image is more powerful than what it is an image of."[4] From the vantage point of fashion, I explore the terms in which alterity was defined in a global setting: how the Chinese Other came to be viewed as not only alien but also inferior in nineteenth-century Europe because she failed to dress à la mode.

In focusing on fashion, my ultimate goal is to examine the manner in which Europe's encounters with China were conducted through the medium of visuality: things purportedly seen (faces, clothing, and hairstyles) became metaphors for things unseen (women's hidden bound feet, power relations, the "real China," and so on.) As we will see, the relation between the seen and the unseen, or between surfaces and ontology, went through a sea change. During the period of first encounter in the sixteenth century, the surface profusion of colors, styles, and symbols that assaulted the traveler's eyes was taken to be a direct revelation of some inner truth, especially the nature of the Chinese government and bureaucracy. In the nineteenth century, however, what Timothy Mitchell has termed the "peculiar metaphysic of modernity" was clearly at work in the traveler's way of seeing: the divorce of "reality" from "representation."[5] All the signs and sights that met the traveler's eyes were construed as deceits, like the women's enameled faces or perfumed footbinders, masking the unseemly inner truths of national cruelty and decay.

Fashion, Change, and Modernity

The myth that clothing never changed in China is a product of this modern metaphysic of seeing. According to a story reiterated in nineteenth-century European accounts of China, Louis XIV once sent for drawings of Chinese costumes. Thirty or forty years later, when readers familiar with these images sailed to China, they were shocked to find that the Chinese were still wearing clothes identical—in color and shape—to those in the pictures. The author of one account exclaimed: "How different amongst the Europeans! The dress of the present year is not only unlike that of the last, but perhaps as different from it as those of twenty years before were, to the fashions of the century preceding. But we not only change the fashions, but the terms, or rather the jargon of them." By contrast, in China "the fashions are not liable to change."[6]

The import of the story lies not in its historical authenticity but in what it can instruct us about attitudes and sensibilities in nineteenth-century Europe. Most suggestive is the storyteller's preoccupation with appearance and change—without which there can be no fashion in the European sense. In particular, his assertion that the essence of fashion in Europe lies not so much in changing styles but in changing "terms" or "jargons" is most perceptive. It bespeaks a heightened awareness of change—linguistically and stylistically—in the age of the Industrial Revolution. To the storyteller and his audience, not only the appearance of the world has changed but also its representation or the terms of describing the world.

In history as in fashion theory, the measurement of change is a necessary albeit treacherous endeavor. The trope of Louis XIV's curiosity about Chinese dress was the sine qua non of the myth, for it is impossible to discern or assess change without a normative baseline. Lacking some prior knowledge of what Chinese dress was like several decades ago, the foreign sojourner would not have been able to discourse on fashion and change. It is evident, however, that the comparison at stake is not between the China of yesteryear and today but between the Europe of today and a China suspended in time.

It is perhaps a truism that descriptions of the alien Other are always, in the final analysis, veiled attempts of self-discovery. Thus, it is not surprising that the discourse of Chinese fashion reveals more about the self-perceptions of an industrializing Europe than about what the Chinese actually wore. This is most apparent in a comparison between the lot of the Chinese seamstress and her European counterpart, which is couched partly in a declaration of the superiority of British technology to even the best of Asian machinery. Yet there are positive aspects to the Asian situation, and the Chinese lack of fashion was used to voice an indirect critique of the lot of textile workers at home: "The Chinese mantua-makers are less splendidly circumstanced than most of the lady dress-makers in either England or France; but their lot is more equal, and their apprenticeship easier."[7] The reason: "The seamstresses of China carry on their profession in a more humble way than the dress-makers of Europe, but on the other hand their business is much sooner learned, and they are liable to few changes; for as the fashion of dress never alters, when they have once learned to form a garment they know how to do it ever after."[8]

Hence, the identification of European fashion with change needed an Other to assume the mantle of "costume." The fashion-costume divide separated the Europeans from the Chinese not only visually but also by placing them on disparate locations on a linear time line. As a historian of China, I was struck by two features of this persistent myth: first, how closely it resembles, in rhetoric and conclusion, the popular U.S. view perpetuated by Pearl Buck and sinologists in the 1950s of China as a nation of toiling laborers trapped in time and perennial suffering who are saved from the tyranny of nature only by their stoic fatalism. So despotic is its government and so corrupt its officials that the only possibility for significant change lies outside the system.

Second, I was struck by how this myth hails from a perceptual and textual universe separate from those of Chinese scholar-officials, who complained vehemently about the caprice and frivolity with which people changed the styles of their attire. Their anxiety has to be understood in the context of the moral and political significance of clothing in the Confucian world. Although Chinese official clothing did change over time—by means of dynastic decrees and adaptation to new habitats—there is no denying that the classical ideal of stability had continued to shape the discourse on fashion and change in China. According to the *Book of Changes,* the mythical Yellow Emperor and sage kings "draped their upper and lower garments, and heaven and earth was put to order." [9] This passage underscores not only the ideal that clothing is an instrument of governance but also the symbolic poignancy of garments: the division between upper and lower garments symbolizes the orderly relationship between the high and the low. In other words, social hierarchy and political order depended on correct clothing. To make social distinctions visible, every dynasty promulgated sumptuary laws and continued to revise them.

No wonder the trope of "changing fashion means moral decay" recurred in Chinese history; it is a reminder that social customs departed from classical ideals all too often, especially in periods of rapid commercial growth. For example, a sixteenth-century resident of Nanjing, the center of the most commercialized region of the empire, observed that the fashion cycle of female dress had shifted from more than ten years to as little as two to three; so changeable were the width and length of sleeves, the height of the collar, and the style of hair ornaments that an outfit barely several years old would be so dated that "everyone has to cover his mouth." [10] Male attire was no different. The same observer listed no less than eighteen names for a scholar's hat, some festooned with jade, some bound with leather and gold, some woven from the hair of a horse's tail. [11] Another scholar from the neighboring city of Songjiang summed up the reasons for his distress: "When slaves vie to dress spendidly, it is hard to be rich; when ladies copy the fashion of prostitutes, it is hard to be upright." [12] The erasure of visible social differences spelled political and moral disaster.

In China, as in Europe, fashion—as the epitome of change—was an indicator of socioeconomic conditions. Chinese Confucian scholars saw changing fashion as symptomatic of the social disorder brought about by rapid commercialization. To Euro-Americans in the nineteenth century, China's lack of propensity to change its clothing was proof of a larger failure: its inability to modernize its society and economy in a race to catch up with the

West. The discourse of fashion, in the East as in the West, is a discourse of modernity.

Tall Tales: The Chinese Are Just Like Us

The elaborateness of Chinese clothing was one of the first things that Europeans noticed after the opening of direct trade with Asia in 1500. "For the first time in history," wrote historian Lach, "sailors, merchants, and missionaries from all parts of Europe sailed to the East themselves and returned to tell tales of the wonders they had personally seen or of the privations which they had individually suffered." The result of this rhetoric of realism was the removal of Asia "from the realm of the mysterious and the exotic." Instead, Asia was placed "within the domain of man . . . subject to the same natural and divine laws which obtained in Europe."[13] As Lach has shown, the heightened pace of European exploits since 1500 has fundamentally changed the nature of European knowledge not just of Asia but of itself. But I think that he has underestimated the power, and indeed the necessity, of the lingering presence of the exotic and mysterious Orient in Europe's definitions of its modern self. Later I will discuss how an enduring fascination with footbinding has served just that purpose. Meanwhile, I hope to demonstrate that sixteenth-century Europeans came to conceive of the Other's shared humanity primarily by way of how the Chinese dressed.

The detailed descriptions of Chinese bodies and dresses captured by sixteenth-century European observers gave the impression that they were trying to gain entry into the world of truth by way of appearances. Thus, in 1515 the Italian Andrea Corsali said of Chinese merchants who landed in Malacca: "For they are people of great skill, and *on a par with ourselves,* but of uglier aspect, with little bit of eyes. They dress *very much after our fashion,* and wear shoes and stockings like ourselves."[14] In this explicit comparison between the Chinese and the Italians, similarities in dress — and well-covered feet — were construed as signs of cultural parity between the two peoples despite the "little bit of eyes."

A subtle awareness of gender and class differences was inserted in a similar description of dress that appeared in Mendoza's *Historie of the Great and Mightie Kingdome of China,*[15] the most widely read treatise on China in sixteenth-century Europe:

> They [noble men] do their coates *according unto our old use* of antiquities, with long sirts, and full of plaites, and a flappe over the breast to

be made fast under the left side, the sleeves verie bigge and wide. . . . They of royall bloode and such as are constituted unto dignitie, do differ in their apparell from the ordinarie Gentlemen. . . . Their women too apparell themselves verie curiouslie, *much after the fashion of Spaine:* they use many jewels of gold and precious stones: their gownes have wide sleeves, that wherwith they do apparel themselves is of cloath of gold and silver and divers sorts of silkes.[16]

This was an age of relatively benign relations, when tales of the bountiful Cathay transmitted by Marco Polo were still vivid in European minds. To our eyes, the clothing of a sixteenth-century Chinese male or female could not have been more different from that of a Spaniard or Italian. Yet through a distortive lens of benign respect, the Chinese were said to resemble Europeans. Suffused with goodwill, many European friars even saw in the Chinese images of their ideal selves: fair skinned, civilized, lavishly attired, and well governed.[17]

To be sure, the Europeans did not fail to notice that the Chinese looked different: "they are all for the most part brode faced, little eyes and flat nose, and without bearde."[18] Apparent differences in facial features and standards of beauty, however, signified parity upon deeper reflection:

It is nevertheless true that Beauty depends upon Taste, and that *it consists more in Imagination than Reality;* they have a Nation of it little different from that of the Europeans, for, generally speaking, that which seems beautiful to us is agreeable to their Taste, and that which appears beautiful to them appears likewise equally to us: That which they chiefly admire [in a man], as making a perfect Beauty, is a large Forehead, short Nose, small Eyes, a Visage large and square, broad and large Ears, the Mouth middle-sized, and the Hair black, for they cannot bear to see it yellow or red; however, there must be a certain Symmetry and Proportion between all the Parts to render them agreeable.[19]

The effect of this lens of parity is most poignant in the European discourse on Chinese skin color. Johann Nieuhof, steward of the first Dutch East India Company embassy to Beijing in 1655–57, declared as a matter of fact: "The Chinese, for the greater part of them, are almost as White of Complexion as the people of Europe." He was particularly impressed by the fairness of the women: "They are for the most part Handsom, Complaisant, and Ingenious, and exceed in Beauty and exact Symmetry of Body all other Heathenish Women; their Complexion tends to whiteness." [20] The same observations were made by Alvaro Semedo (1585–1658) and Matteo Ricci (1552–1610), two of the most influential transmitters of knowledge of things Chinese in sixteenth- and seventeenth-century Europe.[21]

Perhaps it was his appreciation of Chinese taste that led Nieuhof to make a rare remark—for his times and after—on the nature of Chinese fashion: "The fashion of their Apparel *alter as well as here in Europe:* At present they generally wear long Gowns of a blue Colour, which reach down to their Heels . . . but the Women tie them close about their Waists with a girdle. . . . These Forms of Apparel are worn by all without difference, but only in substance they materially differ; for those of the nobler sort are made of the richest Silks, Embroidered with Dragons, whereas the Commonalty wear them made of ordinary Stuffs." [22]

The same spirit of appreciation, however, led other observers to the opposite conclusion:

> As for what is here called fashion, it has nothing at all in it like we call so in Europe, where all the manner of Dress is subject to many Changes. It is not so in China, which is a sign of good Order, and the Uniformity of the Government, even in the most trifling Matters; for which reason the Fashion of Dress has been always the same from the Infancy of the Empire to the Conquest of it by the Tartars [Manchus, in 1644], who without changing the Form of the ancient Chinese Government have only obliged them to dress in the Manner.[23]

Herein lies the beginning of the myth of the absence of fashion in China. It is important to note that in the early stage of interaction, the European traveler considered this lack of change a positive trait, signifying social stability and political order.

Hence, through the relatively benign lens of parity, what appeared to be visible differences were interpreted not as signs of China's Otherness but of a deeper compatibility between China and Europe. The Chinese, with small eyes, flat noses, and thin beards, might have appeared to be different, but they were coeval with Europe and they could be understood in terms of the same ideals: fairness of skin, proportion, symmetry, civility, chivalry, and stability. Yet the European discourse on footbinding in the sixteenth and seventeenth centuries shows how fragile this accommodation was.

The Footbound Women: They See but Are Not Seen

Most Europeans deemed footbinding a uniquely Chinese custom.[24] From the start, footbinding was recognized as a sign of China's uniqueness that destabilized the image of parity. The Italian friar Odoric of Pordenone (d. 1331), who arrived in China in 1322 and stayed at least three years, was the first European to write about footbinding: similar to the male custom of growing long fingernails, both were markers of gentility.[25] Although Chinese sources suggest that the practice began to filter into gentry households from the pleasure quarters in the late twelfth century, Marco Polo failed to mention it. By the sixteenth century, however, footbinding became such a hot topic that it seems as though no knowledge of China was complete without it.

At first glance, the reader today is likely to be struck by the facileness with which sixteenth-century travelers cast footbinding in a positive light. The purpose of the practice appears to have been the enforcement of separate spheres; that China took pains to safeguard female chastity was an admirable sign of its civility and morality. In calling the practice "ingenious," Mendoza set the basic tone:

> Amongst them they account it for gentilitie and a gallant thing to have little feet, and therefore from their youth they do swadell and binde them verie straight, and do suffer it with patience: for that she who hath the least feete is accounted the gallantest dame. . . . They are very secret and honest, in such fort that you shall not see at any time a woman at her window nor at her doors. . . . So that it is a great marvell when that you shall meete a principall woman in the streete, yea you will thinke that there are none in the citie, their keeping in is such: the lameness of their feete is a great helpe ther-unto. The women as well as the men be ingenious.[26]

Although the result of binding was described casually as "lameness," another observer offered a graphic apology of its benefits, contending that the practice hampered neither health nor mobility:

> The girls are no sooner born, than the nurses take care to tye their feet extremely hard, for fear of their growing; but what appears most surprising is, that this violence offered to nature, does not seem to impair their health. Their shoes of satin, embroidered with gold, silver, and silk, are extremely neat; and though they are exceedingly small, yet

they study to shew them as they walk; for walk they do, though one would scarce believe it possible, and indeed would willingly walk all day long, had they the liberty to go abroad.[27]

Thus emerged the enduring image of the secluded footbound woman; so irreproachable and distant was she that foreigners imagined her as a saint and her quarters were said to be a "sanctuary."[28] She was described in adoring terms:

> The Ladies of China are so well bred and so honest, as they give their husbands more cause to cherish them, than to put them out of their Families. . . . The virtue of these Ladies of China, being growne with them is become so solid with time: For from their infancies, they breed them up in the love of honesty, and the hatred of vice; they shut them up perpetually, and implore them without ceasing, to the end that Idleness the nursing mother of Vices, mollifying their spirits, should not draw them into some disorder.[29]

This adoration that borders on longing is understandable in light of a simple fact: by definition, a foreign man could not have seen a cloistered and virtuous Chinese woman.[30] In marked contrast to the discourse of fashion, so dazzling in its minute details of colors, appearances, and surfaces, the discourse of footbinding is essentially that of resistance to that visuality. Under the facade of the same rhetorical strategy of realism conveyed by excessive detailing is hearsay upon hearsay, mythmaking at its finest. In a terse statement, one traveler conveyed his frustration with this economy of a one-sided exchange concerning elite Chinese women: "they see and are not seen."[31] The European looked, but his gaze was not returned. Footbinding as concealment had rendered all objective—foreign—knowledge impossible.

The footbound woman was thus fated to be the perpetual Other to the European man. In stubbornly refusing to be seen, she figured as a nagging reminder of China's alterity: mysterious, exotic, and resistant to foreign terms of understanding. It is no accident that she became the quintessential symbol of China itself in the nineteenth century. So invested were the Chinese and Euro-Americans alike in the victimization script that few people saw through the irony: in refusing to submit to the foreign gaze, the footbound woman could have served as the very site of resistance against foreign encroachment. Instead of adopting this argument, however, the Chi-

Figure 2. Acting Out the Victimization Script: A Chinese girl is liberated from her bondage by a missionary woman, herself clad in a form-fitting dress. In this deliberate pose for the cameras, the missionary adopted a humble posture reminiscent of Jesus washing his disciples' feet. The missionary is Lillian Hale, who served in a town not far from the Great Wall, Zunhua, in 1888–1890. (Courtesy of the Peabody Essex Museum, Salem)

nese nationalists of the twentieth century accepted much of the Western view. Chinese advocates of the antifootbinding movement opted to highlight their parity with the Europeans by calling attention to the shared oppression suffered by women in the form of footbinding in China and tightly laced corsets in the West. We will return to this below.

From Empiricism to Analogy: Origin Myths

Being barred from looking at footbound women, Europeans in the sixteenth century turned to the most fundamental form of knowledge seeking: constructing a myth of origins. The visitors' curiosity and frustration were palpable in the way they besieged their male hosts for explanations; conflicting answers fueled the curiosity even more:

> If you demand a Reason of them, they answer, That they have observ'd this Custom (deriv'd to them about two thousand eight hundred years

since) from the example of *Tachia,* the Wife of the Emperor *Chei,* which Empress for her incredible Beauty they suppose to be plac'd amongst the Goddesses, and therefore she is esteem'd by them for the *Chinesian Venus;* and they feign binding of her Feet, which consequently caus'd the smallness of them. Others say, That this coercitation was Enacted by a Law of the wise Men, that Women may learn to sit at home, which if they do not voluntarily, they are by this means compell'd.[32]

The issue of responsibility and agency is most revealing of the power relations involved in the making of the origin myths. Many Europeans held the men responsible. Most persistent was the view that footbinding was invented by an all-powerful emperor of China and then transmitted by a decree of law or the persuasion of custom. Thus said Mendoza: "This custome hath indured manie yeares, and will indure many more, for that it is established for a law: and that woman which doth breake it, and not use it with her children, shall be counted as evil, yea shall be punished for the same. . . . They say that the men hath induced them unto this custome."[33]

Sometimes the women's foolish pursuit of beauty was said to aid the emperor's project, a reasoning that returned partial responsibility to the women, mothers in particular:

> Another invention of the Kings of China, which have loved the modestie and chastitie of women, hath beene of no small moment to cut off their courses and vaine walkes. They ordained that the Mothers should be carefull, to binde up streight [*sic*] their Daughters feet in the Cradle, to the end they should not grow, [the mothers were persuaded] that the beauty of a woman consisted in having a little foot. . . . It were a difficult thing to persuade them the contrary of this opinion, and to divert their spirits from this foolish crueltie, thus to rack their feet in the estate of innocencie: For if any of them had the face of Angell, and the foot indifferently great, shee will hold herself the foulest creature in the World.[34]

A rare refutation of the commonly held belief that footbinding was invented to maintain separate spheres came in the form of hearsay, one that is strangely evocative of the power that women exerted on Chinese men:

> Some have been persuaded that it was an Invention of the ancient Chinese, who to bring Women under a necessity of keeping within Doors, brought little Feet in fashion. I have more than once inquired about it

of the Chinese themselves, that never heard nothing of it. These are idle Tales, says one of them smiling, our Fore-fathers knew Women but too well, as we do, to believe that in retrenching half of their Feet, they could be deprived of the power of walking, and of longing to see the world.[35]

So the European quest of footbinding's origins ended up where it began: hearsay, rumors, and conjecture. For every plausible explanation advanced, contrary evidence or rebuke could be, and indeed was, summoned. The origin myth, entangled in a web of messy responsibilities and multiple agencies, failed to domesticate the alien female practice or submit it to a European narrative. The problem, however, is not that the Chinese male informants were withholding information from the foreign visitor in the same way that the former barred the latter from casting his eyes on the fairer sex.

The problem, if only the Europeans had known, was that Chinese men themselves found footbinding perplexing if not inexplicable. In fact, one of the earliest chroniclers and critics of the practice, a Confucian scholar called Che Ruoshui (fl. 1274), confessed that he did not know anything about its rationale: "The binding of women's feet, one does not know when this practice began. A little girl not yet four or five is innocent and guiltless, but infinite suffering was inflicted upon her. One does not know what good does it do to have [the pair of feet] bound into such a small size." Che's ignorance is remarkable, for he lived in the very century when footbinding first became popular among women of the domestic gentry. The scholar looked in vain into the classics and histories for an answer: "When Dai Liang of the Later Han dynasty [25–220 A.D.] married out his daughter, she was [dressed in] a silk upper garment and plain skirt, [holding] a bamboo box and [wearing] wooden clogs. That means one cannot blame [footbinding] on the ancients. Or, some say that it started with Consort Yang of the Tang, but no citations can be found about this either."[36]

The enigma continued to haunt Chinese scholars for centuries and had engendered an elaborate origin discourse among philologists by the seventeenth and eighteenth centuries. Armed with the authority of the classics and the power of monopoly over the written word, these scholars combed ancient texts and proposed no less than eleven theories about the timing of footbinding's first appearance, ranging from the prehistoric Xia dynasty to the Five Dynasties period of the tenth century.[37] While these debates are too convoluted to recount in full here, suffice it to note the most salient difference between the Chinese origin myths and their European counterparts: the absence of imperial coercion or punishment as an incentive.

All too aware of the limits of imperial power, Chinese scholars knew better than to ascribe footbinding to an emperor's decree. The men in the Chinese origin myths all appeared as inept and doting rulers; footbinding lost kingdoms in these familiar femme fatale plots. Imperial consorts were said to have bound their feet to enchant and deceive. Hence, there was Daji, consort of the last ruler of the Shang (twelfth century B.C.), who was literally a fox in disguise. She bound her feet to hide her beasty trots. Or Consort Pan, companion of the decadent ruler of the Southern Qi (r. 499–501), who glided on lotuses made of gold leaves. Or Yaoniang, dancer in the court of a dethroned ruler of the Southern Tang (r. 961–75), who wrapped her feet into the shape of the new moon to enhance her grace on a lotus-shaped platform. Che Ruoshui, as we have seen, also mentioned Consort Yang, the voluptuous beauty who was perhaps the most famous femme fatale in history.

The frequent association of footbinding with imperial consorts and palace dancers in these origin myths has led many scholars to hypothesize that the practice originated in the palace, most likely around the tenth century. Modern scholars, aided by archaeology, have further argued that first courtesans and then wives of the gentry imitated the consorts.[38] By the late twelfth century, the practice was common enough to engage the rage and puzzlement of such scholars as Che Ruoshui. Although no historian has furnished evidence on the mechanisms of its spread across class and geographical boundaries, this social history sounds plausible. The most interesting fact, however, is that despite the Chinese scholars' native advantage over the Europeans they were no better informed. It seems as though their classical knowledge had failed them, and they were reduced to grappling with footbinding's meaning by way of analogy: golden lotus, new moon, arch, bamboo shoots.

It is therefore not surprising that travelers to China were left guessing. The import of the European discourse on footbinding lies exactly in its dismal failure to convey objective or useful knowledge, for the alienness of footbinding exposed the limitations of the lens of parity with which the discourse of Chinese fashion was so painstakingly constructed in the same period and by the same observers. The incipient image of the footbound woman being subjected to the law of the emperor and the weight of an age-old and timeless custom was to become, in the much less benign nineteenth century, the metaphor of the Chinese nation under the paws of imperialism. Already, in grossly exaggerating the will and capacity of the Chinese emperor to regulate everyday life, the origin myth of footbinding figured as the harbinger of the two essential elements of the myth of the Chinese lack of fashion that came to full fruition in the nineteenth century: the tyranny of the "Oriental Despot" and the burden of a tradition that did not and could not change.

Peeping into China

The nature of Sino-European relations was fundamentally changed in the mid–nineteenth century, bringing a different crowd of witnesses and chroniclers to the Chinese shore. With the Opium War, which concluded in 1842, British gunboats forced China to open five treaty ports; having lost a second war in 1860, the Chinese had to open more inland river ports to foreign traffic and, significantly, to allow missionaries to buy land and reside in the interior of the empire. Aggressive traders, instructors, and zealous proselytizers from newly industrialized Europe and America, often frustrated by the lack of success of their projects, began to write a different kind of letter.[39]

Indicative of the sea change in the attitude of Euro-American travelers is what they made of Chinese faces and bodies: "The color of their complexion is a brownish yellow; their faces are broad and flat, with very high cheek bones; noses flat, with wild nostrils, and eyes standing far apart, and never opening wide, and placed slanting from the nose up toward the temple. This gives a very silly and insipid expression to the face."[40] The white-skinned Chinese who greeted the traveler two hundred years ago had vanished without a trace; every European now remarked on how yellow and ugly the native was.

The Chinese flat nose was a particular eyesore, and many origin myths sprang up to explain its sorry shape: "At first sight the Chinese is very unattractive. His skin is of yellow hue and his voice is harsh and unmusical. Judged by a Western standard, there is not a feature in his face that could ever by the widest charity be called beautiful. His cheekbones stand out staring and protuberant. His nose is as flat as though his far-off progenitor had had it bruised in some pugilistic encounter, and had transmitted it maimed and battered to his posterity."[41] According to another theory: "A Chinaman always appears to be looking around the corners of his eyes at you, and to have a meaning that you cannot get at. He gives you the impression that somebody when he was born sat on his nose, and that he has been lamenting the calamity ever since." [42]

It is not only the disappearance of the lens of parity that sets these nineteenth-century accounts apart from the early ones. More importantly, it is the directness, without any pretense of politeness, with which the foreigner stared the Chinese in the eye. Contrary to the appearance of the sixteenth-century Chinese as stately actors on a distant stage, the later encounters were laden with immediacy, almost a visceral urgency, as if seeing and being seen were matters of life and death. It is all the more remarkable, given this unabashed aggressiveness of the foreigner, that Chaplain Hardy felt scrutinized by the Chinese and had no way of returning the gaze as hard as he tried to stare back. The Chinese eyes seem to "have a meaning that you cannot get at."

Reverend MacGowan echoed the frustration in describing a typical Chinese: "His eyes, too, which are always black, are narrow and almond-shaped, and the eyeballs, instead of being large and full-orbed, dance and twinkle inside the narrow slits, as though they were playing hide-and-seek with the world." [43] The power of footbound women two centuries ago, who could "see but not be seen," was now being imputed to the entire nation. Instead of turning on the power of imagination in adoring the saintlike natives, however, the modern traveler turned up his or her nose in disgust.

It is in part this difficulty to penetrate the Chinese surface that accounts for the preponderance of voyeuristic-sounding titles when the European wrote books on things Chinese. Indeed, such titles as *China under the Search Light, Glimpses of China, A Peep at Old Asia,* and *Peeps into China,* drawn casually from one library catalog, bespeak not only the primal importance of eyesight and visuality in the modern history of Sino-Western interactions but also the persistent refusal of the Chinese to bare their inner souls. The liminal zone between light and shadow both frustrated and enticed the foreigner. It is no accident that Euro-American onlookers in China were fascinated by the "peep box," puppet shows, lanterns, shadow plays, and ceremonies; many a treatise was published under the title *Chinese Shadow.* Much like the chaotic Egyptian bazaar on display at the World Exposition held in Paris in 1889, everything in China "seemed to be set up before one as though it were the model or picture of something." [44]

Frustrated by this game of the Chinese hiding and the foreigner seeking, the Euro-American resorted to the discourse of the absence of fashion for answers about the inner workings of Chinese society and polity. In addition to the familiar assertion that a stable albeit authoritarian government dictated the styles and colors that people could wear, the lack of fashion was also seen as a result of a family characterized by patrilineal descent: "There is very little change of fashions in China; clothes are handed down from father to son. It is not considered rude to make remarks on the dress of others, nor would it be a bad compliment to say of a handsome dress, 'I suppose that belonged to your grandfather.' "[45]

The observer of Chinese dress also exhibited heightened sensitivity to the difference between form and content, as the looseness of Chinese garments joined unchangeability as a timeless characteristic: "Transparent drapery, or clothes fitted exactly to the shape, would be held in China as outrages upon decency; the police of that correct country never tolerating such public exhibitions. The fashion of the Chinese never vary; they are almost of antediluvian invention, and are perhaps emblematic of the stability of their affections."[46] In concealing the natural body, antediluvian drapes blocked the gaze of the foreigner, who, craning his neck, was still trying to peep into China.

Not only garments, but the skin, face, and even the body of the inscrutable Chinese were seen as instruments of deceit. Under the scientific heading of "Males Head, Chinese and Mongolian," the famed photographer John Thomson related his personal impression of his subject of study:

> No. 20 being that of a boy of the upper or highly educated class, the son of a distinguished civil officer of Canton. He is a fine, attractive-looking little fellow, his full hazel eyes beaming with kindliness and intelligence. . . . The face is altogether a pleasing one, but, as is common among children in China, it will gradually lose its attractions as it grows to maturity. The softness of the eye is then frequently replaced by a cold, calculating expression, the result of their peculiar training, and the countenance assumes a air of apathetic indifference which is so necessary *to veil the inner feelings* of a polished Chinese gentleman.[47]

If every adult Chinese man, acting in the public sphere, donned a mask, the women of the inner chambers were doubly suspicious. The woman who coated her face with makeup appeared to be more ostentatious than real: "The Chinese women are familiar with the art of painting their skins, using a composition of white and red, which imposes a sort of *enamel appearance* upon their complexions."[48] The excessive surface ornamentation that so enchanted European travelers two centuries before now engendered

Figure 3. The Body Concealed: A Chinese seamstress sewing men's socks, whose style supposedly never changed. The bulky socks accentuate the smallness of her bound feet, another product of her handiwork. Produced by a Cantonese artist for export, this print presents the image of Chinese bodies being hidden behind case-like, loose-fitting garments. (From "Women Making Stockings," plate 3, in George Henry Mason, *The Costume of China* [London: W. Miller, 1800]).

the opposite effect. Appearance was no longer charming because it was no longer trustworthy.

Mrs. Archibald Little, a champion of the antifootbinding movement, summed up her sentiments as follows:

> Whilst a roomful of Chinese ladies presents a very pretty appearance, from the exquisite gradations of colour of their embroidered skirts and jackets, the brilliancy of their head ornaments, and their rouge, yet, taken individually, probably no other nation is so deficient in charm. Their idea is that it is indecorous to show the figure; therefore *only their deformed feet, cased, it is true, in beautiful embroidered little shoes,* and their faces, are seen; even the hands, which are small and very elegantly shaped, with tapered fingers and filbert nails, are *concealed* in their large sleeves. Their faces at parties are often so rouged as to *look like masks,* their lips coloured, their eyebrows darkened, and their hair so anointed as to give a *shining, semi-metallic setting* to the face.[49]

Loose-fitting garments and shoes, with all their brilliant design and handiwork, were but a case that masked an imagined natural body that was spontaneous and unspoiled. Not only were the foreigners faster, bigger, and stronger, but they had constructed a nature-culture divide and cast themselves as the embodiment of the natural. In the final analysis, the tyranny of the Chinese emperor and his laws was a mere accomplice to a more pervasive force that immobilized the hapless nation: culture. In maiming the "natural" body, footbinding became the biggest shame of Chinese culture.

Two Kinds of Bondage and a Laugh

Given the prevalence of this discourse of the masked and unfree Chinese in the nineteenth and early twentieth centuries, it is ironic and significant that footbinding lost much of its mystique in the same period. Persistent foreigners, who literally unwrapped the binders to take photographs, destroyed the raison d'être of the practice—concealment—in the very process. Furthermore, internal demographic and cultural developments in China had also rendered footbinding a less genteel practice than before, as binding was increasingly taken up by lower-class women and vulgar prostitutes. For a few coppers, these women were all too willing to expose their crushed bones to the world. The jubilant foreigner had no clue that what he or she saw was not what it seemed: the inner truth of a mysterious China.

John Thomson, the photographer of things Chinese, described the great lengths he went to secure the right not just to peep but to see and document:

> This picture, No.39, shows us the compressed foot of a Chinese lady; and I regard it as one of the most interesting in my collection. Who the lady is, or where she came from, I cannot say. I had been assured by Chinamen that it would be impossible for me, by the offer of any sum of money, to get a Chinese woman to unbandage her foot, and yet gold and silver are arguments in favour of concessions which operate in the Celestial Empire with more than usual force. Accordingly, all my efforts failed until I reached Amoy, and there, with the aid of a liberal-minded Chinaman, I at last got this lady privately conveyed to me, in order that her foot might be photographed. She came escorted by an old woman, whom also I had to bribe handsomely before she would agree to countenance an act of such gross indecency as the unbandaging of the foot of her charge.[50]

Once rid of its ornate facade, however, the bound foot could not live up to its analogical splendor: "And yet, had I been able, I would rather have avoided the spectacle, for the compressed foot, which is figuratively supposed to represent a lily, has a very different appearance and odour from the most beautiful and sacred of flowers." Perhaps unbeknown to the foreigner, he had in fact chanced upon the only truth about footbinding in his disappointment: that its enchantment lies in concealment and its beauty is realized only by the imagination that the literary figurative requires. In first refusing to be seen and then, when seen, refusing to be taken as is, the bound foot mocks the empirical realism of the foreign spectator, represented by the "I saw it with my own eyes" narrative strategy of the travelers of the earlier centuries and the photographic lens of the moderns.

Frustrated by the very visuality that constituted his craft, Thomson turned to a familiar origin discourse to explain away footbinding's alienness. He also introduced two new strategies not available to his predecessors, a scientific medical discourse and a comparison between footbinding and corsetry. While the limitation of space precludes us from pursuing the former here, what Thomson said of the latter is a fitting prelude to the issue of laughter, with which I wish to conclude this essay. Thomson wrote: "We despise so ridiculous a usage as this, but the following extract out of a native work will serve to show that the Chinese return us the compliment, and criticize us for deformities to which the inexorable requirements of fashion have given rise: 'The Yin-keih-le, or English females before marriage, bind their waist, being desirous to look slender.' " [51]

For Chinese and European alike, it was hard to resist a comparison between footbinding and waist binding, both being a travesty of nature in a modern age in which the body has come to be viewed as "natural." This comparison, however, masks the inequalities of power not only between the Chinese and the European but between the man who wrote and photographed and the woman who submitted herself to the tyranny of beauty. Thomson thus said of the secluded Chinese ladies: "Neither are they free to dress as they may choose, for there is an Imperial edict which regulates her attire. I question, however, whether this law, which thus hampers the Chinese lady, is a more rigorous despot than fashion, which in our country sways the gentler sex." [52] Thus, not only was fashion implicitly made a European prerogative, but it was also explicitly gendered female.

As the subject of vision, women seem to be particularly susceptible to slippage into the immobilized bondage mode, and this is the case for both Chinese and European women. If the absence of fashion in China rendered both men and women prisoners in time, women who had their feet bound were made to suffer the additional restriction of bondage in space. European women, although free from the tyranny of the Oriental Despot, could not escape the fate of being slaves of change. The only unencumbered ones, according to this logic, were the Euro-American men, authors of most of the narratives surveyed.

Even in such a predetermined discursive field, Chinese women were seen to occasionally let out a dismissive denunciation or laugh reminiscent of the power that the unseen footbound women exerted on the foreigner two centuries before. One such woman, the empress dowager of the Qing dynasty, had good reason to laugh because she was a natural-footed Manchu with an ungirdled waist. Mrs. Headland, an American who served as physician to the dowager's mother, told her husband a most amusing story about the dowager's audience with a Chinese lady: "This lady was the wife of a Chinese minister to a foreign country, and had adopted both for herself and her daughters the most ultra style of European dress. She one day said to Her Majesty, 'The bound feet of the Chinese women make us the laughing-stock of the world.'

" 'I have heard,' said the Empress Dowager, 'that the foreigners have a custom which is not above approach, and now since there are no outsiders here, I should like to see what the foreign ladies use in binding their waist.'

"The lady was very stout, and had the appearance of an hour-glass, and turning to her daughter, a tall and slender maiden, she said:

" 'Daughter, you show Her Majesty.'

"The young lady demurred until finally the Empress Dowager said:

" 'Do you not realize that a request coming from me is the same as a command?'

"After having had her curiosity satisfied, she sent for the Grand Secretary and ordered that proper Manchu outfits be secured for the lady's daughters, saying:

" 'It is truly pathetic what foreign women have to endure. They are bound up with steel bars until they can scarcely breathe. Pitiable! Pitiable!'

"The following day this young lady did not appear at court, and the Empress Dowager asked her mother the reason of her absence.

" 'She is ill to-day,' the mother replied.

" 'I am not surprised,' replied Her Majesty, 'for it must require some time after the bandages have been removed before she can again compress herself into the same proportions,' indicating that the Empress Dowager supposed that foreign women slept with their waists bound, just as the Chinese women do with their feet." [53]

Thousands of miles away from the Forbidden City, Reverend Hardy heard similar laughter in the British colony of Hong Kong:

> Chinese ladies are also concerned because their European sisters do not wear visible trousers, and they cannot understand how they eat when their waists are girt in. For a woman to show her shape is considered in China most immodest. . . . I saw one day, at the Peak tramway station at Hong Kong, half a dozen Chinese ladies, apparently visitors to the island, dressed in the height of their fashion. Some British ladies stepped out of the cars wearing gowns that showed their figures and hats stuck over with artificial flowers and bits of birds. When they had passed, the Chinese ladies, pointing at their compressed waists and inartistic headgear, laughed in a way that should stagger European complacency.[54]

As has been shown throughout this essay, the discourse of Chinese lack of fashion provided the occasion for Europeans to reflect on, criticize, or celebrate their own devotion to progress. In each case, Europe needed the Chinese Other to complete its image of its modern self. Yet the fact that the empress dowager and the Hong Kong ladies found European fashion laughable and its practitioners pitiable is a useful reminder that China has its own agenda, just as it has its own way of seeing.

The history of Europeans looking at the Chinese presents a paradox: beauty is more than skin-deep, for it informs treatises on such weighty matters as bureaucracy and kinship, yet the meaning of beauty lies in the eyes of the beholder. Nowhere is this paradox more poignant than in the case of footbinding, a practice that so frustrated the foreigner because it cannot be reduced to a core of absolute and timeless meanings. Too busy with unwrapping the binders to reveal the "inner truth," the foreigner has failed to learn that the meaning of footbinding is always constructed and hence always a function of the values of the beholder. If there is any "truth" about footbinding at all, it is a most obvious one: surface ornamentation is all; what you see—the concealment itself—is what you get.

Notes

All translations of Chinese and Japanese are mine, unless otherwise noted.

1 Jennifer Craik, *The Face of Fashion: Cultural Studies in Fashion* (London: Routledge, 1994), 10.

2 William Lockhart, *The Medical Missionary in China: A Narrative of Twenty Years' Experience* (London: Hurst and Blackett, 1861), 335.

3 For the relevant individual titles in this series, see the citations below. This body of travel accounts is a self-referential textual universe. All of the accounts from the seventeenth century and before have been translated and anthologized repeatedly; the same statements on Chinese fashion appear, with slight variations, in a variety of texts from different periods. Due to the limitation of space, I do not trace the history of the transmission of each trope. Instead, I focus on a broad comparison between those familiar to the reading public in the seventeenth century and those popular two centuries later.

4 Michael Taussig, *Mimesis and Alterity: A Particular History of the Senses* (New York: Routledge, 1993), 62.

5 Timothy Mitchell, *Colonising Egypt* (Berkeley: University of California Press, 1991), xii.

6 Breton de La Martinière, "A Thread-Spinner and a Mantua-Maker," in *China: Its Costume, Arts, Manufactures* (London: W. Lewis, n.d. [1812]), vol. 2, unpaginated. See also *China in Miniature* (Boston: Clapp and Broaders, 1834), 53–54.

7 De la Martinière, *China*, vol. 2, unpaginated.

8 *China in Miniature*, 53.

9 *The I Ching or Book of Changes: The Richard Wilhelm Translation from Chinese into*

German, trans. into English by Cary F. Baynes (Princeton: Princeton University Press, 1990), 332.

10 Gu Qiyuan, *Kezuo zhuiyu* (Hearsay from my visitors), in *Baibu congshu jizheng* (Collection of one hundred collectanea) (Taipei: Yiwen yinshuguan, [1617] 1969), 9:16b–17a.

11 Gu, *Kezuo zhuiyu,* 1:23a.

12 Fan Lian, *Yunjian jumu chao* (Chancing upon the world in Songjiang), in *Biji xiaoshuao daguan* (Collectanea of notation books and stories), 22 vols. (Taipei: Xinxing shuju, [1593] 1988), 2:2a.

13 Donald F. Lach, *Asia in the Making of Europe,* vol. 1, *The Century of Discovery* (Chicago: University of Chicago Press, 1965), 16–17.

14 Donald Ferguson, *Letters from Portuguese Captives in Canton Written in 1534 and 1536* (Bombay: Education Society's Steam Press, 1902), 2; emphasis mine.

15 The *Historie* was compiled by the Augustinian monk Juan Gonzales de Mendoza from three sixteenth-century eyewitness accounts by Gaspar da Cruz, Martin de Rada, and Galeote Pereira. Soon after it was published in Rome in 1585, the *Historie* was translated into all of the principal European languages and circulated in thirty editions. Historian C. R. Boxer wrote: "The reading public in those days was small, and it is probably no exaggeration to say that Mendoza's book had been read by the majority of well-educated Europeans at the beginning of seventeenth century" (*South China in the Sixteenth Century* [London: Hakluyt Society, 1953], xvii).

16 Juan Gonzalez de Mendoza, *The Historie of the Great and Mightie Kingdome of China* (London: I. Wolfe for Edward White, 1588), 20; emphasis mine.

17 European sailors and traders tended to be much more negative in their assessments, seeing the Chinese as greedy and dishonest. See, for example, Donald Lach and Edwin J. Van Kley, *Asia in the Making of Europe,* vol. 3, *A Century of Advance* (Chicago: University of Chicago Press, 1993), 1621.

18 Mendoza, *Historie,* 19. See also Louis Le Comte and P. Du Halde, *A Description of China* [1685], in *The World Displayed; or a Curious Collection of Voyages and Travels,* ed. Smart, Goldsmith, and Johnson (Philadelphia: Dobelbower, Key and Simpson, 1796), 214; Louis Le Comte, *Memoirs and Observations, Topographical, Physical, Mathetical, Mechanical, Natural, Civil and Ecclesiastical* (London: Benj. Tooke and Sam. Buckley, 1697), 127.

19 P. Du Halde, *The General History of China* (London: John Watts, 1736), 137–38; emphasis mine.

20 Johann Nieuhof, *An Embassy from the East India Company of the United Provinces to the Grand Tartar Cham, Emperor of China* (London: By the author, 1673), 180.

21 Toshihiko Yazawa, *Seiyōjin no mita 16–18 seiki no Chūgoku josei* (Chinese females in the sixteenth to eighteenth centuries as seen by Westerners) (Tokyo: Tōhō shoten, 1990), 2–4; see also Lach and Van Kley, *Century of Advance,* 1619.

22 Nieuhof, *Embassy,* 181, emphasis mine.

23 Du Halde, *General History of China,* 141. Each successive dynasty, in fact, mandated a change in court clothing. For the queue as a marker of ethnic and political loyalties, see Michael Godley, "The End of the Queue: Hair as Symbol in Chinese History," *East Asian History* 8 (1994): 53–72. The European fascination with the Manchu "Tartars" as the Other of the Han Chinese is an important aspect of the politics of alterity explored in this essay. The Manchus appeared doubly alien and menacing in the sixteenth century, partly because they were seen as successors of the Mongol "Tartars" who had devastated Europe. In the nineteenth century, however, the Manchus appeared to lead a freer and more individualistic life — closer to that of modern Europeans — than the slavish Chinese, whom the Europeans had come to pity and loathe. The Manchu women's freedom from footbinding was often cited as proof. I have discussed this shifting meaning of Manchuness in "The Emperor and His Women: Three Views of Footbinding, Ethnicity, and Empire," in *Life in the Imperial Court of Qing Dynasty China,* ed. Chuimei Ho and Cheri A. Jones, *Proceedings of the Denver Museum of Natural History,* series 3, 15 (1998): 37–48.

24 Le Comte, *Memoirs and Observations,* 128; see also Nieuhof, *Embassy,* 389. The only exception I know is Michel Baudier, who asserted that: "It is true that this vaine beliefe, to hold them faire which haue very little feet, is not only at this day in Asia: some of these Easterne parts, haue followed it with as much passion" (*The History of the Court of the King of China* [London: William Stansby, 1635], 208). Coincidentally, enthography has proven him wrong. Except for a few border peoples such as the Yi in southwestern China, who came under the influence of Han Chinese expansionism, footbinding remained a Han Chinese custom shunned by China's closest neighbors such as Korea.

25 Lach, *Century of Discovery,* 40–41.

26 Mendoza, *Historie,* 21.

27 Le Comte and Du Halde, *Description of China,* 217.

28 Yazawa, *Seiyōjin,* 27.

29 Baudier, *History of the Court,* 206–7.

30 Martin de Rada (1533–78), an Augustinian friar who visited Fujian in southern China in 1575, claimed that footbound women could be seen working in the open fields in the countryside, whereas women in the cities were secluded and virtuous (Boxer, *South China,* 282–83; see also Yazawa, *Seiyōjin,* 14).

31 Baudier, *History of the Court,* 207.

32 Nieuhof, *Embassy,* 389.

33 Mendoza, *Historie,* 21.

34 Baudier, *History of the Court,* 207–8.

35 Le Comte, *Memoirs and Observations,* 129.

36 Gao Hongxin, *Chanzu shi* (A history of footbinding) (Shanghai: Shanghai wenyi chubanshe, 1995), 16.

37 Gao, *Chanzu shi*, 1–6; see also Howard Levy, *Chinese Footbinding: The History of a Curious Erotic Custom* (Taipei: Southern Materials Center, [1967] 1984), 37–63.

38 Gao, *Chanzu shi*, 19–20; see also Patricia Ebrey, *The Inner Quarters: Marriage and the Lives of Chinese Women in the Sung Period* (Berkeley: University of California Press, 1993).

39 One interesting example of contradictory assessments of China can be gleaned from the reception of chinoiserie in mid-eighteenth-century England. At the same time that the "Chinese style" became a fad, critics were denigrating it as false and deceptive. See James L. Hevia, *Cherishing Men from Afar: Qing Guest Ritual and the Macartney Embassy of 1793* (Durham: Duke University Press, 1995), 68–70.

40 *China in Miniature*, 15. For another example, see Mrs. W. H. Collins, *China and Its People: A Book for Young Readers by a Missionary's Wife* (London: James Nisbet and Co., 1870), 61.

41 John MacGowan, *Men and Manners of Modern China* (London: T. Fisher Unwin, 1912), 313–14.

42 Rev. E. J. Hardy, *John Chinaman at Home: Sketches of Men, Manners, and Things in China* (London: T. Fisher Unwin, 1905), 96. Another theory, advanced in the seventeenth century, saw the flat nose as a self-defense tactic of an insular people for, "with the helpe of this great wall they hinder the entry of Strangers into the Realme, and their cares keepe vices out of the Court, which in other places are familiar to Courtiers. If happily any stranger creepes in amongst them, he is presently discovered of every man; for to that end they long since setled a custome amongst them, to cause them to crush and make flat the noses of their Children when they are borne: So as all the Chinois haue flat Noses: Which makes a stranger in their company seeme to haue a different countenance" (Baudier, *History of the Court*, 199).

43 MacGowan, *Men and Manners*, 314.

44 Mitchell, *Colonising Egypt*, 12.

45 Collins, *China and Its People*, 73–74.

46 George Henry Mason, *The Costume of China* (London: W. Miller, 1800), pl. LX.

47 John Thomson, *Illustration of China and Its People* (London: Sampson Low, Marston, Low, and Searle, 1874), vol. 2, pl. 9, nos. 20–25; emphasis mine.

48 Mason, *Costume of China*, pl. LX; emphasis mine.

49 Mrs. Archibald Little, *Intimate China* (London: Hutchinson and Co., 1901), 124; emphasis mine. Marni Stanley has critiqued the Eurocentric assumptions of such critics of footbinding as Mrs. Little in her "Wasp Waists and Lotus Buds: The Corset Looks at Footbinding," in *Pacific Encounters: The Production of Self and*

Other, ed. Eva-Marie Kröller, Allan Smith, Joshua Mostow, and Robert Kramer (Vancouver: Institute of Asian Research, University of British Columbia, 1997), 79–94.

50 Thomson, *Illustration of China,* vol. 2, pl. 14, no. 39.

51 Thomson, *Illustration of China,* vol. 2, pl. 14, no. 39. The source Thomson quoted (n. 1) is F. Neumann, "History of the Pirates," 29.

52 Thomson, *Illustration of China,* vol. 1, pl. 15, no. 29.

53 Isaac Taylor Headland, *Court Life in China: The Capital, Its Officials and People* (New York: Fleming H. Revell, 1909), 105–6.

54 Hardy, *John Chinaman,* 324.

No Questions, No Answers:

China and *A Book from the Sky*

Stanley K. Abe

1

In his book *Brushes with Power,* Richard Kraus tells the story of Yang Bu-wei, the first female doctor of Western medicine in China, who, as a child, was unable to complete an examination essay that was to begin with the words, "Women are the mothers of the race." The recognition of her gendered position and its relationship to the writing of Chinese was later played out as defiance of her father's insistence that she develop her skills in calligraphy: "But I never listened to my father's advice, so today I often write things which people cannot make out, in a true scrawl. Sometimes I even write characters which do not exist, with the result that my friends are puzzled, sometimes thinking me laughable."[1] Yang's deployment of non-existent characters is reminiscent of *nüshu* (literally, "women's writing"), an invented script that was developed by women in an isolated area of southern Hunan province and used exclusively for their private communications.[2] The invention of scripts that are readable only by women or, as in the case of Yang, the refusal to participate in the conventional forms of writing suggest the significance of the Chinese written form within a patriarchal society and the gendered resistance that writing has inspired.

After emigrating to the United States, Yang published a cookbook in 1945 entitled *How to Cook and Eat in Chinese.*[3] In anticipation of a book signing to benefit United China Relief of Boston, Yang was confronted with an unexpected request for calligraphy, as Kraus describes: "An American woman who had been in China enthusiastically suggested that Yang use a brush for signing the copies. Because she dared not say that she had not written with a brush for nearly twenty years, poor Yang was driven to practicing secretly at home. The day after a furtive trip to Chinatown to purchase a brush and ink for a night of practice, she signed three hundred copies." For Kraus, the anecdote indicates the deep hold calligraphy had on Yang: "Yet so mighty is the emotional grip of this art that her calligraphic inadequacies haunted her decades after emigrating to the United States."[4] While the power of the calligraphic tradition is undeniable, tradition is not where the demand made on Yang originates. In China, as an educated, upper-class woman, Yang could display, even flaunt, her lack of calligraphic skill. It was only in the West, and through the invocation of proper Chinese behavior by the "American woman," an "expert," whose knowledge and authority is based on personal experience in China, that Yang abandoned her resistance to calligraphic practice. Rather than the power of tradition, Yang was confronted with the power of Western representations that already knew what was properly Chinese. She was, in a catachrestic moment, inadequate to the authentic Chinese subject that was anticipated in the West. Her capitulation can be understood not as individual weakness but as a desire to resolve the incommensurable demands on her subjectivity. The Chinese cause that the book signing supported should not be overlooked—it reminds us of the way in which the individual is subsumed by the nation-state in times of crisis. Yang is not the first to have the experience of learning what it means to be Asian upon arriving in the West, that is, to experience the effect of encountering the foreknowledge of oneself in the Orientalist West.

2

While it [*A Book from the Sky*] speaks in a national syntax, it disarticulates such a syntax and renders it completely garbled. While it constructs a symbolic national text, it evacuates all meaning from such a text. In this way, the work calls attention to the ongoing crisis of modern China and at the same time calls into question any easy resolution of such a crisis which might be afforded by simple allegiance to culture and tradition. In *A Book from the Sky*, language—a symbolic system fundamental to the integrity and perpetuation of a national culture—is endlessly reproduced but vitiated of any functional value and thus made curiously unproductive.[5]

Writing and the power of the written text are central to one of the best-known works of Chinese art from the 1980s, Xu Bing's installation, entitled in English *A Book from the Sky* (Figure 1). The work consists of books and hanging scrolls with text printed from woodblocks that the artist carved by hand over several years. The books carefully follow traditional conven-

Figure 1. Xu Bing. *A Book from the Sky*. Installation at the Elvehjem Museum of Art, University of Wisconsin–Madison. 30 November 1991–19 January 1992. Photograph provided by the Elvehjem Museum of Art.

tions, from the bibliographic forms, to the stitched bindings, to the wooden storage boxes. All of this pays homage to the long history of Chinese learning and exegesis that is preserved in printed form but with an important twist: all of the characters (*hanzi*) are invented, composed of recognizable elements but illegible as conventional linguistic signs (Figure 2). Xu, tired by the endless philosophical discussions of modernism, pseudomodernism, and postmodernism that consumed young intellectuals in Beijing in the late 1980s, retreated to his studio to carve each of the several thousand invented

Figure 2. Xu Bing. *A Book from the Sky*. Installation at the Elvehjem Museum of Art, University of Wisconsin–Madison. 30 November 1991–19 January 1992. Photograph provided by the Elvehjem Museum of Art.

characters onto individual woodblocks.[6] In the silence of that studio, *A Book from the Sky* was, to borrow the words of Louis Marin, the utopian figure of the neutral: "neither yes nor no, true nor false, one nor the other." For Marin, the utopian neutral is "not the neutral as neutrality" nor the "utopic figure that seems to be freed from society" but the "span between true and false," a theory that "would permit placeless contradiction in discourse to have limitless force."[7] Indeed, Xu's careful re-creation of traditional forms, on the one hand, and the denial of legibility, on the other, produced a powerful work that refuses any singular reading.

When it was first exhibited in Beijing in October 1988, *A Book from the Sky* received considerable attention, along with works of other New Wave (*xinchao*) artists such as Lü Shengzhong.[8] *A Book from the Sky* was shown again in early 1989 as part of the "China/Avant-Garde" exhibition (*Zhongguo xiandai yishuzhan*) (Figure 3).[9] The imagination and beauty of the installation, as well as Xu's serious approach, were often commended. But there was also considerable perplexity over whether to read the work as a critique, or as an instantiation of Chinese culture, or as both; the debate reflected deep concerns and differences over the future direction of Chinese art.[10] Xu and *A Book from the Sky* left China in 1990, and the work was subsequently installed in Taiwan, Japan, South Korea, Australia, Spain, Italy, France, and England, as well as at multiple sites in the United States. Demand for *A Book from the Sky* continues to be strong, and exhibitions have been arranged well into the future.[11] A key question, then, is, How might a work such as *A Book from the Sky*, so powerfully engaging for Chinese viewers, be received in the West? As Yang Buwei learned, knowledge of China and of what is properly Chinese is firmly fixed in the imagination of the West. As a work from China, *A Book from the Sky* is both foreign and already known. As a work of art displayed in a museum, it is made productive through its institutional setting and the language of critical interpretation and contextualization produced from the site of the museum.[12] In what follows, I will be primarily concerned with how *A Book from the Sky* has been read, interpreted, and presented to the public in the United States, both the critical reception of the work and its (re)construction as a representative work of contemporary Chinese art.[13]

A Book from the Sky made its debut in the United States as part of "Three Installations by Xu Bing" at the Elvehjem Museum, University of Wisconsin, from 30 November 1991 to 19 January 1992 (Figures 1 and 2). At first glance, its formal qualities might appear familiar to viewers acquainted with

Figure 3. Xu Bing. *A Book from the Sky*. Installation at the National Fine Art Museum, Beijing. 1989. Photograph provided by Xu Bing.

conceptual installations of the late 1960s and 1970s in Europe and the United States. The work, considerably expanded in comparison to its Beijing installations, features long rows of neatly arranged open books in the central area of the floor. Printed sheets sweep down from overhead, and the side walls are draped with additional text. The manipulation of space, light and shadow, and the orderly arrangement of texts are stunningly evocative, even sublime. What distinguishes this installation from works of conceptual art, however, is its heightened emphasis on visual effect and, most crucially, the complete illegibility of the text.[14] The unreadable signs of Chinese writing have fascinated the Western viewer for many centuries. While the form of the installation points toward modernist visual art practices, the text evokes the role of the Chinese written language in the development of modernist poetics, most closely associated with Ernest Fenollosa and Ezra Pound, and more recently the recuperation of their earlier move by Jacques Derrida.[15] Fenollosa and Pound discovered in the Chinese character what they believed to be an alternative, ideogrammic language to the phonological scripts of the West. Inspired by the Chinese ideogram, Pound, and later poets such as William Carlos Williams, sought to create new modernist forms of expressive language. Many scholars, however, have seized on the manner in which Fenollosa and Pound ignored the phonetic aspects of the Chinese character, and the issue of such a "misunderstanding," which Derrida continued, has generated a significant body of criticism over the last half century, one that is fascinating in its own right.[16] Xiaomei Chen, however, has made the point that such acts of appropriation are always also creative reinterpretations that render the charge of misunderstanding largely irrelevant.[17] This is a point that I would underscore in terms of a work such as *A Book from the Sky*, which not only operates at the juncture of visual and literary production but tests the liminality of concepts such as misunderstanding.

3

The most important attribute of *A Book from the Sky* is the manner in which it offers itself for inscription by the viewer. Gao Minglu puts it this way: "When he establishes a space without meaning in his work, Xu believes, viewers will fill it with their own readings of the confrontations that occur between different cultures and eras."[18] Even the title of the work is slippery, an attribute that Xu encouraged from the beginning: "The name of this artwork, *Tian Shu*, originally refers to the pattern left on the skin of a person who had been struck dead by lightning. People looked at these patterns, which were like words written by the sky, and they couldn't understand them. My original title for the piece was *Fenxi Shijie de Shu* [A book that analyzes the world], but everyone called it *Tian Shu*."[19] Discussions in the Chinese media, however, almost always refer to the work by a third title: *Xishi jian*, sometimes followed by *shijimo juan*. Scholars and critics have translated the first phrase in the title in a number of ways: for example, Britta Erickson has translated it as *An Analyzed Reflection of the World*; Wu Hung, as *Mirror that Analyzes the World*; and Eugene Wang, as *Analytical Mirrors of the World*.[20] Erickson has also suggested an alternative translation: *An Analyzed*

Warning to the World.[21] The second phrase in the title is similarly ambiguous and has been translated as both *The Final Volume of the Century* and *Fin-de-Siècle Volumes.*[22] Xu chose to use the popular title, *Tian shu,* as the basis for the English title of the work, *A Book from the Sky.* But even this name has not gone unchallenged. Wu Hung argues that in colloquial Chinese, *tian shu* means "abstruse or illegible writing that makes no sense to its reader," and that, considering the contents of the work, the English title would be better rendered as *Nonsense Writing.*[23] Interestingly, this translation would bring us close to the disdainful sense of *Tian shu* that was invoked by some critics of the work.[24] The unstable litany of names and translations for the work suggests the manner in which it is able to elicit a multiplicity of readings, something like a Rorschach test, that reveals the interests and politics of the viewer.[25]

In its initial exhibitions in the United States, the openness of the work to a variety of interpretations contributed to a series of politically charged readings. The Tiananmen Square crackdown was still a powerful memory in the United States when the Elvehjem Museum exhibition opened and *A Book from the Sky* was positioned as symbolic of both pre–4 June freedom and post–4 June repression.[26] The catalog of the exhibition, which featured a detailed expository essay by Erickson, clearly was developed in the midst of this emotional and difficult moment. Erickson's essay on *A Book from the Sky* reports that the work was initially "hailed as the definitive work of the New Wave and as a sign that artists could, indeed, find a valid means of expressing themselves in a new China." Soon, however, "as part of the reversal of the temporary freedom of expression in China, just two days before the massacre in Tian'anmen Square," *A Book from the Sky* was vilified in an official publication. In its rush to join "vilified" with "massacre," the essay is blind to its own footnote, which shows that the attack on *A Book from the Sky* was published on 2 June 1990, two days before the first anniversary of the 4 June incident.[27] The slip in the catalog essay points to a widespread desire to reduce *A Book from the Sky* and the events of 1989 to a simple political allegory of good (individual expression) and evil (traditional despotism). The 1990 attack was certainly political and purposefully timed, but its target was continued support for the New Wave as much as *A Book from the Sky.*[28] Unmentioned in any reports is the muted, but no less clear, defense of the New Wave, Xu, and *A Book from the Sky* in a reply to the negative article in the same official publication.[29] Certainly the events of 4 June had a profound negative effect on Chinese artists associated with the New Wave, but Xu continued in his position at the Central Academy of Art in Beijing, and, in May and June of 1990, he was able to organize his project to make a monumental rubbing of the Great Wall.[30] There was clearly less and less room for such works of contemporary art in China, however, and in 1990 Xu accepted an invitation to be an honorary fellow at the University of Wisconsin. He has resided in the United States since that time, although he continues to visit China and produce work there.[31]

Despite the immense complexities and contradictions of the 1989 democracy movement, it is telling that the U.S. print and electronic media representation of the demonstrations — that they were wholly antigovernment and anti–Communist Party — was shared by the hard-line party leaders who suppressed the movement.[32] The goal of the democracy movement was understood by most in this country as the desire for U.S.-style liberal democratic institutions, such as one person/one vote. This form of projection as political analysis also informed early interpretations of *A Book from the Sky*. The Elvehjem catalog states that the set of ten characters used for numbering pages and volumes in *A Book from the Sky* was derived from a special set of numbers used in small-scale Chinese elections. Based on the fact that these are the only intelligible characters among the thousands created by Xu, the Elvehjem Museum catalog suggests the following interpretation:

> All is meaningless except for the opportunity to vote. The Chinese government may make whatever lengthy pronouncements it wishes, but only an announcement that democracy would be enacted would have any meaning: all else is excess verbiage. *Xu denies that this is his intended meaning,* but admits that it is a possible interpretation. It would be an audacious statement for an artist to make, but it is entirely in keeping with the *general desire* for democracy expressed by the young intelligentsia during the later 1980s. Such a reading of *A Book from the Sky* has not been discussed in the Chinese media.[33]

This interesting passage reveals the way in which a liberal ideology is instantiated even as it is forced to disavow the artist's intention and acknowledge the lack of such a reading in China. Not surprisingly, this line of thinking was reiterated in later commentaries on the numbering system, for example: "This aspect of the work might lead one to *speculate* that an underlying theme of the work is that all of the sometimes venerated and ancient Chinese culture based upon written language is meaningless if one cannot vote."[34]

Interpretations such as these are not fanciful; rather, they are overdetermined in the United States, where China has been historically understood as rich in cultural tradition but lacking in modern institutions of civilization, such as liberal democracy. Tiananmen and 4 June are only the latest examples of "Oriental despotism" and the traditional Chinese disregard for human rights. Here one can recall after 4 June the recitation on television by sinologists of the litany of abusive Chinese despots, from Mao back to Qin Shi Huangdi. It seems as though the fact of "Oriental despotism" can never be sufficiently fixed and must therefore be reiterated over and over again.[35] A recent example is an article by Robert Drexler, former U.S. Consul to Hong Kong, on how, "in addition to opening up trade with China, the first visit ever by an American ship to the port of Canton in 1784 also led to the first human-rights struggle between the Asian giant and the United States."[36] The article describes the idealist opposition of a young American against Chinese demands for the execution of a British gunner who was responsible for accidentally killing a Chinese fisherman with a ceremonial salute in Canton in 1784. Such dominant representations of incomprehensible Chinese illiberalism—wholly narcissistic, self-congratulatory, and Orientalist—immensely complicate the field from which to advance criticism of current Chinese government political policies. Orientalism and liberalism combine today to produce the alliance of high-profile dissidents such as Harry Wu with the most right-wing think tanks or the strange bedfellows of the Dalai Lama and Jesse Helms.[37] In a situation where opportunism is so rampant, how does one maintain a principled opposition to injustice that does not simply play into the hands of the most cynical political elements in the United States?

The representation of *A Book from the Sky* as critical of the Chinese government was a product of many historical factors galvanized by the sensational and narrowly polemical media coverage of the 4 June incident.[38] The weight placed on a political reading of *A Book from the Sky* was, in the historical context, inevitable and involved not only museums and curators but Xu himself, who certified such political readings as much by silence as by positive affirmation. It was usually enough for him to simply state that the work had been praised by critics before 4 June and not liked by some after.[39] Interestingly, the characterization of *A Book from the Sky* as an anti-government work was pursued in China just as the Elvehjem installation was being prepared.[40] Xu's U.S. friends and Chinese critics were in complete agreement about the nature of his highly ambiguous work, and this kind of unexpectedly symmetrical political consensus should once again alert us to the continued shared stakes of many strange bedfellows.

4

The aesthetic qualities of the work, heightened by dramatic installations and the exotic subject matter, have made an important contribution to the consistently favorable reception of *A Book from the Sky* after nearly a decade of exhibition. It is natural, then, that recently, when the word *China* is more likely to summon up visions of a billion potential consumers rather than Tiananmen, interpretative readings have concerned themselves more with the form of the work than politics. The eulogy for the earlier political readings of *A Book from the Sky* as representative of dissident politics was delivered by Eugene Wang in 1995: "There is a tendency to pseudo contextualize him by subjugating him to the procrustean bed of facile sociopolitical terms." Instead, Wang adroitly sketches the complex relationship between works of New Wave artists and the politics of the pre-/post-Tiananmen period, for example, the way in which Xu was made "an easy pawn because there are signs in his works that could be everything to everyone." [41]

The aesthetic value of *A Book from the Sky* was never separate from the political, and the unity of the two elements was crucial for its reception in the United States. For example, one of the most compelling arguments for the success of *A Book from the Sky* places emphasis on the excess of labor and concentrated effort that is represented in the work. [42] The representation of oppressive human toil in China — forced (child, women, prison) labor, cheap workers, and the like — has a powerful and alluring aesthetic counterpart: "There is also much to be said for the accumulation of labor, the repetition of simple acts, over and over, for years even, that give both an authority and a reservoir of meaning to Xu Bing's art that would be difficult to achieve with the quick execution usual to western artists." [43] Against numerous examples of Chinese artists who have utilized "quick execution" with spectacular results or Western artists who work quite deliberately, cultural difference is reduced to a matter of tempo, a familiar move for those who have followed the discussion of the relationship between fast and slow economies, where speed marks the modern from the traditional. There is, simultaneously, another direction in which the logic of repetitious labor moves, however. Xu himself has likened the laborious process of creating *A Book from the Sky* to the practice of Zen Buddhism. [44] The fact that a Chinese artist interjects Oriental philosophy into his work, as opposed to Western criticism, adds a touch of authenticity that is indeed impossible for many to resist. It is also significant that Xu has consistently used the Japanese term *Zen* for its Chinese equivalent, *Chan,* a recognition that *Zen* is by far the more widely known term in the West and that the two terms are commonly conflated. By deploying Zen around *A Book from the Sky,* Xu calls up a panoply of cultural traits that represent "ancient China" to the West: solitude, quiet, meditation, wisdom, and, in the visual arts, surface, repetition, pattern.[45] This is not to suggest that the idea of Chan or Zen was not a part of Xu's explanatory vocabulary in China — as it certainly was — but to be reminded that value production is not the sole prerogative of the critic.

Xu has described *A Book from the Sky* as a kind of teasing or joke.[46] The tension produced through the repeated frustration of the desire to read meaning into the text, however, is a strategy that is limited to those who are literate in Chinese. For the Beijing audience who experienced *A Book from the Sky* in 1988 and 1989, there was much force to his no-sense characters. A non-Chinese-reading audience, however, cannot be seduced into the game of searching the text for readable forms, and therefore there is no impulse to read and no shock of illegibility. Rather, there is a doubled alienation from the written forms that makes the joke irrelevant, at least in Xu's original terms. What, then, could be the point to Xu's joke for the non-Chinese reader? The Elvehjem catalog provides a clue in its masterful recuperation of *A Book from the Sky* for the Western viewer: "*A Book from the Sky* frustrates the viewer's inescapable urge to decode the written word, and this frustrated act of viewing ties the viewer in with the work, making his passage through it a part of the work of art." This is the effect on the Chinese-reading viewer. The catalog continues: "Once the viewer can let go of the urge to read, the urge to act upon the work of art, then he can accept and appreciate its beauty." That is, to release oneself from the act of reading is the path to beauty. And finally: "The viewer who does not read Chinese is free to absorb the work's beauty without having to confront its unintelligibility."[47] That is, the non-Chinese-reading viewer is free of the necessity of moving through unintelligibility; he or she is the privileged viewer who can most unproblematically absorb the beauty of *A Book from the Sky*. A lack — the inability to read Chinese — is transformed into a site from which the Western audience can generate singular enjoyment and aesthetic pleasure.

On another level, Jonathan Arac has pointed out that "unintelligibility need not be avoided for the aesthetic power to operate."[48] The productivity of incomprehension has a long history in the West, passing back from Fenol-

Figure 4. Xu Bing. *A Book from the Sky*. Installation at the Massachussetts College of Art, Boston. 1995. Photograph by Stanley K. Abe.

losa and Pound, to Gottfried Wilhelm Leibniz, to Athanasius Kircher and the seventeenth-century fascination with the Chinese written form in the context of the search for an original human language and the construction of a universal written script.[49] In this project, desire and frustration produced a surplus of fantasy, in which Chinese writing "functioned as a sort of European hallucination." [50] The alterity of Chinese writing in relation to romanized scripts is, of course, central, but it is the visuality of the character—the manner in which it is made manifest in highly abstract forms—that most contributes to its enduring effectiveness as a symbol of China.[51] That Yang Buwei was required to produce writing as a sign of China or that *A Book from the Sky* would provide so gripping a spectacle in the West should be considered in light of this venerable tradition of Western fantasy production and willful misrecognition.

The installation of *A Book from the Sky* at the Massachusetts College of Art in 1995 might be taken as a visual allegory for the privileged, aestheticized site of the viewer in the West (Figure 4). In a departure from other exhibitions, Xu did not place text on the walls. He opened the claustrophobic space of the installation, which in turn released the viewer to move around the periphery of the work—there was even a view from above. The shift in the positioning of the audience was subtle but profound. No longer physically enclosed by the work, the viewer faced *A Book from the Sky* from the exterior, an observer always on the outside. This arrangement manifests in visual terms a fundamental aspect of the exhibition of *A Book from the Sky* in the West, where the non-Chinese-reading audience is literally on the "outside" of the point.[52] To be outside of comprehension, however, is where the privilege of the non-Chinese-reading audience is located—a site at which enjoyment of the aesthetic might be substituted for considerations of the political.

The freedom to not engage the difficult issues raised by *A Book from the Sky* for a Chinese audience is a large part of its allure in the West. It is important that the problematic of Xu's work be directed at the Chinese language, Chinese tradition, Chinese culture, or Chinese modernity. And it is equally important that critical commentary on the work confine this critique to China and not allow it to open onto the problematic implications of the role of the West in the very formation of Chinese problems of tradition or modernization.[53] For the typical viewer in the United States, *A Book from the Sky* is not only beautiful; it signifies, through the artist's critique, a problem not for us but for the other country out there.

5

While writing this essay, I happened to look in on a World Wide Web site that some readers may be familiar with—the Han-Shan Tang booksellers in London—and found that works by Xu were featured items in their most recent book list.[54] Four handprinted and bound volumes from *A Book from the Sky*, within a wooden storage case, were offered in a limited edition of one hundred sets for £10,000, or roughly U.S. $16,000. The sale immediately followed the exhibition of *A Book from the Sky* as part of a series of installations and performances of Chinese and British Chinese artists entitled "Fortune Cookies" at the Institute of Contemporary Arts in London.[55] This is not the first sale of part of the work. In 1994, the Queensland Art Museum in Australia purchased scrolls and sets of books from *A Book from the Sky* for $75,000;[56] other portions have been sold to private collectors and museums. Although it remains unclear how many of the books will be sold by Han-Shan Tang, the dispersement of books and scrolls from *A Book from the Sky* will undoubtedly continue. Over the past decade, *A Book from the Sky*, through its insertion into a transnational circuit of exhibition, has been transformed from a limited work that responds to primarily local concerns into a commodified, aesthetic spectacle of contemplation and collection. In this sense, the career of *A Book from the Sky* marks the trajectory of contemporary Chinese visual arts from an engagement with the cultural debates characteristic of the mid-1980s "New Era" to the "postmodernity with Chinese characteristics" of the post-1989 period.[57]

The public offering of books from *A Book from the Sky* marks an important new development in the career of the work. With the sale by Han-Shan Tang, it slips from the category of high art with its attendant exclusivity, marked by limited sales to art dealers, collectors, or museums, to the status of something closer to an ordinary commodity, albeit a high-priced one, available to the general public. There is also a shift in emphasis in the representation of the work, from a monumental installation to an example of print and book arts in which the value of *A Book from the Sky* lies not in its potential critique of traditional Chinese written culture but in the way "it lovingly adheres to all the material-cultural conventions and forms of traditional Chinese book-making and bibliography." The Han-Shan Tang text dwells on the meticulous attention to detail, the extraordinary production of the books from hand-carved movable type, and the faithfulness to traditional Chinese bibliographic forms, and touts the book as having the form of "a 'Classic' or 'Collectanea' of Heaven, a work with a long exegetical history which has deserved and received the close attentions of many scholars for a millennium or more."[58] The advertisement targets a consumer who would most appreciate the antiquarian qualities of the work, and, though there is appended an explanation of the critical potential in the invented characters, it is the book's traditional aesthetic qualities that have been moved to the foreground.

The conversion of *A Book from the Sky* into a celebration of Chinese tradition highlights the continued importance of the Orientalist interest in traditional exotica and the role of sinological expertise in making it an authentic and valuable work of traditional Chinese culture. It is not surprising that the marketing strategy of Han-Shan Tang brings sinological exegesis, fundamental to producing "China" in the West, to bear on *A Book from the Sky*. In fact, the central claim of the work—that its characters were not readable—was taken to be a professional challenge by some sinologists. Charles Stone, a doctoral candidate in Chinese literature, was one of the first to respond. Referring to the cover of a 1993 issue of *Public Culture*, Stone reports, "Undaunted, it took me no more than five minutes of leafing through an unabridged four-corner index of Chinese characters to turn up two real characters. . . . True, they are obsolete orthographies, and no normal person would care to know them, but they are still real characters. I imagine that a careful examination of the whole work would turn up many more." Stone asserts the authority of sinology by claiming a mastery of the Chinese language superior to that of the natives, those Chinese scholars who are said to have spent "hours, even days, at the Beijing exhibition searching in vain for a readable character." [59] However, it has been noted that one of the characters identified by Stone was an invention of the ninth century with no meaning or pronunciation, which indicates something of the difficulty of fixing a "real" or "fake" character in the Chinese language.[60] Sinology's goal of debunking the myths of the natives fuels Stone's final assessment of *A Book from the Sky* as "a study of the layer upon layer of tradition which Xu Bing evidently finds stifling. I do not understand how it is related to the politicization of the meaningless, the prestidigitation of the deconstructed, or the denial of culture. What I see is a hyperesthetic investigation of Chinese culture, and many many words I don't know, except for those two I found in the dictionary." [61] Here one can discern the paramount role of *hanzi* and writing for the maintenance of sinology's essentialized, traditional China — the very same China that rose up to so unexpectedly confront Yang Buwei in the West.

6

> This theory [of the neutral], finally, would entail utopic practice, introducing into narrative history and geography the sudden distance that breaks apart closely held spatial and temporal surfaces. Lightninglike, before coming to a hard and fixed image in the utopic figure and "ideal" representation, the *other* appears: limitless contradiction.[62]

A fundamental structural element of *A Book from the Sky* is its juxtaposition of the past and present, "its reliance on traditional forms to express profound contemporary ideas." [63] The figures of time that constantly recur in interpretations of the work are not surprising, considering the crucial role of temporality for the construction of China as an other of the West. Its traditional elements ensure that old lines of opposition — China/tradition/past versus West/modern/present — continue to operate as a powerful framework for our appropriation of the work.[64]

A Book from the Sky is a work that was created to resist easy interpretation, yet it has been relentlessly inscribed with political and aesthetic significance.

In February 1989 in Beijing, Xu wrote the following about the work: "Nowadays the art world has become an arena. What do I want from it? Handing one's work to society is just like driving living animals into a slaughterhouse. The work no longer belongs to me; it has become the property of all the people who have touched it. It is now concrete and filthy. I hope to depart from it, looking for something different in a quiet place." [65] There is a stunning clarity with which Xu sees what the future holds in store for his work, but what is of interest here is the past that has been lost—a time when *A Book from the Sky* belonged only to the artist, before it was claimed by the "touch" of others, which turned it "concrete and filthy." This is a poignant moment, because we know that circumstances have refused to allow Xu to leave his work behind, that in the West, nearly a decade later, *A Book from the Sky* continues to hold its creator suspended in the past, trapped in our desire to see his "concrete" art reinstalled, again and again.

But even as the "filthy" books and scrolls are sold, the work has experienced one moment of regeneration. The exhibition of *A Book from the Sky* at the University Art Museum in Albany, New York, in early 1996 was the largest installation yet of the work (Figure 5). Because of the size of the hall ($80 \times 60 \times 35$ ft), the work required five hundred new books from China and one thousand feet of additional scrolls, which were printed locally by Xu and two assistants. Lacking enough individual woodblocks to produce the scrolls, Xu's characters were digitally scanned into a computer and transferred onto photosensitive polymer "blocks" for printing.[66] In addition, one new text was added to the installation on the entrance wall: "In the continual trauma that is 'modernity,' the question that returns to haunt the Chinese intellectual is that of continuity and (re)production of Chinese culture. . . . How is culture—in ruins—to be passed on, by whom and with what means?" [67] The insertion of this quotation is still another attempt, of course, to recuperate in legible language exactly what is omitted, left as a blank, in *A Book from the Sky*. Yet even as the quotation returns us to familiar images of "ruin" and "trauma," the crucial role of tradition in the work has been undercut, displaced by the material introduction of the computer-generated and polymer-imprinted characters. Seamlessly inserted into the installation, these characters corrupt the purity of the traditional means of production so beloved in the West. With the intervention of space-age technology, *A Book from the Sky* was given a new life, a second chance to be free of the "hard and fixed" images that were layered on the surface of the work by endless political, philosophical, and aesthetic interpretations.

Figure 5. Xu Bing. *A Book from the Sky*. Installation at the University Art Museum, State University of New York, Albany. 1996. Photograph by Gary David Gold. © Gary David Gold, 1997.

It is no coincidence that it was at this lightninglike instant of material and conceptual disjuncture that the figure of the modern Chinese intellectual appeared in the quotation to confront the wearying dilemma of Chinese culture and modernity.[68] This is the point, after all, from which the work began, and it seems that in Albany, *A Book from the Sky* turned briefly back to a moment in Beijing, when its conception offered nothing more than a utopic space without questions or answers.

Notes

Writing this essay would not have been possible without the cooperation and support of Xu Bing. Parts have been presented at the College Art Association Annual Meeting, Boston, February 1996 (thanks to Richard Powell), and the workshop, "Gender, Visuality, Modernity in Twentieth-Century China," University of Pittsburgh, September 1997 (thanks to Kathy Linduff and Sheldon Lu). The essay has greatly benefited from the comments of Kristine Stiles, Terry Smith, Rey Chow, and Margaret Hattori. Jonathan Arac changed the shape of the essay by raising challenging questions regarding aesthetics, the sublime, and the work of art as "critical." A fortuitous meeting with Marie Aquilino introduced me to Louis Marin's *Utopics*. And special thanks to Yue Gang for urging me to open a space for the utopian in my reading of *A Book from the Sky*. The essay is dedicated to Alice Yang, whom I did not know but whose memory, I hope, is carried in these pages.

1   Richard Curt Kraus, *Brushes with Power* (Berkeley: University of California Press, 1991), 9, citing Yang Buwei, *Yige nüren de zizhuan* (Changsha: Yuelu Shushe, 1987), 63 and 32–33.

2   Thanks to Dorothy Ko for first suggesting the relevance of *nüshu*. For a full-length study of *nüshu* in English, see William Wei Chiang, *"We Two Know the Script; We Have Become Good Friends": Linguistic and Social Aspects of the Women's Script Literacy in Southern Hunan, China* (Lanham, Md.: University Press of America, 1995).

3   Chao Pu-wei Yang, *How to Cook and Eat in Chinese* (New York: John Day, 1945).

4   Kraus, *Brushes with Power,* 9, citing Yang Buwei, *Yige nüren,* 394.

5   Alice Yang, "Xu Bing: Rewriting Culture" (essay for the exhibition of *A Book from the Sky,* University Museum, State University of New York, Albany, 1996), 3.

6   Jonathan Goodman, "Bing Xu: 4,000 Characters in Search of a Meaning," *Art News* 93 (1994): 100.

7   Louis Marin, *Utopics: Spatial Play,* trans. Robert A. Vollrath (Atlantic Highlands, N.J.: Humanities Press, 1984), 9.

8   See, for example, the front-page coverage of the two artists in *Zhongguo meishu bao* 46 (1988): 1.

9   Reviewed in Hang Jian and Chao Xiao'eo, "Zhongguo xiandai yishuzhan ceji" (Record of visiting the exhibition China/Avant-Garde), *Meishu,* no. 4 (April 1989): 5–9.

10 In addition to the references in notes 6 and 7, see " 'Xu Bing xianxiang' yifen-

fen" (Talking about 'Xu Bing phenomenon'), *Meishu,* no. 1 (1989): 20–22; Fan Di'an, "Zhuiqiu yongheng—Xu Bing chuangzuo xiansuo tanxun" (Seeking eternity—Xu Bing's art road), *Meishu yanjiu* 1 (1989) 37–40; Yi Ying, "Xiandai zhuyi de kunjing yu women de xuanze" (The difficult position of modernism and our choices), *Meishu,* no. 4 (1989): 10–13.

11 *A Book from the Sky,* complete or in part, has been exhibited at the National Fine Arts Museum, Beijing, 1988 and 1989; Lung Men Art Gallery, Taipei, 1990; Tokyo Gallery, Tokyo, 1991; Elvehjem Museum of Art, Madison, Wisconsin, 1991; North Dakota Museum of Art, Grand Forks, 1992; as part of *Post-Mao Product: New Art from China,* an exhibition that toured the eastern states of Australia from September 1992 to June 1993; Bellefroid, Paris, 1993; Venice Biennale, 1993; Museo Nacional Centro de Arte Reina Sofia, Madrid, Spain, 1994; Centro de Arte Santa Mónica, Barcelona, 1995; Massachusetts College of Art, Boston, 1995; Queensland Art Museum, Brisbane, 1996; University Art Museum, State University of New York, Albany, 1996; Institute of Contemporary Art, London, 1997; Sonje Museum of Contemporary Art, Kyunju, South Korea, 1996; Prague Castle, 1997.

  In 1998, the work is scheduled for the Guggenheim Museum, New York; the Museum of Far Eastern Antiquities, Stockholm, Sweden; P.S. 1, New York; the Museum of Modern Art, San Francisco; and the National Gallery of Canada, Ottawa.

12 For a discussion of three contemporary museum exhibitions of China, including *A Book from the Sky,* see my "Exhibiting China," in *The Present, and the Discipline of Art History in Japan,* proceedings of the Twenty-First International Symposium on the Preservation of Cultural Property (Tokyo: Tokyo National Research Institute of Cultural Properties, forthcoming).

13 For a primarily quantitative study, see Yan Ma, "A Reader-Response Analysis of *A Book from the Sky*—A Postmodern Educational Enterprise" (Ph.D. diss., University of Wisconsin, Madison, 1993); and Yan Ma, "Reader-Response Theory: An Analysis of a Work of Chinese Post Modern Art," *Journal of Visual Literacy* 15, no. 1 (spring 1995): 39–72.

14 For the sublime and its architectonic materiality, in the Kantian sense, see Paul de Man, "Phenomenality and Materiality in Kant," in *Aesthetic Ideology* (Minneapolis: University of Minnesota Press, 1996), 70–90. Thanks to Jonathan Arac for the reference to de Man. For a discussion of *A Book from the Sky* and its emphasis on visual effect, see Michael Peterson, "A Book that Resists Reading: The Enormous Signs of Xu Bing," *Fine Art Magazine* (January 1992): n.p.

15 For the formative texts and their continued recirculation, see Ernest F. Fenollosa, *The Chinese Written Character as a Medium for Poetry,* ed. Ezra Pound (San Francisco, Calif.: City Lights Books, 1936); Jacques Derrida, *Of Grammatology,* trans. Gayatri Chakravorty Spivak (Baltimore, Md.: Johns Hopkins University Press, 1976); Zhang Longxi, *The Tao and the Logos: Literary Hermeneutics, East and*

West (Durham, N.C.: Duke University Press, 1992); Zhaoming Qian, *Orientalism and Modernism: The Legacy of China in Pound and Williams* (Durham, N.C.: Duke University Press, 1995).

16   For example, see George Kennedy, "Fenollosa, Pound, and the Chinese Character," *Yale Literary Magazine* 126 (1958): 24–36; Hwa Yol Jung, "Misreading the Ideogram: From Fenollosa to Derrida and McLuhan," *Paideuma* 13, no. 2 (fall 1984): 211–27; Guiyou Huang, "Ezra Pound: (Mis)Translation and (Re-)Creation," *Paideuma* 22, nos. 1–2 (spring–fall 1993): 99–114; Jiewei Cheng, "Derrida and Ideographic Poetics," *British Journal of Aesthetics* 35, no. 2 (April 1995): 134–44.

17   Xiaomei Chen, " 'Misunderstanding' Western Modernism: The *Menglong* Movement in Post-Mao China," *Representations* 35 (summer 1991): 143–63; Xiaomei Chen, "Rediscovering Ezra Pound: A Post-Postcolonial 'Misreading' of a Western Legacy," *Paideuma* 23 (fall–winter 1994): 81–106.

18   Gao Minglu, "Meaninglessness and Confrontation in Xu Bing's Art," in *Fragmented Memory: The Chinese Avant-Garde in Exile,* ed. Julia F. Andrews and Gao Minglu (Columbus: Wexner Center for the Arts, Ohio State University, 1993), 28–31.

19   Janelle S. Taylor, "Non-Sense in Context: Xu Bing's Art and Its Publics," *Public Culture* 5, no. 2 (winter 1993): 324.

20   Britta Erickson, "Process and Meaning in the Art of Xu Bing," in *Three Installations* (Madison, Wisc.: Elvehjem Museum of Art, 1992), 15; Wu Hung, "A 'Ghost Rebellion': Notes on Xu Bing's 'Nonsense Writing' and Other Works," *Public Culture* 6, no. 2 (winter 1994): 411; and Eugene Yuejin Wang, "Of Text and Texture: The Cultural Relevance of Xu Bing's Art," in *Language Lost* (Boston: Massachusetts College of Art, 1995), 10.

21   Erickson, "Process and Meaning," 15.

22   Erickson, "Process and Meaning," 15; and Eugene Yuejin Wang, "Of Text and Texture," 10.

23   Wu Hung, " 'Ghost Rebellion,' " 411.

24   Yang Chengyin, " 'Xin chao' meishu lun gang" (A discussion of the main principles of "New Wave" fine arts), *Wenyi bao,* 2 June 1990, 5.

25   The work as a mirror is emphasized in Wu Hung, " 'Ghost Rebellion,' " 411.

26   See, for example, Ina Pasch, "Chinese Printmaker's Work Illustrates Futility," *Wisconsin State Journal,* 8 December 1991, Showcase section, 1I.

27   See Erickson, "Process and Meaning," 11, 15; and Yang Chengyin, " 'Xin chao.' "

28   It should be noted that intense displeasure with the New Wave had been expressed for a number of years and that, indeed, Xu was a target for attack as early as December 1989. See John Clark, "Official Reactions to Modern Art in China Since the Beijing Massacre," *Pacific Affairs* 65, no. 3 (fall 1992): 334–52.

29   Du Jian, "Dui 'Xin chao' meishu lun gang de yijiang" (A discussion of the main principles of the "New Wave" of fine arts), *Wenyi bao,* 29 December 1990, 5.

30 This work was exhibited along with *A Book from the Sky* at the Elvehjem Museum.

31 For example, Xu organized and produced a performance/installation in Beijing in January 1994 entitled *A Case Study of Transference*, which featured two pigs mating in a pen filled with books of invented characters.

32 This is emphasized in Kay Ann Johnson, "The Revolutionary Tradition of Pro-Democracy Students," *Radical America* 22, no. 4 (July–August 1988): 7–12; see also "Documents from the Chinese Democratic Movement," *Radical America* 22, no. 4 (July–August 1988): 13–21. Despite the publication dates, these articles were written soon after the 4 June 1989 events.

33 Erickson, "Process and Meaning," 12; my emphasis.

34 Laurel Reuter, "Into the Dark Sings the Nightingale: The Work of Xu Bing," in *Xu Bing* (Grand Forks: North Dakota Museum of Art, 1992), n.p.; my emphasis.

35 This is reminiscent of the racial stereotype Homi K. Bhabha describes in "The Other Question: The Stereotype and Colonial Discourse," *Screen* 24, no. 6 (1983): 18.

36 Robert W. Drexler, "The Canton War," *American History* 32, no. 1 (April 1997): 42.

37 Helms hosted and embraced the Dalai Lama at Helms's North Carolina alma mater, Wingate University, in 1995. See feature photo and article by Yonat Shimron, "Karma Can Make Strange Bedfellows," *News and Observer* (Raleigh, N.C.), 6 September 1995, A1.

38 An important corrective, though not without its own controversial issues, is the documentary film *The Gate of Heavenly Peace* (Brookline, Mass.: Long Bow Group, 1996).

39 See, for example, Xu's statement in Taylor, "Non-Sense," 324. He was uncharacteristically direct in agreeing that the work was a political critique in Christina Davidson, "Words from Heaven," *Art and AsiaPacific* 1, no. 2 (April 1994): 52.

40 Li Qun, "Dui yu 'Xin chao' meishu zhi wo jian: Jiu shang yu Du Jian tongzhi" (My opinions of "New Wave" fine arts: A discussion with comrade Du Jian), *Wenyi bao*, 30 March 1991, 6.

41 Eugene Yuejin Wang, "Of Text and Texture," 13.

42 Wu Hung, " 'Ghost Rebellion,' " 417.

43 Reuter, "Into the Dark," 4.

44 Jonathan Hay, "Ambivalent Icons," *Orientations* 23, no. 7 (July 1992): 38.

45 Parallel examples are reiterated in popular conceptions of Chinese painting and cinema as grounded in Chan Buddhism, the Dao, or other Oriental philosophies. See, for example, Linda C. Ehrlich and David Desser, eds., *Cinematic Landscapes: Observations on the Visual Arts and Cinema of China and Japan* (Austin: University of Texas Press, 1994).

46 Xu Bing, "Sight, Text, Vision" (paper presented at Duke University, Durham, N.C., 6 November 1995).

47 Erickson, "Process and Meaning," 12.

48 Jonathan Arac, discussant's remarks, "Gender, Visuality, Modernity in Twentieth-Century China" workshop, University of Pittsburgh, Pittsburgh, Pa., 13 September 1997.

49 David E. Mungello, *Curious Land: Jesuit Accommodation and the Origins of Sinology* (Stuttgart, Germany: F. Steiner Verlag Wiesbaden, 1985), 34, 174–207.

50 Derrida, *Of Grammatology*, 80.

51 A spectacular example of the visual allure of Chinese writing can be found on the cover of the paperback version of Derrida's *Of Grammatology*. Interestingly, the publisher, Johns Hopkins University Press, is unable to identify the source of the image.

52 Eugene Yuejin Wang, "Of Text and Texture," 15.

53 One exception is Peterson, "Book that Resists Reading": "[*A Book from the Sky*] is a challenge not only to ancient Chinese writing, the contemporary Chinese art establishment, or the state power of the People's Republic, but also of the discourses of Western art criticism, the 'free communication' of Western democracies, and the meanings encoded in capitalist systems of exchange."

54 Han-Shan Tang, List 82 (June 1997), available from http://www.hanshan.com/.

55 The "Fortune Cookies" series took two years to plan and was coordinated with the 1 July return of Hong Kong to China. Three works by Xu were exhibited from 24–26 May 1997: *A Book from the Sky*, *Square Word*, and a video of *A Case of Transference*. See the Web site of the Institute of Contemporary Art, available from http://www.illumin.co.uk/ica/Bulletin/livearts/fortunecookies/index.html.

56 Goodman, "Bing Xu," 101.

57 Sheldon Hsiao-peng Lu outlines this trajectory in "Art, Culture, and Cultural Criticism in Post-New China," *New Literary History* 28, no. 1 (winter 1997): 111–24.

58 Han-Shan Tang Books, List 82 (June 1997), available from http://www.hanshan.com/x1.html#XUoTS2.

59 Charles Stone, "Xu Bing and the Printed Word," *Public Culture* 6, no. 2 (winter 1994): 407.

60 Wu Hung, " 'Ghost Rebellion,' " 417. The subject of nonstandard Chinese characters is complex and would need to include ancient mistakes that became canonical (see Bai Qianshen, "The Irony of Copying the Elite: A Preliminary Study of the Poetry, Calligraphy, and Painting on 17th-Century Jindezhen Porcelain," *Oriental Art* 41, no. 3 [autumn 1995]: 10–21) and contemporary invented orthographies, such as the previously mentioned *nüshu*.

61 Stone, "Xu Bing," 410.

62 Marin, *Utopics*, 7.

63 Erickson, "Process and Meaning," 11.

64 For a critique of the denial of coevalness in the construction of the other, see Johannes Fabian, *Time and the Other* (New York: Columbia University Press, 1983), 31. For the continued operation of the traditional/modern binary, see

Jonathan Spence, *The Search for Modern China* (New York: W. W. Norton and Co., 1990), and the critical review by Arif Dirlik, "Sisyphus in China," *Transition* 55 (1992): 94–104.

65 Xu Bing, "Looking for Something Different in a Quiet Place," *Beijing qingnian bao,* 10 February 1989, as translated by and quoted in Wu Hung, " 'Ghost Rebellion,' " 418.

66 These details were provided by Zheng Hu, exhibition designer at the University Museum and curator of the installation, in a personal communication, 27 October 1997.

67 Rey Chow, *Writing Diaspora* (Bloomington: Indiana University Press, 1993), 74. Quoted in Peg Churchill Wright, "Xu Bing Art Reveals Persistence of Spirit," *Daily Gazette* (Albany), 1 February 1996, Arts and Entertainment section, 1. Also reproduced on the Web page of the exhibition, available from http://www.albany.edu/museum/www.museum/xb/subing2.html.

68 One might argue that the difference in the Albany installation is also in part due to the Chinese backgrounds of the curator of the exhibition, Zheng Hu, and the author of the never-published catalog, Alice Yang, but this fact is both relevant and inadequate.

International Theory and the Transnational Critic:

China in the Age of Multiculturalism

Michelle Yeh

I begin with the ongoing debate in the field of comparative literature as a point of departure for reflecting on the current state of Chinese literary and cultural studies. There are several reasons for doing this. First, by definition, comparative literature crosses many boundaries—linguistic, national, and cultural, to name only the most obvious ones—therefore, the transnational and transcultural thrust of comparative literature makes it a logical site for discussions on multiculturalism. Second, as a modern Western discipline, comparative literature has exerted a significant influence on Chinese literary studies for decades. Quite a few scholars in the latter field in North America and Europe are trained in comparative literature and play a major role in the introduction of contemporary theory and practice, including multiculturalism, to Chinese audiences. Finally, comparative literature distinguishes itself from other kinds of literary studies by its comparative perspectives, and these perspectives, as I hope to show by the end of this essay, are urgently called for both in the practice of multiculturalism in general and in Chinese literary and cultural studies in particular.

The above-mentioned debate in the field of comparative literature in the United States is effectively summarized in *Comparative Literature in the Age of Multiculturalism,* which centers around the report that Charles Bernheimer was commissioned to write for the American Comparative Literature Association in 1992. The final report, entitled "Report on the State of the Discipline," recognizes, as well as endorses, the expansion of the field to include multiculturalism and cultural studies. In addition, the collection includes three responses to the report that were originally presented on a panel at the 1993 MLA Annual Convention, plus thirteen position papers solicited from a diverse group of scholars who address the pros and cons of the report's recommendations.[1]

The viewpoints presented in *Comparative Literature in the Age of Multiculturalism* are too diverse and rich to be adequately summarized here.[2] Suffice it to say that despite the highly polarized positions, the contributors all agree that comparative literature is at a crossroads, and for quite a few contributors, it is a discipline in crisis. Regardless of whether one is for or against the recommendations of the Bernheimer report, the irony remains that expanding comparative literature in the directions of multiculturalism and cultural studies may well be self-deconstructing and exacerbates rather than resolves the current crisis, for if what distinguishes comparative literature from studies of national literatures are multilingual/multicultural knowledge and comparative perspectives, these two interrelated dimensions, instead of being maintained and strengthened, seem to be disappearing in the process of broadening the field.

It is not the aim of this essay to take part in the debate. What I am interested in are the different implications of multiculturalism when viewed from a non-Western perspective. Primarily a Euramerican vision, multiculturalism now enjoys a global currency and has, in fact, become a buzzword in many parts of the world. For instance, the popularization of the term coincides with the opening of China and the democratization of Taiwan in the 1980s-1990s. Although multiculturalism as it is used in the Anglo-American context may not be familiar to Chinese intellectuals, the respective claim that China and Taiwan are culturally "diverse" (*duoyuan*) societies is so often repeated that it has become a cliché.

On the surface, multiculturalism seems to be the logical extension of comparative literature; after all, in its critique of Eurocentrism, defense of cultures that are traditionally marginalized, and advocacy of diversity and equal respect for all cultures, multiculturalism forcefully articulates the ideal of comparative literature. However, in practice, it is fraught with limitations and contradictions. In her essay, "In the Name of Comparative Literature," included in the Bernheimer volume, Rey Chow points out that while multiculturalism seeks to correct Eurocentrism, the multicultural revision of the curriculum "is precisely the problem . . . because the teaching of, say, Arabic, Hindi, Japanese, Chinese and so forth already has an institutional history in this country" and "our Eurocentric multilingual comparatists have always had their counterparts in the great Orientalists, Sinologists, Indologists, and so on."[3] Paradoxically, without a prior awareness and critique of the Orientalism underscoring the institution of non-

Western studies in the West, multiculturalism helps to reinstate rather than dismantle Eurocentrism.

The case in point is not unlike that of "world literature" in an earlier era. Despite its founding principle of equality of all national literatures on the face of the earth, "world literature," according to Andrew F. Jones, only creates "cultural ghettos" to which non-Western or "minor" literatures are relegated; "the walls around this 'cultural ghetto' [of 'Chinese literature'] were set (and continue to be held) in place by the very entity — 'world literature' — that was supposed to tear them down." [4] It is not surprising, then, to find similar politics of representation in "world literature" and multiculturalism.

Both Chow and Jones direct their attention to Orientalism, which is still prevalent in the West — whether it is found in the institution of the academy or the cultural marketplace. What they do not concern themselves with is the other side of Orientalism: What happens when multiculturalism travels to the non-West? How does it manifest itself in the 1990s? If Western institutions are the culprit for not bringing about true multiculturalism, will we solve the problem by allowing the marginalized to speak for themselves? To answer this question, we need first to understand the impulse behind multiculturalism.

In his recent review article on why multiculturalism appeals to the Americans, K. Anthony Appiah suggests that there is "a connection between the thinning of the cultural content of identities and the rising stridency of their [various cultural groups'] claims." The middle-class descendants of European immigrants, in Appiah's view, "are discomfited by a sense that their identities are shallow by comparison with those of their grandparents; and some of them fear that unless the rest of us acknowledge the importance of their difference, there soon won't be anything worth acknowledging." [5] American multiculturalism, in other words, is symptomatic of an increasing insecurity about self-identity, an anxiety over the submergence of difference in sameness. Insofar as American society becomes more and more homogenized, there is a greater, conscious or unconscious, need to assert difference, which, in turn, gives the assurance of individuality and multiplicity.

One may argue that it is power rather than self-identity that drives multiculturalist agendas. However, the two are opposite sides of the same coin, in that a common impulse is expressed in two spheres, the political and the cultural, and they are mutually enhancing. The implications of Appiah's remark go beyond the American context. Not only the United States but the world as a whole is reaching an unprecedented degree of homogeneity at the end of the millennium. The "global village" that Marshall McLuhan advanced in the 1960s has already become a reality, not only economically and politically but also culturally. If in the 1950s-1960s Western Europe expressed concern about losing its identity to the "Coca-Cola culture," the time-space compression that David Harvey talks about has since made societies more and more alike in many ways. Cultural globalization is most observable at the popular level—for example, "McDonaldization," rock and roll, Hollywood films, media and sports celebrities, designer brands of clothing and accessories, and the like. What is less obvious, at least for the public, however, is that globalization is also taking place in intellectual circles in many parts of the world. If consumers in China or Taiwan are willing to pay several times more for a Mercedes or a Cadillac than what these cars cost in Germany or the United States, a similar phenomenon can be seen among contemporary Chinese intellectuals who are keen on the latest trends in Anglo-European theory. If, according to Mary Louise Pratt, globalization is one of the three historical processes, along with democratization and decolonization, that are changing the way we study literature and culture, it manifests itself first and foremost in critical theory.[6]

In the past two decades or so, critical theory, especially as it originates and is popularized and institutionalized in the Anglo-American world, has spread internationally, enjoying a prestige in the non-West that is unprecedented. Many of the publications in the field of Chinese literary and cultural studies today use theory, often in an extensive and overt fashion, and most tend to be applications of theory to the interpretation of a wide range of Chinese texts (broadly defined). This is a phenomenon common in literary and cultural studies in the West, of course. After all, Western theory has become international in its reception and influence.

When we compare this kind of reception of Western theory among Chinese scholars in the 1990s with the 1970s, the main difference lies in the ubiquity and unchallenged authority of Western theory at the present time. For example, when New Criticism was introduced to Taiwan in the late 1960s and early 1970s, it was clearly based in English or foreign language and literature departments. It was the faculty in those departments that comprised its principal translators, promoters, and practitioners. New Criticism was perceived as a distinctly Western theory and methodology, and was met with much opposition, or simply indifference, from departments of Chinese literature. Questions about the applicability of Western theory to the study of Chinese literature vexed its proponents no less than its opponents. When a professor of English at the National Taiwan University suggested in a close reading that the image of the dripping candle in a classical Chinese love poem was a phallic symbol, he was publicly rebuffed by a leading authority on traditional Chinese poetry.[7] Anecdotes like this suggest the great divide between English and Chinese literary scholars in Taiwan in particular, and the tension between Western theory and Chinese studies in general.

Much has changed, however, in the past two decades. In Taiwan, a wide range of Western theory is commonly practiced across departmental and disciplinary lines, by scholars in Chinese and Western literatures, humanities, and social sciences alike. A few publications from the 1980s suffice to show the widespread impact of Western theory in Taiwan: Zhou Ying-xiong's *Structuralism and Chinese Literature* (*Jiegou zhuyi yu Zhongguo wenxue*); William Tay's edited volume *Phenomenology and Literary Criticism* (*Xianxiangxue yu wenxue piping*), which also includes deconstruction; Liao Binghui's *Deconstructive Criticism* (*Jiegou piping*); Cai Yuanhuang's *From Romanticism to Postmodernism* (*Cong langman zhuyi dao houxiandai zhuyi*); and Lo Qing's *What Is Postmodernism?* (*Shenme shi houxiandai zhuyi?*).

Across the Taiwan Strait, the situation differs only in the degree of compression of time. Since the opening of China in the late 1970s, scholars have been extremely receptive to Western theory. If 1985 was dubbed "the Year of Methodology" (*Fangfa nian*), by 1988, younger intellectuals in China had turned to "Foucault, Derrida and Lacan as their heroes and were engaged in the deconstruction of 'Truth.'"[8] As Zhang Longxi summarized the situation a few years later in "Western Theory and Chinese Reality," "After the Cultural Revolution, Western theory of all kinds—from formalism, New Criticism, and structuralism, to hermeneutics, reception theory, deconstruction, as well as feminism and Western Marxism—generated a great deal of attention and enthusiasm among Chinese scholars and students of literature. In a short span of five or six years, roughly fifty or sixty years' worth of Western theories were introduced to Chinese readers."[9]

Knowledge of Western theory is not only acquired through reading but also through direct contact with theorists. While a sizable number of Chinese students major in literary and cultural studies in North America and Europe, quite a few theorists from the West have visited Taiwan, Hong Kong, and mainland China in the past two decades. The luminaries include Ihab Hassan, Susan Sontag, Fredric Jameson, Terry Eagleton, Charles

Taylor, Tzvetan Todorov, Richard Rorty, J. Hillis Miller, Murray Krieger, Trinh T. Minh-ha, Gayatri Spivak, Umberto Eco, Jonathan Arac, Stuart Hall, and the list goes on. Leading journals and book reviews in Chinese devote generous space to Western theory—in the form of translations, introductions, interviews, and the like—and its applications to Chinese literature and culture.

For instance, the table of contents of *Con-Temporary* (*Dangdai*), a leading humanities and social sciences journal founded in Taiwan in 1986 by Tu Wei-ming of Harvard University, lists (in chronological order) special issues on Foucault, Derrida, feminism, neo-Marxism, Heidegger, Althusser, Benjamin, Baudrillard, Bourdieu, Lacan, and Jameson. The focus on contemporary theory finds another telling example in *Chung-wai Literary Monthly* (*Zhongwai wenxue*), published by the Department of Foreign Languages and Literatures of National Taiwan University. Founded in 1972, it was the stronghold of New Criticism in the 1970s but in recent years has featured deconstruction, postcolonialism, French feminism, psychoanalysis, chaos theory, Rorty, queer theory, and so on. Nowadays, reputable scholarly journals in Chinese don't look much different from their North American counterparts in terms of the range of theories used but differ mainly in the literary and cultural texts under analysis. If there were strong reservations about, and resistance to, Western theory in Chinese studies in the 1970s, by the 1990s, Western theory has come to occupy a uniquely privileged position in Chinese intellectual circles.

However, it is important to qualify the above remarks by pointing out that, strictly speaking, contemporary theory should no longer be labeled as "Western"—that is, Anglo-European—especially in the cases of postcolonial and feminist theories, to which critics of diverse ethnic and cultural origins have made important contributions. Edward Said, Homi Bhabha, Partha Chatterjee, Appiah, Chow, Trinh, and Spivak are only a few of those we might name. They represent a growing number of critics in the West who come from bicultural or multicultural backgrounds that significantly shape their theoretical perspectives and account for the contributions they are able to make. However, scholars in Chinese literary and cultural studies generally make no distinction between those who come from non-Western backgrounds but achieve distinction in the West and Anglo-European critics. Both groups are categorized as Western. In other words, when critical theory, as mediated by scholars in the West, is used by the Chinese, it almost always takes place in a dualistic framework of "East versus West" (*Dong/Xi*) or "China versus the West" (*Zhong/Xi*). The lack of precise differentiation is not due to ignorance but is noteworthy because it is embedded in a particular cultural psychology, which will be the focus of the ensuing discussion.

If contemporary theory can be regarded as a cultural sign, then its role must be defined in relation to other signs in the semiotic system, which in this case is China. It is understandable, and even predictable, that in China, a cultural system vastly different from that of the United States, France, or Germany, theory plays a different role and has a different function. Or, to use another analogy, we may find a parallel between popular culture and theory in China. Although the globalization of theory can be seen as part and parcel of the cultural globalization (of which Americanization is a major element) I mentioned earlier, its consumption inevitably displays local variations that serve local agendas. Rather than seeing China as a passive consumer of Western theory, we may ask how Western theory is appropriated for Chinese purposes.

"What can and does Western theory do in the cultural and political environment of China?" When Zhang Longxi posed this question in 1992, his answer was wholly positive: "All theories willy-nilly found themselves to be both foreign and Western and thereby acquired an oppositional status with radically subversive implications."[10] The government clearly recognized the subversive implications of Western theory and sought to contain its influence, as was evident in such nationwide political campaigns against intellectuals, known as the Anti-Spiritual Pollution Campaign of 1983–1984 and the Anti-Bourgeois Liberalization Campaign of 1987. In a more systematic analysis, Chen Xiaomei defines *Occidentalism* as the Chinese discursive construction of the West, which is "marked by a particular combination of the Western construction of China with the Chinese construction of the West."[11] She distinguishes two types of Occidentalism: the "official Occidentalism" of the state for the purpose of "supporting a nationalism that effects the internal suppression of its own people"; and the "anti-official Occidentalism," which uses "the Western Other as a metaphor for political liberation against ideological oppression within a totalitarian society."[12] Whether the West is understood or misunderstood by Chinese intellectuals is beside the point, Chen suggests, since either way it contributes to the construction of an emancipatory Occidentalist discourse in post-Mao China.

Both Zhang and Chen highlight the positive, subversive import of Chinese appropriations of Western theory in the 1980s. How has critical theory fared as an oppositional discourse in China into the 1990s? It seems that the tables have turned. Although the oppositional edge of theory remains, it is aimed not at the establishment in China but at the West. Sheldon Hsiao-peng Lu observes that the booming Third World criticism in China is the latest manifestation of resistance to the West's cultural and discursive hege-mony. As such, "Third-World criticism empowers the nativist, indigenous critic vis-à-vis the domination of Western theory and culture."[13] The ap-peal of postcolonial theory to Chinese critics is understandable, just as it is in the cases of decolonized nations around the world. However, as many critics (for example, Bhabha, Chatterjee, and Sara Suleri) have pointed out, postcolonialism should not stop at being "a theory of blame" but must take an equally critical look at the complex, ambivalent relationship between the colonizer and the colonized. When postcolonial theory is applied to Chinese contexts, does it go beyond "resistance to the West's cultural and discursive hegemony"? This is the question raised in essays by Zhao Yiheng (Henry Yiheng Zhao) and Xu Ben, both of whom answered with a resound-ing "no."

Zhao's essay, "Post-Isms and Chinese Neo-Conservatism," and Xu's es-say, " 'Third-World Criticism' in Contemporary China," appeared in the February 1995 issue of *Twenty-First Century* (*Ershiyi shiji*), a Chinese-language journal published in Hong Kong. For two years, in subsequent issues of *Twenty-First Century* and elsewhere, the essays drew strong re-sponses from scholars both in and outside China. What started out as a cri-tique of Chinese appropriations of Western theory in the 1990s has turned into a full-scale debate.[14]

Zhao's main argument is that radical Western theory — subsumed under the term *post-isms* to include poststructuralism, postmodernism, and post-colonialism — is appropriated by Chinese intellectuals for conservative pur-poses in the 1990s. He cites four examples to substantiate his point of view: (1) the backlash on the iconoclastic May Fourth movement and the simi-larly critical Cultural Self-Reflection movement of the 1980s; (2) the total-istic negation of modern Chinese poetry written in the vernacular and the call for a revival of classical Chinese by the veteran poet Zheng Min; (3) the Marxist critique of de-ideologization of literature and literary criticism in the 1980s by Liu Kang; and (4) the emergence of "New National Learn-ing." In his conclusion, Zhao argues that Western theory should not be used simply to critique the West, but it should also critique "the institutional cul-ture (official culture, popular culture, and nationalist culture)" in China. The essay ends on a sarcastic note: "Whenever we [Chinese intellectuals] compete with the whole world on being 'radical,' the conservative genes of our culture become active."[15] Although ostensibly radical, the Chinese intellectuals under discussion are actually conservative in that their appropriations of "radical" Western theory implicitly or explicitly defend the status quo in China.

The "taming" of critical theory in China is spelled out more clearly in Xu's essay, which begins by noting that Third World criticism has been the most popular theory in China since 1990. However, in contrast to its practice in such Third World countries as India, where postcolonialism also critiques the complicity between nationalism and colonial discourse, the Chinese version of Third World criticism focuses on the oppression of China by the West as a means of "evading, knowingly or not, the violence and oppression that exist in . . . indigenous society." Avoiding any analysis or critique of official nationalism, postcolonial theorizing in China has only an "international dimension" but no "domestic dimension." Xu concludes that there do not exist as yet the sociopolitical conditions necessary for truly oppositional cultural critique in China. Expressing sympathy for his peers in China who choose "low-risk" or "no-risk" topics, he concludes that "the real oppression of Third World criticism does not come from knowledge relations with the outside world . . . but from the social and cultural structures within."[16]

Although I do not completely agree with their interpretations, Xu's and Zhao's essays raise some provocative questions. Why do some theories appeal to Chinese critics more than others? Is it a historical accident, a reflection of access (for example, translation), a choice based on intellectual affinity, or a reflection of contemporary cultural politics? Most likely there are no definitive answers to these questions, and it may well be a combination of some or all of these factors. Both Zhao and Xu suggest that it is no mere chance that postmodernism and postcolonialism are popular in China in the 1990s. If the critique and deconstruction of Western hegemonies define the main thrust of contemporary theory, the two authors discern a complicitous relationship between Chinese intellectuals and the official ideology of the Chinese Communist Party, whether it be described as neoconservatism or nationalism. If in the 1980s the West provided a counterdiscourse against the ruling ideology in China, the situation has reversed. By Chen's definition, the latest phase of Chinese appropriation of Western theory is much closer to the "official Occidentalism" than to the "anti-official Occidentalism."

During the cold war era, a joke circulated in the United States. It went something like this: an American and a Russian were arguing about who had more freedom in their homeland. To prove his point that the United States allowed more freedom, the American guy says, "I can stand in front of the White House and criticize the President of the United States and not get into any trouble. Can you do that in your country?" The Russian guy retorts: "Of course! I, too, can stand in front of the Kremlin and criticize the President of the United States and not get into any trouble."[17]

The joke works because we all know that meaning is relational rather than absolute; it is determinable only in relation to a certain context, a specific frame of reference. While it proves the point of freedom of speech for the American to openly criticize his president in Washington, D.C., for the Russian to criticize the American president in Moscow is wholly conformist and patriotic, given the open rivalry between the two nations during the cold war era. The joke reminds us how crucial it is, when we study cultures other than our own, to understand their practices and representations. It also serves as an analogue to Zhao's and Xu's arguments summarized above. When Western theory is transported to the Chinese context (that is, China in the 1990s), its cultural significance undergoes a transformation and takes on new meanings that are not only different from, but even opposite to, the original.

Another irony underscores the foregoing discussion, which derives from the fact that the analytical framework of Zhao and Xu is basically no different from that of Chen and Zhang. All of these critics recognize the primacy of context in transcultural and transnational situations, and all of them focus on the meaning of Western theory in Chinese contexts. The fact that Zhao's and Xu's essays set off a widespread controversy both in and outside China over the latest phase of Chinese appropriations of Western theory is in sharp contrast to the absence of controversy with regard to Chen's and Zhang's studies a few years earlier. The contrast is a telling clue that perhaps the Chinese geopolitical space in the 1990s is significantly different from that in the 1980s. Whereas Zhao suggests that cultural discourses in China are shifting from liberalism to conservatism, Xu interprets the change as indicative of acquiescence on the part of Chinese intellectuals to official ideology, of which nationalism is a pronounced component. Ironically, if nationalism is subject to constant critical scrutiny and deconstruction in contemporary theory in the West, the same theory seems to provide many Chinese intellectuals with a rationale for cultural nationalism.

In a 1994 interview in the state-run journal *Strategy and Management*

(*Zhanlue yu guanli*), Wang Hui repeatedly warns against the "merging" of Western theory and Chinese nationalism: "When [postcolonialism] is transplanted to the unique context of China, it *quite naturally* merges with the indigenous tradition of nationalism." Nationalism, according to Wang, is a conscious cultural choice made by those who are deeply committed to national interests. "Introduced to China in the early 1990s, radical Western theory reinforces the mainstream discourse," namely, "the cultural nationalism of some Chinese intellectuals."[18] Why is it "natural" for Western theory to merge with Chinese nationalism? Or, to put it in a different way, why is Western theory so quickly and easily sinicized?

In recent years, there have been extensive discussions on Chinese nationalism in the transnational scholarly communities of Chinese studies.[19] The phenomenon responds, on the one hand, to the proliferation of Western scholarship on nationalism in recent decades (which is itself a response to global politics), and to the changing situation in contemporary China, on the other. Understandably, on a subject as elusive and complex as nationalism, there is little agreement among scholars, and nationalism itself is seen as a "site of contestation and repression of different views of the nation."[20] The "indigenous tradition of nationalism" that Wang alludes to comprises at least two related strains: cultural sinocentrism (*Huaxia zhongxin zhuyi*) and modern nationalism. Scholars have advanced different views that suggest both continuities and discontinuities between cultural sinocentrism and modern Chinese nationalism, and their changing relationship is often shaped by the particular political need at a particular time. Instead of nationalism, perhaps it is less misleading to refer to Chinese nationalisms. Regardless of the nuanced distinctions between them, there seems to be little doubt that traditional sinocentrism and modern nationalism combine to reinforce nationalistic sentiments among the Chinese both at the popular level and among intellectuals in the 1990s.[21]

Nationalist sentiments are clearly at work when we examine some of the negative responses to Zhao's and Xu's essays. For instance, despite the fact that the "conservative" intellectuals whom Zhao criticizes do not all live in mainland China (for example, Liu Kang teaches at Penn State), Zhang Yiwu, a professor of Chinese literature at Beijing University, calls the two authors Eurocentric and Orientalist because they create "a sharp opposition between overseas and indigenous critics."[22] Zhang rightly points out that the picture drawn by the two authors of the Chinese intellectual scene in the 1990s is far from complete, but his criticism displays a tendency to refute Zhao and Xu not so much for *what* they say as for *who* they are, and to dismiss the former on the basis of the latter. And he is not alone in this in the debate. The fact that both Zhao and Xu are originally from mainland China and received advanced education in the West, where they now live, leads to three assumptions shared by their critics.

First, Zhao and Xu are not familiar with the reality in China today since they have been living abroad for years. Second, their criticism of intellectuals in China suggests that they "identify strongly with the mainstream discourse and ideology of the West."[23] Finally, their complicity with the West is allegedly evident in the following ways: their approach to China as an other to be gazed at, interpreted, and "domesticated"; their negative assessments of indigenous intellectuals; and their "pedagogical" or condescending attitude toward indigenous intellectuals. I would like to examine these assumptions briefly and to show how they all stem from a nationalistic, sinocentric framework that reifies China and the West. In problematizing such a framework, I will then suggest an alternative approach for Chinese literary and cultural studies.

The logic behind the critics' claim that Zhao and Xu are out of touch with Chinese reality *because* they are not based in China is flawed. Granted, it is common sense that just as a native speaker has an advantage over foreigners trying to learn the language, living in the country one studies is an obvious advantage in terms of familiarity with home perspectives and access to information. But familiarity with a culture on an experiential basis and abundant data alone do not account for the quality of scholarship, which also depends on the theoretical framework and methodology that one employs. How valid and comprehensive the theoretical framework is and how rigorous the method of investigation is are more important than experience and data per se. While local experience may help, it cannot take the place of scholarly training and does not equal scholarship.

The fundamental problem with this line of argument is that it exalts local experience as a value in itself. Experience is treated, to borrow Joan W. Scott's words, "as incontestable evidence and as an originary point of explanation—as a foundation upon which analysis is based." Further, the "evidence of experience . . . reif[ies] agency as an inherent attribute of individuals, thus decontextualizing it."[24]

Unfortunately, "evidence of experience" is a fairly common argument among scholars of Chinese ethnicity when they criticize their non-Chinese colleagues for their lack of "Chinese experience." For instance, a recent essay in *Dushu,* the most influential journal among intellectuals in main-land China, claims: "Sinologists can speak Chinese, love to taste Chinese cuisine, and often like to hang in their offices or homes a few scrolls of Chinese calligraphy given by their Chinese friends. But hardly any of them can truly appreciate the 'spiritual rhythm' [*shenyun*] and the 'aura and structure' [*fenggu*] of Chinese calligraphy, because calligraphy requires an understand-ing of the spirit of the culture which flows in blood veins; it is not just an intellectual issue." [25] Statements such as this are not only condescending and grossly generalizing, but, more seriously, they present a circular argument about why non-Chinese sinologists can never "really" understand China. In the example cited above, the circularity of the argument hides behind a highly impressionistic language — *shenyun* and *fenggu* — typical of traditional Chinese poetry and art criticism. It is futile to refute this kind of argument because it cannot be substantiated objectively in the first place.

The emphasis on the uniqueness of Chinese experience — but which culture's experience is not unique? — is inseparable from a defensiveness against any criticism of China coming from those not living in China. To give another example, Lung Yingtai is an influential cultural critic who was born and raised in Taiwan. She received her Ph.D. in English from an Ameri-can institution and has been living in Germany for many years, although she has published extensively in Chinese for more than a decade. After pub-lishing an article entitled "A Bottle Filled with 'China China China' " in the Hong Kong–based *Mingbao Monthly* in 1992, she was inundated with criti-cism from readers in mainland China, as she recounts in an interview: "One typical example [of the criticism she received] was, 'Lung Yingtai, since you have not gone through the suffering that we have, you really have no right to criticize us.' " She proceeds to recall an episode that suggests a cultural attitude:

> "I had many chances to meet with Chinese intellectuals [in Germany] after the June 4 massacre in 1989. In my contacts with them, two im-pressions stood out: . . . I discovered that they were so obsessed with China that they had hardly any interest in the rest of the world. I would take them around, show them Goethe's birthplace or the first parlia-ment of modern Germany or Kafka's home, but they would only talk about China. Secondly, they were very defensive about China. That puzzled me a bit, because at home, these were considered the most liberal, outspoken critics of the culture. Now that they were here out-

side China, all of a sudden they were metamorphosed into apologists for China." [26]

The obsession with Chinese uniqueness and the concomitant defensiveness against criticisms of China, especially when they are *perceived as* coming from "the outside," are clearly seen in the debate in *Twenty-First Century,* where some critics of Zhao and Xu create an artificial polarization of émigré Chinese and intellectuals in China. The polarization privileges the intellectuals in China supposedly because they alone have access to the "real" China. In his response entitled "Beware of Artificial 'Pidgin Scholarship,' " Liu Dong pushes this position to an extreme. Not only does he share the above-mentioned assumption that only someone living in China can truly understand China, but, more significantly, he shifts the context of the discussion from scholarship to cultural identity, from objective criteria to subjective identification. Emphasizing the primacy of "personal experience," he predicates scholarship on "the foundation of cultural identity." Liu's use of the mirror metaphor is revealing. The real China, he claims, can only be reflected in the "mirror" of the indigenous scholar, who fully identifies with China ("from the bottom of his heart") and who has "complete, intuitive command of . . . comprehensive experience" so as to " 'reconstruct' the holistic atmosphere of Chinese culture." Native intellectuals are associated with such positive notions as "truth," "identity," "self-conscious identification," and "original facts about China," while émigré Chinese scholars are described as "deviating . . . from the true path of 'assimilating the West into China' " and forming a "harmful counter-current." Émigré Chinese scholars receive scathing criticism for forgetting their "country of origin" (*guguo*) and losing their Chinese identity. According to Liu, "In the continuous experimental process of 'assimilation of the West into China,' the most wrongful thing is the appearance of the 'marginal person' who finds no home on either side of the Pacific Ocean, in other words, the person who has no cultural identity that can endow him with a scholar's real sense of mission." "Marginal" scholars—read *neither Chinese nor Western*—use their "pidgin scholarship" merely to make a living in the West, "a purely private act." [27]

It is irrelevant to counter Liu's argument by noting that there are mediocre China scholars within China as well as outside China. What underscores his vehement assault is the "myth of authenticity" or, to borrow Kristeva's term, "the cult of origin." China is reified as beyond the understanding of those outside China, both literally and metaphorically speaking, and scholarship is equated with an emotional commitment to, and identification with, China based on personal, experiential involvement. It is interesting to note that the "pedagogical" tone that Zhang criticizes in Zhao's and Xu's essays is ubiquitous in Liu's. Being an "authentic" China scholar, Liu describes himself as "heart-aching and head-sickened" (*tongxin jishou*) when he sees how "marginal" scholars create "chaos" and sell out to the West with their "pidgin scholarship."[28] And it behooves him to distinguish unintentional misunderstanding, which characterizes much of the work of non-Chinese sinologists, from "artificial pidgin scholarship" of émigré Chinese scholars.

At one level, the debate is about self-legitimation. By insisting on the uniqueness of Chinese culture and society—but, again, which culture or society isn't?—and the mystique of China, which is impenetrable not only to non-Chinese but even to émigré Chinese scholars, critics such as Liu establish themselves as the legitimate spokespersons for China. Their defensiveness comes to the fore when their territorial authority is questioned or challenged. The need for self-legitimation also reveals an insecurity about Western theory on the part of intellectuals in China. For if we follow the same logic that is used in the insistent claim that those who do not live in China cannot really know China, then we are inadvertently admitting that those who do not live in the West cannot really know Western theory, which until very recently originates from an exclusively Anglo-European context. The globalization of Western theory heightens rather than lessens the insecurity and its concomitant desire to establish "Chineseness." This explains why critics such as Zhang and Liu identify Zhao and Xu with the West; it also accounts for the popularity among some Chinese intellectuals of theories of "Chinese alternatives" to Western models (such as modernization and postmodernity), which assume the posture of self-assertion in the name of hybridity or pastiche but are, for the most part, lacking in substance.[29]

We see this in Zhang's criticism of Zhao and Xu, where he advocates the "new" postcolonial/postmodern position as one that analyzes the hybridity of contemporary China and promises a "transcendence of the hegemony of theory."[30] But despite his repeated denial of subscribing to the China/West dichotomy, Zhang can only fall back on Chinese experience to mount a superficial critique of Western hegemony. Equally problematic is that his description of Chinese experience and his critique of the Western discourse on modernity offer little that is new in comparison with postcolonial and postmodern theory in the West. The fact that the so-called Chinese alternatives often borrow from the latest Western theory (mainly postcolonialism and postmodernism) further illustrates that the West continues to be *the* point of reference for China's self-positioning. In addition, those who see Chinese alternatives as a way of going beyond the West seem to be unaware that the word *alternative* has long been incorporated into consumer culture in the West, as seen in such terms as *alternative rock* and *alternative lifestyle*; any facile use of the term would carry little critical value. It is beyond the scope of this essay to deal with the full implications of Chinese alternatives; I point it out here to illustrate that China's appropriation of Western theory is in direct proportion to its desire to assert Chineseness; the more prevalent the former is, the stronger the latter seems to become.

This perspective also helps us understand why there is a contradiction in the power hierarchy implicit in the criticisms discussed above. For critics such as Liu, China lies at the center of knowledge, which is disseminated centrifugally, first and foremost to native scholars who have an "intuitive" grasp of the true spirit of Chinese culture and then to those outside China. But according to this mode of thinking, émigré Chinese scholars should be placed in the second circle, outside the innermost one of the natives; after all, they come from China and, generally speaking, have closer personal and cultural ties to China than non-Chinese sinologists. Yet in the prolonged debate in *Twenty-First Century,* they receive the harshest criticism. Although it is true that location alone is not the basis of criticism, when an émigré Chinese scholar criticizes China he or she is criticized for being ill-intentioned, "pedagogical," and complicitous with the West. The reason, I reiterate, is that the real issue here is not scholarship but cultural identity, or, more specifically, Chinese cultural identity, which is perceived as feeble and diluted.

China's identity crisis began with its unequal and asymmetrical encounters with Western imperialists in the second half of the nineteenth century. Faced with the grim possibility of falling under foreign domination, China embarked on a long, tortuous course of self-strengthening that was filled with tension and contradictions. Ying-shih Yü views modern Chinese intellectual history as a continuing "process of rapid radicalization," from interpretation and discovery at the turn of this century to wholesale radicalism from the May Fourth period onward. In the first phase, the Chinese discovery of the West was disguised as a reinterpretation of China behind the theory of "Chinese origins of Western learning." In the second phase, radicalism takes the form of "incessantly seeking to import the latest products in the cultural market from the West," or "neoterism," "a mentality obsessed with change, with what is new." [31]

Yü sees the two phases of radicalization of modern Chinese intellectuals as distinct, but it is not clear why and how one gives rise to and is eventually replaced by the other. I would suggest that they are coexistent and interdependent rather than distinct from each other. Throughout the modern period, radical reform is propelled, above all, by nationalist agendas not only to make China "prosperous and strong" but also to restore China's status as a center of culture comparable to that of leading Western nations. The dilemma that Chinese intellectuals face is this: If to import Western learning enables China to catch up with the West, borrowing it also makes China always one step behind. Thus, as China learns from the West, it is necessary at the same time to emphasize the Chineseness of the undertaking, whether in terms of origin (for example, the assertion that such Western concepts as science, democracy, equality, and liberty already exist in ancient China in their embryonic forms) or result (for example, many Chinese intellectuals' acceptance of the theory of the "Western origin of the Chinese race" at the turn of the century).

Nevertheless, the emphasis on Chineseness does not resolve the dilemma, because, if to reinterpret China in terms of Western values assures Chinese intellectuals that "to learn from the West was also the way to bring China back to the center," [32] what often escapes them is that the China that is thus reinterpreted cannot be the "original," "pristine" China that they think they are upholding. "China" is always already implicated in "the West."

My interpretation finds support in some recent work on China. In his study of Yan Fu, the late Qing reformer and influential translator of Thomas Huxley and Charles Darwin, Theodore Huters argues that Yan's work adumbrates the "essential instability of modern Chinese cultural discourse," where we detect the coexistence of two opposite forces: conservatism and iconoclasm. If Yan's pro-reform writings are underlined by the "uneasy need to find some sort of roots within the Chinese past for his reforms," such a need "was itself rooted in the powerful Western narrative of a progressive history that he found . . . indispensable to the possibility for social change." [33] Huters suggests that any effort on China's part to claim an equal status with the West is invariably accompanied by an assertion of China's fundamental differences, which are nevertheless always already framed in Western terms. If conservatism or nationalism seems diametrically opposed to iconoclasm or Westernization, they are both predicated on Western assumptions about the nation-state, national identity, and civilization.

A similar argument is presented by Lydia H. Liu, who points out that such notions as national identity and Chineseness are themselves products of Western influence in the modern period. "The modern notion of *wenhua* or culture has resulted from the recent history of the East-West encounter that forces the questions of race, evolution, civilization, and national identity upon the attention of native intellectuals." [34] One example is the two National Essence (*guocui*) movements in the late nineteenth and early twentieth centuries, in which the models for the conservative ("national learning") and the progressive ("Western humanism") camps are both derived from the West.

Borrowing Mary Louise Pratt's definition of "contact zone" to refer to the encounter between China and the West, Arif Dirlik points out that the space is not only a "zone of domination" but also a "zone of mediation," of distancing from the society of the self as well as the other. Whereas the Orientalist is " 'Orientalized' himself or herself in the very process of entering the 'Orient,' " the same happens with the "Oriental, . . . whose very contact with the Orientalist culminates in a distancing from native society, where s/he becomes an object of suspicion." [35] I will return to this last point shortly.

The above studies show that at least since the late nineteenth century, discourses on China are inextricable from discourses on the West. Paradoxically, to understand Chineseness is to understand how the West is "translated" into Chinese and vice versa. The contact zone between China and the West in the 1990s is no longer limited, as it was in the early decades of the century, to treaty ports in China or Western domains visited by the Chinese but has greatly expanded as a result of the information revolution and increasing transnational experience. Given China's traumatic encounters with the West and the resultant identity crisis, it is understandable why it is always against the West, as the "preferred Other," [36] that China has sought to define and assert itself, but this tendency has also become the source of the problem. For the identity crisis all too often leads to a quest for cultural identity based on a reification of China versus the West. Although historically Chinese culture has always assimilated foreign (for example, Buddhist and Islamic) elements and Western culture was introduced to China long before the nineteenth century, the dichotomy between China and the West is new in the modern period. For the first time in Chinese history, the "identity space" [37] —to borrow from Jonathan Friedman—in which China defines itself is extensively and irrevocably infiltrated by the West, which is seen as an indomitable other. The insistence that there is an authentic and unique China that cannot be really understood by anyone *perceived as* an outsider reflects a deep-rooted uneasiness with, and distrust of, those who are culturally situated between China and the West. There is a long history of tension between native intellectuals and those who are marginalized because they are in the "contact zone," as in the case of those who study abroad or live in treaty ports in China.[38] In this sense, the debate in *Twenty-First Century* is only a contemporary expression of a century-old problematic.

I recognize the deep and natural need, whether at the individual or collective level, for a sense of belonging; cultural identity is a powerful definition of the existential relation between the subject and the constitution of a meaningful world. I also recognize the difficulty of the identity construction process that China has been going through in the past century and a half. What I question are notions of authenticity based on nationalist, essentializing discourses. To the extent that critics such as Zhang and Liu Dong reify China they also reify the West. It is ironic that while Chinese intellectuals rightly criticize Samuel P. Huntington's "Coming Clash of Civilizations?" for his essentializing views on the Islamic and Confucian civilizations, many are completely oblivious to their own assumptions about China's enduring continuities, articulated in such phrases as "holistic atmosphere of China," "the spirit of the culture," and the like.[39] Inasmuch as they are critical of the civilizational approach when it is adopted by Western intellectuals, they have not avoided the pitfall themselves.

If contemporary theory has taught us anything, it is that China is not an unchanging, homogeneous entity and that Chineseness is a continuing process of self-constitution. To interpret China is always already to construct China discursively. More importantly, theory has also taught us that however "objective" scholarly studies may seem, they often operate with implicit political assumptions. The debate in *Twenty-First Century* reveals some of the recurrent politics of identity construction in modern Chinese history. Chinese intellectuals who have emigrated receive scathing criticism from their native counterparts because they are perceived as situated between China and the West, occupying a position that can be variously described as "neither . . . nor," "both . . . and," and "in-between," a position that potentially challenges the nationalist narrative of authenticity and uniqueness exactly because it does not fit into it neatly.

Having said that, let me clarify that I am not suggesting scholars in China alone reify China or are nationalistic, and that émigré Chinese scholars are automatically exempt from these problems. Far from accepting the polarization of indigenous and émigré critics that has unfortunately persisted in the debate in *Twenty-First Century,* I emphasize, first of all, the historicity of the debate, which reveals the resurfacing of a long-standing anxiety of how to assert Chineseness, an anxiety that is exacerbated in a world of accelerated globalization in the age of multiculturalism. Even as Western theory, with its prestige and critical edge, provides Chinese intellectuals with an effective means of self-empowerment (as is evident in the ascendancy of postmodern and postcolonial theory in China since the early 1990s), ultimately it has to be rejected because of its *perceived* "Westernness" (as seen in Zhang's accusation of Zhao and Xu that they have been co-opted by the West and try to impose Western values on China). The debate under analysis fails to go beyond the dualistic framework that characterizes modern China's quest for cultural identity thus far, predicated as it is on an "authentic" China that is to be defended at all costs. Such nationalistic sentiments are worth our attention because, as Etienne Balibar and Immanuel Wallerstein warn us, every nationalism contains "oppressive potentialities," and the other side of "nationalisms of liberation" are "nationalisms of domination." [40]

Going back to our opening discussion on comparative literature, if Chow cautions us that Eurocentrism finds its mirror image in multiculturalism "in the name of the other," then what I am suggesting is that the other side of Eurocentrism is sinocentrism, and that the other side of Orientalism is cultural nationalism. I do not undervalue how important and, indeed, necessary it is to continue to critique Orientalism wherever it is practiced. I am also well aware of the economic and material inequalities between those of us working in the United States and scholars working in mainland China, which renders the issue of power relations between China and the West even more sensitive. But I believe cultural nationalism cannot be an effective critique of Orientalism because it replicates and perpetuates the latter epistemologically, and, in doing so, it falls short of fully deconstructing the Orientalism without and elides the Orientalism within. If Chinese cultural nationalism appears to be the antithesis of Orientalism, they are coterminous at a deeper level because both operate in a dualistic framework that reifies self and other, Chineseness and Westernness, and both oppress dissenting approaches. This point is demonstrable not only in China but in other non-Western cultures as well. For instance, Tapati Guha-Thakurta's study of Indian art shows how, in the institutionalization of modern Indian art, Orientalism is inseparable from the nationalist discourse that establishes the "Indianness" of Indian art; both "mystify and rarify" the "Indian essence." [41]

In the final analysis, such notions as China and the West must be used with caution and qualification so that they facilitate rather than impede cross-cultural communication and understanding. While critics chastise the West for Orientalizing China, they must not treat the West as an indomitable other by reifying its perennial, fundamental differences from China. If terms such as *Asian values* and *the Asian way* only really make sense in English, as Ian Buruma suggests, the West is all too often similarly perceived by the Chinese as monolithic and undifferentiated. In a 1995 interview, Chen Maiping, a writer-critic from China who teaches at the University of Stockholm, observes, "Concepts such as Asia, Europe, the West, etc., are so large that generalizations easily become misleading. I have noticed, for example, that people in Scandinavia often become irritated if I refer to a certain attitude as typically European. In such cases they often reply that what I speak about is not a European attitude but a French, a German or an English attitude. Europe covers so much." [42] Ironically, when Chinese scholars, whether based in or outside China, claim that non-Chinese sinologists can never really understand China because of their entrenched Eurocentrism or lack of "intuitive" grasp of the Chinese spirit, they show such uncritical confidence in their own knowledge of the West to the extent that they decide peremptorily what the West can and cannot understand.

For anyone who studies the non-West in the West, it is important to be wary of Orientalist assumptions. But there is a delicate balance between studying the non-West in its proper context and privileging the non-West over the West; the latter merely reverses the Orientalist hierarchy and is just as imperialistic as historical Orientalism. Appiah remarks, "The West has no hard edges." It is equally true of China. China has no hard edges; culturally, it is always already "impure." Furthermore, when we speak of China, especially contemporary China, it refers to a complex configuration of transnational and transcultural realities. By *China,* do we mean mainland China or both mainland China and Taiwan? How do we place Hong Kong culturally, which has only recently become part of China again? What about the Chinese diaspora, or "Chinese overseas"? [43] When we speak of twentieth-century Chinese literature, are we referring to works from mainland China or do we also include those from Taiwan, Hong Kong, and Chinese communities around the world where literature in Chinese is written and read? What kind of hierarchy exists, implicitly or not so implicitly, in our study of modern Chinese literature, and why?

When we realize that cultural identity is not an immutable set of beliefs and practices, it is perhaps easier to transcend the limitations of nationalism. Clearly there are differences in linguistic, social, and cultural backgrounds among Chinese scholars all over the world, and they entail different vantage points, strengths, and limitations. We need to work together not only because our different perspectives may well complement and balance each other but also because we all share a pressing responsibility to study Chinese literature and culture across geopolitical boundaries and to resist the temptation of nationalistic, sinocentric premises.

What I am advocating, then, is a transnational identity or positionality that challenges and problematizes the reification of China and the West, inside and outside, native and foreign. China provides an excellent example of theory's ability to travel, often with the transnational critic, who serves as the translator and transmitter between the West, where most contemporary theory originates, and the culture under study. Granted, the existence of transnational critics has always been a given of comparative literature, but the worldwide consciousness of ongoing globalization and growing multicultural awareness have catapulted them into a position that is more prominent and complexified than before. All of us are willy-nilly transnational critics situated between languages, cultures, and nations. By the transnational critic, I am thinking of "the intellectual in exile" that Said describes as "between domains, between forms, between homes, and between languages." I also have in mind Frederick Buell's "new global cosmopolitan," one who evokes and yokes together "two very diverse, even opposed, legacies" and tries to find "a new constitutive, not exclusionary, logic of order." [44] The more we participate in the transnational economy of literary and cultural studies, the more open the field will be, as we tear down old fences and resist, at the same time, erecting new ones, such as the fence of nationalism in the name of multiculturalism.

I think this is where comparative literature has much to offer and is, in fact, urgently needed. What is often lost in the actual practice of multiculturalism and the globalization of theory are comparative perspectives, which, by alerting us to the pitfalls of ethnic or cultural nationalism, bring us closer to a more viable multiculturalism. I fully agree with Andrew Hatfelder that "the nation [has to be read] against both other nations and other forms of 'imagined community.'" In her study of the construction of cultural identities in South China, Helen F. Siu remarks, "If Beijing does not occupy the privileged position as the center of Chinese history, that cultural distance from it does not mean marginality or anomaly, then the entire process of becoming Chinese needs to be seen as involving a much wider range of players and voices." Chow identifies the crux of the issue in her comments on the papers presented at a recent conference, "Cultural Studies: China and the West": "Any discussion of cultural studies and China would be inadequate without some attempt to address—not the well-worn theme of China's relation to the West, but—the scarcely touched issue of China's relation to those whom it deems politically and culturally subordinate. I am referring specifically to Tibet, Taiwan, and Hong Kong, cultures which, despite their own histories, are simply denied identity and validity in the eyes of the People's Republic." [45]

Although the domains that Chow mentions are all "Chinese," to subsume them under such a rubric as "Cultural China" is dangerous so long as it presumes the centrality of mainland China, thus putting a cultural hierarchy firmly in place that is at least potentially repressive. The cultural hegemony that Chow critiques is unfortunately evident in the transnational field of Chinese literary and cultural studies, anywhere from college curricula to scholarly publications having to do with modern China. The absence, in most cases, of Taiwan and Hong Kong is simply taken for granted. To cite two specific examples, despite the increasing attention to popular culture in mainland China, few scholars study it alongside Hong Kong and Taiwan, even though, as Thomas Gold has pointed out, the popular culture of Hong Kong and Taiwan—"Gangtai"—has been a major influence on mainland China and is "corrosive and potentially destabilizing" to the establishment. Another example would be the critique of modern Chinese poetry launched by the poet-critic Zheng Min in 1993–1994. [46] Zheng dismisses modern Chinese poetry in toto on the ground that it severs itself from the linguistic and literary resources of classical Chinese. Her historical survey of modern Chinese poetry encompasses the May Fourth pioneers, the experimental poets of the 1930s–1940s, the bleak poetry scene during the Mao period, and the rejuvenation of poetry in the 1980s–1990s. Nowhere in her discussion, however, does she consider the remarkable artistic innovations in Taiwan and Hong Kong. Regardless of the genre or topic, Hong Kong and Taiwan are simply nonexistent in many literary and cultural studies of modern China.

In many cases, our understanding of China can benefit a great deal from comparative perspectives across geopolitical boundaries. For instance, almost all the critics who participated in the debate in *Twenty-First Century*, regardless of their positions and despite claims to the contrary, operate in a dualistic framework of China versus the West, or indigenous versus overseas, and show little critical awareness of its problematic assumptions. Although it has become common among scholars to study post-Mao literature and culture in terms of the dichotomy of official and unofficial, hegemonic and oppositional, I doubt if the analytic scheme is as viable for the 1990s as it has been in earlier eras. In view of the rapid commercialization, the rise of a vital popular culture, and the gradual formation of a private, civic sphere in mainland China over the past decade, it is conceivable that cultural discourses can no longer be adequately described within this kind of framework, in which such scholars as Zhao, Xu, Chen, and Zhang base their arguments. In her pioneering study of modern fiction in Taiwan, Sung-sheng Yvonne Chang draws on Raymond Williams's work on hegemony to develop a tripartite paradigm for studying the cultural discourses in postwar Taiwan. She differentiates between the discourse created by the Nationalist government as "hegemonic," modernist literature as "alternative," and nativist literature as "oppositional." While the modernists of the 1960s "adopted literary concepts developed in Western capitalist society" and shared the government's drive toward modernization, they simultaneously harbored a skepticism toward the dominant culture's neotraditionalist discourse" and took "such bourgeois social values as individualism, liberalism, and rationalism as correctives for the oppressive social relations derived from a traditional system of values." [47] In other words, despite its divergence from the oppositional discourse of the nativists in the 1970s, modernist discourse was a subversive force vis-à-vis official ideology.

The Williams model that Chang develops in her book suggests an alternative perspective from which to view Chinese literary and cultural studies in the 1990s. Even if we agree with Zhao and Xu that some Chinese critics, both in and outside China, display nationalist tendencies, this does not necessarily lead to the conclusion that they endorse official ideology or that they do not, in fact, try to develop an independent position that only intersects with official ideology on the issue of nationalism. In other words, a more nuanced study of cultural discourses in contemporary China may require that we go beyond the dualistic cultural logic and pay more attention to existing or emergent alternative positions.

Obviously, Taiwan is not the only vantage point from which China may be studied comparatively. With regard to the debate in *Twenty-First Century*, even a cursory glance at Russian intellectuals may yield meaningful comparisons with China. When Liah Greenfeld gave a seminar at the Davis Humanities Institute in 1994, I asked her about Russian intellectuals' reception of critical theory in the post-Soviet era. Greenfeld, who came from a family of Russian intellectuals, answered that in her frequent contact with Russian academics, none of them showed any interest in contemporary theory. The sharp contrast with Chinese intellectuals could raise some interesting questions.

Consider another comparative perspective. Local appropriations of Western theory in different Chinese contexts may provide a unique perspective on Chinese societies and cultures. For instance, in Taiwan, feminism and postcolonialism have been especially influential not only in intellectual circles but also in the public sphere in general. Besides books, magazines, conferences, and newspaper columns devoted to feminist issues, feminism has been a major force behind Taiwan's legal reform and social movements. In recent years, feminism in Taiwan has directed much attention to queer theory; in 1995, a gay rights group advanced (or revived) the theory that Qu Yuan (338–278 B.C.), "the father of Chinese poetry," was a homosexual. As to postcolonialism in Taiwan, one of its agendas is to give voice to the underrepresented aborigines against dominant ethnic groups on the island, including the Fukienese, the Hakka, and the Mainlanders (those who moved from mainland China to Taiwan after World War II).

In contrast, both homosexuality and the empowerment of ethnic minorities are still by and large neglected (forbidden?) areas of intellectual inquiry in China. In comparison, postcolonialism plays a much more prominent role than feminism in mainland China, despite the fact that feminism has been around longer. According to a 1992 survey by Zhang Jingyuan, while we find many histories and anthologies of women writers published in mainland China, there are few books on feminist theory and criticism. Of the three that she mentions, only one, published in 1989, "signal[s] the independence and maturity of Chinese feminist literary criticism." [48] Why has feminism not made a more significant impact in mainland China? In what way are feminist critiques undermined by the official, nationalist ideology that, in claiming to subsume gender equality under its objectives, elides it? What is the relation between feminism and "mainstream" scholarship in mainland China? In contrast to feminism, does not an implicit affinity with official nationalism explain the easy acceptance of postcolonialism and its high visibility and prestige? When seen in a comparative context, these and other questions will contribute to a better understanding of Chinese social, political, and cultural conditions.

To return to my opening discussion on comparative literature and multiculturalism, neither globalization nor the fear of the obliteration of cultural differences as a result of the former is new. But there is little doubt that the decline in Western hegemony, decentralization of capital accumulation, and fragmentation of the former world order in our time contribute to the latest round of quests for, and debates about, national, ethnic, and cultural identities in many parts of the world. The transnational identity of the intellectual that I am proposing is defined neither by national, ethnic, or cultural origins nor by geopolitical locations. It is the comparative perspective across these boundaries that gives one that identity. As such, it is the foundation of true multiculturalism. Without comparative perspectives, multiculturalism exists only in name.

Notes

I thank Professors A. Owen Aldridge, Rey Chow, Prasenjit Duara, Lydia H. Liu, Marjorie Perloff, and Wen-hsin Yeh, as well as the audiences at the University of Notre Dame, University of Georgia, Athens, and University of California, Berkeley, for their valuable comments on earlier versions of the paper.

1 Charles Bernheimer, ed., *Comparative Literature in the Age of Multiculturalism* (Baltimore, Md.: Johns Hopkins University Press, 1995).

2 For instance, on the positive side, Mary Louis Pratt celebrates the removal of "fences" (58) and the new openness in the discipline; Françoise Lionnet sees multiculturalism and cultural studies not as an attempt to "replace the old with the new but to make room for those ancient civilizations that had been marginalized and for those subcultures and countercultures that question the authority of the past" (170–71). Others, however, are concerned about how it can be done in reality when comparative literature becomes, in Jonathan Culler's words, "a discipline of overwhelming scope" (117). Or, as Marjorie Perloff puts it, "For common sense tells us that no one can in fact learn all there is to know (or even a smattering) about 'global' literature and culture; no one can study high and low, First World and Third World, anthropology and sociology, political economy and feminist theory, as well as specific literary texts" (177). The result of such an "overwhelming scope," according to K. Anthony Appiah, is that "what we are going to get is not interdisciplinarity—the disciplines will have disappeared—but an unstructured postmodern hodge-podge" (57). By the same

token, although virtually everyone agrees that there is no hard-and-fast line between literary and cultural studies, there is no consensus on how cultural studies
should be incorporated into comparative literature. If some see the emphases on
gender, race, and class as ways of opening up the field, others feel uneasy about
the shift of focus from literary to cultural studies, which ignores the specificities
of literature and, in Peter Brooks's words, "risks replacing the study of literature
with amateur social history, amateur sociology, and personal ideology" (100).
To Tobin Siebers, it signals that "comparative literature as a discipline is dying"
(196).

3   Rey Chow, "In the Name of Comparative Literature," in Bernheimer, *Compara-*
    tive Literature in the Age of Multiculturalism, 108, 111.

4   Andrew F. Jones, "Chinese Literature in the 'World' Literary Economy," *Modern*
    Chinese Literature 8 (1994): 171.

5   K. Anthony Appiah, "The Multiculturalist Misunderstanding," *New York Review*
    of Books, 9 October 1997, 32.

6   Mary Louise Pratt, "Comparative Literature and Global Citizenship," in *Com-*
    parative Literature in the Age of Multiculturalism, 59.

7   For a summary of the controversy, see Chen Fangming, "A Close Reading of
    Yan Yuanshu's Poetry Criticism" ("Xidu Yan Yuanshu de shi ping"), in *Poetry and*
    Reality (*Shi yu xianshi*) (Taipei: Hongfan Bookstore, 1977), 9–39, esp. 19–21.

8   Zhang Yiwu, "Land of Confusion" ("Kunhuo zhi yu"), *Reading* (*Dushu*) 124–25
    (July–August 1989): 100.

9   Longxi Zhang, "Western Theory and Chinese Reality," *Critical Inquiry* 19, no. 1
    (autumn 1992): 109.

10 Longxi Zhang, "Western Theory," 129.

11 Xiaomei Chen, *Occidentalism: A Theory of Counter-Discourse in Post-Mao China*
    (New York: Oxford University Press, 1995), 5.

12 Xiaomei Chen, *Occidentalism,* 5, 8.

13 Sheldon Hsiao-peng Lu, "Art, Culture, and Cultural Criticism in Post–New
    China," *New Literary History* 28, no. 1 (winter 1997): 129.

14 Zhao Yiheng, "Post-Isms and Chinese Neo-Conservatism" ("'Houxue' yu
    Zhongguo xin baoshou zhuyi"), *Twenty-First Century* 27 (February 1995): 4–15; Xu
    Ben, "'Third-World Criticism' in Contemporary China" ("'Disan shijie piping'
    zai dangjin Zhongguo de chujing"), *Twenty-First Century* 27 (February 1995): 16–
    27. An English version of the essay and a Chinese-language summary of the
    prolonged debate, entitled "How to Face the State of Contemporary Chinese
    Culture?—A Debate," were prepared for the International Workshop on the
    Literary Field of China, at the International Institute of Asian Studies, Leiden,
    Netherlands, on 24–27 January 1996. However, because of illness, the author did
    not attend. The various points of view were published in *Twenty-First Century,*
    Tendency, and *Today,* all of which are published outside mainland China. A work-

shop devoted to the debate was sponsored by the Chinese Department of the University of Stockholm in May 1995.

15 Zhao Yiheng, "Post-Isms," 14.

16 Xu Ben, " 'Third-World Criticism,' " 17. The last quotation in this paragraph is also from this essay, 27.

17 I thank Professor Wen-hsin Yeh for reminding me of the joke.

18 Wang Hui and Zhang Tianwei, "Cultural Critique Theories and Contemporary Chinese Nationalism" ("Wenhua pipan lilun yu dangdai Zhongguo minzu zhuyi wenti"), *Strategy and Management* (*Zhanlue yu guanli*) 3 (April 1994): 17; my emphasis.

19 For instance, an international conference, "Nationalism and Modern China," was sponsored by the Chinese University of Hong Kong in December 1992. Forty papers were presented, some of which later appeared in *Twenty-First Century*. In November 1995, the state-run journal *Strategy and Management* sponsored a conference, "Nationalism at the Fin de Siècle" ("Shiji zhi jiao de minzu zhuyi"), in Shenzhen, China. Some of the papers were published in the journal. A special issue of the *Far Eastern Economic Review* also came out in November 1995, entitled "Chinese Nationalism: New Hopes, Old Fears." *Mingbao Monthly* in Hong Kong published a special issue on new Chinese nationalism in March 1996. In English, see Harumi Befu, ed., *Cultural Nationalism in East Asia: Representation and Identity* (Berkeley: Institute of East Asian Studies, University of California, 1993); and Jonathan Unger, ed., *Chinese Nationalism* (Armonk, N.Y.: M. E. Sharpe, 1996).

20 Prasenjit Duara, "De-Constructing the Chinese Nation," in *Chinese Nationalism,* 43.

21 For a discussion of widespread nationalist sentiments in Chinese popular culture in the 1990s, see Geremie R. Barmé, "To Screw Foreigners Is Patriotic: China's Avant-Garde Nationalists," in *Chinese Nationalism,* 183–208.

22 Zhang Yiwu, "The Anxiety of Interpreting 'China' " ("Chanshi 'Zhongguo' de jiaolu," *Twenty-First Century* 28 (April 1995): 129.

23 Zhang Yiwu, "Anxiety of Interpreting 'China,' " 129.

24 Joan W. Scott, "Experience," in *Feminists Theorize the Political*, ed. Judith Butler and Joan W. Scott (New York: Routledge, 1992), 24, 25.

25 Xu Zhangruen, "Layman's Words from Specialists" ("Neihang de waihang hua"), *Reading* (*Dushu*) 216 (March 1997): 104.

26 See the interview conducted by Torbjörn Lodén, "Chinese Identity in Flux: An Interview with Chen Maiping and Lung Yingtai," *Stockholm Journal of East Asian Studies* 6 (1995): 21.

27 Liu Dong, "Beware of Artificial 'Pidgin Scholarship' " ("Xiaoxin renwei de 'yang-jingbang xueshu' "), *Twenty-First Century* 28 (April 1995): 7–11.

28 Julia Kristeva, *Nations without Nationalism*, trans. Leon S. Roudiez (New York: Columbia University Press, 1993), 3; and Liu Dong, "Beware," 10.

29 See, for instance, Liu Kang, "Globalization and the Chinese Alternative to Modernization" ("Quanqiuhua yu Zhongguo xiandaihua de butong xuanze"), *Twenty-First Century* 27 (October 1996): 140–46; Zhang Yiwu, "Facing the Challenge of Globalization" ("Miandui quanqiuhua de tiaozhan"), *Twenty-First Century* 28 (December 1996): 138–42; Sheldon Hsiao-peng Lu, "Global POSTmodernization: The Intellectual, the Artist, and China's Condition," *boundary 2* 24, no. 3 (1997): 65–97.

30 Zhang Yiwu, "Anxiety of Interpreting 'China,'" 135–36.

31 Ying-shih Yü, "The Radicalization of China in the Twentieth Century," *Daedalus* 122, no. 2 (spring 1993): 125–50.

32 Ying-shih Yü, "Radicalization of China," 139.

33 Theodore Huters, "Appropriations: Another Look at Western Ideas and Modern China" (paper presented at the Center for Chinese Studies, University of California, Berkeley, April 1995), 19, 10. I thank the author for giving me permission to quote from this paper.

34 Lydia H. Liu, *Translingual Practice: Literature, National Culture, and Translated Modernity—China, 1900–1937* (Stanford, Calif.: Stanford University Press, 1995), 240.

35 Arif Dirlik, "Chinese History and the Question of Orientalism," in *The Postcolonial Aura: Third World Criticism in the Age of Global Capitalism* (Boulder, Colo.: Westview, 1997), 118–19.

36 Rey Chow, "Can One Say No to China?" *New Literary History* 28, no. 1 (winter 1997): 151.

37 For a discussion of the concept, see Jonathan Friedman, *Cultural Identity and Global Process* (London: Sage, 1994).

38 Zhang Qing and Yü Ying-shih both illustrate clearly how Hu Shi, as an overseas Chinese student, gained legitimation and acceptance by intellectuals in China by establishing himself as a scholar of "Chinese learning." Lucian W. Pye discusses how Chinese intellectuals in treaty ports were regarded as compradores or sellouts; he sees the discrimination as an impediment to China's modernization. See Zhang Qing, "The Dialogue between the Native Land and 'Beyond the Realm': A Historical Perspective" ("Cong lishi kan bentu yu 'yuwai' de duihua"), *Twenty-First Century* 34 (April 1996): 113–20; Yü Ying-shih, *Hu Shi in the Intellectual History of Modern China (Hu Shi zai jindai Zhongguo sixiang shi shang de diwei)* (Taipei: Lianjing, 1984), especially 35–42; and Lucian W. Pye, "How China's Nationalism was Shanghaied," in *Chinese Nationalism*, 86–112.

39 Samuel P. Huntington, *The Clash of Civilizations and the Remaking of World Order* (New York: Simon and Schuster, 1996); Chinese translation: *Wenming de chongtu mu shijie zhixu de chongjian* (Beijing: Xinhua Press, 1997). A collection of responses by Chinese intellectuals, edited by Wang Hui and Yu Guoliang is forthcoming from the Chinese University of Hong Kong Press.

40 Etienne Balibar and Immanuel Wallerstein, *Race, Nation, Class: Ambiguous Identities,* trans. Chris Turner (New York: Verso, 1991), 46.

41 Tapati Guha-Thakurta, *The Making of a New 'Indian' Art: Artists, Aesthetics, and Nationalism in Bengal, c. 1850–1920* (Cambridge: Cambridge University Press, 1992), 184.

42 Ian Buruma, "The Singapore Way," *New York Review of Books* (19 October 1995): 67. For the interview with Chen Maiping, see Torbjörn Lodén, "Chinese Identity in Flux," 23.

43 K. Anthony Appiah, "Geist Stories," in *Comparative Literature in the Age of Multiculturalism,* 57. On "Chinese overseas," a term coined by Wang Gungwu as an alternative to "overseas Chinese," see Wang's "Greater China and the Chinese Overseas," in *Greater China: The New Superpower?,* ed. David Shambaugh (New York: Oxford University Press, 1995), 274–96.

44 Edward Said, *Culture and Imperialism* (New York: Knopf, 1993), 332; and Frederick Buell, *National Culture and the New Global System* (Baltimore, Md.: Johns Hopkins University Press, 1994), 341.

45 Andrew Hatfelder, *Literature, Politics, and National Identity: Reformation to Renaissance* (New York: Cambridge University Press, 1994), 1; Helen F. Siu, "Cultural Identity and the Politics of Difference in South China," *Daedalus* 122, no. 2 (spring 1993): 27; and Rey Chow, "Can One Say No to China?" 151.

46 Thomas Gold, "Go with Your Feelings: Hong Kong and Taiwan Popular Culture in Greater China," in *Greater China: The New Superpower?* 273; and Zheng Min, "A Fin de Siècle Reflection: The Linguistic Revolution of the Chinese Language and the Creation of New Chinese Poetry" ("Shijimo de huigu: Hanyu yuyan biange yu Zhongguo xinshi chuangzuo") and "What Problems Has Our New Poetry Encountered?" ("Women de xinshi yudao le shenme wenti?"), originally published in *Literary Criticism (Wenxue pinglun),* March 1993 and February 1994. They are reprinted respectively in *Chinese Poetry Annals: 1993 (Shige nianjian)* (Chongqing: Xinan Shida Chubanshe, 1994), 353–80, and *Chinese Poetry Annals: 1994* (Chongqing: Xinan Shida Chubanshe, 1995), 308–24.

47 Sung-sheng Yvonne Chang, *Modernism and the Nativist Resistance: Contemporary Chinese Fiction from Taiwan* (Durham, N.C.: Duke University Press, 1993), 2.

48 Zhang Jingyuan, *Comparative Literature Newsletter* (1992): 386.

Can One Say No to Chineseness?

Pushing the Limits of the Diasporic Paradigm

Ien Ang

William Yang was born in 1943 and grew up in Dimbulah, a small mining town in northern Queensland, Australia. Today a celebrated photographer working and living in Sydney, he is presented—classified—as "a third-generation Australian-Chinese." In an autobiographical account of his life, he recounts:

> One day, when I was about six years old, one of the kids at school called at me "Ching Chong Chinaman, Born in a jar, Christened in a teapot, Ha ha ha." I had no idea what he meant although I knew from his expression that he was being horrible.
>
> I went home to my mother and I said to her, "Mum, I'm not Chinese, am I?" My mother looked at me very sternly and said, "Yes you are."
>
> Her tone was hard and I knew in that moment that being Chinese was some terrible curse and I could not rely on my mother for help. Or my brother, who was four years older than me, and much more experienced in the world. He said, "And you'd better get used to it." [1]

This is a classic tale of revelation that can undoubtedly be told in countless variations and versions by many people throughout the world, articulating the all-too-familiar experience of a subject's harsh coming into awareness of his own, unchosen, minority status. "Chineseness" here is the marker of that status, imparting an externally imposed identity given meaning, literally, by a practice of discrimination. It is the dominant culture's classificatory practice, operating as a territorializing power highly effective in marginalizing the other, that shapes the meaning of Chineseness here as a curse, as something to "get used to." Yang reveals that for most of his life, he has had negative feelings about "being Chinese." But what does his Chineseness consist of? "We were brought up in the western way," explains Yang. "None of us learned to speak Chinese. This was partly because my father, a Hukka [*sic*], spoke Mandarin, whereas my mother, a See Yup [*sic*], spoke Cantonese, and they spoke English at home. My mother could have taught us Cantonese but she never did—frankly she couldn't see the point."² This glimpse into one ordinary family's history indicates the apparent lack of interest Yang's parents had in transmitting their Chinese roots and cultural traditions to their children. This would have been a difficult thing to do in Australia in the forties and fifties, when the official ideology was still one of "white Australia" and required the few nonwhite people in the country to assimilate. But at the same time, Yang's family obviously never lost a sense of certainty about the self-declared *fact* of their Chineseness. But are they indeed Chinese? What makes them so? And how do they know?

■   ■   ■

Scholars have always been bewildered by China. The intricate empirical multifariousness and historical complexity of the country is hardly containable in the sophisticated (inter)disciplinary apparatus and theoretical armory of Western researchers. Language, culture, civilization, people, nation, polity—how does one describe, interpret, and understand China, that awesome, other space that has never ceased to both fascinate and infuriate its dedicated scholar? The difficulty has grown exponentially, however, with the emergence of a so-called diasporic paradigm in the study of Chineseness. The booming interest in what is loosely termed the *Chinese diaspora* has unsettled the very demarcation of China as an immensely complex yet ontologically stable object of study. The view from the diaspora has shattered the convenient certainty with which Chinese studies has been equated, quite simply, with the study of China. "China" can no longer be limited to the more or less fixed area of its official spatial and cultural boundaries nor can it be held up as providing the authentic, authoritative, and uncontested standard for all things Chinese. Instead, how to determine what is and what is not Chinese has become the necessary preliminary question to ask, and an increasingly urgent one at that. This, at least, is one of the key outcomes of the emergent view from the diaspora.

Central to the diasporic paradigm is the theoretical axiom that Chineseness is not a category with a fixed content—be it racial, cultural, or geographical—but operates as an open and indeterminate signifier whose meanings are constantly renegotiated and rearticulated in different sections of the Chinese diaspora. Being Chinese outside China cannot possibly mean the same thing as inside. It varies from place to place, molded by the local circumstances in different parts of the world where people of Chinese ancestry have settled and constructed new ways of living. There are, in this paradigm, many different Chinese identities, not one. This proposition entails a criticism of Chinese essentialism, a departure from the mode of demarcating Chineseness through an absolutist oppositioning of authentic and inauthentic, pure and impure, real and fake. The anti-essentialism of the diasporic paradigm opens up a symbolic space for people such as Yang, a distant member of the diaspora, to be Chinese in his own way, living a de-centered Chineseness that does not have to live up to the norm of "the essential Chinese subject." [3]

I am entering into this discussion from the perspective of cultural studies, where the new theorization of diaspora has most energetically taken place.[4] One of the distinctive characteristics of cultural studies is its recognition of the positionality of any mode of intellectual practice or style of knowledge production. Such a recognition implies a de-universalization of knowledge and an emphasis on the particular historical and cultural coordinates that inform the enunciation of discourse and the formation of knowledge. For cultural studies, as Lawrence Grossberg puts it, "there can be no separation between theory, at whatever level of abstraction, and the concrete social historical context which provides both its object of study and its conditions of existence." [5] Importantly, this is both a political and an epistemological statement. Thus, any intellectual investment in an object of study—say, Chineseness—is not the innocent reflection of a natural reality that is passively waiting to be discovered; rather, the very quest for knowledge actively brings into being, in the knower's experience and understanding of the world, slices of reality he or she then calls and classifies as Chinese. Furthermore, there are stakes involved in the ongoing ontological confirmation of Chineseness, just as nineteenth-century Western science had a stake, beyond the noble one of scientific progress, in producing the existence of distinct, and hierarchically ordered, human "races." This analogy should provoke us to interrogate the political and ideological significance of the ongoing currency, as well as shifting currents, of discourses, claims, and disclaims to Chineseness in the modern world. How Chineseness is made to mean in different contexts, and who gets to decide what it means or should mean, is the object of intense contestation, a struggle over meaning with wide-ranging cultural and political implications.

I also have a personal investment in this interrogation of Chineseness. Like Yang, though along a rather different historical trajectory, I am intimately familiar with the injunction to "get used to being Chinese." I was born into a so-called Peranakan Chinese family in Indonesia, a country that has always had a problem with its long-standing and economically significant Chinese minority (as, of course, is the case throughout Southeast Asia, except Singapore).[6] In Indonesia, from the sixties to the present, I have found being Chinese a profoundly ambivalent experience, fraught with feelings of rejection (by the majority of Indonesians) and alienation (from an identity that was first and foremost an imposed one). The need to come to terms with the fact of my Chineseness remained a constant after I relocated—in a peculiar diasporic itinerary informed by the historical connections established by European colonialism—to the Netherlands, where I spent my teenage and young adult years, and later, after I transferred to Australia (where I live now). In these different geocultural spaces, the meaning of being Chinese was both the same and different, shaped by changing specific contexts, yet enduringly framed by the fact that I could not take my Chineseness (or lack of it) for granted. In short, the status of Chineseness as a discursive construct—rather than as something natural—is a matter of subjective experience to me, not just a question of theory.[7]

Conceiving Chineseness as a discursive construct entails a disruption of the ontological stability and certainty of Chinese identity; it does not, however, negate its operative power as a cultural principle in the social constitution of identities *as* Chinese. In other words, the point is not to dispute the fact that Chineseness exists (which, in any case, would be a futile assertion in a world where more than a billion people would, to all intents and purposes, identify themselves as Chinese in one way or another, either voluntarily or by force), but to investigate how this category operates in practice, in different historical, geographical, political, and cultural contexts. As Stuart Hall remarks, the fact that race is not a valid scientific category does not undermine its symbolic and social effectuality. The same could be said about Chineseness. What highlighting the constructed nature of categories and classificatory systems does, however, is shift "the focus of theoretical attention from the categories 'in themselves' as repositories of cultural [meaning] to the process of cultural classification itself."[8] In other words, how and why is it that the category of Chineseness acquires its persistence and solidity? And with what political and cultural effects?

What I call the view from the diaspora, which will be my starting point, is necessarily unstable. After all, the spirit of diasporic thought, motivated as it is by notions of dispersal, mobility, and disappearance, works against its consolidation as a paradigm proper. Contained in the diasporic perspective itself, therefore, are the seeds of its own deconstruction, which provides us with the opportunity to interrogate not just the different meanings Chineseness takes on in different local contexts but, more fundamentally, the very significance and validity of Chineseness as a category of identification and analysis.

■ ■ ■

The process of de-centering the center, which is so pivotal to diasporic theory, has been forcefully articulated in the recent influential collection *The Living Tree: The Changing Meaning of Being Chinese Today,* edited by Tu Weiming, professor of Chinese history and philosophy at Harvard.[9] In this collection, Tu elaborates on the contours of a symbolic universe he calls "cultural China,"[10] a newly constructed cultural space "that both encompasses and transcends the ethnic, territorial, linguistic, and religious boundaries that normally define Chineseness."[11] For Tu, the project of cultural China is one designed to de-center the cultural authority of geopolitical China, an intellectual effort to redefine "the periphery as the center" in current engagements with what it means to be Chinese.[12] This project is critical insofar as it aims to break with static and rigid, stereotypical and conventional definitions of Chinese as "belonging to the Han race, being born in China proper, speaking Mandarin, and observing the 'patriotic' code of ethics" (preface, vii). Instead, Tu wants to "explore the fluidity of Chineseness as a layered and contested discourse, to open new possibilities and avenues of inquiry, and to challenge the claims of political leadership (in Beijing, Taipei, Hong Kong or Singapore) to be the ultimate authority in a matter as significant as 'Chineseness' " (preface, viii). The impetus for this intervention is a certain disillusion, if not despair, about the political reality of mainland China, the People's Republic of China. As Tu observes, "Although realistically those who are on the periphery . . . are seemingly helpless to affect any fundamental transformation of China proper, the center no longer has the ability, insight, or legitimate authority to dictate the agenda for cultural China. On the contrary, the transformative potential of the periphery is so great that it seems inevitable that it will significantly shape the intellectual discourse on cultural China for years to come" ("Cultural China," 33–34).[13]

It is important to note the political implications of Tu's project. His position is known to be explicitly neo-Confucianist and largely anticommunist, which we need to keep in mind when assessing his critiques of "the center." Placed in the context of Chinese *cultural* history, however, the assertion of the periphery as the center is a radical one. The notion of a single center, or cultural core, from which Chinese civilization has emanated—the so-called Central Country complex—has been so deeply entrenched in the Chinese historical imagination that it is difficult to disentangle our understandings of Chineseness from it. Yet the very emergence of a powerful discourse of cultural China enunciated from the periphery and formulated to assert the periphery's influence at the expense of the center is a clear indication of the increasingly self-confident voice of some Chinese intellectuals in diaspora, such as Tu Wei-ming himself. This growing self-confidence has much to do with the historical and economic state of affairs in global modernity at the end of the twentieth century. As Tu puts it, "While the periphery of the Sinic world was proudly marching toward an Asian-Pacific century, the homeland seemed mired in perpetual underdevelopment" ("Cultural China," 12). Indeed, it is precisely the homeland's seeming inability to transform itself according to the ideal image of a truly modern society—an image still hegemonically determined by the West—that has led to the perceived crisis of Chineseness, which the project of cultural China aims to address.

Central to the intellectual problematic of cultural China is what one sees as the urgent need to reconcile Chineseness and modernity as the twentieth century draws to a close. There are two interrelated sides to this challenge. On the one hand, the question is how to modernize Chineseness itself in a way that will correct and overcome the arguably abject course taken by the existing political regime in China, a course almost universally perceived as wrong and, provocatively, as somehow having a debilitating effect on the fate of Chineseness. According to Tu, the Chinese diaspora will have to take the lead in the modernization of Chineseness. "While the overseas Chinese may seem forever peripheral to the meaning of being Chinese," he writes, in an implicit attack on the center, "they [can] assume an effective role in creatively constructing a new vision of Chineseness that is more in tune with Chinese history and in sympathetic resonance with Chinese culture" ("Cultural China," 34).

On the other hand, there is also the reverse question of how to sinicize modernity—how, that is, to create a modern world that is truly Chinese and not simply an imitation of the West. The radical iconoclasm of the May Fourth movement—which was based on the assumption that China's modernization could only be realized through a wholesale process of Westernization and a simultaneous renunciation of Chinese culture—is now regarded as completely outdated. Instead, inspiration is drawn from the economic rise of East Asia to look for models of modernity—Chinese modernity—which pose challenging cultural alternatives to the Western model. Tu refers specifically to Taiwan, Hong Kong, Singapore, and the Chinese communities in Southeast Asia. The experiences of these countries suggest for Tu that "active participation in the economic, political, social, and cultural life of a thoroughly modernized community does not necessarily conflict with being authentically Chinese," signaling the possibility that "modernization may enhance rather than weaken Chineseness" ("Cultural China," 8).

The privileging of the periphery—the diaspora—as the new cultural center of Chineseness in Tu's discourse is an important challenge to traditional, centrist, and essentialist conceptions of Chinese culture and identity. Yet I want to suggest that the very postulation of a cultural China as the name for a transnational intellectual community held together not just by a "common awareness" but also by "a common ancestry and a shared cultural background, . . . a transnational network to explore the meaning of being Chinese in a global context" ("Cultural China," 25), is a move that is driven, and motivated, by another kind of centrism, this time along notionally cultural lines.

An important element here is the continued orientation of, if not obsession with, the self-declared periphery-as-center in the discourse of cultural China in relation to the old center, even if this center is so passionately denied its traditional authority and legitimacy. "What mainland China eventually will become remains an overriding concern for all intellectuals in cultural China" ("Cultural China," 33), writes Tu, and in this ongoing preoccupation with the center, the periphery not only reproduces unintentionally its own profound entanglement with the former; it also, by this very preoccupation, effects its own unwarranted internal homogenization and limits the much more radical potential that a diasporic perspective allows. In other words, while the aim would seem to be to rescue Chineseness from China, to de-hegemonize geopolitical China, which is found wanting in its own, heavy-handed politics of modernizing Chineseness/sinicizing modernity, the rescue operation implies the projection of a new, alternative center, a de-centered center, whose name is *cultural* China, but China nevertheless. It is clear, then, that the all-too-familiar "obsession with China," which has been a key disposition in the work of Chinese intellectuals in the twentieth century, remains at work here with undiminished intensity.[14] This obsession, which is so profoundly inscribed in the psychic structure of a wounded Chinese civilizationalism, "privileges China's problems as uniquely Chinese, which lays absolute claim to the loyalty of Chinese in all parts of the world."[15]

According to Leo Ou-fan Lee, who came from Taiwan to the United States as a graduate student more than thirty years ago and who describes himself as "a voluntary exile situated forever on the fringes of China," the "excessive obsession with their homeland has deprived Chinese writers abroad of their rare privilege of being truly on the periphery." For Lee, it is only by being truly on the periphery that one can create a distance "sufficiently removed from the center of the obsession," allowing one to "subject the obsession itself to artistic treatment."[16] From this point of view, cultural China definitely does *not* occupy a truly peripheral position at all. On the contrary. An overwhelming desire—bordering, indeed, on obsession—to somehow maintain, redeem, and revitalize the notion of Chineseness as a marker of common culture and identity in a rapidly postmodernizing world is the driving force behind Tu's conception of cultural China. While the meaning of Chineseness is defined explicitly as fluid and changeable, the category of Chineseness itself is emphatically not in question here: Indeed, the notion of cultural China seems to be devised precisely to exalt and enlarge the global significance of Chineseness, raising its importance by imbuing it with new, modernized meanings and heightening its relevance by expanding its field of application far beyond the given spatial boundaries of geopolitical China.

The Chinese diaspora, as we have seen, is posited as one of the key pillars of the imagined community of cultural China. It is noteworthy that Tu persistently accentuates the quest for Chineseness as a central motif in his wide-ranging discussion of variant diaspora narratives. In the case of Southeast Asian families of Chinese descent remigrating from Malaysia or Vietnam to North America, Western Europe, or Australia, he sees the "irony of their not returning to their ancestral homeland but moving farther away from China with the explicit intention of preserving their cultural identity" ("Cultural China," 24). In mainland Chinese intellectuals' decision not to return to China after the Tiananmen event in 1989, he reads a "conscious and, for some, impulsive choice to realize one's Chineseness by moving far away from one's homeland" ("Cultural China," 24). But isn't Tu being too insistent in foregrounding the salience of Chineseness in the configuration of these diasporic flows and movements? Doesn't this emphasis unduly confine diverse strands of the diaspora to the narrow and claustrophobic shaft of a projected, if highly abstract, "obsession with Chineseness"?

The organic metaphor of "the living tree" to describe cultural China provides us with a clear insight into the problem I am hinting at here. A living tree grows and changes over time; it constantly develops new branches and stems that shoot outward, in different directions, from the solid core of the tree trunk, which in turn feeds itself on an invisible but life-sustaining set of roots. Without roots, there would be no life, no new leaves. The metaphor of the living tree dramatically imparts the ultimate existential dependence of the periphery on the center, the diaspora on the homeland. Furthermore, what this metaphor emphasizes is continuity over discontinuity: In the end, it all flows back to the roots.

In thus imputing an essential continuity and constancy in the diaspora's quest for Chineseness, the discourse of cultural China risks homogenizing what is otherwise a complex range of dispersed, heterogeneous, and not necessarily commensurable diaspora narratives — a homogeneity for which the sign of Chineseness provides the a priori and taken-for-granted guarantee. But in this way, the hegemony of "China" (cultural, if not geopolitical, China) is surreptitiously reinforced, not undercut. As Tu rightly notes, "Hegemonic discourse, charged with an air of arrogance, discriminates not only by excluding but also by including. Often it is in the act of inclusion that the art of symbolic control is more insidiously exercised." (preface, vii). Tu refers here to the coercive manner in which the People's Republic includes a variety of others (such as the non-Han minorities inside the borders of China) within the orbit of its official political control. But a wholesale incorporation of the diaspora under the inclusive rubric of "cultural China" can be an equally hegemonic move, which works to truncate and suppress complex realities and experiences that cannot possibly be fully and meaningfully contained within the singular category of "Chinese."

Ironically, Tu recognizes the fact that not all members of the diaspora would feel comfortable with their inclusion in the grand design of cultural China. Indeed, he writes, "learning to be truly Chinese may prove to be too heavy a psychological burden for minorities, foreign-born, non-Mandarin speakers, or nonconformists; for such people, remaining outside or on the periphery may seem preferable" (preface, vii–viii). Let's ignore the surprising return to cultural essentialism — the ghost of the "truly Chinese" — here.

What we must start to question is the very validity and usefulness of the spatial matrix of center and periphery that is so constitutive of the conventional thinking about the Chinese diaspora; we must give the living tree a good shake.

■ ■ ■

The condition of diaspora—literally, "the scattering of seeds"—produces subjects for whom notions of identity and belonging are radically unsettled. As James Clifford puts it in his very useful discussion of contemporary theorizing on diasporas, "Diasporic subjects are distinct versions of modern, transnational, intercultural experience." In this sense, diasporic subjects are exemplary cases of the multiple and hybrid subjectivities so favored by postmodern and poststructuralist theory. Interestingly, however, as I have discussed above, a dominant tendency in thinking about the Chinese diaspora is to suppress what Clifford calls "the lateral axes of diaspora," the ways in which diasporic identities are produced through creolization and hybridization, through both conflictive and collaborative coexistence and intermixture with other cultures, in favor of a hierarchical centering and a linear rerouting back to the imagined ancestral home. Such a conceptual focus on the center, Clifford notes, inhibits an understanding of the significance of diaspora cultures in the late twentieth century. As he puts it, "The centering of diasporas around an axis of origin and return overrides the specific local interactions (identifications and ruptures, both constructive and defensive) necessary for the maintenance of diasporic social forms. The empowering paradox of diaspora is that dwelling *here* assumes solidarity and connection *there*. But *there* is not necessarily a single place or an exclusivist nation."[17]

Indeed, for Clifford, the most important aspect of diasporic formations is the multiplicity of "here's" and "there's," which together make up "decentered, partially overlapping networks of communication, travel, trade, and kinship [that] connect the several communities of a transnational 'people.'"[18] The metaphor of the living tree is not at all suited to capture the features of such dispersed, discontinuous, fractal cultural formations. Interestingly, Paul Gilroy has chosen the image of ships as a starting point for his groundbreaking work on the African diaspora: "ships in motion across the spaces between Europe, America, Africa, and the Caribbean as a central organizing symbol" for the particular diasporic formation that has developed historically as a result of the transatlantic slave trade, a formation he calls "the black Atlantic."[19] What is highlighted in this image is a virtual space of continuous mobility, of crisscrossing flows and multiple horizontal exchanges between different sites of black diasporic concentration, in which there is no center. I am not suggesting here that a similar image should be adopted for the Chinese diaspora—indeed, the image of the ship is particularly appropriate in Gilroy's context for its evocation of the African diaspora's founding moment of the Middle Passage—but this comparative note might serve to illuminate the fact that the metaphor of the living tree is by no means ideologically innocent. It could encourage us to problematize the predominance of centrist and organicist conceptions of Chineseness, Chinese culture, and Chinese identity in diaspora.[20]

Leo Lee, with his claimed desire to be "truly on the periphery," comes close to embodying the diasporic Chinese subject who has renounced the debilitating obsession with the center. "By virtue of my self-chosen marginality I can never fully identify myself with any center," he writes. He defines his marginality in relation to two centers, China and America: "On the peripheries of both countries, I feel compelled to engage actively in a dialogue with both cultures." Freed from the usual obsession with China, Lee declares himself "unbounded" by his homeland. Instead, he advocates what he calls a "Chinese cosmopolitanism," a cosmopolitanism "that embraces both a fundamental intellectual commitment to Chinese culture and a multicultural receptivity, which effectively cuts across all conventional national boundaries."[21] Cosmopolitanism, of course, is an idea warranting a discussion of its own (which I cannot provide here), but what is the surplus gained in the addition of the word *Chinese* to *cosmopolitanism* here? And what does Lee mean by a fundamental (that is to say, a priori, fundamentalist) intellectual commitment to *Chinese* culture? What makes Lee's vantage point so interestingly contradictory is that while he places himself on the margins of both "China" and "America," he does this from a position of unquestioned certainty about his own ontological Chineseness and his (inherited?) proprietorship of "Chinese culture." Once a Chinese, always a Chinese?

Ouyang Yu, a poet and a specialist in English and Chinese literature, who moved from mainland China to Australia many years ago, actively resists such ethnic determinism. "Where is the way out for people such as me?" he asks. "Is our future predetermined to be Chinese no matter how long we reside overseas?" Ouyang expresses a desire to contribute to his present culture—Australian culture—"more than as just a Chinese." But, he tells us, he has been prevented from doing so: "My effort to 'English' myself has met with strong resistance from all sorts of people ever since I came here. Even if I wanted to be English, they wouldn't let me be. I would find my frequent criticism of China was not appreciated. On many occasions, I found people preaching that I should be proud of being a Chinese. . . . I was made to feel uneasy with my disloyalty."[22]

This story highlights how difficult it can be for people like Ouyang to embrace a truly diasporized, hybrid identity, because the dominant Western culture is just as prone to the rigid assumptions and attitudes of cultural essentialism as is Chinese culture. In other words, there seems to be a cultural prohibition of de-sinicization, at least for intellectuals from mainland China or Taiwan, such as Ouyang Yu and Leo Lee, who have moved to the West. It would be interesting to speculate why this should be so. It would be easy—and perhaps too simplistic—to suggest the antagonizing work of racism or Orientalism here; their capacity as forces that perpetuate and reinforce essentialist notions of the Chinese other should not be underestimated. However, the important point to make here is that Lee's ideal of "being truly on the periphery" is inherently contradictory, if not a virtual impossibility, because his notion of the periphery is still grounded in the recognition of a center of sorts, the de-territorialized center of Chinese culture or, perhaps, of Chineseness itself.

While Lee and Ouyang now live in different parts of the (Western) world, their diasporic Chineseness is still clearly linked to their obvious biographical rootedness in the cultural formations of the territorial center. Moreover, even though they no longer live in the center, their subjectivities are still steeped in Chineseness: Being first generations migrants, they possess the linguistic and cultural capital that is generally recognized as authentically Chinese. Lee and Ouyang *know* that they are Chinese, and they are known by others as such. While both express a desire to go beyond their Chinese identities (Lee, by staking a claim to a Chinese cosmopolitanism, and Ouyang, in wanting to be more than *just* Chinese), their bottom-line Chineseness is not in doubt. Theirs, in other words, is a relatively straightforward narrative of (self-)exile from the homeland, and as such they are still easily incorporated in Tu's cultural China and firmly attached to one of the branches of the living tree.

Without wanting to devalue the de-centering discourses articulated by intellectuals such as Lee and Ouyang, I would nevertheless argue that there are other narratives that tell of much more radical, complicated, and checkered routes of diasporic dispersal. In these narratives, the very validity of the category of Chineseness is in question, its status as a signifier of identity thrown into radical doubt. It is in these narratives that the diasporic paradigm is pushed to its limits, to the extent that any residual attachment to the center tends to fade.

The Peranakan Chinese in Southeast Asia are often mentioned as one distinct group of Chinese people who have lost their Chinese cultural heritage and have gone "native." The Peranakans are an old diaspora. From the tenth century onward, traders, mostly men from South China, visited various Southeast Asian ports. At first they remained temporarily and rarely established permanent Chinese communities, but between the sixteenth and nineteenth centuries, Chinese trading quarters in cities such as Bangkok, Manila, and Batavia became large and permanent, aided by the ascendancy of European colonialism in the region. Over the course of centuries, they intermarried with local women, began to speak the local languages, and adapted to local lifestyle (while selectively holding on to some Chinese traditions). This is not the place to enter into a detailed historical discussion of this important diaspora; the question to ask here is, Why are they still called Chinese? As David Yen-ho Wu observes, "While the 'pure' Chinese may question the legitimacy of the *peranakans'* claim to being authentic Chinese, the *peranakans* themselves are quite confident about the authenticity of their Chineseness. They are often heard referring to themselves as 'we Chinese.' "[23] Having been born into a Peranakan family myself, I can testify to the correctness of this observation: There is an instinctiveness to our (sometimes reluctant) identification as Chinese that eludes any rationalization and defies any doubt.[24] Yet it is a fraught and ambivalent Chineseness, one that is to all intents and purposes completely severed from the nominal center, China. In contemporary Indonesia, for example, where the state deploys a strict assimilation policy to eradicate Chinese difference within the national culture (for example, by banning the use of Chinese characters from public display), Peranakan Chinese are said to "see themselves as Indonesian rather than Chinese, [but] recognize their Chinese origin, albeit knowing very little of Chinese culture and tradition."[25] And for many Peranakans, "China" has no relevance at all in their lives, so what meaning does the notion of "Chinese origin" still carry?[26]

Wu argues that two sentiments identify those who see themselves as Chinese. The first, a culturalist sentiment, is a feeling of connectedness with the fate of China as a nation, a patriotism associated with "a sense of fulfillment, a sense of being the bearers of a cultural heritage handed down from their ancestors, of being essentially separate from non-Chinese."[27] But it is clear that this sentiment does not apply to those in the diaspora who not only have lost most of their cultural heritage, language being chief among them, but also do not have a great attachment to the ancestral homeland at all, while still identifying themselves (and being identified) as Chinese. The Peranakans in Indonesia are a case in point, but so, for that matter, is William Yang, the "Australian-Chinese" photographer, with whose story I began this essay.

Yang's story illuminates the precarious meaning of Chineseness at the outer edge of the diaspora. If Yang, brought up the Western way in small-town Australia, can be described as Chinese at all, then his is a Chineseness that is stripped of any substantial cultural content. This, of course, is the case with millions of "ethnic Chinese" throughout the West, those who have settled in all corners of the world in a checkered history of several centuries of dispersal from the original "homeland." To undersand Yang's Chineseness in terms of his imaginary and subjective relationship to this imputed homeland, which can only be an extremely tenuous relationship anyway, would be missing the point altogether. As his own account of the formative event shows, he came to know about his Chinese identity only because someone else, arguably a non-Chinese, labeled him as such, to Yang's own initial surprise and to his later chagrin, when his mother confirmed that he *was,* indeed, Chinese. In other words, Yang's identification as Chinese took place in a context of coexistence and copresence with others, others who were *different* from him. Yang's Chineseness, then, is fundamentally relational and externally defined, as much as it is partial. Its boundaries are fuzzy. Its meaning, uncertain. Yang both is and is not Chinese, depending on how he is perceived by himself and by others. But what is it, we might ask, that still ultimately determines the possibility of Yang's categorization as Chinese in the first place?

This brings us to the second sentiment, which, according to Wu, is common to those identifying themselves as Chinese. This is the sentiment that Chinese share of seeing themselves as members of "the Chinese race" or "the Chinese people."[28] We are returned here to a concept that, as I remarked earlier, refuses to go away from social discourse despite its repudiation as a "scientific" concept in the West: race. So when Yang's mother affirmed sternly that he *was* Chinese, his brother adding insult to injury by informing him that he'd "better get used to it," the only tangible markers of distinction could only have been those associated with "race." The glee with which the schoolkid, most probably white, could yell "Ching Chong Chinaman" at Yang was based on the former's dominant positioning within the prevailing social network, which gave him the *power* to offend in this way, but it also depended on the availability of some clues that enabled him to single out the guileless William as an appropriate object of such an attack: What else could it have been but his "yellow skin" and "slanty eyes," the key "racial" markers for Chineseness in the West?

While scientific racism has long been discarded, then, it is in situations like these that the notion of race continues to thrive in everyday life, where race theories operate in practice as popular epistemologies of ethnic distinction, discrimination, and identification — which are often matched by more or less passionate modes of self-identification. The idea of being part of a race produces a sense of belonging based on naturalized and fictive notions of kinship and heredity; in Chinese discourse, of course, this is eminently represented by the enduring myth of the unity of the Chinese people as children of the Yellow Emperor.[29] What Rey Chow calls the "myth of consanguinity"[30] has very real effects on the self-conception of diasporic subjects, as it provides them with a magical solution to the sense of dislocation and rootlessness that many of them experience in their lives. Yang describes it this way: "I've been back to China and I've had the experience that the expatriot [*sic*] American writer Amy Tan describes; when she first set foot in China, she immediately became Chinese. Although it didn't quite happen like that for me I know what Amy's talking about. The experience is very powerful and specific, it has to do with land, with standing on the soil of the ancestors and feeling the blood of China run through your veins."[31]

In this extraordinary narrative of return to the imposing center, Yang constructs himself as a prodigal son who had lost his way, a fallen leaf that has blown back to the soil where the living tree has its roots. In this narrative, race — blood — operates as the degree zero of Chineseness to which the diasporic subject can resort to recover his imaginary connectedness with China and to substantiate, through the fiction of race, what otherwise would be a culturally empty identity.

But, as Chow has rightly pointed out, "the submission to consanguinity means the surrender of agency"[32]: The fiction of racial belonging would imply a reductionist interpellation (in the Althusserian sense of the term) that constructs the subject as passively and lineally (pre)determined by blood, not as an active historical agent whose subjectivity is continuously shaped through his or her engagements within multiple, complex, and contradictory social relations that are overdetermined by political, economic, and cultural circumstances in highly particular spatiotemporal contexts. Race, in other words, provides a reductionist, essentializing discursive shortcut, in which, to paraphrase Stuart Hall, the signifier *Chinese* is "torn from its historical, cultural and political embedding and lodged in a biologically constituted racial category."[33] In the imagining of "the Chinese race," differences that have been constructed by heterogeneous diasporic conditions and experiences are suppressed in favor of illusory modes of bonding and belonging. Recently, I had a taxi ride in Sydney with a driver who was from mainland China. We mutually recognized each other as Chinese, but I had to tell him that, unfortunately, I couldn't speak Chinese. "Well," he said, "it will be easy for you to learn. After all, you have Chinese blood." As if my imputed racial identity would automatically and naturally give me access to some enormous reservoir of cultural capital!

As Balibar has remarked, "The racial community has a tendency to represent itself as one big family or as the common envelope of family relations."[34] Indeed, there is an equivalence between the organicist metaphor of the living tree and the lineal notion of race-as-family that is profoundly problematic if we are to interrogate Chineseness effectively from the diasporic point of view. In his work on the African diaspora, Gilroy has criticized "the dubious appeal to family as the connective tissue of black experience and history," as it disables black intellectuals from developing alternative perspectives on black lives in diaspora, which, in Gilroy's view, must be grounded in explicitly disorganic, hybrid, and synthetic notions of identity and community, not in some cozy, familial notion of blackness.[35] Similarly, Hall has argued against "reaching for an essentialized racial identity of which we think we can be certain" as a guarantee for political solidarity or cultural unity. Instead, the very category of "black" needs to be interrogated: "Blackness as a sign is never enough. What does that black subject do, how does it act, how does it think politically . . . being black isn't really good enough for me: I want to know what your cultural politics are."[36]

In the same vein, if we are to work on the multiple, complex, overdetermined politics of "being Chinese" in today's complicated and mixed-up world, and if we are to seize on the radical theoretical promise of the diasporic perspective, we must not only resist the convenient and comforting reduction of Chineseness as a seemingly natural and certain racial essence; we must also be prepared to interrogate the very significance of the category of Chineseness per se as a predominant marker of identification and distinction. Not only does the moment of pure Chineseness never strike; there are also moments — occurring regularly in the lives of those "truly on the periphery," in Leo Lee's words — in which the attribution of Chineseness does not make sense in the first place. The liberating productivity of the diasporic perspective lies, according to Rey Chow, in the means it provides "to *unlearn* that submission to one's ethnicity such as 'Chineseness' as the ultimate signified." [37] This will allow diasporic subjects to break out of the prisonhouse of Chineseness and embrace lives — personal, social, political — "more than as just a Chinese" (Ouyang), to construct open-ended and plural "post-Chinese" identities through investments in continuing cross-influences of diverse, lateral, unanticipated intercultural encounters in the world at large. As it happens, Yang, who now calls himself "bicultural," does occupy such a position in his public life. His celebrated photographs of friends suffering from AIDS testify to his identification with Western gay culture, which he represents as entangled with, but also distinct from, the cultural identifications derived from his ethnicity, and articulate a hybrid, disaggregated, multiple identity that is uncontainable, in any meaningful sense, by the category of "Chinese." [38]

As I have put it elsewhere, "If I am inescapably Chinese by *descent,* I am only sometimes Chinese by *consent.* When and how is a matter of politics." [39] The politics involved here reaches far beyond the identity politics of individual subjects, in diaspora or otherwise. What is at stake are the possibilities and responsibilities of these subjects to participate, as citizens of the world, in the ongoing political construction of world futures. As we enter the twenty-first century, we face ever greater challenges in light of growing global economic disparity, continuing environmental degradation, rapid technological change, increasingly massive transnational migrations, and shifting geopolitical (im)balances of power. There is no necessary advantage in a Chinese identification here; indeed, depending on context and necessity, it may be politically mandatory to refuse the primordial interpellation of belonging to the largest race of the world, the "family" of "the Chinese people." In such situations, the significant question is not only, Can one say no to China? but also, Can one, when called for, say no to Chineseness? [40]

298 · Ien Ang

Notes

1 William Yang, *Sadness* (St. Leonards, Australia: Allen and Unwin, 1996), 65.

2 William Yang, *Sadness*, 63–64.

3 See Stuart Hall's similar critique of the notion of the essential black subject, for example, in his essays "New Ethnicities" and "What Is This 'Black' in Black Popular Culture?" reprinted in *Stuart Hall: Critical Dialogues in Cultural Studies,* ed. David Morley and Kuan-Hsing Chen (London: Routledge, 1997), 441–49 and 465–75.

4 For some examples of the wide-ranging emergent body of work on the Chinese diaspora along these theoretical lines (which can be described loosely as informed by postmodern, poststructuralist, and postcolonial theory), see, for example, Rey Chow, *Writing Diaspora: Tactics of Intervention in Contemporary Cultural Studies* (Bloomington: Indiana University Press, 1993); Ien Ang, "On Not Speaking Chinese: Postmodern Ethnicity and the Politics of Diaspora," *New Formations* 24 (winter 1994): 1–18; Aihwa Ong, "On the Edge of Empires: Flexible Citizenship among Chinese in Diaspora," *Positions: East Asia Cultures Critique* 1, no. 3 (winter 1993); Allen Chun, "Fuck Chineseness: On the Ambiguities of Ethnicity as Culture as Identity," *boundary 2* 23, no. 2 (summer 1996): 111–38; and Yao Souchou, "Books from Heaven: Literary Pleasure, Chinese Cultural Text and the 'Struggle against Forgetting,'" *Australian Journal of Anthropology* 8, no. 2 (1997): 190–209.

5 Lawrence Grossberg, "History, Politics, and Postmodernism: Stuart Hall and Cultural Studies," in *Stuart Hall: Critical Dialogues in Cultural Studies,* ed. David Morley and Kuan-Hsing Chen (London: Routledge, 1996), 153.

6 For a recent discussion on the position of Chinese in Southeast Asia, see, for example, Leo Suryadinata, ed., *Ethnic Chinese as Southeast Asians* (Singapore: Institute of Southeast Asian Studies, 1997).

7 See my "On Not Speaking Chinese."

8 Stuart Hall, "For Allon White: Metaphors of Transformation," in *Stuart Hall: Critical Dialogues in Cultural Studies,* 302.

9 Tu Wei-ming, ed., *The Living Tree: The Changing Meaning of Being Chinese Today* (Stanford, Calif.: Stanford University Press, 1994). This book is a reprint (with some additions) of a special issue of *Daedalus* 120, no. 2 (spring 1991).

10 The emergence of a discourse on cultural China, as launched by Tu, is closely related to the growing prominence of the discourse of "Greater China." The latter is the most commonly used term, in English at least, for "the system of interactions among mainland China, Hong Kong, Taiwan and people of Chinese descent around the world" (Harry Harding, "The Concept of 'Greater China': Themes, Variations and Reservations," *China Quarterly* 136 [1993]: 683. Harding distinguishes three key themes in the contemporary discourse of Greater China:

the rise of a transnational Chinese economy; the (prospect of a) reunification of a Chinese state; and the emergence of a global Chinese culture, to which Tu's discussion of cultural China is an important contribution.

11 Tu Wei-ming, preface to *The Living Tree,* v. Subsequent references to the preface are cited parenthetically.

12 Tu Wei-ming, "Cultural China: The Periphery as the Center," in *The Living Tree,* 1–34. Subsequent references to this essay are cited parenthetically.

13 It should be noted that Tu's paper first appeared in 1991, only two years after the crushing of prodemocracy demonstrators at Tiananmen Square in June, 1989, by the People's Liberation Army. This event has arguably had a massive impact on the fate of representations of Chineseness in the contemporary world and has been of major significance in the emergence of the dissident discourse of cultural China.

14 C. T. Hsia, "Obsession with China: The Moral Burden of Modern Chinese Literature," in *A History of Modern Chinese Fiction,* 2d ed. (New Haven, Conn.: Yale University Press, 1971), 533–54.

15 Leo Ou-fan Lee, "On the Margins of Chinese Discourse: Some Personal Thoughts on the Cultural Meaning of the Periphery," in Tu Wei-ming, *The Living Tree,* 232.

16 Leo Ou-fan Lee, "On the Margins of Chinese Discourse," 226, 232.

17 James Clifford, "Diasporas," in *Routes: Travel and Translation in the Late Twentieth Century* (Cambridge: Harvard University Press, 1997), 266, 269, Clifford's emphases.

18 Clifford, "Diasporas," 269.

19 Paul Gilroy, *The Black Atlantic: Modernity and Double Consciousness* (London: Verso, 1993), 4.

20 Gilroy explicitly and passionately rejects Africa-centered discourses of the black diaspora, which are highly influential among some African American intellectuals in the United States (as in the idea of Africentricity).

21 Leo Ou-fan Lee, "On the Margins," 231, 229.

22 Ouyang Yu, "Lost in the Translation," *Australian Review of Books* 2, no. 9 (October 1997): 10, 35, 10.

23 David Yen-ho Wu, "The Construction of Chinese and Non-Chinese Identities," in Tu Wei-ming, *The Living Tree,* 161.

24 See my "On Not Speaking Chinese."

25 Mely G. Tan, "The Ethnic Chinese in Indonesia: Issues of Identity," in *Ethnic Chinese as Southeast Asians,* ed. Leo Suryadinata (Singapore: Institute of Southeast Asian Studies, 1997), 51.

26 Suryadinata mentions a survey that reveals that most Southeast Asian Chinese capitalists who have invested in mainland China are those who are "culturally Chinese." Peranakan Chinese have, by and large, been prevented from this "re-

turn" for economic purposes because, "having lost their command of Chinese, [they] are unable to communicate with the mainland Chinese" (Suryadinata, "Ethnic Chinese in Southeast Asia," in *Ethnic Chinese as Southeast Asians*, 16). Sadly, as has been made all too clear by the recent anti-Chinese mass violence that erupted throughout Indonesia in early 1998 as a consequence of a severe economic downturn, which saw massive price increases, a rise in unemployment, and social chaos in the country, the meaning of being of Chinese origin in this context can all too easily become related to fear and scapegoatism. I partly address the complex and ambivalent positioning of Indonesian Chinese in the Chinese diaspora in a forthcoming paper entitled "Indonesia on My Mind: Diasporic Intellectualism and the Politics of Hybridity."

27 David Yen-ho Wu, "Construction of Chinese and Non-Chinese Identities," 149.

28 David Yen-ho Wu, "Construction of Chinese and Non-Chinese Identities," 150.

29 See Etienne Balibar, "The Nation Form: History and Ideology," in Etienne Balibar and Immanuel Wallerstein, *Race, Nation, Class, Ambiguous Identities* (London: Verso, 1991), 99. For a discussion of Chinese conceptions of race, see Frank Dikötter, *The Discourse of Race in Modern China* (Stanford, Calif.: Stanford University Press, 1992).

30 Rey Chow, *Writing Diaspora*, 24.

31 William Yang, *Sadness*, 23.

32 Rey Chow, *Writing Diaspora*, 24.

33 Hall, "What Is This 'Black' in Black Popular Culture?" 472.

34 Balibar, "The Nation Form," 100.

35 Paul Gilroy, "It's a Family Affair," in *Small Acts: Thoughts on the Politics of Black Cultures* (London: Serpent's Tail, 1993), 203.

36 Hall, "What Is This 'Black' in Black Popular Culture?" 474. The quotation on blackness is attributed to black British filmmaker Isaac Julien.

37 Rey Chow, *Writing Diaspora*, 25; Chow's emphasis.

38 Yang's book *Sadness* (which was originally presented as a one-man slide show) alternately traces two stories of his life—one about his Chinese family and the other about his gay community in Sydney.

39 Ien Ang, "On Not Speaking Chinese," 18.

40 The first question is posed by Rey Chow, "Can One Say No to China?" *New Literary History* 28, no. 1 (winter 1997): 147–51. On the second question, I am thinking of, for example, the ideological role Chinese essentialisms and chauvinisms have played in the rising power of ethnic Chinese business networks throughout the Asia-Pacific region and its exclusionary and potentially oppressive implications for non-Chinese Asians. See Aihwa Ong and Donald M. Nonini, eds., *Ungrounded Empires: The Cultural Politics of Modern Chinese Transnationalism* (New York: Routledge, 1996); and Arif Dirlik, "Critical Reflections on 'Chinese Capitalism' as a Paradigm," *Identities: Global Studies in Culture and Power* 3, no. 3 (1997): 303–30.

Afterword: The Possibilities of Abandonment

Paul A. Bové

The literary and cultural humanities are not very old disciplines, and in the not too distant past they were marked by high passion, intellectual rigor, and cultural ambition. These disciplines have declined; it is not just that the status of their objects—literature and culture—have lost value; the practitioners in the fields have adopted facile models of professional work. Mostly, this decline means little except in the fact of teaching poorly; mostly, it results from and extends a professional model, especially but not only within the United States, according to which what matters is to "take a position" on an already recognized continuum of legitimate positions, thereby identifying oneself with a faction, a mode of talking, a professional cadre. Often there is nothing at stake and so this matters little. Symptomatically, it represents real reasons to worry about the state of the university as an institution capable of seriously studying or thinking about our world, its needs, and the needs for any future. Sometimes a great deal is at stake, not just professionally but immediately for the political and intellectual future of large institutions and numbers of people. At times, in other words, and to put it simply, the kinds of knowledge produced and the standards according to which they are produced—these things can matter.

Rey Chow's edition of essays revising and laying bare the working of modern Chinese studies has, I believe, as one of its legitimate motives anger at the intellectual laziness and normal practice of "critics"—wherever they are to be found—who mouth inherited, commonsensical, and (professionally) normal phrases that are patently unsupportable by anyone who pauses for a moment to think clearly about the words and their apparent referents. Reimagining the field of Chinese studies in the current geopolitical climate matters enormously to virtually everyone now alive or soon to be born. If there is a fact of life inescapably consequent upon globalism and the end of the Cold War it is simply what appears to be the "fact of China," that idea for two centuries in such proximity to U.S. power and the history of

Western global domination. Equally important, this "fact" resolves upon humanistic culture workers an obligation as pressing as any since the formation (and, more recently, the breakup) of the great European empires and the emergence of literatures, nations, and related modes of thought and language. In other words, although American critics feel they can still safely mumble and muse over the largest pieties such as nation and God with little to fear other than the approval of a newspaper reviewer,[1] serious cosmopolitan intellectuals see the dangers of such habitual humanistic disinterest and carelessness, especially when it extends into areas of real political and societal danger.

Of course, such passionate criticism often is the seemingly easy target of well-accommodated academics. Stanley Abe lets us see this when he discusses how Xu Bing's installation, *A Book from the Sky,* devalues the cultural capital of traditional sinologists. In a "text" made of thousands of nonexistent "ideograms," as Fenollosa taught many American critics to call these characters, a work of art that sets aside the racist and orientalist identification of written characters with "Chinese authenticity," one forlorn doctoral student in Chinese literature, Charles Stone, discovers "two real characters." Abe says: "Stone asserts the authority of sinology by claiming a mastery of the Chinese language superior to that of the natives" (242). Abe's Stone thinks he made a significant discovery because it allows him to say something like "See! You just don't know enough. There's something you've forgotten. There are exceptions to your 'theoretical' statement." Where Abe rightly sees sinology, I see, in instances like this, the last claim of the reactionary, namely, the appeal to the empirical exception supposedly proving that the challenger does not know the field or its protocols. The aim of this all too common gesture is to delegitimate critique, not to advance knowledge or thinking. It is an effort to defend old thought habituated and sedimented into cultural-capital-producing value for its acquisitor.[2] Nietzsche's genealogist grew pale from years buried studying in the archive—a whiteness redeemed only by surfacing long enough to hurl a lightning bolt. Stone's time with a dictionary—short as it might seem—is an eon's embrace of the already well known from the mines of which some nugget appears to assure the faithful that panning the load can still produce hard currency.

Chow's injunction to her contributors and readers to "reimagine a field" masks a very violent and potentially creative gesture: light up the night and smash the icons with a hammer. The intent behind such a gesture refreshes; given that the local target happens to be one of great geopolitical and historical importance adds to the matter and provides an objective correlative to the urgency:

> The essays collected in this volume make it clear that the old model of area studies—an offshoot of U.S. Cold War political strategy that found its anchorage in higher education—can no longer handle the diverse and multifaceted experiences that are articulated under the study of Chineseness, be that study through texts of fiction, film, history, art, subtitling, standup comedy, criticism, geographies of migration, or cultural studies. Instead, in the age of theory, new linkages and insights that may be at odds with more acceptable or naturalized conventions of interpretation continue to emerge, extending, redrawing, or simply traversing and abandoning existing boundaries of the field as such. (17)

Catachreses have marked all the developing new knowledges within the confines of the academy as discourses cross and disciplines slip, but Rey Chow is not interested in letting mere rhetoric stand in the place of serious and prolonged work to bring about an intellectual, discursive, and political transformation.[3] Indeed, she is so wary of the critical commonplace that mistakes rhetorical "subversion" for careful reading that, like Edward Said, she insists upon the complexly woven and finely textured nature of lived experience, lines of power and desire, in cultures more compound than our standard criticisms—whether they be essentialist or identity based— can acknowledge. It is the compound nature of historical reality that gives force to the charge repeated by essayists throughout this volume that the work of too many of their predecessors depends upon "reductive" formulations. Of course, in recent years, poststructuralism and cultural studies have led us to expect this charge against naturalizing and dehistoricizing forms of knowledge, resting their claims on essentializing universals. Moreover, we have come increasingly to understand that cultural and ethnic studies equally poorly distill out impurities in any compound in pursuit of the new stabilization that their models and ways of talking can provide.

Like other important critics, Chow tries to find a way to continue to make use of the notion of "experience." This is a challenging ambition since the term so easily aligns itself with phenomenologies, psychologisms, and discourses of subjection as well as pragmatist notions of the valued already known. I take it that Chow has solicited these essays and urged her contributors precisely to take experience as a compound so that the techniques of the humanities—so capable of reduction—find themselves not merely adjusted and, as it were, made more "complex"—what could be more modernist than complexity?—but forced onto an apparently different terrain wherein they recognize their active part in the construction of knowledge itself as part of this experience rather than merely as a spectatorial or reflective gaze upon it.

Dorothy Ko's provocative essay, "Bondage in Time," makes this clear: her point is not the merely clichéd cultural studies claim that whatever "footbinding" might be depends upon the "situation" of the constructive knower; rather, this weak perspectival model gives way to a much more nuanced reading of the participatory nature of the distant technician who aspires to know. Having entered within the object in the act of subjecting it, the knower differs from the known only by belatedness, by the differential displacement that shifts the knower not to a different spatial site from which to see and so construct and reflect back for nativist consumption; rather, the knower stands within but at a temporal moment askew to the known. Ko ends her analysis with a citation from Rev. E. J. Hardy's *John Chinaman at Home:*

> Chinese ladies are also concerned because their European sisters do not wear visible trousers, and they cannot understand how they eat when their waists are girt in. For a woman to show her shape is considered in China most immodest. . . . I saw one day, at the Peak tramway station at Hong Kong, half a dozen Chinese ladies, apparently visitors to the island, dressed in the height of their fashion. Some British ladies stepped out of the cars wearing gowns showing their figures and hats stuck over with artificial flowers and bits of birds. When they had passed, the Chinese ladies, pointing at their compressed waists and inartistic headgear, laughed in a way that should stagger European complacency. (221)

Although this passage records cultural difference and, like Montaigne in his essay on cannibals, racially marks the decline of Europe by contrast with the healthier "primitive," Ko gives us a scene with an emphasis on the passing, not of gender or race or ethnicity, but of temporality: the Westerner is seen from behind, within the scene even as he or she attempts to narrate it. Unknown to himself, Hardy creates an object outside of which he does not and cannot stand. He hopes to assign himself the masterful position of external reflection, but he has himself there, the passing object of laughter—an undeconstructed version of reflection that Foucault's Velasquez expertly represents.[4] His knowing, his knowledge object—these are too late; they come as a moment always later than the reality they claim to describe. How too late? Because they do not see themselves as what they are, namely, an essential part of the process constituting that which they claim to report. In this instance, there is an intense irony in that the writer claims the superior position, claims to be aware of how to the "Asian" the "Westerner" looks provincial and out of place—whereas the very efforts of observation and reporting stand within that very structure of "Westernness" it takes to be neutral and natural. We are given a narrative about an object that exists only so the narrative can be a truth-telling story. When read with a little care, the story shows itself to be a belated fragment of an experience compounded by its participation in that of which it has no immanent knowledge at all—except what it produces as fiction!

Rey Chow and Ien Ang have produced brilliant writings to surpass this entire construct. Most important, Rey Chow has shown that it is a construct of humanistic knowledge as such unless and until it becomes willing to abandon the very fields it must bound in order to exist. For what is "Chineseness" but an object organizing a field structured by the protocols of the disciplines that take the field as their own? After Saussure took the trouble to announce that linguistics, to be a science, had to have its object, can there be anything more obvious or critically boring than the mere facticity of the object of a "human science" as having been "constituted" by that science in the very act of studying, forming, narrating, compiling, interpreting, analyzing, and so on? One senses that Rey Chow hopes to sweep aside not only all the essentialisms, open and covert, at work in forming Chineseness as an object of discussion but also the tiring need to declare the demystification, time and again, of the erroneous habits of a nonreflexive criticism that, rather than thinking, mechanically redeploys politically or professionally familiar counters and patterns of writing.

Chineseness affords an extraordinary opportunity to reform knowledge practice and do so in relation to a problematic so important as to have consequences far beyond its seeming disciplinary limits. Americanists, for example, old and new, might well take seriously Chow's injunction that critics must abandon existing fields and their boundaries. This is no soft call for interdisciplinarity—that bane of serious scholarship that both keeps the disciplines in place (just use two!) and justifies not amateurism but superficiality. Nor is it a call merely to alter the forms of existing fields such as area studies, although no one familiar with the history of this model and its Cold War origins would lament its passing. Rather, it is a call to adopt abandonment as a critical practice, a call to give up the already known as a sacred value effectively working like Stone's scruple, to rub raw the daring trespasser or anarchist. Can there be a more frightening cry to the human scientist than to abandon the field? Does this not imply cowardice, a giving up and running away? Nor does it mean something trivial like leaving the field and training in another. It means, rather, taking seriously abandoning the organization of knowledge into fields as such and making an effort to hollow out any given field for the knowledge it provides.

Chow's deepest historical claim, one testified to by Ang in her remarkable essay in this collection, has to do with the error humanists make in believing that knowledge made possible by, organized and preserved in, reproduced through, and circulated by "field" models actually has value as anything other than a powerful device for impoverishing the store of images, thoughts, intellectual practices, and so on by means of which we live the experience we otherwise think we record or mirror. Ang's essay gives us the familiar story of a child inaugurated into racism, what she calls "a classic tale of revelation" (281), in a context that, like Chow's, compels humanists to see the role fields and discourses play in ontologically stabilizing their knowledge objects even when their own protocols, as in this case, admit the nonscientific nature of their borders and effects—racism based on "inescapable" phenotypes. Field formation forces a question that Ang testifies has been made compulsory by the effort to struggle successfully with and against its effects: "how to determine what is and what is not Chinese has become the necessary preliminary question to ask, and an increasingly urgent one at that. This, at least, is one of the key outcomes of the emergent view from the diaspora" (282). This question is especially urgent for a postcolonial theorist who has lived through the complexities of liberation struggles or any of the new political movements of the last thirty years. Yet the question comes clothed in academic field related terms. Of course, we are all working within the large humanistic paradigm that universities and states once encouraged in order to support each other in the effort to build national models for their own related interests. Forces of globalization and the power of emergent cultures, knowledges, and literatures record the way order autopoetically develops in odd and truly chaotic, that is, surprisingly unpredictable, forms around and through us. When Chow speaks of experiences compelling the need to abandon, creating the moral and libidinal desire to abandon, she tells us that Chineseness means this experience as an autopoeisis that cannot rest within the domain of a field or any boundaries. The question Ang feels is essential reflects her strong sense that disciplinarity affronts knowledge in its emergence, but, tempted by the formative power of knowledge, she transforms the diasporic discovery of emergence back into outcomes and determinations. What she has gained by struggle — the indeterminate signifier whose "emergence," unexpected, into the world she has helped free from the prejudice of racist common sense and scholarly discourse alike — Ang writes of in terms of will, in terms that belong to the very forces forming fields and knowledge. Rather than abandonment, she focuses her efforts on the production of outcomes and determinations.

Whereas Chow calls for abandonment, Ang calls for a new paradigm. These are not the same, although under the right circumstances the second is a necessary ally of the first. Abandonment is a difficult notion with which to live and think. Cultural studies discourse seems already to have adopted it in other forms. The following quotation from Ang makes both points necessary to understand the weighty consequences of Chow's thinking: "Central to the diasporic paradigm is the theoretical axiom that Chineseness is not a category with a fixed content — be it racial, cultural, or geographical — but operates as an open and indeterminate signifier whose meanings are constantly renegotiated and rearticulated in different sections of the Chinese diaspora" (282–83). Theoretically inflected critics know the long history of this kind of powerful talk and realize that, at least since Derrida spoke of logocentrism and Lacan of phallus, certain utopian or liberatory possibilities have been thought to reside in the discovery or uncovering of "indeterminate signifiers." The familiarity of the notion has little effect per se upon its value within a struggle to do away with the worst naturalizations of ethnicity and cultural authenticity in talking about Chineseness, so Ang's use of this notion, placed within a strong and complex essay, explains how these erroneous figures of Chineseness have their hegemonic hold on so many discourses.

It is worth noting, however, that Rey Chow's entire collection flies under the sign of abandoning the boundaries of knowledge fields, including even cultural studies: Leung, Chang, and Lupke, for example, all, in their different ways, historicize Chineseness by constructing alternative genealogies of literatures called Chinese; their essays show, in themselves, how such concepts as Chinese, in part, are constructs produced by institutionalized scholarly work. When Ien Ang quotes Lawrence Grossberg's talismanic and symptomatic remark that "there can be no separation between theory, at whatever level of abstraction, and the concrete social historical context which provides both its object of study and its conditions of existence," she seems not to realize that Chow's critical project cannot set out upon such a familiar, universalistic, and assured basis. Certainly, one would want to know more than just where Grossberg stands in making his timeless claim; more interesting would be to question the possible grounds on which his "no" might not hold. But, to take such actions would mean that the critic, engaged in combat with the deadly enemies of racism and essentialism, would need to surrender one of the most powerful tools in the conflict of knowledge: the cultural studies claim for the context-based nature of all discourse. What is this claim? Simply put, it involves deconstructing any essentialist or universalizing claims about the "natural" or "timeless" essence of any substance or subject. As many of the essays in this collection show, for example, "Chinese" is not a natural or given essence; rather it is a concept and social reality formed by various practices of life and knowledge. Lo's essay shows, for example, how the legal and cultural power of the state and society compel certain language practices as Chinese in Hong Kong while delegitimating other practices as either inauthentic or colonial: politics, carefully traced, forms the parameters within which what is Chinese about literature can be identified. Understanding such things allows scholars and critics to do important historical work showing how such apparent "essences" as Chineseness are deeply historical and the result of often quite historical events and processes. (This is certainly true of Berry's careful analysis of how the nation itself underlies our readings of not only film but all media.) This poststructuralist idea that human agency and discourse create essences has been mocked by reactionaries, made heavy use of by cultural studies, and been taken up as a serious matter of intellectual reflection by others concerned with method. Chow's project rests on something appreciably more daring and demanding than any of these efforts. Real intellectual rigor in the arena of compound and autopoetic experiences—this requires the courage of surrender.

To abandon fields of knowledge means, after all, not only to leave behind, as in "abandoning a friend in need," or to withdraw from a previously securely held place or position; it also means two other things that the mind finds it extremely difficult to hold together at the same time: first, "to give up to the control or influence of another person or agent; to give up with the intent of never again claiming a right or interest in"; and, second, "to give (oneself) over unrestrainedly." [5] Ang's essay is quite interesting for its testimony; she not only gives us a painful story of revelation to open her essay but confirms it from a personal experience present throughout as one of the motives of her writing and career. The essay is most important for highlighting the topic of not just freedom and the possibility of self-determination within racist practice and culture but of the will as a matter of individual and political consent. The will matters because racism remains empowered within the interpolation "You are Chinese—and you had better get used to it." This inflexible other speaking voice, no matter how cultural and historical in its existence and power, functions as nature to the point that Ang, as a person and critic, might be by descent Chinese without choice but she strives mightily to effect a world in which she, the symbolic subject, can be Chinese at those moments when she consents to carry that sign.[6] When she can be indeterminate as a signifier and not automatistically coded as Chinese, as now she must be. Oddly, this desire to come to consent resonates poorly with the universal "no" of Grossberg and better with Chow's powerful commitment to abandonment. Ang would like to be able to give herself over to being Chinese when she consents, not when she is forced. Violence is not abandonment, but she surely abandons herself to the necessary and hard struggle to attain the conditions for consent. This very fact of struggle requires the will to sustain itself as the highest value as the power that says yes and no. It does not yet appear as the power to renounce the desire to control, to be an agent, to have an interest in or to claim something as a right. The problem Chow poses is how intellectuals might help achieve the moment when the right to assent to being Chinese is not the highest aim for which one struggles—for, dispersed or specified, such abilities to assign yes or no relate all of intellectual work and life still to the tyrannical ruling sign "Chinese," which, like a law of nature, rules as tyrannical sovereign over thought and experience. One must abandon the indeterminate signifier to the power that one has already abandoned oneself—otherwise one becomes the slave of what one beholds. In other words, once Ang's work is successfully completed and she herself, or "Chinese," is made into a free-floating and indeterminate signifier, she runs the risk of becoming the intellectual prisoner of her own success. Oddly, to progress from the point she has earned she must let go of the signifier she has freed or she will remain forever the captive of the effort to sustain it, as it were, over and against the seemingly constant encroachment of the "essentializers" and "racists." Moreover, she would commit herself to a life of work unable ever to leave this signifier and the battles over it behind: in short, she would remain incapable of abandonment and would sustain the dialectical field of Chinese discourse.

Of course, such abandonment occurs not all at once in a sweep of the theoretical broom. It requires labor, much of which will look like the ordinary detailed work of humanistic scholarship. Many of the essays in this collection, no matter their topic, must do this. As I understand Chow's plan, all this work, no matter what its intent, is catechretical — perhaps as I have just begun to suggest about Ang's essay. *Cata-*, we recall, is a prefix that suggests all the powers of tradition, of being able to carry on or over. *Cata-* means not only down or from but also "in accordance with." *Catachresis,* by contrast, etymologically implies acts of abuse, misuse, or, indeed, more significant in this context, using up.[7] Catachresis is a misuse that uses up, forcing abandonment for an intellect not enamored of death and repetition. To abandon by using up requires a passionate commitment to work; committing oneself to induce work in the hope that catachreses will use up the protocols that sustain the boundaries — this is an act of intellectual struggle and faith that inspires a reconsideration of the value of error. By contrast, signifiers, no matter how indeterminate, always tempt scholars to stabilize them in acts of affirmation. Experience, in the terms of this collection, warns us against signification; it tells us, as I have suggested in reading Ang, that signifiers seduce our will into the double effort to "free" them into their indeterminacy — so that bodies are no longer phenotypically inscribed as Chinese — and to redetermine them as a constructed outcome that the self (as subject) desires as security for its own being and agency, for its freedom to "assent" only at a substantial time of the subject's "own" choosing.[8] Chow's introduction to this volume concludes by drawing attention to the ways in which the reimagined field will require detailed, close, and exacting work. Yet, as I take Chow's text, her desire is not for a newly established field discipline but for the liberating effects that intellectual responsibility embodied in rigorous acts of reading will have in suspending — nor merely defining — Chineseness, itself one of many names for the violent repetition of ignorance that form stable fields of inquiry. Instability of field — the much hailed self-reflexivity of contemporary talk — promises nothing more than the ideological liberal commitment to what Chow calls "the act of pluralizing."[9] Multiplication and addition might make for mannerism but they do not give us more than sums of erroneous parts, the consequences of liberal individualism masked as weak perspectivism. Indeed, pluralism gives us much less than we get from Ang's traditional poststructuralist trope of the indeterminate signifier.

As I have been suggesting, however, it is precisely not *what we get* from Chow's desire that matters but *what we abandon* (or, if you will, what abandons us, we passionate lovers). Professionalism is such, of course, and academic knowledge formations require it as well, that Chow's discourse will come to ground a new imaginary field for "reimagined Chineseness studies." Certainly, her work's strong critique of the inadequacies of existing practice and her posing of new, strong questions—these gestures beg for repetition, as they authorize work and set the direction for others to proceed. There is a diabolism to this, however, a deep irony that appears when we realize that the work Chow calls for, and which this collection so excellently begins, produces not a positivity but its erasure, that

> the poststructuralist theoretical move of splitting and multiplying a monolithic identity (such as *China* or *Chinese*) from within, powerful and necessary as it is, is by itself inadequate as a method of reading, that the careful study of texts and media becomes, once again, imperative, even as such study is now ineluctably refracted by the awareness of the unfinished and untotalizable workings of ethnicity. . . . Only with such close study, we may add, can Chineseness be productively put under erasure—not in the sense of being written out of existence but in the sense of being unpacked—and reevaluated in the catachrestic modes of its signification, the very forms of its historical construction. (18)

This conclusion seems to be constructed by a return: we now know the poststructuralist trope, and we enact it as a commonplace because it is powerful, but it is insufficient and "once again," we must go back to the careful study of our media. But this conclusion is more sinuous than a simple return. It begins with a recognition of the value of plurality against the monolith. It then worries that the newer trope's insufficiencies will not appear to those who rely upon it (as I have shown in my brief comments on Ang's adoption of Grossberg). It passes on to satisfy the desire not simply for adequation but to meet the intellectual and historical "imperative." Unable to rest in a proliferating pluralism, this desire, this critical project, would go on to erase Chineseness by unpacking its contents from within the field so they can be analyzed and seen as the catachreses they are. Unpacking as erasure means showing how the contents of the field have already used themselves up but have not had the passionate abandon to let themselves go. Such compelling erasure reveals the self-embracing narcissism of a field and its practitioners, a self-denying embrace hiding the historicality of its own belated exhaustion. At its worst, such a field must be abandoned because, when put in contact with the act of reading, its necrophilic nature becomes too evident—at least too evident for the living to deny.

What Chow hopes for cannot be achieved all at once, despite her text's theorization of the problem. We can see elements of what her project wants to achieve in various essays in this collection: Laughlin's demonstration of the lingering utopian potential of socialist criticism in the face of many new critical movements; Yeh's examination of the varying ideological underpinnings of debates among intellectuals—within the People's Republic and overseas—about what forms "Chinese" literature and criticism, or what sort of theory, can fit within a rubric of Chinese studies; and Wang's use of multiple feminist models to offer varying interpretations repositioning well-known and neglected texts alike within a reformed "canon" of Chinese literature and writing.

Stanley Abe's "China and *A Book from the Sky*" develops most elaborately the basic elements of this collection's project and rewards extended attention. Indeed, it has important elements of a futural essay dancing over an already erased and unpacked field. In important ways, it contrasts with Ang's equally powerful but differently inflected essay. If, as Ang's title suggests ("Can One Say No to Chineseness?"), the issue is (sovereign) will within the (natural and political) spaces of authority and power, then the same issues clearly form the space within which Abe's essay begins its work. Tracing the ways in which the free-floating signifier, *A Book from the Sky*, acquires a wide range of readings by varied audiences over different times and continents, Abe's essay perfectly establishes how the automatism of field practice controls and determines reading. At first, the essay looks like a story of the fall of the signifier into power and social construction. Yet Abe's essay also has a movement of return, if you will, of redemption, for *A Book from the Sky*, digitalized and reinstalled (at SUNY Albany) remakes itself away from tradition, the traumatic ruin of tradition, and the purity of aesthetic effort—all tropes that have regulated its interpretation and placement. In a sense, *A Book from the Sky* reauthorizes its own indeterminacy in a second life that unpacks and erases the codes that had constrained and recontained it. Abe's ending coalesces with Chow's: erasing as unpacking creates an empty space, as Abe says, "without questions or answers," a desire Chow's project conjures and a power that would, once and for all, make impossible the seemingly eternal racist question, the "moment of revelation," that marks the opening of Ang's essay. Abe's reading of *A Book from the Sky* brings the mind to a space where the principal issue is not the will, where the ambition to be able to say yes or no — to overcome descent in consent — will be left behind as a mark of the utopian become real.[10]

Achieving such a moment means, as Chow presents it here, that critics and intellectuals must accept their part in the struggle to realize this possibility. Not naively believing that this is merely a matter of textual or critical practice, Chow (and this collection as a whole) show that there are both powerful political obstacles to achieving this end — the United States and China as states exemplify the difficulty — and social and intellectual reasons to believe that certain forces, as yet disunited, might make possible the moment when the harsh realities that compel Ang's desire to be able to assert or deny her Chineseness might be at an end. Post-Chineseness is not, itself, the ambition or declaration of this collection. These essayists show their strong commitment to complex and difficult long-term intellectual projects, which, unlike those they hope to displace, will not forget their necessary ties to historicalities much too compounded for any reductive distillation — essentialist or merely strategic — to pass muster on the path to erasing Chineseness. These essays span a notable and wide expanse of experience, production, history, and movement. To deal with these matters, they reach for the tools at hand, terms borrowed from theory, postcolonial studies, cultural studies, and so on. They worry the relationship between these highly capitalized Western notions and the traditions and emergences within their range. These are all real problems that will require considerable time to develop and solve; terms like *hybridity,* justifiably controversial, will need to be taken to the limits of their utility when good reasons for their abandonment appear. The time this conceptual, rhetorical work will take is part of the larger project this collection imagines: finding better ways to establish relations between such words and the things within their historico-intellectual expanse of study. If working at Chineseness in this way succeeds, much good will have been done for all the world. It is hard to imagine, for example, that Americanness can survive the unpacking of Chineseness. Not only is "American" increasingly constructing itself as the dominant figure in a binary relation with "Chinese," but the same tactics and strategies useful in advancing the critique of Chineseness will allow those interested in unpacking the force of Americanness to undo as well this hegemon, this "last remaining superpower." Learning how to bring words and things into proper alignment for our increasingly globalized future of relations between locales—this will be a contribution the successful achievement of which will require taking a fully cosmopolitan view of the very expanse Chineseness reveals and hides. A new type of intellectual will be born in the process, one not given to will the right to yes or no but to the making real what are now only utopian spaces. The value of this project lies in its having set this effort in motion.

Notes

I want to thank Rey Chow for taking the time originally to edit this collection of essays for *boundary 2;* for talking me into writing the afterword to this volume, and for her careful reading of my drafts, guiding me away from many unnecessary obscurities.

1 See, for example, Richard Rorty, "I Hear America Sighing: Andrew Delbanco Ponders the Possible Solutions to Our Postmodern Melancholy," *New York Times Book Review,* 7 November 1999 (http://www.nytimes.com/books/99/11/07/ reviews/991107.07rortyt.html). Rorty is reviewing Andrew Delbanco, *The Real American Dream* (Cambridge, Mass.: Harvard University Press, 1999); as Rorty tells us, these essays by "one of America's most acute and perceptive cultural critics" were Delbanco's 1998 Massey Lectures in American Civilization at Harvard.

2 On this general point, see Paul A. Bové, "Giving Thought to America: Intellect and *The Education of Henry Adams," Critical Inquiry* 23 (autumn 1996): 80–108; and "Policing Thought: On Learning How to Read Henry Adams," *Critical Inquiry* 23 (summer 1997): 939–46.

3 Sometimes this marking seems little tied to realities larger than those of academic words, as, for example, when oppositional critics come near announcing that catachresis will end imperialism.

4 Michel Foucault, *The Order of Things: An Archeology of the Human Sciences,* trans. unknown (New York: Vintage Books, 1994), 3–16.

5 *WWWebster Dictionary* (http://www.m-w.com/cgi-bin/dictionary).

6 For some deeper understanding of what Ang enacts here, see Giorgio Agamben, *Home Sacer: Sovereign Power and Bare Life,* trans. Daniel Heller-Roazen (Stanford: Stanford University Press, 1998), 181–83. In effect, Ang does not want to be treated as a creature of nature (descent) but of politics. Agamben brings his own thinking about this matter to the point of understanding the Nazi extermination of the Jews as the part of the logic of sovereignty that sees the Jews as creatures available for death, as "lice." Agamben's book (188) concludes by articulating a

program differently directed than what I am reading here as Rey Chow's and one that allows us to understand Ang's efforts and their motives from the point of view of perhaps a larger conceptual reach.

7   *WWWebster Dictionary* (http://www.m-w.com/cgi-bin/dictionary).

8   In raising this issue, I merely draw upon the well-known Derridean reading of the proper self, the self as one's own and as property. See, for example, *Of Grammatology,* trans. Gayatri C. Spivak (Baltimore and London: Johns Hopkins University Press, 1974), esp. 107–17.

9   Chow notes: "White feminism, which has taught us that the problems inherent in the term *woman* have not disappeared with the introduction of the plural, *women,* is the best case in point here" (18).

10 It is precisely this movement that I suggest coalesces with the ending of *Home Sacer.* Agamben writes there: "If we give the name form-of-life to this being that is only its own bare existence and to this life that, being its own form, remains inseparable from it, we will witness the emergence of a field of research well beyond the terrain defined by the intersection of politics and philosophy, medico-biological sciences and jurisprudence" (188).

Index

Contributors

Stanley K. Abe is Assistant Professor of Art History at Duke University. He has written on colonialism and the study of Buddhist art and is completing a book, *Ordinary Images,* on Chinese Buddhist and Daoist art of the fifth and early sixth centuries C.E.

Ien Ang is Professor of Cultural Studies and Director of the Research Centre in Intercommunal Studies at the University of Western Sydney, Nepean, Australia. Her most recent book is *Living Room Wars: Rethinking Audiences for a Postmodern World.*

Chris Berry teaches in the Department of Film Studies at the University of California, Berkeley. He is the author of *A Bit on the Side: East-West Topographies of Desire* and the editor of *Perspectives on Chinese Cinema.*

Paul A. Bové is Professor of English at the University of Pittsburgh and editor of *boundary 2.* The author of several books on modern literature, criticism, and theory, he is currently completing a book on Henry Adams.

Sung-sheng Yvonne Chang teaches in the Department of Asian Studies and the Program in Comparative Literature at the University of Texas, Austin. She is the author of *Modernism and the Nativist Resistance: Contemporary Chinese Fiction from Taiwan* and the editor of *Bamboo Shoots after the Rain: Contemporary Stories by Women Writers of Taiwan.*

Rey Chow is Andrew W. Mellon Professor of the Humanities at Brown University. Her books in English include *Woman and Chinese Modernity; Writing Diaspora; Primitive Passions;* and, most recently, *Ethics after Idealism: Theory–Culture–Ethnicity–Reading.*

Charles A. Laughlin is Assistant Professor of Chinese Literature at Yale University. His specialty is modern Chinese prose literature. He is currently working on a book entitled *Chinese Reportage: The Aesthetics of Historical Experience.*

Leung Ping-kwan is Professor of Chinese at Lingnan University, Hong Kong. The author of many poetry and fiction collections in Chinese, he has also written scholarly essays both in English and Chinese on postcolonialism and contemporary Chinese literature and cinema. He is currently working on a book on Hong Kong culture.

Dorothy Ko teaches Chinese history and women's studies at Rutgers University. The author of *Teachers of the Inner Chambers: Women and Culture in Seventeenth-Century*

China, she is at work on a history of footbinding. Beginning in spring 2001, she will be Professor of History, Barnard College, Columbia University.

Kwai-Cheung Lo teaches in the Department of English Language and Literature at Baptist University, Hong Kong. He is the author of numerous fiction pieces and critical essays and the first book-length study of Gilles Deleuze in the Chinese language.

Christopher Lupke is Assistant Professor in the Department of Foreign Languages, Washington State University. He is currently working on modern Chinese literature in the diaspora and issues of postcoloniality.

David Der-wei Wang is Professor of Chinese Literature at Columbia University. His most recent publications include *Fictional Realism in Twentieth-Century China: Mao Dun, Lao She, Shen Congwen; Xiaoshuo Zhongguo* (Narrating China: Chinese Fiction from the Late Qing to the Contemporary Era); and *Fin-de-Siècle Splendor: Repressed Modernities of Late Qing Fiction, 1849–1911.*

Michelle Yeh is Professor of East Asian languages and cultures at the University of California, Davis. Her books in English include *Modern Chinese Poetry: Theory and Practice Since 1917; Anthology of Modern Chinese Poetry;* and *No Trace of the Gardener: Poems of Yang Mu* (cotranslated with Lawrence R. Smith).

Library of Congress Cataloging-in-Publication Data
Modern Chinese literary and cultural studies in the age of theory :
reimagining a field / [edited by] Rey Chow.
p.   cm. — (b2 books and Asia-Pacific)
Includes index.
ISBN 0-8223-2584-5 (alk. paper)
ISBN 0-8223-2597-7 (pbk. : alk. paper)
1. China — Civilization — 20th century.   2. Popular culture — China.
I. Chow, Rey.   II. Series.
DS775.2.M63   2000
951 — dc21   00-029425